Peterson
Institute for
International
Economics

The Great
Tradeoff
**Confronting
Moral Conflicts
in the Era of
Globalization**

Steven R. Weisman

Washington, DC
January 2016

MIX
Paper from
responsible sources
FSC
www.fsc.org
FSC® C005010

In memory of
Edward Tureen
ഔ ര

Steven R. Weisman is vice president for publications and communications at the Peterson Institute for International Economics. He previously served as a correspondent, editor, and editorial board member at the *New York Times*, based in New York, Washington, New Delhi, and Tokyo. His book *The Great Tax Wars: How the Income Tax Transformed the Nation* received the Sidney Hillman Award in 2003. He is editor of *Daniel Patrick Moynihan: A Portrait in Letters of An American Visionary*, a Washington Post bestseller listed by the Times as one of its best books of 2010.

PETERSON INSTITUTE FOR INTERNATIONAL ECONOMICS
1750 Massachusetts Avenue, NW
Washington, DC 20036-1903
(202) 328-9000   FAX: (202) 328-5432
www.piie.com

Adam S. Posen, *President*
Steven R. Weisman, *Vice President for Publications and Communications*

Cover Designed by Fletcher Design, Inc./ Washington, DC

Editorial Photos: © Adam Stoltman—Corbis, pg. 17; Andrew Winning—Reuters/Corbis, pg. 67; and Timothy Fadek—Corbis, pg. 123.

Printing by Versa Press, Inc.

Printed in the United States of America
18   17   16   5   4   3   2   1

Library of Congress Cataloging-in-Publication Data
Weisman, Steven R.
 The great tradeoff: confronting moral conflicts in the age of globalization / Steven R. Weisman.
   pages cm
 Includes bibliographical references.
 ISBN 978-0-88132-695-6
 1. Economics—Moral and ethical aspects.
 2. Externalities (Economics) 3. Social choice.
 4. Equality. I. Title.
 HB72.W445 2015
 172—dc23
                        2014041814

This publication has been subjected to a prepublication peer review intended to ensure analytical quality. The views expressed are those of the author. This publication is part of the overall program of the Peterson Institute for International Economics, as endorsed by its Board of Directors, but it does not necessarily reflect the views of individual members of the Board or of the Institute's staff or management.

The Peterson Institute for International Economics is a private nonpartisan, nonprofit institution for rigorous, intellectually open, and indepth study and discussion of international economic policy. Its purpose is to identify and analyze important issues to make globalization beneficial and sustainable for the people of the United States and the world, and then to develop and communicate practical new approaches for dealing with them. Its work is funded by a highly diverse group of philanthropic foundations, private corporations, and interested individuals, as well as income on its capital fund. About 35 percent of the Institute's resources in its latest fiscal year were provided by contributors from outside the United States. A list of all financial supporters for the preceding four years is posted at http://piie.com/supporters.cfm.

Contents

Preface   ix

1 What We Talk about When We Talk about   1
   Globalization
   What Is Globalization?   3
   What Is the Great Tradeoff?   8
   Moral Absolutes and Pragmatism   14

I The Conflicts of Liberty and Justice

2 Economic Liberty: From Freedom of the Seas to   19
   Freedom of Capital
   Origins of Economic Liberty   20
   Free Markets and Liberty in the New World   24
   Liberty in Crisis   28

3 The Wolves and the Lambs: "Justice, Justice Shalt   33
   Thou Pursue"
   A Short History of Economic Justice   35
   The Powerful Appeal of Economic Justice   44

4 Justice for All: Defining and Measuring Inequality   47
   Rawls Redux   48
   Piketty's Charge: Sorting Through Different Definitions of   49
      Economic Justice
   Measuring Inequality as a Symbol of Economic Injustice   56
   The Bottom Line?   64

II   The Conflicts over Instilling Virtue

5   The Hazards of Moral Hazard   **69**
The European Fallout of the Global Financial Crisis   70
Is Virtue Essential to Capitalism—or Antithetical to It?   73

6   Government and Just Deserts: A Brief US History   **81**
The Early Days   82
From Virtue to Charity: The Deserving and Undeserving Poor   86

7   Bubbles, Panics, Crashes, and Bailouts: Moral Hazard   **95**
in the Marketplace
"By Every Possible Means" versus "Purging the Rottenness Out of   96
the System"
Debt as a Morality Play: A Brief History   103

8   Who's Afraid of Debt? Debt as a Public Policy Tool   **109**
The Keynesian Revolution   110
Debt Morality Tale: How the East Asian Crisis Raised Doubts   114
about Rescues
Must Virtue Be Its Own Reward?   120

III   The Conflicts over Loyalty

9   The Moral Imperative of Loyalty   **125**
Three Categories of Loyalty   126
Who Is a Communitarian? The "Mystic Chords of Memory"   130
Who Is a Cosmopolitan? "I Am a Citizen of the World"   137

10 Grappling with the Communitarian-Cosmopolitan   **143**
Tradeoff
Offshoring and Reshoring   144
Trade and Globalization: Lifting All Boats or Only Yachts?   146
Case Study of Loyalty: Divided over NAFTA   150
The Continuing Trade Debate   154

11 Loyalties in Conflict: Jobs, Communities, and   **159**
Multinational Corporations
The Special Case of Immigration   162
The Special Case of Multinational Corporations   165
Role of US Consumers?   171
Search for Corporate Tax Havens   173

12 Who Governs? The Role of Liberal Internationalism   **177**
Mediating Moral Principles in the Era of Globalization   178
Enter the NGOs   182

13 Pulling Together the Threads   **187**
The "Comfortable Beds of Dogma"—Sorting Out Liberty,   190
Justice, Virtue, and Loyalty

Notes   **193**

Bibliography   **227**

Acknowledgments   **247**

Index   **249**

Figures

4.1   Economic growth brings millions out of poverty   58
4.2   Globally, the middle class and the superrich gained the most while   60
the upper middle class gained the least between 1988 and 2008
7.1   Financial crises create lasting pain: Increase in unemployment   97
rate following precrisis peak, selected countries
9.1   Trade's share of the US economy is increasing   128
9.2   Global trade has reached new highs   128

Preface

The dramatic opening and integration of the world economy over the last quarter century have undeniably advanced the welfare and living standards of billions of people around the world, especially its poorest citizens. But globalization has put new competitive pressures on workers and businesses, especially on the rich world's lower-skilled citizens. This poses challenges to policymakers seeking to address the grievances of those who are or feel left behind. The rapid rise of global financial flows has also contributed to financial crises in Asia, Latin America, Europe, and the United States over the same time frame, while fueling the investment required for growth. These capital flows have decreased the stability of asset markets, with tough conditions for small savers. Those challenges in turn have required some policy measures— including unprecedentedly large monetary and fiscal interventions—that have ignited fierce debates among the rescued and rescuers alike.

Over the years, in many of our books, papers, and projects, the Peterson Institute for International Economics has tried to assess these trends, understand their moral as well as economic weight, and convey the needed policy responses to the engaged public. Now in *The Great Tradeoff: Confronting Moral Conflicts in the Era of Globalization*, Steven R. Weisman undertakes a direct discussion of some of the pressing moral dilemmas posed by the increasing flows of goods, services, capital, technology, and even people across borders. The world as a whole and the majority of human beings are richer because of globalization, but the current state of distribution and the policies pursued remain open to question. Weisman asks whether the economic system has produced the right balance between preserving freedom in markets and fostering economic justice. He also examines whether rescuing market participants—whether individuals, institutions, or governments—from their reckless behavior to save the economic system as a whole is properly balanced with the need for individuals to suffer risk as well as reward. Finally, he addresses the multifold moral dimensions of the debate over trade and investment liberalization—how to think about and balance the benefits to poor countries and to rich countries' consumers against the possible costs to the livelihood of less-skilled workers in rich countries.

The Great Tradeoff is an unusual book by an author who is experienced in bringing both economics to the public and broader concerns to economics. As the Institute's vice president for publications and communications, Weisman oversees the editing and production of the full range of PIIE publications. Before coming to the Institute in 2008, he served for many years as a correspondent for the *New York Times*, covering economic issues in New York, Washington, Tokyo, and New Delhi. He is the author of *The Great Tax Wars: How the Income Tax Transformed the Nation*. This volume combines economic and political analysis, history, moral philosophy, psychology, law, and basic journalism about how these moral issues are being debated around the world.

Weisman argues that while it is widely recognized how globalization has brought labor, capital, businesses, and occasionally countries into conflict as well as cooperation, the moral implications that arise from these encounters are less thoroughly explored and more politically salient than ever to sort out. The book further documents that throughout human history—indeed since antiquity and running through the Middle Ages and modern times—economic and moral issues have always been intertwined in public debate. Weisman concludes that it is as unreasonable to expect to live in a world of moral absolutes as it is to expect one or another economic interest to always be paramount. Sensible adjustments can be made in a given issue area, but none of these issues will ever be settled, certainly not to widespread satisfaction.

The Institute is grateful to the Stavros Niarchos Foundation for its generous support of this project, an ambitious risk jointly taken by the Foundation, the Institute, and the author. Earlier, the Institute held a high-level conference and published a collected volume on *Ethics and Globalization: The Tradeoffs Underlying Our Policy Choices*, with the Foundation's support. All of the participants that day contributed to the background for this book, and many of them generously provided comments and guidance on this work.

The Peterson Institute for International Economics is a private nonpartisan, nonprofit institution for rigorous, intellectually open, and indepth study and discussion of international economic policy. Its purpose is to identify and analyze important issues to making globalization beneficial and sustainable for the people of the United States and the world and then to develop and communicate practical new approaches for dealing with them.

The Institute's work is funded by a highly diverse group of philanthropic foundations, private corporations, and interested individuals, as well as income on its capital fund. About 35 percent of the Institute resources in our latest fiscal year were provided by contributors from outside the United States. A list of all our financial supporters for the preceding year is posted at http://www.piie.com/supporters.cfm.

The Executive Committee of the Institute's Board of Directors bears overall responsibility for the Institute's direction, gives general guidance and approval to its research program, and evaluates its performance in pursuit of its mission. The Institute's President is responsible for the identification of topics that are likely to become important over the medium term (one to three years) that should be addressed by Institute scholars. This rolling agenda is set in close consultation with the Institute's research staff, Board of Directors, and other stakeholders.

The President makes the final decision to publish any individual Institute study, following independent internal and external review of the work. Interested readers may access the data and computations underlying Institute publications for research and replication by searching titles at www.piie.com.

The Institute hopes that its research and other activities will contribute to building a stronger foundation for international economic policy around the world. We invite readers of these publications to let us know how they think we can best accomplish this objective.

ADAM S. POSEN
President
November 2015

The Great Tradeoff

Confronting Moral Conflicts in the Era of Globalization

We cannot be, in any casual way, "in touch" with moral truth.
But we can nevertheless think well or badly about moral issues.

—Ronald Dworkin, *Justice for Hedgehogs* (2011)

1

What We Talk about When We Talk about Globalization

> *Happy are those ... who have, by their own methods, arrived at clear and unshakeable convictions about what to do and what to be that brook no possible doubt. I can only say that those who rest on such comfortable beds of dogma are victims of forms of self-induced myopia, blinkers that may make for contentment, but not for understanding of what it is to be human.*
>
> —Isaiah Berlin, "The Pursuit of the Ideal" (1988) in *The Crooked Timber of Humanity* (2013).

Images of despair from the Great Depression in the early 1930s are etched in the American consciousness: shantytowns, farmlands turned into dust bowls, beggars and apple sellers on city streets, vagrants drifting through back roads, and families gathered around the living room radio to listen to a president's reassuring voice. "Remember my forgotten man" went the mournful anthem of a popular 1933 movie, lamenting the desperate plight of jobless doughboys a dozen years after World War I. "You put a rifle in his hand/You sent him far away/You shouted 'Hip-hooray'!/But look at him today."

By contrast, the much fresher pictures and videos of the global financial crisis and Great Recession that began three quarters of a century later, in 2008, conjure up shattered complacency and black humor over what was supposed to have been permanent if uneven prosperity. The modern depictions of economic distress are padlocked suburban shopping malls and foreclosed homes, shuttered factories and businesses, long lines at job fairs, crumbling working-class neighborhoods in bankrupt cities, sober-suited men and women lugging boxes of belongings from Wall Street offices, and corporate executives on the defensive at congressional committee hearings, where they explain how it all happened. "Robin Hood was right," read one sign at the 2011 Occupy Wall Street protest in Zuccotti Park in lower Manhattan. "If only the war on poverty was a real war, then we would actually be putting money into it," said another.

The images and slogans from both of these turbulent eras have one thing in common: they inspire moral indignation, feelings of betrayal, and a pervasive sense that the misery resulted from failings that were not just economic but ethical in nature. From the improvised tent cities of Occupy Wall Street to the rallies and talk radio and cable television rants by the Tea Party, people caught up in the latest crisis and downturn have focused their criticism not simply on the perpetrators but also on the steps taken by government to alleviate it or rescue those caught up in its tentacles. Critics on the right, the left, and in between all seem to acknowledge that somehow the global economic system, which has become increasingly integrated over the last few decades, is at the root of the suffering. These critics suggest that the system itself has yielded a morally defective and unfair universe in which businesses, workers, consumers, policymakers, international financial institutions, and multinational corporations are all to blame.

But if moral outrage has intensified, it is also, as this book argues, often unfocused and even confused. On the one hand, the system of market economics, which governs most of the world in the era of globalization, has brought the competing interests of labor, capital, business, and countries together into a convergence that has elevated the living standards of hundreds of millions, if not billions, of people worldwide, including some of the world's poorest citizens. On the other hand, globalization has left large numbers of people behind in many countries, particularly advanced countries in the West, and produced disastrous shocks that have thrown millions out of work and vaporized trillions of dollars in assets and savings. The surge of emotions about immigration in the United States, an early debating point among candidates for president, and the flood of refugees and asylum seekers in Europe in 2015 have also driven home the perils and opportunities of globalization.

This book maintains that there is a moral case to be made for globalization. But that case must be based on a greater understanding of how moral imperatives as well as economic interests contend, converge and conflict with each other.

Humans are moral creatures. The impulse to assign moral values to the marketplace is as old as the impulse to assign such values to war and politics. Indeed from ancient times to the present, economists, historians, philosophers, political scientists, and other writers often debate economics in moral terms, whether the subject is the treatment of the poor, the obligations of buyers and sellers or the just distribution of rewards and costs in everyday life. It has long been tempting as well to think about economic forces as representing absolutist moral principles, such as freedom, justice, virtuous behavior, and patriotism. This book argues that such absolutist approaches are unrealistic. What people talk about when they talk about globalization may be centered on moral principles, but a doctrinaire pursuit of such principles in isolation of competing values has an unfortunate and even tragic record historically. In the last 150 years, the "comfortable beds of dogma," as the political philosopher Isaiah Berlin calls them, have led to hatred, persecution, totalitarianism, and war.[1]

The dangers of dogma aside, globalization seems to have brought on a global political movement for a new type of ethically charged economics. Some call it inclusive capitalism; others call it inclusive prosperity. Whatever the label, the goal would seem to be a system in which opportunities are more equal, the distribution of rewards is fairer to those buffeted or left behind, and the preservation of communities and national sovereignty is more respected.

Three types of moral conflicts, or tradeoffs, lie in the universe of any set of economic issues: (1) the conflicts between liberty and justice in society and the marketplace; (2) the conflicts between the need to sustain virtuous behavior and trust (by governments, individuals, and banks) and the need to recognize the realities of the modern global economy; and (3) the conflicts between ensuring economic justice for one's own community and ensuring it for others in the world at large, especially the world's poorest citizens. These three tradeoffs form the basis of this study.

This book ranges over history, philosophy, politics, economics, and social science, with an objective of applying understandable moral principles to the complexities and, for many, the mysteries of the modern global economy. There is no easy way to bring these disciplines together, except by recognizing one fundamental conclusion: the only moral outcome in a conflict of moral principles is compromise—that is, a tradeoff, or what this book refers to collectively as The Great Tradeoff. The purpose of this book is to deepen readers' understanding of *morality in the modern economic world*. Its premise is that only after such recognition can policies be devised that open the doors of opportunity and prosperity while avoiding the trapdoors of blinkered and absolutist thinking. A greater understanding of the moral issues at stake and how they connect with economic imperatives can make the goal of morally based globalization more reachable.

What Is Globalization?

The word *globalization* sprang into common usage in the early 1990s. Its popularity as a term grew in the wake of the collapse of communism and the rapid spread of market capitalism that many saw as a harbinger of a new epoch of prosperity and world harmony. As a catchword used in books and newspapers and favored by market theorists and protesters alike, globalization refers generally to the growing interdependence of the world economy, the cross fertilization of the world's many cultures, and of course the expansion of cross-border flows in trade, investments, capital, technology, knowledge, culture, and people (immigrants). Although globalization and the ease of cross-border commerce and population shifts have been blamed for the proliferation of terrorism, disease, crime, human trafficking, environmental degradation, loss of biodiversity, and invasions of personal privacy, this study focuses strictly on the economic aspects of worldwide interaction, speeded by the growth of technology and the expanding acceptance of liberalized markets for goods and capital.

The expansion of economic activity throughout the world is not new. Globalization has been under way since the first humans migrated from East Africa some 60,000 years ago. Over subsequent millennia they searched for hospitable places to settle, produce, and exchange goods in places such as Mesopotamia and the Indus, Yangtze, and Yellow River valleys. Each new phase of globalization has been accelerated by important breakthroughs such as the domestication of the horse and the camel, advances in river craft, ocean sailing, the steam engine, telegraph, air travel, and most recently the astonishing leap in information technology. Each new technology has also been disruptive, subversive, or revolutionary. Indeed, in his history of globalization, *Bound Together*, Nayan Chanda draws an analogy between the spread of trade and commerce in antiquity and the transmission of the religions and ethical systems espoused by Buddhism, Judaism, Christianity, and Islam, all embracing some tenets that challenged the established political order.[2]

From antiquity to about 1500, the world straggled along with negligible economic growth, little technological innovation, scant capital resources, and some but not a lot of geographic interaction. War, famine, disease, and the seizure of property by warlords and church and political figures were the norm. With the late Renaissance (1520–1600) and the Enlightenment (1650s to 1780s) came the glimmerings of commercial revolution, business innovation, science, greater education—and higher economic growth, driven by mercantilism. What is generally recognized as the first modern era of globalization was facilitated by a technology revolution—rail, steamship, telegraph—and an explosion of international trade, investment, and immigration. But that epoch of the Industrial Revolution and its Gilded Age complacency crashed in the outbreak of World War I with its massive debts and death. The period 1914–80 (labeled "the short 20th century" by the economist Brad DeLong) was disrupted by World War II, but then that war led to a remarkable recovery, the new rules and norms governing the global economic system established at Bretton Woods, and a series of progressive social welfare steps in many countries.[3]

The most recent phase of globalization began in the late 1970s and early 1980s, a time of growing belief in market economics and conservative economic philosophies. It was symbolized by the election of Ronald Reagan to the presidency in the United States, the rise of Prime Minister Margaret Thatcher in Britain, and the ascendency of Deng Xiaoping to the leadership in China. This period, hastened by the fall of communism in the Soviet Union and Eastern Europe a decade later, saw the adoption of policies that encouraged the expansion of markets, business, and wealth, particularly in poorer countries that followed China's lead in moving away from state-directed economies. Not only did world trade and investment grow at an even faster rate as free markets, rather than the state, were granted control of the "commanding heights" of economies across the globe,[4] but also a new ideological era was introduced, equating these forces with the cause of liberty and freedom. "Communism collapsed, and the mixed economy failed," said Lee Kuan Yew, the founder of modern Singapore. "What else is there?"[5]

The economic results have been impressive. From 1990 to the middle of the first decade of the 21st century, world exports as a percentage of global GDP rose from 19.2 percent to nearly 30 percent (figure 9.2 in chapter 9). US exports as a share of US GDP rose to 9 percent in 2010 (from 4 percent in 1960), and total trade exceeded 20 percent of the US national economy as of 2013 (figure 9.1 in chapter 9). Since the liberalized trade agreements of the

1990s and 2000s, exports and imports have generated more than 38 million US jobs, or one out of five US jobs, according to the Business Roundtable.[6] Annual world merchandise trade has reached $18 trillion,[7] and international capital investments amount to more than $4 trillion a year.[8] From 1990 to 2012, the cumulative amount of foreign direct investment in the world grew more than tenfold, from $1.8 trillion to $23 trillion.[9] As a partial result of this activity, standards of living have risen across the globe and more of the world's citizens have been lifted out of poverty than at any comparable time in history. "We have never seen this kind of rapid and sustained development across so many countries," Jim Yong Kim, president of the World Bank Group, has declared. "We can fairly say that the concept of a development decade that eluded us for 50 years was finally achieved.[10]

The Backlash

It is not as if the growth in economic activity has been without criticism and misgivings. There is nothing new in that. The pursuit of material gain through business or commercial activities has long been denigrated in Western literature, going back to the ancient Greeks. Religious figures, moreover, have leveled a moral critique of money lending and money making that is symbolized well by the story of Jesus chasing the traders and money changers from the temple, Jesus' own declaration in the Beatitudes (Matthew 5:3,5) "blessed are the poor in spirit: for theirs is the kingdom of heaven," and the first epistle of Paul to Timothy, "for the love of money is the root of all evil." The prohibition of usury, or *riba*, has been powerfully fixed in Muslim societies since the Koran was revealed to Mohammed in the 7th century, on the grounds that charging interest is corrupting, unjust, and destructive—although the ban has often been circumvented.[11]

But the economic trends of the past decades have produced an unusual backlash, or at least ambivalence, accelerated by the global economic crisis that began in 2007–08. This hostile or questioning response has raised issues of justice and equity as well as liberty and freedom, discussed in this book.

Americans seem to like worldwide economic integration in theory more than in practice, for example. The Pew Research Center, a respected polling organization, found in 2013 that although the US public had grown tired of their country trying to solve world problems, "support for closer trade and business ties with other nations stands at its highest point in more than a decade." Fully 77 percent believed that such growing trade and business ties with other countries were either very good (23 percent) or somewhat good (54 percent). But the public debate reflects deeper anxieties about, among other things, corporations transferring their investments to locations where labor is cheaper and taxes and regulations are lighter. Wariness of "offshoring" by US companies extends to trade deals such as the North American Free Trade Agreement (NAFTA) and more recently to the prospect of a Trans-Pacific Partnership (TPP) trade deal between the United States and 11 countries in

Asia and the Western Hemisphere.[12] In 2010 another poll found that 69 percent of Americans felt that trade agreements such as NAFTA had cost American jobs.[13]

To be sure, much of the antiglobalization movement overseas is simply anti–United States, anti-West, or anti–multinational corporation. Many people around the world see globalization as an American project, while in the United States many see it as symbolized by Chinese, Japanese, or European acquisition of American companies. The generalized backlash against globalization has also taken on added impetus because of the speed of modern communications, degradation of the environment, global warming, and the visible spread of disease and other phenomena associated with an integrated world economy.

The heightened concern of recent vintage has focused on whether globalization, along with labor-saving technology innovations, has helped suppress the incomes of low-skilled middle-class workers in rich countries and widened the perception of a gulf between the superrich and multinational corporations on the one hand, and everyone else on the other. It would be hard to deny the evidence of the destruction of American jobs, for example—a trend that has contributed to inequality and wage stagnation in rich countries. But critics of globalization go further, charging that it has exploited workers in Asia, weakened environmental and food safety protections in the United States and its trading partners, and permitted megacorporations to reap record profits (10 percent of the US domestic economy in 2014) at the expense of consumers and workers. Hundreds if not thousands of nongovernmental organizations have rallied around the cause of turning back the growing interdependence of the world economy. One of them, the International Forum on Globalization, puts it this way in an all-inclusive indictment that is part of its mission statement: "All over the world, evidence points to the failure of globalization and the so-called 'free trade' policies of the last decade—loss of jobs and livelihoods, displacement of indigenous peoples, massive immigration, rapid environmental devastation and loss of biodiversity, increases in poverty and hunger, and many additional negative effects."[14]

Concerns about the malign effects of the global economy reached an initial peak at the World Trade Organization's Ministerial Conference held in late 1999 in Seattle, where tens of thousands of demonstrators descended on the conferees meeting at the Washington State Convention and Trade Center, overwhelming the police. Demonstrators chained themselves together and blocked intersections, demanding better treatment for the people they asserted had lost their jobs or had seen their environment ravaged by trade. President Bill Clinton sought to empathize with the dissidents, telling the conference that most of them had legitimate grievances. He later recalled that even though the process of globalization could not be reversed, he realized that the protests would impede the work of governments "until we addressed the concerns of those who felt left out and left behind."[15]

For much of the first decade of the 21st century, following the protests of the 1990s, a certain complacency settled in and surrounded the idea of globalization, especially among leadership elites. It was previously widely accepted among economists and political leaders, for example, that the interdependent global economy could stabilize political conflicts and cushion the blow when a traumatic meltdown in one part of the world affected citizens far away. That self-satisfaction was blasted away by the crisis that began in 2007–08, which demonstrated that the world economy had become so interdependent that its vulnerabilities to economic shocks were in fact magnified, with the result that blameless victims around the world were devastated when the crash occurred.

Within Europe since 2010, complacency was heightened by arrogance. European leaders, who initially blamed the financial practices of the United States on the crisis in 2008, became engulfed in their own similar problems of state sector spending without regard to the ability to pay for it and lax regulatory practices two years later. Just as Americans rebelled against programs that rescued banks, the citizens of Portugal, Spain, Italy, and especially Greece expressed outrage over diminished services and safety net programs, imposed in the view of many by the lords of finance in Germany and northern Europe. Europe's moral indignation was thus aggravated by nationalist fervor and resentment.

Even before President Barack Obama's embrace of liberalized trade and investment agreements in his second term, the critics saw markets not as liberating but as a new tyranny, imposing discipline, austerity, and weaker protections for the poor and helping to spread terrorism and cyberwarfare.[16] Anger has especially been directed at the organizations that help support globalization—the World Bank, International Monetary Fund (IMF), and World Trade Organization (WTO). Their rules, critics claim, are trampling on local laws and prerogatives.

Following the global financial crisis, the criticism of capitalism and free markets became especially acute among religious figures. Pope Benedict XVI's 2009 encyclical, *Caritas in Veritate* (Charity in Truth), declared that both had their place, but that they had also led to greed, selfishness, "wasteful and consumerist" luxuries, and "dehumanizing deprivations" of the poor.[17] He added, "The economy needs ethics in order to function correctly—not any ethics whatsoever, but an ethics which is people-centered."[18] His successor, Pope Francis, has been an even more acerbic critic of the global economic system and capitalism in general. His 2015 encyclical on climate change, *Laudato Si'* (Praise Be to You), excoriated greed and free markets as sources of the global environmental crisis. "We need to reject a magical conception of the market, which would suggest that problems can be solved simply by an increase in the profits of companies or individuals," he declared.[19] He went so far as to criticize the mobilization of market economics to cap greenhouse gases and trade them for credit, declaring that such a system—which is supported by many environmental advocates—is "a quick and easy solution under the guise of a certain commitment to the environment."[20] In another speech, Pope Francis referred to the "unfettered pursuit of money" as "the dung of the devil." [21] But speaking to the US Congress in September 2015, he tempered his denunciation of capitalism, saying that "business is a noble vocation" that nonetheless must serve "the common good." A line in his prepared text saying that politics "cannot be a slave to the economy and finance" was omitted from his actual address.[22]

Francis's call in *Laudato Si'* for "wealth redistribution," opposition to corporations outsourcing production to places where they are less regulated and taxed, and denunciation of "downsizing of social security systems" and weakening of rights of workers has been especially striking.[23] But Catholics are hardly the only religious leaders to speak this way about the modern global economy. In a 2009 speech, Rowan Williams, the former Archbishop of Canterbury, deplored the exaltation of the marketplace above other values, which he said was creating "a ruinous legacy for heavily indebted countries, large-scale and costly social disruption even in developed economies; and, most recently, the extraordinary phenomena of a financial trading world in which the marketing of toxic debt became the driver of money-making—until the bluffs were all called at the same time."[24]

What Is the Great Tradeoff?

An axiom of modern economics is that individuals, organizations, governments, and indeed societies must confront material tradeoffs—that is, to choose some things, they must give up other things, and every benefit or gain comes with some kind of cost. These tradeoffs can sometimes be measured and sometimes not. Two famous generalized *economic* tradeoffs are "You can't have your cake and eat it too" and "There is no free lunch." To assess tradeoffs, economists apply metrics and formulas to the empirical observations of gains, losses, and efficiencies that flow from the alternatives posed in ordinary life, such as whether to save or to spend, whether to work or to play, whether to combat inflation or to fight unemployment, whether to devote public resources to national security or to support the social safety net (better known as the guns versus butter debate). In the economic analysis of free market systems, tradeoffs may cause some people to win and some to lose, but in the end market economics is justified as the system that most efficiently delivers goods and services to those who want and need them, spreading wealth to communities and nations.

Yet, however efficient the system is at delivering economic benefits, it has its shortcomings, arising from what economists call "externalities" such as pollution and the inability of the marketplace to adequately deliver public benefits such as schools, law and order, and infrastructure (roads, ports, and highways, among other things).[25] Mere use of the term *externality* to describe what non-economists might regard as moral shortcomings (such as harming the planet and the human race through pollution or global warming) suggests a certain discomfort in the field of economics with the notion of morality. But surely the economic consensus of most of those who support free markets includes the need for regulation to curb abuses and ensure transparency, competition, and a level playing field. With its welter of federal agencies, for example. the United States is hardly an unregulated economy. "The market needs a place," the economist Arthur Okun argued in the 1970s, "and the market needs to be kept in place."[26]

Moral tradeoffs are obviously more difficult to quantify than economic tradeoffs. More important, they cannot be isolated or understood apart from the messy, complex, and ambiguous realities of history, human behavior, politics, culture, and faith. Compromises and solutions must derive from politics and political institutions and leaders, however imperfect they may be, because absolute moral principles, when expanded or extrapolated, invariably come into conflict. Choices must be determined by experience, history, and the implications of what might be true in one context but not in another.

Economics and moral philosophy have gone hand in hand at least since the days of Adam Smith, the 18th-century founding father of modern free-market economics. Smith, in fact, taught moral philosophy, not economics (which did not exist as a discipline), at the University of Glasgow. In *The Theory of Moral Sentiments* (1759), he wrote of the conflicting ethical impulses of personal strength of will, "dignity and honour," on the one hand, and "indulgent humanity," on the other—his own version of the conflict between justice and mercy.[27] In the 1920s, John Maynard Keynes, already famous for his warnings about the harsh economic penalties imposed on Germany after World War I, asserted that the goal of any society is to balance economic efficiency against two moral values—social justice and individual liberty.[28] Okun, a leading proponent of the "mixed economy" of government and private sector who served as the chief economic adviser to President Lyndon Johnson during the Great Society, captured the tradeoff differently. In his book *Equality and Efficiency: The Big Tradeoff* (1975), he asserted that it was between economic efficiency (and the economic growth that would come with it) and the moral goal of achieving social and economic *equality*.[29] (The title of this book is an homage of sorts to Okun's formulation.)

According to Okun, there is no easy way to resolve the tradeoff between economic efficiency and economic equality. Programs intended to bring about social justice, for example, come at a cost. That cost, Okun asserted, comes in the form of slower economic growth when some of those receiving assistance work less than they might otherwise, or when waste results from government aid programs. He evoked the image of a "leaky bucket" in which some of the money transferred from the rich to the poor "will simply disappear in transit."[30] The leaky bucket idea of inefficiency in government programs has had staying power and is endorsed by economists of varying political persuasions, even many of those who favor government intervention to assist the needy. On the other hand, a staff paper by the International Monetary Fund (IMF) in 2014 argued that for poor countries, at least, programs aimed at redistributing wealth are "generally benign" in terms of their impact on economic growth and that "only in extreme cases" do such programs harm growth. "We should be careful not to assume that there is a big tradeoff between redistribution and growth," the staff concluded. "The best available macroeconomic data do not support that conclusion." Indeed, the staff pointed out that some government intervention, such as taxes to prevent risk taking in the financial sector and programs to encourage education of young people, can actually encourage economic growth.[31]

The sections that follow describe in more detail the moral conflicts, encompassed by The Great Tradeoff, studied in this book.

Liberty versus Justice

The principles of liberty and justice spring from Western tradition and the Enlightenment. Freedom of movement of goods, services, capital, people, and technology is rooted in both ancient mythology and modern political theory. In the words of Milton Friedman, one of the most influential modern proponents of the virtues of capitalism, "I know of no example in time or place of a society that has been marked by a large measure of political freedom, and that has not also used something comparable to a free market to organize the bulk of economic activity."[32] Justice, in the sense of reward for good behavior or punishment for bad behavior, has also been an issue since antiquity, in scripture and Greek philosophy, although the notion of a just distribution of economic benefits in a society is of much more recent vintage.

In the modern era of globalization, freedom of choice enables consumers to buy goods made in other countries at lower cost and enables investors to channel funds anywhere they believe will yield a return. But since at least the 18th century, a countervailing principle has been the imposition of social and economic justice to tame the excesses and unequal consequences of freedom. Whether the same dynamism that has encouraged economic growth throughout the world has also contributed to increased economic inequality between countries and within countries—and has been driven deeper by the global economic crisis—is the subject of reams of books over the last several years from widely read authors such as Joseph Stiglitz, Jeffrey Sachs, and Thomas Piketty on the left.

Liberty and justice, which are loaded terms in an economic context, mean different things to different people. Liberty can refer to freedom from external constraints by government, or it can refer to government intervention to ensure that all individuals have the ability to mobilize their own resources and gifts to fulfill their individual potential, possibly with the intervention of government. In recent years, the goal of economic justice has been equated in American political discourse with the concern over reducing economic inequality. But is economic justice in fact achieved by increasing economic equality? Or is it achieved when those at the bottom gain a greater standard of living for themselves, even if inequality increases in some countries along with these gains? To explain further, in his work A Theory of Justice (1971) the eminent Harvard philosopher John Rawls said a just social order must embody economic justice and economic liberty.[33] But Rawls is most famous for the principle holding that the first priority of any society is to devise a distribution acceptable only if the worst-off members of that society are helped, not hurt. What happens, however, if the worst-off members of a society are helped, but those at the higher end of the ladder are helped even more, widening the economic gulf overall?

Instilling Virtue versus Recognizing the Realities of the Modern Global Economy

In the era of globalization, does capitalism require virtuous behavior by countries, corporations, and individuals—or does it undermine such conduct? Since the dawn of modern capitalism, part of the system's legitimacy has rested on the widespread view that it encourages self-discipline, trust, hard work, saving, self-improvement, ingenuity, and delayed gratification (while discouraging laziness and recklessness). The Founders of the United States were determined to create laws and charters that would encourage upstanding habits and conduct. "To suppose that any form of government will secure liberty or happiness without any virtue in the people is a chimerical idea," wrote James Madison at the Virginia Ratifying Convention in 1788.[34] From this idea has come the belief that any government must ensure that economic incentives encourage virtuous behavior among citizens.

That idea was challenged—among those on both the left and the right—by the actions taken during the recent financial crisis to bail out banks, financial institutions, homeowners, and governments. Indeed, these rescues were widely seen as excusing and even encouraging recklessness, corruption, and heedless greed—the very shortcomings that caused the crisis in the first place. Economists define this problem as "moral hazard." A furor similar to that arising from the recent rescues occurred in the late 1990s when the IMF, supported by the United States, went to the rescue of the East Asian countries in trouble. The IMF's actions were doubly unpopular, both among those who opposed the bailouts and among the countries themselves, which were resentful of the harsh measures they had to endure as the price for rescue.

The belief that government should not undermine incentives toward virtue has extended to tax policies, to the welfare state, and to charity for the "undeserving" or to those at risk of becoming dependent on outside aid. Even President Franklin Roosevelt opposed the "dole." The 2012 presidential election campaign between Democrat Barack Obama and Republican Mitt Romney exploded over Romney's assertion that nearly half of the US population did not pay federal income taxes and, depending on government for transfer payments, had lost the willingness to take responsibility for their own lives. The other side of the argument is that government must help, if not as a matter of charity or justice then as a matter of preserving stability and avoiding unrest.

All this said, is it moral to invoke the risk of contagion and rescue the financial institutions that behaved irresponsibly by borrowing heavily and packaging dubious housing loans to unsuspecting customers? Is it moral to do the same for errant governments, businesses, and homeowners who take on too much debt? Or is it immoral to invoke moral hazard and bring down a system to the harm of countless innocents? Again the danger is in following moral absolutes to disastrous ends. This book concludes that just as justice is tempered with mercy, moral hazard must be tempered by whether innocents are harmed in the process.

Loyalty to Community versus Loyalty to the World

The tradeoff between doing what is best for one's own country or community and the demands of the world as a whole is debated by economists and philosophers in terms of "communitarian" versus "cosmopolitan" loyalty. The dilemma is choosing between protecting the welfare of one's own community or country from unwanted immigrants, foreign-made goods, and the loss of investments to locations or tax havens overseas, or seeking a system of trade, capital flows, and immigration that produces the greatest prosperity for all, and particularly benefits the poorest individuals and countries in the world. Loyalty can be expressed in different ways: the French Revolution, after all, enshrined *fraternité* as equivalent to *liberté* and *égalité*.

The morally unassailable economic goals for any society, and indeed for the world as a whole, should be to provide the greatest good for the greatest number while doing the most for those most in need. The modern global economy has delivered an unprecedented level of economic gains and improvements in living standards for vast numbers of once-destitute people, especially in Asia and more recently in Africa. But these gains have not been so helpful to the working class in the United States and Europe. There, globalization has lowered middle- and lower-income wages, leading to a decline in median household incomes, even as the wealthiest and those deriving income from their investments have done exceptionally well in terms of both income and possessions.

Support for free trade and liberalized investment has eroded in advanced countries over the last few decades because of this dilemma. The 1993 debate over the North American Free Trade Agreement (NAFTA) among Canada, Mexico, and the United States accelerated that trend, which is invoked by opponents of pending trade agreements between the United States and its partners in Europe and Asia. To whom should Americans be loyal? This question is even more difficult to answer because trade and investment are increasingly taking place between and among corporations rather than countries. Indeed 80 percent of all transfers of goods and services across borders is undertaken by multinational corporations through their affiliates or networks of providers,[35] blurring the distinction between "us" and "them" in global commerce. "We no longer simply trade what we make for what we do not make but need," wrote Stephen Carmel, a senior executive at Maersk Line, Ltd., the giant Danish container ship concern. "We now trade in order to get what we need *to make what we make*." He also noted that more than 50 percent of containerized trade is in components of goods rather than goods themselves.[36] A plane or automobile may be labeled as "Made in America," but it often contains parts made in many other countries. The iPod, for example, has 451 different parts produced in companies, factories, and assembly operations spread throughout Japan, China, the Philippines, and other places in Asia, although most of the value added is by Apple in the United States.[37] Americans who embrace the moral obligation to "Buy American" find it increasingly hard to do so. Similar conflicts arise over the obligations of the biggest US corporations—should they be "loyal" to their workers, their investors, their home countries, or their customers, whether in the United States or in distant countries?

The "communitarian" school of thought holds that one's obligation to one's own community has a high moral standing equal to the primacy of helping the poor, especially in other communities. Cosmopolitan moral judgment requires that one's obligation to others around the world be equal to the loyalty one feels toward one's neighbors or compatriots. In reality, citizens are always pulled in opposite directions and find it difficult to reconcile these two demands.

An important aspect of these conflicts is that it is difficult to go from judgment to implementation and solutions. The political scientist Ethan Kapstein has written, "One of the great weaknesses in the application of moral philosophy to international politics is that it has almost exclusively been exploited by scholars as a normative tool for asserting what some imagined world *should* look like, as opposed to a methodology for helping us to understand the world as it *is*."[38] This book does not seek to lay out practical solutions, except to invoke another kind of "cosmopolitan" loyalty in the form of the legitimacy and authority of international organizations. What Kapstein and others call "liberal internationalism" applies to the post–World War II order of the United Nations and global diplomacy and the supranational political and financial institutions that represent attempts at global economic governance. These institutions, through which the modern rules of globalization must be negotiated, include the World Bank, IMF, World Trade Organization (WTO), and similar, lower-level organizations structured to stabilize the international system. Flawed as many of these organizations are, their goals are to try to avoid another round of ruinous economic "beggar thy neighbor" warfare, elevate the values of economic freedom and openness, and introduce new rules, norms, and buffers to achieve economic justice. Yet the irony is that these same institutions are depicted by antiglobalization critics as agents of the rich and powerful.

However flawed, the international system of free markets needs these institutions because, with the end of the Cold War especially, governments around the world have come to see the management of their economies as their most important function, alongside the obligation to provide security.[39] The work of these agencies is supplemented by nongovernmental organizations (NGOs) that seek to elucidate and elevate the research necessary to make the worldwide market system work. NGOs are also an important counterweight to the role of multinational corporations on the global stage.

Moral Absolutes and Pragmatism

The attraction of moral absolutes has been prevalent at least since antiquity. Tales of heroism, national purpose, and war can hardly exist without that attraction. But in the real world, justice is often tempered by liberty, punishment is moderated by mercy, and discipline is offset by compassion. Utilitarianism (the greatest good for the greatest number) runs up against the rights of the minority. Liberty conflicts with security and stability. Tolerance is balanced with the need for social order. Action is weighed against reflection. Honesty and truth telling are mitigated by sympathy and benevolence. Resisting tyranny at all costs is balanced against sparing the lives of the innocent, particularly children. The psychologist Joshua Greene speaks of "the two moralities" of head and heart that he labels "abstract" and "sympathetic."[40] He applies the label "metamorality" to the balancing of moral imperatives. Other writers have used other terms.

The shadowy world of ambiguous choices is inhabited by civilization's greatest writers and thinkers. The poet John Keats employed the term *negative capability* to describe the rare but vital ability to accept the world's complexities and contradictions and to reject forced and permanent theories or categories— "when a man is capable of being in uncertainties, mysteries, doubts, without any irritable reaching after fact and reason."[41] F. Scott Fitzgerald's formulation of this capacity is also well known: "The test of a first-rate intelligence is the ability to hold two opposed ideas in mind at the same time and still retain the ability to function. One should, for example, be able to see that things are hopeless and yet be determined to make them otherwise."[42] David Herbert Donald, historian and biographer of Abraham Lincoln, associated this "negative capability" with the 16th president, who ended slavery but violated civil liberties, made crass political deals, and tolerated scorched earth warfare to achieve his goals.[43] Isaiah Berlin has written in the same vein: "The notion of the perfect whole, the ultimate solution, in which all good things coexist, seems to me to be not merely unattainable—that is, a truism—but conceptually incoherent. We are doomed to choose, and every choice may entail an irreparable loss."[44]

Reconciling the conflict between hard realities and moral absolutes gave birth in the late 19th century to the American philosophical tradition of pragmatism, described by the literary historian Louis Menand as "an effort to unhitch human beings from what pragmatists regard as a useless structure of bad abstractions of thought."[45] The term *pragmatism* was introduced by the philosopher William James, and its approach was adopted by leading lights and thinkers of the era such as Charles Sanders Pierce, John Dewey, and US jurist Oliver Wendell Holmes Jr.

Pragmatism holds that "the ultimate test for us of what a truth means is indeed the conduct it dictates or inspires," in James's words.[46] Or as he subsequently rephrased it, "A pragmatist turns his back resolutely and once for all upon a lot of inveterate habits dear to professional philosophers. He turns away from abstraction and insufficiency, from verbal solutions, from bad *a priori* reasons, from fixed principles, closed systems, and pretended absolutes and origins. He turns towards concreteness and adequacy, towards facts, towards action, and towards power."[47]

In the 20th century, pragmatism went into something of an eclipse for intellectuals—they turned to other schools of thought such as Marxism, psychoanalysis, and existentialism—but it has undergone a revival in recent decades with a new generation of writers. In that spirit, this book is guided by the principles enunciated by Holmes, an intimate of James though he did not call himself a pragmatist. In 1886 Holmes told an audience at Harvard Law School, "to make a general principle worth anything, you must give it a body. You must show in what way and how far it would be applied actually in a system. . . . Finally, you must show historic relations to other principles, often of very different date and origin."[48]

If there is a moral case for globalization, as stated at the outset of this chapter, it must be rooted in a spirit of pragmatism. Thus to explore the Great Tradeoff, one must proceed in the pragmatic spirit of Holmes, with an examination of the origins, evolution, and context of what has been meant historically and economically by liberty, justice, virtue, and loyalty.

THE CONFLICTS OF LIBERTY AND JUSTICE

Demonstrators in Lower Manhattan near Zuccotti Park taking part in the Occupy Wall Street protests on October 5, 2011.

© Adam Stoltman—Corbis

Liberty! What crimes are committed in thy name!
—Mme Marie-Jeanne Roland de la Platière, before her execution (1793)

There is no crueler tyranny than that which is perpetuated under the shield of law and in the name of justice.
—Charles de Montesquieu, *Considerations on the Causes of the Greatness of the Romans and Their Decline* (1734)

2

Economic Liberty:

From Freedom of the Seas to Freedom of Capital

The following most specific and unimpeachable axiom of the Law of Nations, called a primary rule or first principle, the spirit of which is self-evident and immutable, to wit: Every nation is free to travel to every other nation, and to trade with it.

—Hugo Grotius, *The Freedom of the Seas: The Right Which Belongs to the Dutch to Take Part in the East Indian Trade* (1608)

Freedom has its risks. But are they greater than those of complex administrative rules and capricious changes in their design?

—Michel Camdessus, managing director, IMF (1997)

In the early morning of February 25, 1603, in the Strait of Singapore near the strategic Strait of Malacca, a Dutch ship captained by the explorer Jacob van Heemskerck attacked the Portuguese square-rigged carrack *Santa Catarina*, seizing cargo that included copper from Japan, silk and porcelain from China, and bullion from Mexico and Peru.

The Dutch auctioned everything off for more than 3 million Dutch guilders, a sum that enriched the newly formed United Dutch East India Company. To proclaim a high-minded rationale for attacking the ship—one that would impress the French, British, and other rival powers suspicious of Portugal—van Heemskerck hired an ambitious young lawyer in The Hague, who had only recently graduated from Leiden University, to prepare a legal case for his action. The lawyer, Hugo Grotius, just happened to be a cousin of the Dutch captain.[1]

Dutch authorities wanted Grotius to build his case on a narrow basis, by saying that the captain's attack was necessary to punish the Portuguese for their harassment and intimidation of Dutch merchants over the years. Instead Grotius wrote a treatise on "universal laws" asserting that freedom of the seas and of commerce was a matter of natural law derived, not from God, but from human reason. Because it applied to all nations, such a natural law justified Dutch action in the ship's seizure.[2] Grotius's theory, outlined in a book called *Commentary on the Law of Prize and Booty*, led later to his more ambitious and influential works *The Freedom of the Seas* (1608) and *The Rights of War and Peace* (1625). The seas, he argued in the 1608 book, were common to all, like the air and the sky. No one nation can possess them or prevent another nation from traversing them, the argument went. Defending the right of the Dutch to preempt the Portuguese from interference with their trade, he asserted that "every nation is free to travel to every other nation, and to trade with it."[3]

Origins of Economic Liberty

The globally integrated economy has been evolving since antiquity, but the Dutch-Portuguese encounter near the strategically vital Malacca Strait chokepoint for East Asian trade demonstrates that only since the 17th century have nations tried to establish rules about the free flow of goods and investments. These rules have been modified countless times since the Dutch, Portuguese, British, French, Spanish, and others competed for commerce on the open seas. Today, they reflect an evolved understanding on an international level that the world cannot march under the banner of economic liberty alone. As the global crises of recent decades have unfolded, proponents of free flows of trade and investment have understood that liberty must be combined with justice on an international scale. This chapter traces the history of the concept of economic liberty and the problems that concept has begun to encounter today.

Economists since Adam Smith have argued—and argue today—that impediments to trade should be reduced for the sake of efficiency and economic prosperity, not morality. But the *idea* and *ideal* of trade and commerce conducted freely and held out as moral principles have shaped the destinies and arguments of global trading participants. On the one hand, in stories, histories, songs, and legends, the activities of markets have been described as leading to wealth, influence, and progress. On the other, since antiquity, poets, philosophers, and historians have viewed the untrammeled marketplace with distaste and moral condescension.

Long before Grotius, some Greek and Roman authors claimed that because the winds and the oceans were created by Divine Providence, humans were meant to engage freely in commerce.[4] Plutarch wrote of the sea's power in providing goods that would not otherwise have been available, such as wine, grain, and parchment or paper. Plato spoke of prosperity in the ideal Republic depending on "importers and exporters, who are called merchants."[5] But other writers feared that the commerce brought by trade was divisive because it brought contact with people of bad manners and corrupt behavior. Many Greek writers looked down on traders and merchants as lower in status. "The life of money-making is one undertaken under compulsion, and wealth is evidently not the good we are seeking," Aristotle wrote in *Nicomachean Ethics*.[6] Philosophers in Rome wrote that traders who bought goods at one price and sold them at a higher price without upgrading their value were engaged in vulgar conduct.[7]

Hebrew scripture and subsequent rabbinic interpretations enshrine both the justice and freedom of markets. The many biblical teachings in favor of moral behavior, such as dealing honestly in business, giving charity to the poor, and treating servants, slaves, and even animals properly, are underpinned by a basic understanding that engaging in commerce is a moral good. "Judaism has tended to favor the free market, while subjecting it to criticism in the light of its ideal," wrote Lord Jonathan Sacks, the former chief rabbi of the United Hebrew Congregations of the Commonwealth. "The rabbis favored markets and competition because they generated wealth, lowered prices, increased choice, reduced absolute levels of poverty, and in the course of time extended humanity's control over the environment, narrowing the extent to which we are the passive victims of circumstance and fate."[8]

In the first centuries of the Common Era, a doctrine of "universal economy" was enunciated by some philosophers and theologians who held that Providence scattered resources and goods across the globe in order to promote commerce and peaceful cooperation. "God did not bestow all products upon all parts of the earth, but distributed His gifts over different regions, to the end that men might cultivate a social relationship because one would have need of the help of another," wrote Libanius, a 4th-century teacher and friend of the Roman emperor Julian. "And so He called commerce into being, that all men might be able to have common enjoyment of the fruits of the earth, no matter where produced."[9]

But throughout much of early and medieval Christian teachings, the marketplace, money lending, and especially usury were morally equivalent to lying and blasphemy, which was evoked in the story of Jesus chasing the money changers and merchants from the temple, crying: "Take these things hence; make not my Father's house a house of merchandise!"[10] St. Augustine suggested that good Christians should avoid the world of commerce, that the rich should distribute alms to the poor, and that the poor should be satisfied only with what they need to survive.[11] In the 13th century, St. Thomas Aquinas, in *Summa Theologica*, declared that producing goods was "more dignified" than buying and selling them. The idea of a "just price"—not one dictated by markets— flourished especially in the Middle Ages, even as various writers disagreed on how to calculate it. Some scholars, however, argue that reckoning such a price was more influenced by market economics than is commonly supposed.[12] For example, many early philosophers held that a seller is obliged to not exploit the existence of a monopoly, and the buyer must not take advantage of the seller's straitened circumstances.[13] In the 15th century, theologians such as John Calvin and Martin Luther spoke of the necessity of trade but warned against the excesses of wealth, greed, and dishonesty that could come from it.[14] In the 19th century, Honoré de Balzac, Charles Dickens, Fyodor Dostoevsky, Anthony Trollope, Émile Zola, and other novelists stirred popular consciousness with their lacerating portraits of wealthy misers and predatory businessmen.[15]

But these teachings and portrayals were no match for the power of wealth and the philosophies that justified it. The rise of the big trading companies in the 16th and 17th centuries coincided with nations' pursuits of imperial conquests and also with the emergence of modern concepts such as free labor, private property, and the mobility of capital. The Dutch East India Company, British East India Company, and others became so powerful that they administered territories and even issued their own currency. Thus they served the interests of the nations that chartered them but also implicitly challenged the authority of those nations by insisting on rules that benefited the companies' interests. Trade delivered by these companies brought ancillary benefits to the nations that sponsored them. Governments in turn spent money to build up their ports, construct roads, and dredge navigable rivers to enhance commerce (something that the United States did in earnest throughout the 19th century). Thus locking in markets and possessing colonies were viewed as imperative. English prosperity, for example, was first built in this period on the sale of raw wool and woolen cloth to continental Europe. But when European markets became glutted with wool, England searched for new markets, trade routes, and investments. Spain sent its conquerors on board galleons to the New World in search of gold and other riches. The French, Dutch, Italians, Portuguese, and other rival empires rested on the need to exploit economic, political, and military gain.[16] A similar trajectory was followed in the Muslim world. The ban on usury had remained throughout the Middle Ages, but because trading was allowed, the concept that one could sell something and buy it back for a higher price effectively relaxed the ban. By the rise of the Ottoman Empire, banks had sprung up throughout the Arab world, charging interest and enabling commerce to expand.[17]

In this environment, the concept that merchants must charge a "just price" became obsolete, yielding to a new concept of economic freedom. In France, legend has it that when a group of businessmen met with Jean-Baptiste Colbert, finance minister under Louis XIV, they were asked how the government could best help their efforts. "Laissez-nous faire," one of the guests replied—get out of the way! As one example, French tailors in the 17th century had been barred from making cloth buttons because of protests by button makers. The force of free markets pushed back and gave innovators a free hand in the new era.[18]

But that hand was free only up to a point. France under Louis XIV was also the leading proponent of what became known as "mercantilism," the economic concept that a state should gain economic power from encouraging private business to prosper and support its political and military ambitions. The force of mercantilism fed the rise of the European nation-state after the Thirty Years' War ended with the Treaty of Westphalia in 1648—the moment in history generally regarded as solidifying the nation-state in the international system. The wealth of that state was usually measured by its stores of gold and silver. But because England had no gold (Sir Francis Drake and Sir Walter Raleigh, among its pirates, were only intermittently successful at capturing that symbol of wealth), the only alternative in the view of its treasury chiefs was to build up reserves of gold from favorable balances of trade.[19]

Yet as trade expanded, the underlying mercantilist idea that exports are good and imports unhealthy was increasingly challenged. Many economic thinkers pointed out that a nation seeking to export would provoke a reciprocal reaction in other countries, jeopardizing their ability to do so. Some writers spoke of the inefficiency of government subsidies for export industries. Calls for "free trade" or "freedom to trade" arose. A century after Grotius, the author Henry Martyn published anonymously in 1701 another early prescient tract in favor of free trade. Entitled *Considerations upon the East India Trade*, it argued that protectionism increased costs and wasted labor by employing more people than necessary to make something that could be made more cheaply overseas. In 1744 the English merchant and writer on trade Matthew Decker called for Britain to become a free port, waiving customs fees for all imports and exports. He even called for a scheme in which the beneficiaries of free trade would compensate those domestic producers hurt by it.[20]

By the 18th century, the counterreaction to mercantilism was starting to unleash a new era of moral thinking about market economics as a whole. The term *mercantilism* was coined by, among others, Adam Smith. His arguments against the system were based on the growing concept that free trade benefits both parties, creates efficiencies, and produces overall economic growth by allowing participants to specialize in what they can produce best—the so-called principle of comparative advantage discerned by Smith and later refined by the economist David Ricardo. Equally, Smith argued that mercantilism derived from a collusive, corrupt relationship between government and the barons of land ownership and industry in ways that were harmful to the general population.[21]

Thus the rise of markets contributed to overthrowing the Christian and medieval teachings on the dangers of selfishness and self-seeking behavior. In 1714, well before Adam Smith, the philosopher and political economist Bernard Mandeville wrote the *Fable of the Bees: Private Vices, Publick Benefits*, which invoked the metaphor of hard-working and greedy bees forming a prosperous, productive and harmonious society: "Bare Virtue can't make Nations live/In Splendor; they, that would revive/A Golden Age, must be as free." But it was Smith who changed the course of history because he presented a view of the world that was coherent both morally and economically. In *The Theory of Moral Sentiments* (1759) and *An Inquiry into the Nature and Causes of the Wealth of Nations* (1776), Smith did not ignore the innate characteristics of empathy and justice shared by all humans. His intellectual innovation derived from the idea that freedom was an enabling force spurring the creation of wealth and social welfare for everyone. Barriers to free commerce and trade, he argued, give undue advantage to certain industries and individuals, thereby encouraging inefficiency, and also to moral failings such as laziness and complacency.

In Smith's classic formulation, an individual acting in the marketplace does not seek to promote the public interest but rather his own economic interests, and "by directing that industry in such a manner as its produce may be of the greatest value, he intends only his own gain, and he is in this, as in many other cases, led by an invisible hand to promote an end which was no part of his intention."[22] Government intervention, Smith suggested, not only impeded efficiency and freedom but also often proved counterproductive, reinforcing waste and corruption.[23] He opened the eyes of the world to understanding markets as an increasingly efficient "system" that could be analyzed apart from the individual conduct of buyers, sellers, lenders, and borrowers in the marketplace. "It is not from the benevolence of the butcher, the brewer, or the baker that we expect our dinner, but from their regard to their own interest," he wrote in *The Wealth of Nations*.[24] Smith is thus rightly considered the founder of modern economic theory and of *homo economicus*, which is a far cry from the earlier teachings in scripture and Greek literature and by Aquinas and others that it is somehow sinful to pursue gains selfishly.

It took some time for Smith's ideas to be realized. Only in 1846, for example, did Britain take the dramatic step of repealing the so-called Corn Laws, which imposed import duties effectively barring competition from less expensive imported grain. The action relegated the interests of British landowners and grain producers to a secondary place as the people of Britain and Ireland struggled with hunger, unable to pay the high price of grain resulting from the protectionist policies. Repeal of the laws was supported by manufacturers, who argued that they would not have to raise the wages of factory workers if food prices could be kept under control.

In the context of contemporary debates, to conservatives Smith is an uncompromising advocate of liberty in all aspects of society and something approaching the status of a saint. But some conservatives conveniently forget the sympathy for the downtrodden and for social justice also expressed by the great author of *The Wealth of Nations*. Far from being an antigovernment absolutist, Smith contended that government, and taxes, had an important supporting role to play in producing a society's "public goods." The historian Emma Rothschild argues that Smith was "different and more skeptical" of markets than his followers claim and that his concerns about poverty among workers and other forms of inequality have been ignored by ideological conservatives and libertarians, starting almost immediately after his death and continuing up to the contemporary debates about social welfare programs.[25]

Free Markets and Liberty in the New World

Our interest will be to throw open the doors of commerce and to knock off all its shackles, giving perfect freedom to all persons for the vent of whatever they may choose to bring into our ports, and asking the same in theirs.
—Thomas Jefferson (1782)

When he enshrined the values of "life, liberty and the pursuit of happiness" in the Declaration of Independence, Thomas Jefferson, who served as president of the United States from 1801 to 1809, was influenced by, among other things, the treatises of John Locke favoring the "natural rights" of "life, liberty and property."[†] As the young nation emerged as an economic power in the

---

† To be in favor of a liberalized economy is understood traditionally and in many parts of Europe to be a "liberal," although the word *liberal* is now used by most Americans to describe the opposite—that is, policies calling for more government control and intervention in the economy.

19th century, however, it practiced its own brand of mercantilism called the "American System," which was established by Alexander Hamilton, the first US Treasury secretary, and later embraced by House Speaker Henry Clay of Kentucky. The system's three pillars were a national bank, federal spending for "internal improvements" such as roads, canals, and railroads, and high tariff walls to promote US industry.

Armed by this system, the United States could participate in the first great era of globalization, which expanded in the latter part of the 19th century and the early 20th century with the advent of modern forms of communication and transport. Meanwhile, European countries flooded their colonies in South America, Asia, and Australia with manufactured goods while importing farm products and raw materials from them. These powers had long adopted the practice of mobilizing armies to protect their interests and, in some cases, to force other countries to trade with them. Nations in the West thus demanded that Turkey open its doors to trade and that China maintain an "Open Door" to imperial exploitation. The United States, not yet an imperial power, nonetheless insisted on protecting its interests in China's open door and elsewhere. In 1854 Commodore Matthew Perry's "black ships" arrived in Tokyo Bay and forced the ruling Tokugawa shogunate to open itself to trade.

The age of the empire brought benefits to imperialists and subjugated alike, however.[26] Typical of a certain nostalgia for the era is the comment by the historian Niall Ferguson, "No organization in history has done more to promote the free movement of goods, capital and labor than the British Empire in the nineteenth and early twentieth centuries."[27] There was also a belief in that era that liberty in commerce was a guarantor not simply of wealth but also of peace, which would come from a stabilizing economic interdependence. "Free trade is God's diplomacy," wrote Richard Cobden, a British politician and owner of a manufacturing plant, in 1857. "There is no other certain way of uniting people in the bonds of peace."[28]

But for all the optimism embodied by Cobden's axiom, what often has been described as the first great era of globalization exploded and collapsed with the outbreak of World War I. The European powers borrowed massively to finance their armies, compounding the economic disaster that struck in the late 1920s, sweeping in the Great Depression and before long an even more horrific global conflict in the form of World War II. The Great Depression had been accompanied by exactly the wrong policy responses—higher tariff barriers and the competitive devaluation of currencies—all to discourage imports from other countries. In the United States, the notorious Smoot-Hawley tariff of 1930 elevated barriers to astronomical levels, choking off commerce as other countries retaliated. The collapse of world trade, coupled with demands for reparations from Germany, worsened the economic plight of the West, sending European countries into hypernationalism, fascism, and, in Germany, Nazism.[29]

In July 1944, a few weeks after the D-Day invasion of France on June 6, delegates from 44 nations gathered in the White Mountains of New Hampshire at Bretton Woods and vowed to create an economic system that would avoid a repetition of the earlier mistakes. They established a more liberalized regime of open economic flows of goods and created the International Monetary Fund (IMF), the International Bank for Reconstruction and Development (which later added other institutions to become the World Bank), and the General Agreement on Tariffs and Trade (GATT), which evolved into the World Trade Organization (WTO) in the 1990s. The founders of these institutions saw free markets as far more than a symbol of liberty. Rather, they saw such an open system as a path to efficiency, prosperity, and mutual economic dependence that could fortify Europe against authoritarianism, war, and the rising power of communism and the Soviet Union in the East (see chapter 12). John Maynard Keynes, the British envoy at Bretton Woods, joined with others in expressing ambivalence about free-flowing investment capital, but there was little doubt about the need for reciprocity in the trade of goods. Europe needed machinery, equipment, and other capital goods, and its ability to import such materials depended in part on its ability sell its own goods to Americans.[30]

In Europe, the French statesmen Jean Monnet and Robert Schuman believed that economic integration, cooperation, and free-flowing goods would further safeguard Europe against a return to ruinous conflict. Thus France, Germany, and others established the European Coal and Steel Community in 1951 as a first step toward the still-evolving economic federalization of Europe. The Treaty of Rome, signed in 1957, created the European Economic Community, which expanded and established a parliament in 1979. The Maastricht Treaty of 1992, signed only a few years after the fall of the Berlin Wall and the end of communism in the Soviet Union and Eastern Europe, established a European Union (EU) in which there would be not only freer trade and freer capital movements but also a common currency, the euro. The success of the EU in establishing peace and stability as a function of economic freedom was recognized with the Nobel Peace Prize in 2012, although ironically the accolade was awarded while the euro area was undergoing its gravest economic crisis since the Great Depression. Indeed, it was a period of tumult that raised new doubts about the costs of free-flowing goods, services, capital, and people.

The Soviet Union and its satellites went their own way in the decades after World War II. As soon as the new Bretton Woods system was established, the cleavage deepened over the nature of global and economic openness, pitting the belief in capitalism and free markets in the West against the state-controlled socialist or communist states of the Soviet Union, China, and their allies. In many parts of the postwar world, developing countries that were ostensibly neutral in the battle for loyalties between East and West nonetheless turned to state-controlled economies as the best means to combat the influence of corporations and private wealth, especially the investment class, which for these countries was simply a new version of imperialist oppression under which they had already suffered.[31]

State regulation or control of economies remained part of Western political thought during this period as well. The dominance of social democrats and socialism in weaving a strong government safety net, and avoiding another

Great Depression, remained a factor in Europe and the United States until the economic, energy, and political shocks of the 1970s sparked a crisis in Western capitalism. Inflation and the expanding private capital outflows in the United States in the late 1960s (despite trade surpluses) and the 1970s put new pressure on the US Treasury's gold stocks. In response, the Nixon administration imposed price controls, offered an economic stimulus, and abandoned the peg of the dollar to gold, letting the dollar depreciate in order to spur exports and raise the price of imports.

In 1973 the Middle East erupted in war, compelling Arab oil-producing countries to impose an embargo that raised the price of energy for Americans. A lethal combination of inflation and stagnation strangled the US and British economies. In Britain, a wave of industrial unrest, highlighted by coal mine strikes from South Wales to Scotland, inspired the defenders of free markets to find their voice. A growing number of economists and political leaders thus blamed the West's economic woes on government regulation, state ownership, labor unions, rigid labor markets, and high taxes. President Ronald Reagan in the United States and Prime Minister Margaret Thatcher in the United Kingdom vaulted into power and prominence, reviving the old idea that free markets and property rights were a "natural right" of humankind as Locke and the US Founders had declared centuries earlier. As Reagan memorably declared in his inaugural address in 1981, "In this present crisis, government is not the solution to our problem. Government is the problem."[32] The conservative tide spread to developing countries. Many of them also returned to market fundamentals. Under Deng Xiaoping, China opened its previously self-contained system to investment, competition, and free enterprise, which led in turn to export-led economic growth. India and other countries in Asia followed suit. A new category of success stories was found in the "emerging market" countries or economies (including Hong Kong, Singapore, and Taiwan). Once again, the renewed belief in economic interaction was fulfilled by a dizzying new array of improvements in technology and communication.[33]

The political successes in turn rekindled interest in the writings of longtime advocates of free markets and freedom of transaction such as Ludwig von Mises and Friedrich Hayek. Hayek was a contemporary of Keynes whose 1944 book, *The Road to Serfdom,* was a postwar conservative cult classic for decades. (Keynes told Hayek at the time it was published that he was "not only in agreement, but in deeply moved agreement" with Hayek's warning that central economic planning might lead to totalitarianism. But he said the proper conclusion was to improve government's role, not abandon it.[34])

Many observers found competitive markets to be both a reflection of and a source of political freedom. In the pantheon of heroes were Ayn Rand, author of the novels *The Fountainhead* (1943) and *Atlas Shrugged* (1957), both paeans to the individualist's pursuit of rational self-interest; and Milton Friedman, renowned University of Chicago economist and author of *Capitalism and Freedom* (1962) and *Free to Choose* (1980). The new catechism was that free markets and political freedom were inextricably intertwined. In the words of Vaclav Havel, the Czech poet, playwright, and politician, "a government that commands the economy will inevitably command the polity; given a commanding position it will distort or destroy the former and corrupt or oppress the latter."[35]

The collapse of communism, starting in Poland in 1989, reinvigorated the world's faith in markets, especially global markets, as governments in the United States and elsewhere embraced the value of deregulation, privatization, and lower taxes—a consensus that was shaken by the global economic collapse after 2007–08 but, at least so far, has not fundamentally changed. The spread of the gospel of markets after the fall of communism extended to countries in the developing world that had previously embraced socialism and communism, producing the benefits of export-led growth for China, India, and other parts of what used to be called the Third World. Economic freedom, markets, capitalism, and ultimately globalization have become perhaps the most powerful forces in the world today.

Liberty in Crisis

Yet the crises, shocks, and downturns of the last 25 years—attributed by many economists to the deregulation of capital flows enabling investors to send funds around the world in an instant—are now viewed as a factor in deepening poverty in countries caught up in those events. In the 1970s and 1980s, for example, a crisis of confidence in liberty in the economic sphere began seeping into the era of relative growth as Brazil, Argentina, and other countries of Latin America embarked on a ruinous accumulation of debts. Their problems were aggravated by rising oil prices, interest rates, and inflation in the West. Together they produced massive unemployment, poverty, and increased crime and instability. The fact that many of the debts were run up by dictatorship regimes hardly softened the impacts in these countries.

Subsequent debt crises in East Asia in the 1990s and Europe and the United States in the last decade have forced rich and poor countries alike to cut social safety net programs, a trend that has drawn criticism from the advocates of social welfare from the parties of the left in Europe to Pope Francis.[36] The pope declared in 2013, "Just as the commandment 'Thou shalt not kill' sets a clear limit in order to safeguard the value of human life, today we also have to say 'Thou shalt not' to an economy of exclusion and inequality."[37] Finally, skeptics of globalization worry that economic integration may be destroying national, regional, religious, and ethnic cultures, or alternatively it may be aggravating anger and resentment and violent attacks among these groups.[38]

The International Monetary Fund and World Bank eventually moved in to help countries restructure their debts and restore their devastated economies. But with the support of the United States, these two institutions also encouraged the most troubled countries to move toward greater openness to investment and the development of export-oriented industries. The desperate leaders of many Latin American countries readily agreed. The phrase "Washington Consensus" was coined in 1989 by the economist John Williamson to refer to these policies. By citing Washington, he was referring not simply to the IMF and the World Bank but also to the US Treasury and the Federal Reserve, all of which are headquartered in the same neighborhood of the nation's capital, although the consensus was shared by a new generation of Latin American economists as well.

In moral terms, the phrase "Washington Consensus" reflects the twin principles of liberty and justice as building blocks. Several of Williamson's consensus principles fall under the heading of liberty. These include calls for freeing or liberalizing interest rates, trade, foreign direct investment, and regulations, while privatizing government enterprises establishing private property rights. What many forget is that several other principles would fall under the heading of economic justice, an essential ingredient if the public is to support such efforts. These principles include greater spending on basic health and education for poor or troubled countries, and tax reform, specifically broadening taxes to combat crony capitalism and corruption and to ensure that the wealthy pay their fair share.[39]

The conflicting demands of liberty and equality resurfaced in the 1990s in the Mexico debt crisis, which spread because markets in many countries were opening up to trade and investment in the hopeful era of globalization ushered in by the fall of communism. The Clinton administration embraced the idea of lowering tariff barriers by supporting the North American Free Trade Agreement (NAFTA), which had been negotiated by the administration of President George H. W. Bush. NAFTA was the first US bilateral trade agreement with a poor country, and it was followed by the global trade negotiations that led to the establishment of the World Trade Organization (WTO), replacing the General Agreement on Tariffs and Trade of the Bretton Woods era.

Meanwhile, beyond trade Clinton's aides debated the wisdom of lifting the longtime curbs on the flow of capital, loans, and investments across borders. The Clinton-era Treasury Department under Secretaries Robert Rubin and Lawrence Summers was also eager for the US banking and finance industries to gain greater access to the emerging markets in the developing world. Inside the administration, however, the secretaries faced skepticism and even opposition. Two other advisors, Joseph Stiglitz and Alan Blinder, argued that, in Blinder's words, "it was dangerous to put this fancy finance into these countries with underdeveloped financial systems."[40] Nonetheless, the idea of liberalizing capital flows gained currency in many circles, including the IMF. In the 1990s, the Fund began to promote capital liberalization informally, even though it had no specific mandate to do so.[41] The logic was compelling. "Poor countries need funds to develop, and rich countries tend to have a surfeit of savings; so why deprive the less fortunate of financial resources?" wrote Paul Blustein, author of several books on international capital flows and crises. "Moreover, when investors are restricted from putting their capital into an investment overseas that offers more attractive returns than they can get at home, the world's overall resources are presumably being used less efficiently than they might."[42] Many free-market economists joined the chorus of those encouraging the Treasury and the IMF to lift capital restrictions, in part to enable investors from rich countries to seize opportunities in poor countries and in the process to help them develop. Rudiger Dornbusch, an economist at the Massachusetts Institute of Technology (MIT), was widely quoted after he called the Bretton Woods–era curbs on capital flows "an idea whose time is past."[43]

Under Michel Camdessus, the IMF'S managing director, the leadership sought to amend the IMF's charter to give it expanded jurisdiction to press for greater openness of capital accounts, which would have altered its identity and perhaps its mandate. "Freedom has its risks," Camdessus declared in 1997. "But are they greater than those of complex administrative rules and capricious changes in their design? Freedom has its risks. But is there any more fertile field for development and prosperity? Freedom has its risks! Let us go then for an orderly liberalization of capital movements."[44] Although Camdessus no doubt advocated changing the system to achieve growth and efficiency, it was important that again he invoked the moral value of freedom and liberty. In the end, the effort to change the IMF charter failed, in part because of ambivalent feelings in the Clinton administration, which was divided over the issue, and also in some developing countries that feared the threat of foreign domination of local industries. It did not take long for a counterreaction over free-flowing capital to set in.

The East Asian financial crisis in the late 1990s gave ammunition to those economists who had warned that capital flows were risky and the cause of shocks as financing flowed out just as easily as it flowed in. The crisis started in Thailand and quickly spread to several other countries, which were forced to accept tough austerity measures that imposed their greatest hardship on the poorest citizens.

Looking back, a range of scholars have wondered why experts did not predict the dangers of an open-ended liberalizing of capital flows. To some, the crisis raised the question of whether developing countries were "incapable of managing the explosive combination of capital mobility and political democracy," as the economist Barry Eichengreen has put it.[45] One implication of that comment is whether liberty and justice are compatible in countries with poorly developed democratic institutions. "The age of financial liberalization has, in short, been an age of financial crises," Martin Wolf of the *Financial Times* wrote in 2004, citing a World Bank estimate of 112 systemic banking crises in 93 countries between the late 1970s and the end of the 20th century. "The overall conclusion is that finance is different from trade," he observed. "While openness to trade is normally beneficial and requires relatively few complementary policy changes, the same is not true of finance."[46]

Jagdish Bhagwati, professor of economics at Columbia University and a well-known champion of free trade, charges further that proponents of such flows have been in the thrall of an ideological commitment to the notion that everything in economics should be unfettered and free, an idea that sounds principled but has "in effect, been hijacked by the proponents of capital mobility" and "used to bamboozle us into celebrating the new world of trillions of dollars moving about daily in a borderless world, creating gigantic economic gains, rewarding virtue and punishing profligacy."[47] The economists Dani Rodrik and Arvind Subramanian studied the literature on the subject in 2008 and concluded that there was little evidence to support the benefits of freeing up the movement of capital. "Depending on context and country, the appropriate role of policy will be as often to stem the tide of capital flows as to encourage them," they wrote. "Policymakers who view their challenges exclusively from the latter perspective will get it badly wrong."[48] In *The Globalization Paradox* (2011), Rodrik notes the huge surge in capital flows and concludes that "financial globalization has failed us" because the greater risks did not deliver "compensating benefits in the form of higher economic growth."[49] A dissenting view has been advanced by William Cline of the Peterson Institute for International Economics, whose research into dozens of empirical studies has indicated a "positive growth effect of openness." He has found that sudden stops produced the most damage in countries with poor governance institutions and closed rather than open capital markets.[50]

In his memoirs, Treasury secretary Rubin said that while in the Clinton administration he later had second thoughts about the devastating economic impact of the financial shocks, which were followed by the tough terms imposed in international rescue programs on the countries hit by the East Asian economic crisis.[51] Stiglitz, who had earlier chaired the Council of Economic Advisers at the White House, wrote scathingly about the IMF's harsh measures in bailing out countries that he maintained had gotten into trouble through no fault of their own, and he went on to question the benefits of globalization generally.[52] The IMF's second thoughts led to various self-examinations. For example, an internal staff evaluation noted many years later that the Fund had no explicit mandate to promote capital account liberalization, but that its staff focused on the advantages of such a step in the 1990s only to realize the dangers later.[53] The East Asian crisis had made them "increasingly wary of the risks" that Camdessus had spoken of earlier.[54]

As the rethinking unfolded at the IMF, it held a conference in 1998 on "Economic Policy and Equity" at which Stanley Fischer, the first deputy managing director, declared that the Fund's commitment must be to promote equitable policies. He had earlier supported a liberalization of capital movements but later acknowledged that, as a general rule, boom times tend to make the rich richer, and busts tend to make the poor poorer. "Sometimes, reforms designed to achieve macroeconomic stability and growth may impact negatively on the poor, especially in the short run," Fischer said.[55] Accordingly, the IMF would tailor its programs to cushion the blow for the most vulnerable and to yield a more equitable distribution of benefits as a matter of social justice. "We believe that open world markets are in the long-run interests of all countries," he said, but attention must now be paid to policies that promote equity as well as growth if the system were to be sustained in the future.[56]

The Fund's evolution away from "liberty" and toward greater economic justice reached a new peak in the post-2010 period. Two important IMF staff papers examined the relationship between growth and inequality, concluding that they were deeply interconnected. Contrary to the axiom of the "leaky bucket" proposed by Arthur Okun, which held that programs aimed at the redistribution of income (through tax or spending policies) dampened economic growth, the empirical evidence suggested that such an effect was true only in extreme cases. In fact, the papers (discussed earlier) concluded that efforts to redistribute incomes and wealth in developing countries would spur economic growth, not impede it. These papers, issued in 2011 and 2014, were widely discussed in the development community and contributed to an important shift in attitudes just as rising inequality was becoming a major issue around the world.[57] Then in 2014 the IMF issued an important additional paper, *Fiscal Policy and Income Inequality,* which found that income inequality had increased in both advanced and developing economies in recent decades. The report attributed this phenomenon to the usual suspects: globalization, liberalization of markets, technologies that favored people with skills and left unskilled workers with less remunerative work, declining tax rates for the rich, and the increased bargaining power of well-to-do workers in their environments. It noted that many of these developments had also spurred growth and reduced poverty, but that there was "growing evidence" that inequality itself hampered growth and may have contributed to the financial crisis of the previous half-decade. It called on the Fund to incorporate into its studies the effects of its policies on equality, and it called for "fiscal policy" to alleviate the problem of maldistribution of wealth and income—a euphemism for higher tax rates on the rich and more government spending on the poor.[58]

In 2014 there was a poignant exchange related to this problem at a conference of the IMF honoring Stanley Fischer. Lawrence Summers, the former Treasury secretary and Obama economic adviser, said in a speech that there had been fewer financial crises in the decades after World War II than recently because people were more prudent back then. "Larry," Fischer responded, "I wonder whether the 35 years after World War II had something to do with the fact that financial liberalization hadn't yet happened."[59]

For many years, a popular joke among the staff at the IMF was that its initials stood for "It's Mostly Fiscal," meaning that its mandate was primarily to require countries to balance their budgets. The IMF's newfound interest in combating inequality was defended in 2014 by its leadership as less a change in policy than a new emphasis on social justice as a factor in economic growth and stability. "I hear people say, 'Why do you bother about inequality? It is not the core mandate,'" observed Christine Lagarde, managing director of the fund. "Well, sorry, it is also part of the mandate. Our mandate is financial stability. Anything that is likely to rock the boat financially and macro-economically is within our mandate."[60]

3

The Wolves and the Lambs:
"Justice, Justice Shalt Thou Pursue"

Both liberty and equality are among the primary goals pursued by human beings through many centuries; but total liberty for wolves is death to the lambs, total liberty of the powerful, the gifted, is not compatible with the rights to a decent existence of the weak and the less gifted.
—Isaiah Berlin, *The Crooked Timber of Humanity* (2013)

Justice is the first virtue of social institutions, as truth is of systems of thought. A theory however elegant and economical must be rejected or revised if it is untrue; likewise laws and institutions no matter how efficient and well-arranged must be reformed or abolished if they are unjust.
—John Rawls, *A Theory of Justice* (1971)

Few phrases are more familiar to Americans than the twin goals proclaimed by the Pledge of Allegiance—"liberty and justice for all." The moral imperatives of both have roots in the Bible. "Proclaim liberty throughout the land. . ."—the inscription on the Liberty Bell—derives from Leviticus. "Justice, justice shalt thou pursue" is from Deuteronomy. The Pledge of Allegiance dates from 1892. It was written by a Christian socialist minister, Francis Bellamy, who was commissioned to draft a set of inspirational words for the 400th anniversary of Christopher Columbus's discovery of America. Bellamy spent "two sweating hours" trying to express his thoughts. As a champion of worker rights—and a cousin of the utopian novelist Edward Bellamy—he had considered including those now-famous words from the French Revolution—"liberty, equality, fraternity"—but he discarded the phrase as too obscure and perhaps provocative.[1]

Economic *justice* and economic *equality* do not mean exactly the same thing, but for the purposes of the argument in this book they are aligned as objectives. In 1755, more than three decades before the French Revolution, Jean-Jacques Rousseau declared that "one of the most important functions of government [is] to prevent extreme inequality of fortunes."[2] At the same time, an inherent contradiction exists between *liberty* and *equality*, and many political philosophers have recognized the dangers of trying to enforce the latter over the former. The "doctrine of equality" is a "fallacious" one, the lexicographer Noah Webster declared in 1802. "That one man in a state, has as good a right as another to his life, limbs, reputation, and property, is a proposition that no man will dispute. . . . But if by equality, writers understand an equal right to distinction, and influence; or if they understand an equal share of talents and bodily powers; in these senses, all men are not equal."[3]

An insightful early contribution to understanding the dichotomy between liberty and equality was offered in this same era by another Frenchman, Alexis de Tocqueville, the aristocrat who documented his fateful journey in 1831 to examine the prison system in the United States. In *Democracy in America*, a two-volume work of enduring insights into the American character, Tocqueville found that the new nation embodied an egalitarian spirit far stronger than that in the Old World. But he also displayed a certain cynicism about the willingness of Americans to favor equality over liberty. "I think that democratic communities have a natural taste for freedom," he wrote. "But for equality, their passion is ardent, insatiable, incessant, invincible: they call for equality in freedom, and if they cannot obtain that, they will still call for equality in slavery."[4]

That anyone would prefer "equality in slavery" over freedom is doubtful. But some evidence suggests that Tocqueville's analysis persists in shedding light on European versus American values. In a 2011 survey, for example, 58 percent of Americans indicated they believed that "freedom to pursue life's goals without state interference" is more important than a government that "guarantees nobody is in need" (35 percent). Surveys conducted in Britain, France, Germany, and Spain revealed virtually the reverse in priorities.[5]

Globalization has reinforced the tension between economic equality, in the form of a more equal economic distribution of a society's goods, and economic liberty, in the form of ever freer flows of goods, services, and people. Globalization, labor-saving technology, immigration, tax policies, aging populations, and the winner-take-all dynamics of modern business (i.e., the ability of highly skilled, highly productive, or highly gifted people to command huge salaries) have all been generally cited as contributing to wage stagnation in the US middle and working classes and higher incomes for those among the top 1 or 5 percent of wage earners, translating into a level of inequality that more and more people find socially and economically unjust.

As mentioned earlier, economic justice and economic equality are not exactly synonymous. Some would argue that economic justice is more a matter of equal opportunity than equality of results. The contemporary debate on economic inequality is thus both complex and confusing, with moral, political, and economic dimensions. Many Americans find today's rising economic inequality morally unacceptable. In political terms, these Americans maintain that the spiraling incomes for the rich give them special advantages in determining or influencing government policies and priorities. But in economic terms, some argue that inequality is a by-product of economic growth, whereas others cite evidence that it impedes growth.

A Short History of Economic Justice

Justice has been invoked as an ideal since the time of ancient philosophy and the early scriptures. But when justice is discussed in the literature of antiquity, it usually relates to whether the rewards of life should be proportionate to one's behavior, particularly how one treats one's fellow humans. Consider, for example, the parable of misfortune meted out to Job in the Bible and whether it attests to God's justice. The goal of distributing wealth and resources justly, fairly, or even more equally within a society as a whole is a much more modern concept. The Bible features many appeals for charity for the poor as a matter of humanitarian benevolence, but not in the context of a vision of distributive justice for society as a whole. Philosophy professor Samuel Fleischacker notes that for most of human history "practically no one held, even as an ideal, the view that everyone should have their basic needs satisfied."[6] The idea that there could be systematic alternatives to a commercial system was not introduced to the world until the early phases of the Industrial Revolution in the 18th and early 19th centuries, with experiments in places such as New Lanark in Scotland, where the community itself owned the cotton mills. Robert Owen, a Welsh philanthropist and social reformer, turned the New Lanark experiment into a scheme designed to stand athwart the tide of history. It drew famous visitors such as Grand Duke (later Czar) Nicholas of Russia and a flood of writers, emissaries, reformers, and business people to observe what the historian Robert Heilbroner said "was living proof that the squalor and depravity of industrial life were not the only and inevitable social arrangement."[7]

Owen called his arrangement a "cooperative movement." The French theorist Henri de Saint-Simon called it "socialism." Karl Marx used the terms *socialism* and *communism* interchangeably. Socialism has since evolved, especially since the fall of communism in the late 1980s and early 1990s, into what proponents call social democracies. (In Europe, some political parties on the left have long preferred to call themselves Social Democrats rather than Socialists.) But the goal of adherents of those terms is to achieve greater economic equality—and therefore a more economically just society—in a spirit of liberty and freedom. This assertion is tested again and again throughout history in a cyclical pattern that is usually compelled by economic crises.

In the United States, the first American confrontation between the demands of open finance, on the one hand, and equality, on the other, surrounded the establishment in 1791 of the Bank of the United States by Treasury secretary Alexander Hamilton. Hamilton saw the bank as essential to the establishment of efficiency, economic stability, and trade in an infant nation aspiring to compete with the Old World. Thomas Jefferson argued against the bank on the basis of economic justice in that it enriched investors at the expense of the yeoman farmers whom he saw as the backbone of US prosperity. Along with James Madison, Jefferson also charged that the bank infringed on the individual liberties enshrined in the Bill of Rights. The bank's charter expired in 1811. It was later revived before being killed by President Andrew Jackson, who distrusted banks because of their involvement in booms and busts such as the South Sea Bubble of the early 18th century. Such busts, known as "panics," erupted in the United States in 1857, 1873, 1893, and 1907, each time bringing demands for curbs on the power of banks, trusts, railroads, and other powerful elements of the private sector.

The Panic of 1893, at the time the worst economic downturn in US history, was in fact a product of the first era of globalization, a dramatic example of the collision of free-flowing capital with the anxiety over distributive justice in the Gilded Age. The crisis began with speculative investments, followed by the bankruptcy of several railroad companies, which triggered in turn thousands of additional failures of banks and businesses. The British and European financial institutions that had helped fuel the great westward expansion of the post–Civil War era faced insolvency and demanded payment in gold, but Wall Street banks were unable to meet that demand. Meanwhile, farmers, hit by the plunging prices of wheat, cotton, and other exports, also sank into debt. Destitute and desperate, the victims of hard times sought help from Washington. A rabble of jobless workers and farmers known as "Coxey's Army" marched from Massillon in Ohio, through Pennsylvania, before descending on Washington in 1894 to demand a federal relief program. They were ousted by the police from their encampments on the steps of the Capitol.

Out of the late 19th-century travails of an expanding US role in the first era of globalization was born the Populist movement and political party. The Populists, who represented both farmers and workers, primarily in the West and South, sought to promote, among other things, a bias toward inflation by introducing concepts such as grain-backed and silver-backed currency to supplement currency based on gold.[8] They also supported lower tariffs as well as an income tax to replace the lost revenue from the tariffs and to level the economic imbalances of that era. Meanwhile, in this epoch there was growing awareness of the disparity between rich and poor. One widely disseminated study in 1889 concluded that 50,000 families "owned" half of the nation's wealth, whereas four-fifths of American families earned less than $500 a year.[9] To address the growing economic inequities while raising revenues for the Civil War, Congress approved Abraham Lincoln's request for an income tax in 1862, but it was repealed when the war was over. In response to the Panic of 1893, Congress reenacted the income tax in 1894, but the Supreme Court threw the tax out the following year, criticizing it as a violation of economic liberty. Representative William Jennings Bryan of Nebraska delivered his famous speech against the gold standard while launching his campaign for president in 1896, railing against the financial interests for crucifying mankind "on a cross of gold." But he also made the income tax a major feature of his campaign, assailing the Supreme Court for invalidating it.[10]

Bryan lost his crusade in 1896 to William McKinley. A half-decade later, Theodore Roosevelt, who became president after McKinley's assassination in

1901, renewed the cause for economic justice with his "trust busting" assault on railroad, oil, and banking combines, as well as promoting new food safety laws, an expansion of worker rights and nature conservation, and attempts (with limited success) to lower tariffs. Roosevelt also advocated an income tax, but not until after another banking crisis, the Panic of 1907, did the idea regain footing to overcome the constitutional issue. Like its predecessors, the 1907 panic grew out of a speculative binge that collapsed and caused a banking and stock market meltdown. JP Morgan and a consortium of fellow financiers stepped in to rescue the system with more loans, but the crisis accelerated demands for reform to curb the "money trusts," which culminated in the election of Woodrow Wilson to the presidency in 1912. His victory was followed by a sweeping reduction in tariffs, enactment of an income tax (after a constitutional amendment that passed the same year), and creation of the Federal Reserve system, intended to regulate and backstop the nation's financial network.

The Supreme Court was late in catching up to the historic trend, however. In a series of decisions dramatizing just how important the tension was between liberty and justice, the justices embraced the "natural rights" of freedom of commerce that had become a part of Western philosophical thinking since the age of Locke, Adam Smith, and the Declaration of Independence. Indeed, the Court was heavily influenced by the so-called social Darwinists and their belief that laissez-faire economics were not only part of nature's law but also an important element of progress. Just as Darwin's theories explained advancement of the human species, the concept of "survival of the fittest"—a phrase coined not by Darwin but by the English philosopher Herbert Spencer—was understood to explain the dominance of big business as the engine of economic development.[†]

Embracing this Darwinist view of the interplay between liberty and progress, the Supreme Court, under Chief Justice Melville Fuller (who served 1888–1910), struck down a variety of laws and regulations aimed at establishing just rules for economic activity, including use of the Sherman Antitrust Act to break up the sugar cartel. The Court not only threw out the income tax as unconstitutional, but also barred New York State from limiting the hours of work of a baker, saying in *Lochner v. New York* that the statute was an "unreasonable, unnecessary and arbitrary interference with the right and liberty of the individual to contract."[11]

In his powerful dissent from *Lochner*, Justice Oliver Wendell Holmes Jr. declared that the Constitution was "not intended to embody a particular economic theory, whether of paternalism and the organic relation of the citizen to the State or of laissez faire."[12] The *Lochner* decision was viewed as a landmark in the triumph of individual rights over a society's conception

---

† One reason Bryan was a lifelong opponent of Darwin's theory of evolution—arguing in 1925 in favor of prosecuting the high school teacher John Scopes—was that he despised social Darwinism for allegedly justifying the unequal power of the wealthy. See Michael Kazin, *A Godly Hero: The Life of William Jennings Bryan* (New York: Anchor Books, 2006).

of justice.[13] Decades of conservative Court rulings ensued, and in the 1930s the Court struck down the New Deal's National Recovery Administration (NRA) and the Agriculture Adjustment Act (AAA) as overly intrusive in their establishment of production quotas in industry and on farms. Following President Franklin Roosevelt's pursuit in 1937, after his reelection, of an ill-advised and ill-fated scheme to expand and "pack" the Supreme Court, the composition of the justices evolved and became more hospitable to the ends of government intervention on behalf of justice.

The Fuller Court's categorical embrace of economic liberty has been compared by scholars to the similarly sweeping expansion of political and social liberties established by the Supreme Court under Chief Justice Earl Warren in the 1950s and 1960s. Whereas the Fuller Court invoked the sanctity of property and free market rights, the Warren Court argued that the primary importance of individual political and social rights, as well as the equal protection of the law, was a rationale for upholding one-man, one-vote in the states and striking down racial segregation, school prayer, and what were ruled as violations of "the right of privacy," including bans on abortion and contraceptives. "The substantive values propounded by the Court in the 1960s differed radically from those of the Court at the turn of the century," wrote Owen Fiss, a Yale law professor, in his history of the earlier Court decisions. But what they had in common, he explained, was the Court's determination to play the role of "guardian of a public morality that was anchored in and made authoritative by the Constitution." In this view, the dialectic across the century between one Court's embrace of "property rights" and another's embrace of "human rights" is a great illustration of the never-ending redefinitions in US history of what constitutes liberty and justice.[14]

The dialectic between the definitions of liberty of the Fuller and Warren Courts remains a major part of the fabric of modern political discourse. On the one hand, Democrats and liberals tend to favor government intervention in the economic sphere but not in the social sphere, especially when it comes to reproductive choice, privacy, and equal rights and nondiscrimination for minorities and gays. Some libertarians and Republicans, on the other hand, channel the philosophy of the Fuller Court, tending to oppose government intervention in the economy in the name of freedom while often favoring government-sponsored school prayer and restrictions on abortion, contraception, and sexual relations. The legacy of this Fuller-Warren tension on individual liberty was most recently illustrated by Chief Justice John Roberts's dissent in the Supreme Court's 2015 ruling that the Constitution barred laws against gay marriage (*Obergefell v. Hodges*). Roberts cited the *Lochner* decision 16 times, saying it was a classic example of the Court construing individual rights too broadly in the economic sphere, leading the Court to make the same mistake on gay marriage.[15]

Because of the dichotomy between economic and personal rights, the words *freedom* and *liberty* often fall prey to distortion. President Franklin Roosevelt invoked the word *freedom* and expanded it in his 1941 State of the

Union message with an eye toward the war in Europe, calling for "four freedoms" that should be guaranteed for all. "As men do not live by bread alone, they do not fight by armaments alone," the president declared.[16] The first two "freedoms"—freedom of speech and freedom of worship—were predictably rooted in the Bill of Rights. But the second two were designed to justify the emergence of the modern national security and welfare state. They were "freedom from fear" and "freedom from want." Thus these "freedoms" expanded the definition of the word *freedom* to justify more government intervention at home and abroad. Borrowing from the World War I–era state intervention in the economy such as the War Industries Board, the New Deal included attempts to limit production in the farming and industrial sectors based on the theory that oversupplies had caused prices to collapse. Also part of the New Deal was an array of emergency relief programs, public works projects, and regulations of the industrial, farming, and banking sectors, as well as the enactment of Social Security, the Securities and Exchange Commission, the Federal Deposit Insurance Corporation, the Tennessee Valley Authority, the Federal Housing Administration, and income support payments to the poor through the Aid to Families with Dependent Children (AFDC) program.[17]

In the 1950s, Isaiah Berlin formulated in a scholarly essay two forms of liberty that sounded much like FDR's four freedoms. He differentiated between "negative" liberty, providing equal opportunities for all, and "positive" liberty, creating conditions in which everyone can take advantage of those opportunities. If someone is too poor to afford a loaf of bread or recourse to the judicial system, "he is as little free to have it as he would be if it were forbidden him by law," Berlin reasoned. But enforcement of a uniform system of justice that tries to equalize economic status in the name of such freedom can lead to an unjust system of coercion and dictatorship, as he characterized communism.[18]

In the 1960s, on the heels of the civil rights movement, the Berlin formulation evolved into a debate over equality of opportunity versus equality of results. At Howard University in 1965, President Lyndon Johnson noted the passage of civil rights legislation in the name of freedom, and then he added,

> But freedom is not enough. You do not wipe away the scars of centuries by saying: Now you are free to go where you want, and do as you desire, and choose the leaders you please. You do not take a person who, for years, has been hobbled by chains and liberate him, bring him up to the starting line of a race and then say, 'you are free to compete with all the others,' and still justly believe that you have been completely fair. . . . This is the next and the more profound stage of the battle for civil rights. We seek not just freedom but opportunity. We seek not just legal equity but human ability, not just equality as a right and a theory but equality as a fact and equality as a result.[19]

Daniel Patrick Moynihan, then serving as an assistant secretary in the Labor Department, fired a warning shot about such talk. He effectively turned on its head Alexis de Tocqueville's argument that Americans would prefer equality over freedom. "Liberty has been the American middle-class ideal par excellence," Moynihan wrote in a memo to the White House. "It has enjoyed the utmost social prestige. Not so equality. Men who would carelessly give their lives for Liberty, are appalled by equality. . . . [T]he great movements for equality in our history—from Jacksonian Democracy through Populism to the Trade Union Movement—have invariably been met with fierce opposition."[20] In fact, Moynihan's political analysis has held up in recent years. At a time when rising inequality in the United States has become a major political issue for many, the evidence suggests that Americans have become less, not more, inclined to support government programs to address the problem. "Both the absolute level and the changing structure of inequality have long been a force promoting conservatism," one student of opinion surveys, Matthew Luttig, concluded in 2013. Among the reasons cited was concern, even among those in the middle class whose incomes have stagnated in recent decades compared with those at the top, that government programs aiding the poor would hurt their own standing.[21] In a separate example, the Gallup Organization reported in 2000 that 59 percent of Americans claimed it was the federal government's responsibility to make sure all Americans have health care, but more recently, in 2014, 52 percent of Americans said the federal government had *no* such responsibility.[22]

A parallel history of torturing the meaning of *liberty* is seen in the way the word has evolved since the 19th century. In Europe, the word *liberal* is still generally understood in its earlier sense of support for economic liberty—that is, a "liberal" opposes government intervention aimed at achieving justice or any other objective in the free market–oriented economy. This was the meaning favored in the early days of the United States. Thomas Jefferson was an agrarian "liberal" who stood with farmers to oppose government action aimed at building up a productive manufacturing-based economy as espoused by his rival, Treasury secretary Alexander Hamilton.

The term *liberal* has evolved, in the United States at least, into describing advocates of *more* government to promote social justice—that is, in the words of Herbert Croly, the Progressive Era writer and founder of the *New Republic* magazine, using Hamiltonian means (government intervention) to achieve Jeffersonian ends (equality of opportunity).‡

Johnson's presidency was another high-water mark for the newly defined liberalism, with its establishment of vast government intervention in health care through Medicare (for the elderly) and Medicaid (for the poor). In subsequent years, President Richard Nixon, while primarily focusing on international affairs, continued the tradition of state intervention and even sought to expand

---

‡ The term *liberal* has confused many political scientists on opposites sides of the Atlantic. After Pope John Paul II denounced liberalism in a 1991 encyclical, Daniel Patrick Moynihan, by then a senator from New York, tried to convince the Vatican to understand that to American ears it sounded like the pope was opposing government help for the poor, when he was actually stating the opposite. See Steven R. Weisman, ed., *Daniel Patrick Moynihan: A Portrait in Letters of an American Visionary* (New York: PublicAffairs, 2010), 588.

it with a proposal for a guaranteed income for the poor championed by his outspoken domestic policy adviser, Moynihan. The Kennedy-Johnson-Nixon eras also marked the ascendancy of Keynesianism and advocates of a "mixed economy" of private markets and government intervention, redistribution through spending and tax policies, and regulation to deliver the best mix of liberty, justice—and prosperity—to the postwar United States. A major figure in legitimizing the mixed economy was the economist Paul Samuelson, coauthor of perhaps the most influential economics textbook ever written, *Economics*.[23] When it came out in 1948, John Kenneth Galbraith, then an editor at *Fortune* magazine, predicted that it would educate the next generation of economists. It no doubt did. But Samuelson became caught up in the red-baiting recklessly pursued by Senator Joseph McCarthy in the 1950s and was targeted by the right as a communist sympathizer. Some conservative alumni at the Massachusetts Institute of Technology, where Samuelson was teaching, tried to have his textbook banned or censored. "It all seems slightly comical four decades later, but it was no joke to be a teacher at a public university when many of the fashionable textbooks of the time were being denounced as subversive," Samuelson later recalled.[24]

By the time Jimmy Carter entered the White House in 1977, the revival of conservatism and the drive to restore "freedom" to the marketplace was in full roar, spurred by the disastrous combination of recession and inflation in the 1970s. Carter embraced some of the libertarian agenda, lifting regulations in air transportation and energy, for example. But the recession and inflation toward the end of his term paved the way for the election of Ronald Reagan in 1980 and the return of faith in free markets. Freedom was back on the agenda, and free markets were deemed by the White House to be the best guarantor of justice (although the Reagan presidency left the fundamentals of the social welfare state intact). A surge of interest in more government occurred at the outset of the presidency of Bill Clinton in 1993, but he failed to enact a sweeping expansion of government-sponsored health care and, under pressure from Republicans and conservative Democrats, ended welfare as an entitlement program.

President George W. Bush angered conservatives by enacting a Medicare prescription drug program and taking initial steps to rescue the auto industry. Then, with Democratic majorities in both houses of Congress in his first term, President Barack Obama presided over a return to a more activist government with three major initiatives: (1) massive government spending to stimulate the economy and bail out the banks, auto industry, and (to a limited extent) mortgage holders; (2) broader regulation of the financial sector under the Dodd-Frank Act; and (3) the Affordable Care Act, which expanded health care to millions of Americans, partly through a "mandate" that businesses provide health insurance and partly through incentives for individuals to obtain coverage. Obama's initiatives, coupled with others to curb greenhouse gases and expand government monitoring of telephone and computer usage, inevitably provoked a backlash by conservatives and libertarians, epitomized by the Tea Party. More than that, Obama built his political proposals increasingly around the issue of inequality. He signaled his intentions first in 2011 in Osawatomie, Kansas, a site chosen because it was the scene of a fiery address in 1910 by former president Theodore Roosevelt, who was labeled a socialist and even a communist by critics. There, Obama declared that "over the last few decades the rungs on the ladder of opportunity have grown farther and farther apart, and the middle class has shrunk."[25] He pursued the theme in successive State of the Union messages, and his administration often noted that the recovery from the Great Recession had not translated into middle-class income gains.[26]

The cycles of US history therefore demonstrate, if nothing else, a swinging back and forth between the goals of liberty and justice, and in some sense between freedom and government, as the vehicle to achieve economic justice. As the political scientist Michael Mandelbaum has pointed out, free markets tend to be egalitarian, decentralized, voluntary, and driven by individual initiative, whereas governments tend to be hierarchical, centralized, potentially coercive, and reflective of collectivity. Accordingly, markets symbolize liberty and governments symbolize justice.[27]

In recent years in the age of globalization, the issue of economic justice has been pursued with religious fervor by many. For example, Rebecca Blank, an economist who became chancellor of the University of Wisconsin at Madison after serving as acting secretary of commerce under President Obama, has also been a leader in the United Church of Christ and was the author of *Do Justice: Linking Christian Faith and Modern Economic Life* (1992). The book is an outgrowth of efforts by the Church of Christ in the 1980s to commission theologians, economists, pastors, businesspeople, and others to write a "public theology" of economics. The church's efforts were undertaken in parallel with *Economic Justice for All: A Pastoral Letter on Catholic Social Teaching and the US Economy*, which was issued by the United States Conference of Catholic Bishops in 1986. "Throughout the Bible, God manifests a deep concern for economic justice and economic well-being among God's people," wrote Blank, citing many passages of scripture from the Old Testament and also the Gospels. The United States, in her view, should favor distributive justice not only globally but also in poor countries receiving help from outside.[28] Gary Dorrien, Reinhold Niebuhr Professor of Social Ethics at Union Theological Seminary, may speak for many in his denunciation of capitalism as a system that thrives on the "selfish impulses that Christian moral teaching condemns," arguing that "neo-classical economic theory mythologizes a supposedly 'natural' free market that never existed anywhere." Globalization, he asserts, "has unleashed the predatory logic of capitalism, devastated trade union movements and shrunken the restraining capacities of government."[29]

In his 2012 book *What Money Can't Buy: The Moral Limits of Markets*, Michael Sandel contended that the United States had moved from having a "market economy" to becoming a "market society" in which free markets have led to everything being up for sale. Prisoners, for example, can pay for an upgrade of their cells in California; solitary commuters can pay to use car pool lanes in Minneapolis; Western couples can pay $6,250 for the services of a surrogate mother in India; foreigners who invest $500,000 and create 10 jobs or more can emigrate to the United States; a hunter can shoot an endangered black rhinoceros in South Africa for $150,000; companies can pay for the right to emit carbon into the atmosphere in Europe; and, although the policy never appears in print, wealthy parents can effectively pay to have their children admitted to prestigious universities. There is "a widespread sense that markets have become detached from morals," Sandel has written, allowing those with the ability to pay to buy access to schools and hospitals, nature, health care, the arts, and even comfort in prisons.[30]

Conservatives historically argue that even talking about inequality raises the specter of "class warfare" in the United States—a charge House Speaker John Boehner has leveled many times at President Obama's budget and equality statements.[31] Indeed, there is a long tradition of conservatives warning against such talk. In 1962, for example, Bryce Harlow, a onetime aide to Presidents Dwight Eisenhower and Richard Nixon, told the Merchants and Manufacturers Association, "The Achilles' heel of every democracy has been the drive to use the mighty weapon of political equality to enforce economic equality." Years later, William Simon, who served as both energy secretary and Treasury secretary in the 1970s, declared that "egalitarianism is a morbid assault on both ability and justice."[32] Finis Welch, a professor of economics at Texas A&M, wrote in 1999, "Without inequality of priorities and capabilities, there would be no trade, no specialization, and no surpluses produced by cooperation."[33] Thomas Garrett, then an economist at the Federal Reserve Bank of St. Louis, wrote in 2010, "Income inequality should not be vilified, and public policy should encourage people to move up the income distribution and not penalize them for having already done so."[34] Richard Epstein, a senior fellow at the Hoover Institution and professor of law at New York University, has asserted that because "inequality creates an incentive for people to produce and create wealth, it's a wonderful force for innovation."[35] More recently, Edward Conard, a retired head of Bain Capital and former business partner of Massachusetts governor Mitt Romney, the 2012 Republican presidential candidate, claims in his book *Unintended Consequences: Why Everything You've Been Told about the Economy Is Wrong* (2012) that for every $1 invested by the wealthy, the public gets $20 in value.[36] As for all those high corporate salaries deplored by liberals, Holman Jenkins Jr. has noted in the *Wall Street Journal* that pay for executives is a reflection of the rise in value of a company's shares. "Executive compensation is better understood as executive incentive," he wrote, and to punish executives by limiting their pay will end up limiting economic growth and the value of the companies they lead.[37]

In the end, however, the values of both liberty and justice must underlie the purpose of government. "No government is legitimate unless it subscribes to two reigning principles," the legal scholar Ronald Dworkin wrote in *Justice for Hedgehogs*. "First, it must show equal concern for the fate of every person over whom it claims dominion. Second, it must respect fully the responsibility and right of each person to decide for himself how to make something valuable of his life."[38]

The Powerful Appeal of Economic Justice

Justified or not, the bashing of wealthy economic elites has never gone out of fashion in US political history. However, the Great Recession and the ensuing protests thrust the issue of economic inequality to the forefront emotionally and to a level not seen in recent decades. Even as the economy was improving in 2015, Americans were found in polls to remain concerned about it. A June 2015 *New York Times*/CBS News Poll found that nearly 6 in 10 respondents agreed that the government should do more to reduce the gap between rich and poor—only a third of Republicans supported such a role, whereas 8 in 10 Democrats did. Meanwhile, the proportion of respondents who said everyone has a fair chance to get ahead fell to 17 percent; 6 in 10 felt that only a few people at the top had an opportunity to advance.[39]

In terms of inequality of income, the United States is the 41st most unequal country in the world, according to the US Central Intelligence Agency's *World Factbook*. Not surprisingly perhaps, in the European Union as a whole incomes are considerably less unequal, as are those in the United Kingdom, Switzerland, Germany, and Sweden (the most economically egalitarian country on the list). Income equality in Nigeria, Albania, Indonesia, Russia, and Ukraine also surpasses that in the United States, where the economic growth rate has been higher than in many countries where income is distributed more evenly.[40] Clearly, then, greater equality of incomes is likely not the only criterion that someone wanting to live in the United States might consider.

The trend toward greater economic income inequality, especially in some advanced countries, has been under way for several decades. The phenomenon became more prominent in the 1980s, slackened in the late 1990s, and accelerated in the slow recovery after the Great Recession. Emmanuel Saez, a French-American economist at the University of California at Berkeley, reported in March 2012 that from 1993 to 2010, an average of 52 percent of the total growth in income in the United States was captured by the top 1 percent of wage earners. In the Clinton-era expansion of the late 1990s, the top 1 percent captured 45 percent of the total growth, 65 percent in the Bush-era expansion of 2002–07, and 93 percent in the recovery of 2009–10.[41]

Reams of books on inequality have been published, the most influential of which is perhaps *Capital in the Twenty-First Century*, by Thomas Piketty, professor at the École des hautes études en sciences sociales (EHESS) and the Paris School of Economics.[42] His book became a best-seller in the United States in mid-2014. Its neo-Marxist critique is based on vast amounts of census data and other surveys that were used to compile a database showing that earnings accruing to the upper classes from their ownership of capital had exceeded—and would continue to exceed—earnings from labor in the West. Piketty's work with Saez has become a standard reference point for debates on the subject, even among those who disagree with the diagnosis.[43] The remarkable and perhaps unprecedented flood of other books relating to the issue of economic justice have included two by Nobel Laureates, Joseph E. Stiglitz (*The Price of*

Inequality: How Today's Divided Society Endangers Our Future, 2012) and Paul Krugman (*End This Depression Now!* 2012).[44]

The perception of extraordinary benefits for the top 1 percent of earners has been reinforced by findings that the executive compensation of leading firms has far outstripped the salaries of their workers. The Economic Policy Institute (EPI), studying data on compensation drawn from government statistics and Capital IQ Compustat, a private consulting company, concluded that the growth of CEO and executive compensation overall was a major factor in the doubling of the income shares of the top 1.0 percent and top 0.1 percent of households from 1979 to 2007. In a measure of 350 top firms, this study found that CEOs earned 18.3 times more than typical workers in 1965 and 26.5 times more than those in 1978. The ratio, EPI said, grew to 136.8 to 1 in 1995 and peaked at 411.3 to 1 in 2000. In 2012 CEO pay was back down to 202.3 times more than typical worker pay, but the trend toward disparities over the long term is striking.[45]

But it is not just labor advocates and liberals who have worried about the problem and the dangers of undertaking the wrong policies in response. In 2005, for example, Alan Greenspan, then chairman of the Federal Reserve, said in response to a question at a congressional hearing about growing inequality, "This is not the type of thing which a democratic society—a capitalist democratic society—can really accept without addressing."[46] Income inequality "is where the capitalist system is most vulnerable," Greenspan later asserted. "You can't have the capitalist system if an increasing number of people think it is unjust."[47] Greenspan's comments are notable because he is a well-known opponent of government regulation and redistributionist social welfare programs. His successor as Fed chief, Ben Bernanke, also a Republican, though perhaps less ideologically libertarian than Greenspan, was also asked about rising inequality in the United States. "It's a very bad development," he said in a 2010 interview, adding that the danger was two separate societies based on educational attainment differences, with those possessing only a high school degree or less stuck at the middle or bottom.[48] In 2007 Bernanke spoke of the "questions of ethics and values" that the problem of inequality posed for Americans.[49] The market system should not be expected to deliver "equality of economic outcomes," he maintained, that approach would undermine the free enterprise system. But he nonetheless argued, "If we did not place some limits on the downside risks to individuals affected by economic change, the public at large might become less willing to accept the dynamism that is so essential to economic progress."[50]

But does the achievement of greater economic equality necessarily lead to economic justice? Or is economic justice better served by lifting the incomes of the poor than by achieving greater economic equality? The difficulty in reconciling these two propositions is discussed in the next chapter on the writings of the philosopher John Rawls and the economist Thomas Piketty.

4

Justice for All:
Defining and Measuring Inequality

This disposition to admire, and almost to worship, the rich and powerful, and to despise or, at least, neglect persons of poor and mean conditions, though necessary both to establish and to maintain the distinction of ranks and the order of society, is, at the same time, the great and most universal cause of the corruption of our moral sentiments.
—Adam Smith, *The Theory of Moral Sentiments* (1759)

When professional economists think about economic problems we generally start with the Pareto principle that a change is good if it makes someone better off without making anyone else worse off. . . . A change that increases the incomes of high-income individuals without decreasing the incomes of others meets that test: it makes some people better off without making anyone else worse off.
—Martin Feldstein, "Is Income Inequality Really a Problem?" (1998)

John Rawls (1921–2002) grew up in a family of modest means in Baltimore. His father lacked a law degree but managed to practice law and even argue before the Supreme Court, and his mother was a powerful advocate for women's rights. He initially aspired to become a minister but gave up that goal after serving as a combat infantryman in the South Pacific in World War II. Perhaps more influential on his life and sense of justice was the fact that during his youth two younger brothers died of infectious diseases that some biographies said were caught from him. Self-effacing and understated, Rawls often recalled that he turned to moral philosophy because he was not good enough in music or mathematics. It was in graduate school at Princeton that Rawls began his inquiry into the subject that preoccupied his career and led him to become the preeminent modern theoretician of justice.[1]

While teaching at Harvard, Rawls outlined his philosophical vision in his book *A Theory of Justice*, published in 1971. He later amplified that vision in his works *Political Liberalism* (1993) and *The Law of the Peoples* (1999).[2] Rawls set forth two major principles of justice: (1) an equitable social order must secure basic liberties for its citizens, and (2) any action taken by a society must not hurt the least well-off of its most vulnerable citizens. The attribute of social and economic justice, however, is evoked by what is known as Rawls's "difference principle," which holds that an unequal distribution of the benefits of a society is morally justified only if its worst-off members accept their own gain as a result.

This chapter discusses the importance of Rawls in the debate over economic justice and why he might have surprising things to say about the issue of inequality introduced in recent years—in US political discourse especially—by a parade of economic writers, most notably Thomas Piketty. Although lifting the lives of the poor and achieving economic equality throughout a society are not necessarily incompatible goals, they do not necessarily go hand in hand based on recent economic history. Indeed, economic justice may hinge more on lifting the lives of the poor than on eliminating inequality per se.

Rawls Redux

Rawls's noteworthy metaphor for thinking about justice was his definition of the so-called veil of ignorance—that is, the idea that the social arrangement must be acceptable to someone who would not be able to know where he or she was in the system. Thus citizens must accept a system only if it is predicated on their theoretically not knowing whether they would be its beneficiary or its disadvantaged party. Economists might compare the difference principle in such a society to the term *Pareto-optimal*, named after the Italian economist Vilfredo Pareto (1848–1923). A Pareto-optimal improvement posits an allocation of resources in which no one is made worse off even if some are better off. Rawls's insight was so striking that Robert Nozick, the libertarian critic of Rawls's philosophy and a proponent of the free exercise of personal liberty and property rights, paid homage to its importance. In his book *Anarchy, State, and Utopia* (1974), Nozick declared, "Political philosophers now must either work within Rawls' theory or explain why not."[3]

Although he is not considered a political philosopher, French economist Thomas Piketty's writings have certainly fostered a somewhat different perspective on economic justice, in part because his book *Capital in the Twenty-First Century* tapped into the zeitgeist created by the Occupy Wall Street movement's anger directed at "the 1 percent" of wealthiest Americans. Piketty's implicit assumption is that the most important measure of economic justice is income inequality rather than how the poor fare in a given society. Using reams of tax records and other statistical measures of wealth and income going back 200 years, Piketty argues that economic justice is weakened when the expansion of the wealthy class permits it to dominate the political system. He finds, for example, that the share of national income in the United States for the richest 1 percent grew from 9 percent in the 1970s to 20 percent in the decade 2000–2010, with inevitable consequences for the nature of US democracy.[4]

According to Piketty, the growing enrichment of those at the top derives from three sources: (1) the increasing share of income from salaries and wages paid to the super rich and corporate "super managers," accounting for two-thirds of inequality in the United States; (2) the disproportionate share of capital held by those at the top of the ladder; and (3) the increasing share of national incomes derived from capital as opposed to wages and salaries. In particular, Piketty focuses on what he calls "patrimonial capitalism"—that is, the fact that owners of assets—whether equity, bonds, retirement accounts, homes, or other kinds of property—have become a larger portion of society than wage earners owning and saving little or nothing. These disparities, he asserts, "radically undermine the meritocratic values on which democratic societies are based."[5]

Is it too much to say that Rawls and Piketty symbolize two schools of thought about the nature of economic justice? Not really.

Rawls has spawned a variety of critics. On the one hand, Nozick and other libertarians argue, as just noted, that inequality in society is an acceptable outcome of a system that allows its citizens to pursue their economic freedoms and reap the advantages of their talents, hard work, discipline, and gifts. Rawls and his supporters argue, on the other hand, that many of the rewards in such a system stem from luck, birth status, and other arbitrary advantages. A second line of criticism—advanced by Amartya Sen, the Nobel Laureate economist, among others—is that Rawls's definition of a just distribution of goods is overly restrictive because people have different wants, needs, and capabilities. Like Nozick, Sen has also argued that Rawls overlooks the obvious importance of a poor person's responsibility for his or her own state of affairs, or of the possibility that individuals, including the poor, may have goals other than economic gain or self-interest.[6] A third category of critics of Rawls, no less influential than the libertarians, belongs to the "communitarian" and "cosmopolitan" schools of thought, discussed later in this book, which hold that justice must also factor in loyalty to one's own community (communitarian) or to the world as a whole even if the effect on one's own community is detrimental (cosmopolitan).

Piketty's Charge: Sorting Through Different Definitions of Economic Justice

Of the tendencies that are harmful to sound economics, the most seductive, and in my opinion the most poisonous, is to focus on questions of distribution.

—Robert E. Lucas Jr., Nobel Laureate economist (2004)

In warning of a calamity or revolution if inequality is not addressed, Thomas Piketty has become heir to a tradition of economic doomsaying dating at least from Reverand Thomas Malthus, whose doctrines in the late 18th and early 19th centuries theorized that disaster was in the offing as population growth outstripped society's ability to feed the masses, especially the poor. Malthus's contemporary, David Ricardo, predicted equally pessimistically that landed elites would become increasingly and perhaps dangerously wealthy and dominant. And, of course, Karl Marx later forecast a system that would relentlessly enrich the owners of capital, impoverish the masses of workers, and spark a revolution of the proletariat. "Let the ruling classes tremble at a communist revolution," Marx and Friedrich Engels declared in their *Manifesto of the Communist Party* in 1848. "The proletarians have nothing to lose but their chains. They have a world to win."[7]

Piketty's goal is more analytical than prophetic. But he does explicitly make a case against what he terms the "fairy tale" put forward by the Nobel Laureate economist Simon Kuznets, who theorized in the 1950s that economic growth in the United States would lead to greater economic *equality*. In the first decades after World War II, the Kuznets theory seemed true, in part because so much wealth had been wiped out in the previous decades by the Great Depression and two world wars. But in recent decades, Piketty's evidence demonstrates, the trend in the United States and other advanced countries has gone back to the Gilded Age of the pre–World War I era. The top 10 percent of earners claimed 45–50 percent of national income in the 1910s and 1920s, for example. Their share dropped to 30–35 percent after World War II, but has now returned to what it was a century ago.

Piketty's central point revolves around the formula that r (return on capital) is and will continue to be 4–5 percent, whereas g (economic growth) is likely to remain stuck at about 2 percent. Thus with $r > g$ likely to prevail for the foreseeable future, capital becomes increasingly important, and the owners of capital will increasingly be those who inherited it rather than those who built it up in the first place. After its release, Piketty's book, *Capital in the Twenty-First Century*, was widely praised for its path-breaking assemblage of data. But some of that praise was qualified by questions about his methodology and even some of his basic assumptions. The *Financial Times* argued that flawed statistics and extrapolation led Piketty to conclude incorrectly that inequality had risen in Britain.[8] Conservative-leaning economists found additional grounds for dispute. Harvard professor Martin Feldstein contended that Piketty misread the US tax code as it applies to small business owners, in particular a revision that encourages individuals to shift their income out of taxable corporations and onto their personal tax returns, which would show an increase in their income on paper but not in reality.[9]

A noteworthy aspect of *Capital in the Twenty-First Century* is that, despite the title, Piketty's research reveals that two-thirds of inequality in the United States results from skewed labor compensation, not capital—that is, skyrocketing compensation for those in the top income brackets. Conservatives argue that such high-end earners are generally compensated in relation to the value they add to their companies and therefore the economy in general. "When a high-frequency trader figures out a way to respond to news a fraction of a second faster than his competitor, his vast personal reward may well exceed the social value of what he is producing," asserts economist Gregory Mankiw. "The key issue is the extent to which the high incomes of the top 1 percent reflect high productivity rather than some market imperfection. . . . My own reading of the evidence is that most of the very wealthy get that way by making substantial economic contributions, not by gaming the system or taking advantage of some market failure or the political process."[10]

But even among economists sympathetic to Piketty's concerns, questions have been raised about, for example, his certitude that $r > g$ would continue in the same proportion as in the past. Robert Solow, the Nobel Laureate economist, has said that "maybe a little skepticism is in order" in light of the probability that the rate of return may decline in the future.[11] Still others have cited a number of countries where $r > g$ has persisted for decades without increasing inequality. Lawrence Summers expressed "serious reservations" about Piketty's theories, contending that $r > g$ could easily be undermined by the dissipation of fortunes over generations and by returns being consumed rather than reinvested. "As capital accumulates, the incremental return on an additional unit of capital declines," Summers argued, contending that Piketty misread the literature on the subject.[12] Two widely cited studies by an economics graduate student at the Massachusetts Institute of Technology (MIT), Matthew Rognlie, also have found that Piketty greatly overstates the inevitability of growth in the returns from capital. Moreover, by breaking down capital into disaggregated categories, Rognlie has shown that the growth in both capital and wealth contributing to inequality (in the United States as well as in other developed countries) has been driven almost entirely by the housing sector—not the stocks, bonds, or other assets usually thought of as capital. Because housing is owned more broadly by the public, Rognlie has suggested that "the consequences for inequality may be less severe" than Piketty claims.[13]

An important shortcoming in Piketty's analysis is his exclusion of the impact of existing redistributive government programs such as food stamps, housing assistance, free health benefits, Pell grants for undergraduate education, income support (i.e., welfare), the earned income tax credit (EITC), heating subsidies, and other transfer payments that put cash or the equivalent in the pockets of low-income Americans. The Congressional Budget Office, in its measurements of inequality, has tried to compensate for these omissions and has shown that after the late 1970s Americans in the bottom fifth of the income ladder saw their incomes climb by almost 50 percent, whereas the incomes of Americans in the middle fifth grew by 36 percent. "To disregard the impact of transfers and progressive taxation on the distribution of income and family well-being is to ignore America's most expensive efforts to lessen the gap between the nation's rich, middle class, and poor," wrote Gary Burtless, a senior fellow and labor economist at the Brookings Institution.[14] A separate Brookings study found that, after adjusting for inflation, spending on the 10 biggest means tested federal programs had increased from $126 billion in 1980 to $626 billion in 2012. Part of this increase was driven by an increase in the population and the number of poor people, but spending had increased from about $516 to $13,034 per person over the previous five decades, the Brookings study said.[15] Because the wealthiest 1 percent of Americans pay nearly a quarter of all federal taxes, one could well argue that, far from gaining greater political control as a result of their wealth, their tax dollars are being used to redistribute income to the poor and even the middle class through entitlement programs.

An even more deeply puzzling aspect of Piketty's work is his dismissal of the importance of investment in a modern industrial economy. His disdain is symbolized by his use of the word *rents* to describe all earnings derived from profits, dividends, interest, royalties, or capital gains, including the gain in value of one's home.[16] He acknowledges that the word *rents*—and the class of people the French would call *rentiers*—is used by economists nowadays to refer to "undue or unjustified income" derived from a monopoly or lack of competition.[17] But Piketty prefers to apply the term to any income other than that derived from labor, noting that over the centuries it has been considered "an affront to common sense" that people should earn income without working.[18] (The American usage would be "earned" versus "unearned" income, but most Americans would regard their pension income as "earned" over a lifetime of work.) Piketty thus dismisses the value of private investment in creating jobs—implying perhaps that the only legitimate investment should be undertaken by government or government-controlled companies—while he consigns people who work hard and use their earnings to save and invest, even pensioners, as a less legitimate sector of society. That sector is what he describes as rent seekers, *rentiers*, the "patrimonial class." The middle 40 percent of the national income range is labeled the "patrimonial middle class."[19]

Yet for many years economists and policymakers have worried that Americans do not save and invest sufficiently for themselves or for the nation, which needs their savings to invest productively in new businesses (thus the logic behind "supply side" tax cuts). Although it is true that the poorest half of the US population owns very little and cannot save or invest, the United States does not have the elaborate government pension systems that France or other European countries enjoy, and so Americans do have to save.

Piketty also rarely acknowledges or discusses whether capital can be a valuable thing. Nowhere does he address the argument that capital is needed to promote entrepreneurship, innovation, modernization, advances in technology, increases in productivity, and standards of living except in a backhanded way, such as when he notes that capital "is always risk-oriented and entrepreneurial, at least at its inception, yet it always tends to transform itself into rents as it accumulates in large enough amounts—that is its vocation, its logical destination."[20] So capital, in his view, starts out as legitimate but quickly ends up less so as it grows.

Piketty's writing seems laced with a bit of religious fervor that is reminiscent of ancient writings against profits. His bottom line is to consign all savers, pensioners, people with 401(k)s and other retirement systems, not to mention homeowners—that is, people who work hard during their working years and use their earnings to save and invest—as belonging to a less legitimate sector of society.[21] Indeed, Piketty's aversion to income earned from capital was likened by a reviewer in the *Wall Street Journal* to "an almost medieval hostility to the notion that financial capital earns a return."[22] Elsewhere, the columnist Clive Crook suggested that Piketty's message seems to be that inequality overwhelms all other moral imperatives or considerations, as if everyone is better off in a more equal society even if the poor are less well off. As Crook saw it, moreover, Piketty seemed almost ghoulishly nostalgic about the fact that greater equality in the postwar years resulted from the wiping out of wealth by two world wars and the Great Depression. "In the frame of this book, the two world wars struck blows for social justice because they interrupted the aggrandizement of capital," the columnist commented sarcastically. "We can't expect to be so lucky again."[23]

Piketty is not the only one to note the rise of income derived from capital as opposed to labor. In 2011 the Organization for Economic Cooperation and Development (OECD) reported that from the early 1990s to the late 2000s income from labor declined as a share of overall national income in virtually every advanced economy—in fact, more in other countries than in the United States. Specifically, it found that the median labor share of income dropped from 66.1 percent in the early 1990s to 61.7 percent in the late 2000s, following a trend that began 30 years ago. Blaming the forces of technology and globalization for causing the shift to capital, the OECD cited another factor as well, the privatization of many formerly government-owned companies, especially in energy, transportation, and telecommunications.[24] In another report, the OECD said, "Young people who see no future for themselves feel increasingly disenfranchised. They have now been joined by protesters who believe they are bearing the brunt of a crisis for which they have no responsibility, whereas people on high incomes appear to have been spared."[25]

However, there is much evidence that growth resulting from globalization and other factors has reduced inequality on a global scale, not increased it. In a rare admission but almost as a throwaway line, Piketty acknowledges as much: "To be sure, the very rapid growth of poor and emerging countries, especially China, may well prove to be a potent force for reducing inequalities at the global level."[26] As Branko Milanović, former lead economist at the World Bank's Development Research Group and more recently a visiting professor at the City University of New York Graduate Center, has demonstrated, those in the bottom third of the world's population except for the very poor, who earn as little as $1.25 a day, have become significantly better off in recent decades.[27] The gains have affected as well the middle third of the world's population and, of course, the very richest 1 percent. Left behind is the working class in advanced countries, which is the equivalent of the upper middle class on a global scale.

What all these figures add up to is a paradox economically, but also morally.

A pointed criticism that could be directed at the focus on inequality is that it leaves out Rawls's definition of an acceptable result: that it must help, or at least not hurt, the condition of those at the bottom of the income ladder. Leaving aside the condition of those at the very bottom, it appears that the majority of the world's poor are better off in recent decades, despite widening inequality within countries and in some cases among them. Does it matter that the rich are a lot better off if there is a payoff in the improved livelihoods of most of those at the bottom? Piketty argues that for all the gains in the economic status of the poor, their losses in a more unequal society derive from a diminished ability to participate in it. Even if a rising tide were to lift all boats, according to this view, there is a danger when it also widens the gap between rich and poor in poor countries. "I am not convinced . . . that the least advantaged would not choose truly equal opportunity over an increase in their relative income," argues Nancy Birdsall, president of the Center for Global Development. The dangers of inequality go beyond the moral challenge, she asserts—inequality not only dampens growth but also limits the equal opportunity necessary in a stable and democratic society.[28]

China offers an especially compelling case study. According to Thomas Pogge, professor of philosophy and international relations at Yale University and director of its Global Justice Program, China's growth in per capita income was a spectacular 236 percent from 1990 to 2004, but there was also "a stunning increase in inequality" over the same period. The national income share of the top 10 percent of the Chinese population rose from 25 to 35 percent in this period. By contrast, the share of the poorest 5 percent fell from 7.3 to 4.3 percent. On the other hand, the poorest fifth of the population saw their income grow by 98 percent over the 14-year period. "Not bad at all," Pogge comments. But he adds that "China's poor paid a high price for it in terms of marginalization, humiliation, and oppression by the emerging economic elite whose greatly expanded share of Chinese household income gives them much greater opportunities to influence political decisions, to give unfair advantages to their children, and to dominate the poor in direct personal interactions. They would have been much better off with more equal economic growth, even if this would have been somewhat less rapid."[29]

It can, of course, be argued that the Chinese generally have better access to medical care and better life expectancies under their currently more unequal economic system. Indeed, there is empirical evidence that in China and other emerging-market economies, as opposed to more developed countries in the West, the very rich have added to economic efficiencies and job opportunities for the poor, especially peasants who had formerly eked out hard livings in the agriculture sector. The economist Caroline Freund of the Peterson Institute for International Economics studied the examples of hundreds of billionaires and concluded that in many countries their riches resulted from innovation, competition, and entrepreneurial genius rather than "rent-seeking" behavior or inheritances, as is often the case in the West.[30]

In recent years, some leading liberals in the United States have sought to defuse the sensitivity of the inequality issue by focusing more on helping the poor with government programs than on whether to tax the rich for having allegedly benefited excessively from the modern economy. For example, in 2015 Governor Andrew Cuomo of New York, in calling for a higher minimum wage, declared, "Some argue that we can close the income gap by pulling down the top. I believe we should do it by lifting up the bottom."[31] And as Senator Charles Schumer of New York, a Democrat who represents the nation's financial capital, has commented, Americans "don't mind if incomes of people at the top go up 20 percent as long as theirs go up 3 to 4 percent."[32] Bill Clinton has defended his presidency on the grounds that those at the lower end of the income scale improved their income status even as the rich may have benefited even more.

"You can say, 'Well, inequality has still increased,' because the top 1 percent did better," he commented at a forum on his presidency. "But I don't think there's much you could do about that unless you want to start jailing people."[33]

In fact, reinforcing this point of view, some evidence suggests that the incomes of the wealthiest Americans are so great that lifting the economic lives of the poor is not enough to reduce inequality. An analysis by the *New York Times* in 2015 revealed that if the United States had increased the minimum wage to $15 between 2009 and 2014, such a move would have been insufficient "to undo the escalation in the income gap" over that period. The reason, the *Times* said, is that the incomes of the top 10 percent of families "rose by much more over the same period." The conclusion reached was that "if reducing inequality is the goal, there's no alternative to slowing the income growth of the highest earners, say, by raising upper-income tax rates or limiting the favorable tax treatment of pay for corporate executives."[34]

Psychologists have weighed in on the issue of whether people in fact care more about equality than about elevating their own material well-being. A well-known survey of graduate students and staff members at the Harvard School of Public Health in the 1990s asked which status respondents would prefer: (1) earning $50,000 a year if their peers earned only $25,000 a year or (2) earning $100,000 if their peers earned $200,000. Perhaps surprisingly, 50 percent of the respondents preferred to earn a *lower* salary if it placed them at a *higher* level among their peers. "Many seemed to see life as an ongoing competition, in which not being ahead means falling behind," the study said. "In their view . . . a higher relative standing leads to such desirable outcomes as access to better jobs and education, improved marital prospects and the opportunity to pass these advantages to one's children. . . . Both absolute well-being and relative position seem to matter to people."[35]

The study noted its implications for public policy by quoting from a comment made by Martin Feldstein, former chairman of President Reagan's Council of Economic Advisers, who wondered why anyone would oppose a cut in the capital gains tax, since such a cut, while helping the rich, would not hurt the poor. "But benefits to the rich will hurt the poor if the poor, like everyone else, care about their relative standing," said the Harvard School of Public Health study. "The majority of respondents to our survey rejected the prospect of everyone becoming richer if it was accompanied by a fall in their own relative standing. For them, a policy that increased their absolute income but lowered their relative income did not make them feel better off."[36]

Other academic studies have addressed the same issue as the one at Harvard. In what is known as the "ultimatum game," a player is given $10 and told to bargain with another player (not known to the first player) over dividing up the money. If they do not agree, neither side gets to share the $10. Presumably, the first player might first offer the second $.01 and keep the $9.99. Why would the second player reject that offer? After all, he (or she) would be one penny richer. But in three experiments in one study, the minimum acceptable offer for the second player was $3 (or more). In other words, the second person would rather not have anything if it amounted to only a small portion of what was to be allocated. "The willingness of people to resist what they consider to be unfair allocations has implications for economics that go well beyond bargaining theory," observed Richard Thaler, behavioral economist at the University of Chicago. "In general, consumers may be unwilling to participate in an exchange in which the other party gets too large a share of the surplus. . . . *Homo economicus* is usually assumed to care about wealth more than such issues as fairness and justice. . . .The research on ultimatum games belies such easy characterizations."[37]

Measuring Inequality as a Symbol of Economic Injustice

> *This [inequality] is not the type of thing which a democratic society—a capitalist democratic society—can really accept without addressing.*
>
> —Alan Greenspan, testimony before the Joint Economic Committee, US Congress (2005)

How helpful are moralistic tenets in making judgments about the actual effects of globalization on the world's economic distribution? Has globalization produced the inequalities that critics claim? Inequality in the world economy, and within countries, can be criticized on moral, political, and ethical grounds. Morally, it clearly offends many people that there is such a wide chasm between rich and poor throughout the world. Politically, such inequality can give rise to instability, protest, and even war. Ethically, the question arises as to whether inequality is a necessary by-product of economic growth and the price that must be paid for a system based broadly on markets, trade, and investments. The evidence of the economic consequences of inequality is mixed and a matter of dispute, and that dispute is unlikely to be resolved by the evidence presented here. But one must begin somewhere, presenting at least some of the evidence.

To deepen understanding of a highly complex (and morally charged) issue, Milanović has applied analysis to three concepts of global inequality. Each is based not on dollar terms but on what economists call purchasing power parities (PPPs). PPPs are used instead of market exchange rates to convert currencies, which makes it possible to compare the output of economies and the welfare of their citizens in real terms—that is, controlling for differences in price levels.[38] Measured by the so-called Gini index, in which a value of 0 expresses total equality and 100 expresses maximum inequality, the three categories of inequality are as follows:

1. inequality between and among the world's nations, drawing on information from 150 countries, irrespective of the size of their populations,

2. inequality between and among the world's nations, weighted according to the size of their populations, and

3. inequality based on the condition of a cosmopolitan or "imaginary community" of all the world's individuals, irrespective of the nation in which they live.

Efforts to measure these types of inequality, along with the trend over time, have been hampered by a lack of data, particularly on households. In a 2013 update of his studies, Milanović found that inequality among nations, undifferentiated by size (first category), has *risen* in the era of globalization. In the second category, however, inequality has *declined*, largely because of the success of Brazil, China, India, Indonesia, and some other countries in achieving higher growth rates as a result of their integration into the global economy. Inequality among the world's citizens, undifferentiated by where they live (third category), can be calculated only from the mid-1980s because of the unavailability of comprehensive data. However, the trend shows a moderate *increase* in inequality after 1990 and a moderate *decrease* in inequality since the middle of the first decade of the 21st century. Thus over the last several years, says Milanović, "we see something that may be historically important: perhaps for the first time since the Industrial Revolution, there may have been a decline in global inequality. . . . [W]e do not know if the decline in global inequality will continue over the next decades. So far it is just a tiny drop, a kink in the trend, but it is indeed a hopeful sign. For the first time in almost 200 years—after a long period during which global inequality rose and then reached a very high plateau—it may be setting onto a downward path."[39]

A similar conclusion was reached in 2015 by Tomas Hellebrandt and Paolo Mauro of the Peterson Institute for International Economics. They studied household surveys in more than 100 countries and found that the Gini index of worldwide global inequality improved from 69 in 2003 to 65 in 2013. And it was projected to improve further to 61 in 2035, indicating that on a worldwide basis inequality was declining, not rising—again in large part because of gains in China, India, and sub-Saharan Africa (see figure 4.1). This future decline, they said, is likely to increase worldwide consumption or use of consumer goods such as cars and appliances and of food and natural resources.[40]

Taking a longer view, Milanović recognizes that global inequality has been a growing fact of life since the dawn of the Industrial Revolution and the first phase of the integrated global economy that reached a peak in the late 19th century. His findings force a rethinking of the earlier conclusions of Kuznets, whose empirical research, largely in the 1950s and 1960s, delineated the dramatic expansion of growth globally, starting in the mid-18th century. That expansion led to a remarkable new era of prosperity that the world—previously dependent on agriculture and before that on hunting, gathering, and fishing—had never before seen. The trend was driven by industrialization, of course, but also the growth of individual incomes and the resettlement of populations to take new jobs in the manufacturing and services sectors. Kuznets found, however, that in poor countries this growth had widened the gap between rich and poor. In wealthier countries, especially the United States, economic growth was producing greater economic *equality* and would continue to do so. Using what was deemed to be the best data available at the time, Kuznets put forward the comforting idea that in the new age of postwar prosperity, the rising tide not only lifted all boats, but also lifted them in fairly equal proportion. Kuznets

Figure 4.1 Economic growth brings millions out of poverty

percent of world population

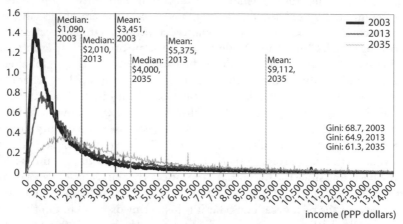

Note: The percentage of world population for each $20 interval is reported on the vertical axis. Individual incomes on the horizontal axis are expressed in US dollars at 2011 international prices (purchasing power parity, PPP). Figure shows that in 2003 nearly half of the world's population had incomes of less than $1,000, adjusted for PPP. Their incomes increased to $2,000 in 2013. As economic growth brings millions out of poverty, the global income is more equitably distributed. This process is expected to continue into the future. The Gini index is the most commonly used measure of inequality in income or consumption expenditure. The index ranges from 0, which reflects complete equality, to 100, which indicates complete inequality (one person has all the income or consumption, while all others have none).

Sources: Tomas Hellebrandt and Paolo Mauro, *The Future of Worldwide Income Distribution*, Working Paper Series 15-7 (Washington: Peterson Institute for International Economics, April 2015). Forecasts for growth: Organization for Economic Cooperation and Development, Consensus Forecasts, International Monetary Fund/World Bank, and authors' forecasts; population projections: United Nations; household survey data on income distribution: Luxembourg Income Study (LIS) and World Bank.

acknowledged that much of his basis for this conclusion was speculative and even "wishful thinking."[41] However, his findings were certainly politically important in an era in which Communists were trying to denigrate the fruits of capitalism and threatening to bury the West economically.

Although in the first decades after World War II the Kuznets theory seemed true and thus was widely accepted, more recent data suggest that inequality within countries such as the United States has grown. Thus the issue of the stagnant or declining wages in the advanced countries has become a major cause of concern over the last several years, underscoring the existence of winners and losers.

The Winners

Living standards for hundreds of millions of the world's poorest people have risen in the globalization era. The World Bank estimates that nearly 2 billion people lived on less than $1.25 a day (World Bank's poverty line) in 1981, but that by 2008 that number had dropped to under 1.3 billion (even as the world population increased from 4.4 billion to 7 billion).[42] (A similar finding was reached by the International Labour Organization.[43]) A separate report at the end of 2014 by the World Bank and the IMF found that the share of the world's population living on $1.25 a day dropped from 36.4 percent in 1990 to 11.5 percent in 2015—and that this share was projected to drop to less than 5 percent by 2030, all because of global economic growth.[44]

According to development experts at the United Nations, these higher incomes have brought about dramatic improvements in health, education, and opportunity in recent decades.[45] The once-poor countries are now home to about 2 billion people earning $3,000 to $20,000 a year, which translates into $12 trillion of purchasing power, just a bit below the size of the US economy.[46] In 2015 the United Nations hailed the halving of the number of people living in poverty and the tripling of people in "the working class" since 1991 as "profound achievements" that had also promoted gender equality and reduced the child mortality rate by more than half.[47] A separate study projected that a billion people are likely to enter the global "consuming class" between 2010 and 2025. Six hundred million of this class are expected to live in 440 cities in emerging-market countries, where they will likely generate nearly half of global GDP growth between 2010 and 2025.[48]

The McKinsey Global Institute estimates that by 2025, out of a projected 8.2 billion people around the world, 1.8 billion (more than 20 percent) will be part of this "consuming class," spending $30 trillion a year compared with $12 trillion today, thereby creating huge new demands for global production that could help nearly everyone.[49]

Immigration, another feature of globalization, is also believed to have brought benefits to poor countries. More than 200 million people have sought livelihoods outside the country of their birth, many of them sending remittances back home, in the process helping their families weather the storms of downturns, crises, stagnating poverty, and lack of opportunity.[50]

Thus there is clear evidence that over the last few decades globalization has fueled advances toward global equality, not inequality, even though there is greater inequality *within* the United States and many other countries, as documented in myriad other studies.

Milanović, for example, finds that the big winners over the last two decades have been the very wealthy in rich and poor countries alike, and also the hundreds of millions of people in the middle classes of emerging-market economies, especially Brazil, China, India, and Indonesia, who account for perhaps a third of the world's population (see figure 4.2). In addition, the bottom third of the global income distribution has also made "significant gains, with real incomes rising between over 40 percent and almost 70 percent."[51] An important exception is the very poor, or the poorest 5 percent of the world's population, even though the number falling under the World Bank's definition of "absolute poor"—those living on less than $1.25 per day in PPP dollars—has declined over the last two decades. Not that the number is anything to be satisfied with. According to the World Bank, nearly 1.3 billion people remain below

Figure 4.2 Globally, the middle class and the superrich gained the most while the upper middle class gained the least between 1988 and 2008

real PPP income change (percent)

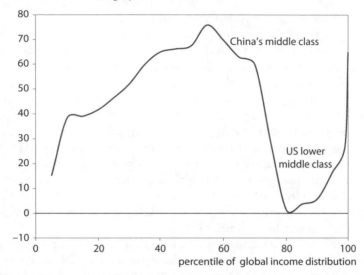

PPP = purchasing power parity

Note: The vertical axis shows the percentage change in real income measured in constant 2005 international dollars. The horizontal axis shows the percentile position in the global income distribution. The percentile positions run from 5 to 95 in increments of five, whereas the top 5 percent are divided into two groups: the top 9 percent and those between the 95th and 99th percentiles. The figure shows that those in the middle ranges of global income distribution—for example, the emerging global middle class—gained the most in those two decades. Those in the upper ranges of world income—but in the global upper middle class—gained the least. The super-rich in the world also gained the most.

Source: Christoph Lakner and Branko Milanović, *Global Income Distribution: From the Fall of the Berlin Wall to the Great Recession*, Policy Research Working Paper 6719 (Washington: World Bank, December 2013).

the extreme poverty line, living on $1.25 or less a day. Another 2.6 billion live on less than $2 a day.[52] All in all, the glaring inequities of the world economy remain shocking. A recent study by Oxfam concluded that nearly half of the world's wealth, or $110 trillion, was owned by the top 1 percent of the population. Indeed, "the bottom half of the world's population owns the same as the richest 85 people in the world."[53]

The Biggest Losers (or Nonwinners)

Along with the absolute poor, the biggest losers or biggest nonwinners in the era of globalization are those whose income is between the 75th and 90th percentiles of the global income distribution. This category applies to the working class or middle class of more advanced countries, particularly those in the former Soviet Union, whose welfare plummeted after the fall of communism. It is this category that also captures the wage and income stagnation and declines in the United States, which have become an urgent matter of concern for politicians and policymakers, many of whom eye globalization as the cause of these problems.

Thus a dramatic reshuffling has occurred in global income, with the evidence suggesting that globalization has contributed at least some of the change. With the exception of the very poor, the bottom third of the world's citizens have gained, with many of them escaping destitution. The middle third or more have become much richer, with their incomes growing at a remarkable 3 percent a year. The top 1 percent, and to a lesser extent the top 5 percent, have gained significantly. The next 20 percent down have gained very little or have had stagnant real incomes. They are at the high end of the world's income distribution because of the wealth of the United States, where even the poorest Americans have incomes higher than those of most of the world's population. But they represent the working class in the United States and other advanced countries.

Implications of a Mixed Bag of Winners and Losers

The mixed bag of winners and losers around the world raises profound questions about the relationship between equality and economic growth in the era of globalization—and between justice and liberty on the broadest possible scale. It would be easy to say that globalization-driven economic growth, underpinned by the freeing up of trade and investment, would be morally unacceptable if it benefited the rich and hurt the poor. But growth that benefits both the rich and the poor (leaving out the middle class in the developed world) is harder to assess on a moral scale. Even harder to assess is whether inequality is a necessary by-product of economic growth or an impediment to it. In other words, is the unequally distributed economic growth in the world today good for the poor?

Since Adam Smith and the dawn of capitalism, economists have agreed that wealth translates into capital investment, and that capital is one of the three primary factors of production, or inputs, that energize an economy. (The other two primary factors are land and labor.) The implication is that capital is essential to the equation because it spurs growth and jobs while providing incentives to investors. Thus the economist John Maynard Keynes, in his landmark *The General Theory of Employment, Interest, and Money,* observed in 1935 that "there is social and psychological justification for significant inequalities of incomes and wealth," although he insisted that the disparities in the Great Depression were not justifiable.[†] In light of the crucial role of wealth and

---

† Keynes argued, for example, that it was better for humankind that "dangerous human proclivities" be channeled into wealth accumulation rather than finding "their outlet in cruelty, the reckless pursuit of personal power and authority, and other forms of self-aggrandisement." John Maynard Keynes, *The General Theory of Employment, Interest, and Money* (1935), chap. 24.

investment in an economy, conservatives and libertarians therefore contend that government and tax policy must encourage the accumulation of capital, or wealth, as a force for job creation and as a hallmark of economic liberty.

A 2013 study by the World Bank argued that because of the recent unprecedented economic gains for the world's poorest people, economic growth in the era of globalization has been good for the poor.[54] The Bank reported that absolute poverty has fallen dramatically in the developing world over the most recent three decades. In 1980, 52 percent of the world's population lived below the World Bank's poverty line, defined as $1.25 a day. By 1990 the incidence of poverty had fallen to 42 percent, and then to 21 percent in 2010. Based on these favorable trends, the World Bank broadened its focus to helping those in the bottom 40 percent, not simply those below the poverty line. The Bank's study of 118 countries over four decades concluded that the bottom 20 percent and 40 percent tended to grow economically in proportion to overall economic growth. "The result holds across decades, including in the 2000s—hence the conclusion that 'growth still is good for the poor.'" The study did find that growth was somewhat better than average in Latin America and somewhat worse in Asia, but that growth at the bottom did rise along with the tide that lifted all boats. However, it did arrive at an even more important and startling conclusion: Measured on a country-by-country basis, the fact that so many previously poor countries had lifted themselves out of poverty and achieved economic gains indicated that "there is no worldwide trend towards greater inequality."[55]

Many economists support the "growth is good for the poor" axiom, even when such growth also heavily benefits the rich. "More people have exited poverty globally in the past 30 years than in all of prior human history, precisely because the rich world steadily grew at potential rates for most of the time," Adam Posen, president of the Peterson Institute for International Economics, wrote in a debate in the *Economist* in 2015. "That rich-country growth led to the diffusion of innovation to poorer countries and the expansion of markets for their exports."[56] Lawrence Summers, while serving as Treasury secretary, tried to make the same point in a speech in 2000 at Oberlin College, although he was drowned out by protesters. "No country has achieved significant and lasting reductions in poverty without rapid economic growth," he declared. "No country has grown rapidly in the past 50 years without substantial growth in exports, supported by integration with the global economy and a move to accept the norms of the global marketplace."[57] Summers later told an interviewer that jobs created by globalization for poor people represented the best opportunities they had ever had. "There are children who are working in textile businesses in Asia who would be prostitutes on the streets if they did not have those jobs," he said. "Of course we should be appalled by, revolted by, and turn absolutely against slave or coerced labor of any kind, but where goods are produced by workers who are free and who make their choices, [it] seems to me very wrong for us to say that those choices are wrong and to limit them."[58]

Accordingly, as a simple matter of moral justice, some economists argue that it is misplaced to concentrate on equality rather than poverty reduction. Martin Feldstein calls such priorities "spiteful egalitarianism," arguing that a result that makes everyone better off without making the poorest worst off is morally acceptable. (This is not to say, Feldstein notes, that tax and spending programs that redistribute income further to the poor are inappropriate.[59]) "Inequality of outcomes is said to be the Achilles Heel of globalization," adds Anne Krueger, the former first deputy managing director of the International Monetary Fund. "This characterization is misleading in several respects. At the very outset, one has to wonder about the preoccupation with inequality . . . . Poor people are desperate to improve their material conditions in absolute terms rather than to march up the income distribution. Hence it seems far better to focus on impoverishment than on inequality."[60]

Yet the evidence that excessive inequality does indeed impede growth has grown in recent years. A series of empirical studies by the staff of the IMF have led to the conclusion that lengthy periods of economic growth are "robustly associated with" more rather than less equality in income distribution, for example. "Some inequality is integral to the functioning of a market economy and the incentives needed for investment and growth," said one such study in 2011, echoing the long-standing view of economists since the rise of capitalism. "But inequality can also be destructive to growth, for example, by amplifying the risk of crisis or making it difficult for the poor to invest in education."[61] The staff paper concedes that some efforts to help the poor and reduce inequality can impede growth, an echo of the Arthur Okun axiom of the "leaky bucket" in which some of the money transferred from the rich to the poor simply disappears in transit. The evidence is mixed as to whether growth is good for equality, or equality is good for growth, the study says. But on balance, it finds that "attention to inequality can bring significant longer-run benefits for growth."[62]

Echoing that point, the Nobel Laureate economist Joseph Stiglitz has argued that inequality has been a significant factor in holding back the recovery in the United States. He asserts that because of inequality, the middle class is too weak to support consumer spending, invest in the future of their children, and generate tax revenues, and their excessive borrowing has contributed to the volatility America's economic performance.[63] Similarly, Raghuram Rajan, governor of the Reserve Bank of India since 2013 and a former chief economist at the IMF, contends that increased inequality helped precipitate the Great Recession by encouraging people to go too deeply into debt, only to suffer the consequences when the housing and debt bubbles burst in 2008.[64]

Does this mean that government efforts to reduce inequality will work and will automatically produce greater growth? Not necessarily. Not only are many programs aimed at alleviating inequality compatible with economic growth, but they can actually encourage growth. "Poorly designed" programs intended to aid the poor, such as massive subsidies for consumers and for inefficient state-owned enterprises or restrictions on certain economic activities, however, can undermine growth *and* hurt the poor. In such cases, "inequality may impede growth at least in part *because* it calls for efforts to redistribute that themselves undercut growth," such as imposing high taxes, regulations, and wasteful subsidies, according to IMF studies, which argue that the best way to help the poor without introducing costly inefficiencies into the economy is to improve infrastructure and access to education and health care for the poor.[65] The United States and other advanced countries seeking to do the same should, meanwhile, consolidate social assistance programs to target the neediest, offer more cash transfer programs, improve pensions and education and health programs, as well as implement a more progressive income tax system.[66] Not everyone favoring such programs agrees that they come without a tradeoff, however. Douglas Elmendorf, former director of the Congressional Budget Office, has evoked Okun's leaky bucket and cautioned that paying for worthwhile government programs might require more borrowing, higher taxes, or lower government spending for other purposes. "Those changes might well *hamper* growth or equity," he said.[67]

The Bottom Line?

Piketty's book presents a number of proposals for leveling off inequality, suggesting that there is an overriding interest in curbing the growth of wealth and capital as a public good in individual countries as well as the world as a whole. Staff experts at the International Monetary Fund argue similarly that rich and poor countries should adopt tax, fiscal, and regulatory policies that curb the power and wealth of those at the top of the ladder while distributing help to the lower half so they have greater opportunities to gain in their societies. Whether the use of taxes to curb the influence of capital is workable is a matter of dispute. Instead of advocating curbs on the expansion of economic globalization or technological progress, the OECD recommends investing in *human* capital to counter the trend, reducing school dropouts, and promoting tax and transfer policies to help those at the lower end.

There is no doubt that inequality matters, even if its injustice results from what Martin Wolf, the *Financial Times* columnist and editor, calls a "just process" such as economic liberty. And despite inequality, many poor people around the world in increasingly unequal societies are better off than they used to be, and many struggling Americans have a higher standard of living and enjoy many goods and services that were unavailable even to the rich of decades ago. "For me the most convincing argument against the ongoing rise in inequality is that it is incompatible with true equality as citizens," Wolf concludes. "Inequality cannot be eliminated. It is inevitable and to a degree even desirable. But, as the Greeks argued, there needs to be moderation in all things. We are not seeing moderate rises in inequality. We should take notice."[68]

But how much curbing of inequality's excesses is too much? Piketty advocates an 80 percent marginal income tax rate in advanced countries and a global wealth tax of 2 percent. He estimates that 80 percent is the "optimal" tax rate for developed countries, but that rate would not be acceptable to most mainstream American economists, to say the least.[69] Milanović has proposed three sensible rules to achieve greater progressivity among income groups. First, ensure that funds generally flow from rich countries to poor countries. Second, ensure that the beneficiary in the poor country does not turn out to be a rich person in that country: "It is precisely the perception that many transfers end up in the pockets of the rich elite in poor countries that is fueling the current discontent with multilateral and bilateral aid." Third, reduce inequality *within* countries by, for example, creating a global governing body financed by a tax raised from the rich in rich countries—similar to Piketty's global wealth tax—to oversee assistance for poor people in poor countries. Preferably, such assistance would be in the form of cash transfers rather than cumbersome programs that would benefit those running them.[70]

It is not the purpose of this book to explore or define ideal government programs to help the neediest. But it would seem that helping those at the lower end of the income scale achieve economic benefits is a far more likely path to success than making the reduction of inequality the be-all and end-all of public policy. That objective should guide the economic and moral imperatives in rich countries and poor countries alike.

That said, how do countries pursue the goal of helping people in need without discouraging them from helping themselves? This is the subject of part II. The larger question of what rich countries owe poor countries, or what rich individuals in rich countries owe the poorest of the poor in poor countries, is addressed in part III on how globalization has redefined citizenship in the modern world economy.

II

THE CONFLICTS OVER INSTILLING VIRTUE

A worker carries a box out of the newly defunct US investment bank Lehman Brothers offices in the Canary Wharf district of London on September 15, 2008. © Andrew Winning—Reuters/Corbis

Any polis which is truly so called, and is not merely one in name, must devote itself to the end of encouraging goodness.
—Aristotle, *The Politics*

To suppose that any form of government will secure liberty or happiness without any virtue in the people is a chimerical idea.
—James Madison, Virginia Ratifying Convention (1788)

No moral philosopher, from Aristotle and Aquinas, to John Locke and Adam Smith, divorced economics from a set of moral ends or held the production of wealth to be an end in itself; rather it was seen as a means to the realization of virtue, a means of leading a civilized life.
—Daniel Bell, *The Cultural Contradictions of Capitalism* (1976)

The Hazards of Moral Hazard

People see economic issues through moral frames and people think there's an extent to which recessions are punishment for sins—mainly sins of excess— and you don't expiate sins by binges.

—Lawrence H. Summers, former White House economic adviser (2011)

Liquidate labor, liquidate stocks, liquidate farmers, liquidate real estate. . . . It will purge the rottenness out of the system. . . . People will work harder, live a more moral life.

—Andrew Mellon, US Treasury secretary, as reported by President Herbert Hoover in his memoirs (1952)

European leaders responded with condescension to the bankruptcy of the US financial services firm Lehman Brothers in September 2008 and the ensuing global financial crisis. Gathering in Paris, they went out of their way to deplore US-style excesses and express nervous confidence that Europe had set a better example. "We want a capitalism of entrepreneurs, we don't want speculators," declared President Nicolas Sarkozy of France. Prime Minister Gordon Brown of Britain claimed that the crisis "has come from America." Prime Minister Silvio Berlusconi of Italy insisted that "Europe is not facing and never faced the risks in the American system."[1] American capitalism fostered selfishness and misconduct, they suggested. European capitalism promoted self-discipline and virtue.

The self-satisfaction did not last long. The shock that originated in the United States soon exposed many European banks to the vulnerability of their own investments and loans. In 2010 Greece's government debts and deficits were revealed to be greater than previously thought. Unbeknownst to incurious creditors, including many leading European banks, the debts and deficits had been covered up for years by deceptive accounting practices. Meanwhile, rescue programs had to be launched, not only for Greece but also for Ireland, Portugal, and Cyprus, and the financial contamination spread to Italy and Spain. Only after Mario Draghi, president of the European Central Bank (ECB), pledged to do "whatever it takes" in 2012—just as the Federal Reserve had done in the United States in 2008–09—was the situation stabilized. By early 2015, after rounds of tough austerity in many European budgets, most of the continent was still struggling to lift itself out of the worst economic downturn since the 1930s. The notable exception to that stability was Greece, which was compelled to accept a tough new regimen of budget cuts, tax increases, privatizations, and reforms of its labor, product, and business regulations in return for a third program of loans from Europe and the International Monetary Fund (IMF) following earlier loan rescues in 2010 and 2012.

This chapter introduces the concept that modern capitalism, including capitalism on a global scale, rests on the widely shared premise that such a system cannot survive without the encouragement of virtuous behavior by participants—whether they are individuals, businesses, financial institutions, or governments. From the European crisis, the chapter traces some of the origins of this fixed idea that capitalism depends on ethical conduct.

The European Fallout of the Global Financial Crisis

Like the aid provided by the Bush and Obama administrations for insolvent or troubled financial institutions, homeowners, and auto companies in 2008-09, Europe's efforts to stabilize its financial system after 2010 left a pungent residue of moral unease. That unease has grown in recent years.

A generation of Europeans grew up under the rift between East and West during the Cold War—a rift that was revived somewhat by Europe's concerns about Russia's intervention in Ukraine beginning in 2013. The newest significant rift in Europe, however, is between North and South—that is, the stable countries of northern Europe, most prominently Germany, and the supposedly errant debtor countries of southern Europe such as Italy and Spain, and especially Greece.

The financial lifeline preventing a Greek collapse after 2010 involved the transfer of many of its liabilities from banks onto the shoulders of European taxpayers, who in turn—through the institutions of the European Commission, ECB, and IMF—imposed harsh requirements that Greece return to balanced budgets. "One really must question whether we can go on receiving less than we spend, so that our debts keep on growing," German chancellor Angela Merkel observed in 2014, saying "we" when she clearly meant "they," and adding, "Indeed, a whole crisis of confidence has grown out of that."[2]

To understand the European crisis, it is important to remember that the Economic and Monetary Union, when creating the euro as a common currency, required member countries to harmonize their fiscal policies. The commitment to fiscal balance was not always honored, but in the case of Greece its failure to reach that goal was compounded by deception—that is, the discovery in 2009 that Greece had covered up its massive deficits with dubious bookkeeping. In 2015 German loss of confidence and Greek defiance led to a nerve-wracking showdown between European and IMF creditors and the leftist government in Athens of Prime Minister Alexis Tsipras. Voted into office in January 2015 with a promise to ease his country's years of economic hardship, Tsipras quickly repudiated many of the fiscal and structural reforms accepted by the leaders he had ousted. His election gave him a mandate to demand relief, Tsipras contended. But Germany and other European countries countered that they also had a mandate from voters and taxpayers—who were, after all, providing the loans that Greece needed. Their obligation, they said, was to ensure that Greece would take steps toward fiscal balance, enabling it to pay back its creditors. (Without further loans, Greece would have faced default, the collapse of its banking system, and an exit from the euro area, which most analysts said would have brought inflation, massive unemployment, and economic ruin.)

The confrontation ended in mid-2015 with an agreement by Europe and the IMF to extend €86 billion to Greece for three more years. In return, Tsipras convinced Greek lawmakers to approve a tough regime of fiscal, budgetary, and structural measures—steps he had previously termed unacceptable. Neither side was happy with the accord. Sullen Greek citizens faced the possibility of many more years of hardship, although European officials said they were willing to consider an IMF proposal for additional debt relief for Greece in order to ease what the Fund called an unsustainable debt burden exceeding 175 percent of Greece's GDP (in part because its economy had shrunk so dramatically). Germans were unhappy that Merkel seemed to be rewarding the Greeks for their record of reckless fiscal and financial failures. All sides were unhappy that European banks—which had extended loans in the first place but were saved by intervention from European government institutions—had not been punished for their own improvident conduct. Europe had become a festival of moral hazard accusations on all sides.

Even before the latest crisis, Germans had developed a habit of seeing aggressive financial institutions as a predatory arm of capitalism suitable for the City of London and Wall Street perhaps, but not Frankfurt, and of seeing the scourge of debt as a moral issue. Indeed, they often referred to private investment firms as parasites that preyed on companies and spat them out while firing workers. In 2005 German labor minister Franz Muntefering, a Social Democrat, compared private equity investors to "swarms of locusts that fall on companies, stripping them bare before moving on."[3] The term *locusts* in fact became quite popular, and German politicians became fond of using it to refer to the financial sector that had enabled countries to pile up mountains of debt.

Underlying the moral concern about paying debts was the parallel concern that if creditors were forced to write off part of their loans, such "haircuts" would rattle the credit markets and force up interest rates for everyone else. Indeed, after ensuring that European banks were spared the worst of the crisis, including their reckless loans to Greece, French president Sarkozy and German chancellor Merkel met at Deauville in October 2010 and called for *future* costs to be imposed on creditors of the troubled countries. That pledge alarmed bondholders and drove up Spain and Italy's interest rates, compounding their difficulties in closing their fiscal deficits.

A mixture of almost religious fervor and cultural disdain infused the discussion, underscored by Germany's particular scorn for anyone accumulating debts—an attitude that stemmed from history, culture, and even language. For example, the German word for debt, *Schuld*, is also used for the concept of "sin" or "fault."[4] Chancellor Merkel, the daughter of a Lutheran pastor in East Germany, appeared to uphold a traditional attitude that debts are an invitation to irresponsible conduct and that even poor people must take responsibility for themselves. Her apparent belief was traced by some to her Lutheran education. "She admits that austerity is the toughest road home but hastens to add that it is also the surest and quickest way to recover the economy and gain full emancipation from the crisis," wrote Steven Ozment, a historian of the Protestant Reformation in Europe. "Luther would agree. According to the polls, so do Ms. Merkel's fellow Germans."[5] In 2015 two German economists asserted in an academic paper that countries with Catholic majorities had a tendency to run into fiscal problems, whereas countries with Protestant majorities such as Germany avoided those problems. After all, they noted, it was a sociologist and philosopher, Max Weber, who coined the term *Protestant work ethic* to explain the hypothesis that "Protestants were more hard-working than Catholics."[6]

It was not hard to see that some of these attitudes bordered on ethically and religiously tinged contempt. Throughout the confrontation with Greece, it was often suggested in Germany, for example, that Greece should auction the Acropolis to meet its loan obligations.[7] "Why should we help rescue the Greeks from their sham bankruptcy?" asked the German playwright Rolf Hochhuth. "Ever since Odysseus, the world has known that the Greeks are the biggest rascals of all time."[8] The Obama administration told Germany's leadership that Berlin's support of only minimal lending to Athens—combined with harsh demands for tax hikes, spending cuts, and wage freezes—was both parsimonious and risky for the region's financial system, and for the NATO alliance as well. But Chancellor Merkel and her cabinet were hardly ready to listen to advice from Americans, who, in their view, caused the crisis in the first place.[9] Later, an American economist attending a conference in Munich in 2015 wrote in the *New York Times* that he was shocked to hear German officials portray themselves as dupes of the corrupt, incompetent, tax-evading, and even irreligious behavior of Greeks.[10]

Greeks responded to German tight-fistedness with invective of their own. They routinely evoked Germany's notorious history, comparing Merkel and German finance minister Wolfgang Schäuble to Otto von Bismarck and even Adolf Hitler. Posters depicted the finance minister with a Hitlerian mustache and Twitter comments called the chancellor "Angela Lecter," after the flesh-eating movie villain Hannibal Lecter. Opponents of Tsipras's concessions to Germany likened him and his team to Nazi collaborators.[11] More soberly, Greek leaders and others pointed out that Germany benefited itself from generous bailout terms by the victors in World War II, avoiding the mistake of the post–World War I victory of imposing on Germany what John Maynard Keynes described as a "Carthaginian Peace" (a term arising from the time legions of the Roman Empire burned Carthage to the ground, seized its armies, forced its citizens into slavery, and exacted huge sums of tribute). It was a fair point. Following World War II, US president Franklin Roosevelt rebuffed US Treasury Secretary Henry Morgenthau Jr. and his plan for a deindustrialized—a "pastoralized"—Germany. Instead, he and other Western leaders launched the Marshall Plan, cancelling large amounts of Nazi-era debt, fearing that a destitute Germany would become vulnerable to Soviet influence.[12] Thus faced with whether to rescue Greece and relieve its debts, at least some Germans argued that doing so would be "morally justified" in light of their own history. "After all, Germany also benefited once from public-sector debt relief," said an editorial in the daily *Handelsblatt*. "At the start of the 1950s, the US wrote off a large part of Germany's war debts, making Germany's famous 'economic miracle' possible."[13]

The debt crisis in Cyprus in early 2013 provoked similar anguish, compounded by Cyprus's dubious business model as a tax haven for foreign depositors, many of them Russians using Cyprus to launder money gained from crime and corruption. Yet the distaste of "rewarding" Cyprus for its bad behavior had to be balanced against destabilizing the system. "At what point does a debt-ridden country endanger the entire financial system, and how can allowing it to go bankrupt still be the right approach?" asked the German magazine *Der Spiegel*.[14] To many, the enmities exposed by these questions were frightening.

"The way some German politicians have lashed out at Greece when the country fell into the crisis has left deep wounds there," concluded Jean-Claude Juncker, at the time prime minister of Luxembourg before he took office as president of the European Commission in 2014. "I was just as shocked by the banners of protesters in Athens that showed the German chancellor in a Nazi uniform. Sentiments suddenly surfaced that we thought had been fully relegated to the past. . . . I am chilled by the realization of how similar circumstances in Europe in 2013 are to those of 100 years ago."[15]

Former German chancellor Helmut Schmidt, a champion of the "European project" of ever-greater economic and political union, also counted himself among the chilled. European unity was a vital German objective to reassure a continent with a blood-soaked history that it must never again worry about German ambitions. Now German economic success, driven by its export-based economy and trade surpluses, was provoking envy and fear in the rest of Europe, especially the countries in the southern tier, Schmidt said. "This time the issue at stake is not a central power that is exceedingly strong in military and political terms, but a centre that is exceedingly powerful in economic terms," he noted in a speech in 2011. German willingness to help those less fortunate—including Greece, Portugal, and Ireland—had become essential: "We must have a compassionate heart for our neighbours and partners."[16]

Is Virtue Essential to Capitalism—or Antithetical to It?

> *Get money, money still! And then let virtue follow, if she will.*
>
> —Alexander Pope, *An Essay on Man* (1734)

Philosophers divide the process by which humans elucidate the rules of moral conduct into three major schools of thought. The first, known as deontology, emphasizes the purity and power of moral reasoning, which is associated with its most important historical practitioner, Immanuel Kant (1724–1804). The second school of thought is utilitarianism, supposing that moral behavior can be understood in terms of the consequences of a set of actions—for example, whether such behavior enhances the social welfare of the greatest number of people. And the third school of thought is virtue ethics, which emphasizes the virtues, or moral character, of an individual in behaving benevolently toward fellow humans. This approach was promoted by, among others, Jesus, Confucius, and the Buddha. Of the Golden Rule, for example, the deontologist would say that doing unto others as you would have them do unto you derives from moral reasoning. A utilitarian would say it flows from the obvious practical need for a society to function. And a virtue ethicist would say it stems from the honorable and virtuous behavior of an individual.[17]

All three schools of thought contribute to the enduring idea that a society cannot function successfully if its citizens do not cultivate virtuous behavior—and to its corollary, that market economies also depend on virtuous conduct by those engaged in commercial transactions. Adam Smith viewed markets as dependent on self-interest, as previously discussed. But his writings also argued that markets and society in general depend as well on trust. He regarded commercial society as having evolved from the earliest phase of hunting and gathering to the domestication of animals, agriculture, and finally market transactions. Economic progress for each of these stages depended on the assumption, or at least the goal, that participants would not deliberately hurt or cheat one another, he wrote. For Smith, an important guarantor of trust in the commercial stage was found in agreed-on rules, in many cases established or arbitrated by government.[18] The need for trust and virtuous behavior in commercial transaction is evident in the use of the word *credit*, derived from the Latin word for belief, as in credibility. Thus as American sociologist Daniel Bell asserts, "No moral philosopher, from Aristotle and Aquinas, to John Locke and Adam Smith, divorced economics from a set of moral ends or held the production of wealth to be an end in itself; rather it was seen as a means to the realization of virtue, a means of leading a civilized life."[19]

What Is Moral Hazard?

Probably since Noah and the flood humans have tended to believe—rationally or not—that disasters in life occur because of sinful behavior, and that the path out of crisis is to return to the straight and narrow road of virtue. The challenge of Western religions has long been to reconcile the belief in a God of justice with the fact that the innocent and sinful suffer alike in a fallen world. Yet the powerful idea of punishment and reward based on one's conduct has endured. It was one of the original definitions of justice in Greek philosophy and scripture. It is thus no surprise that the financial crises of the modern era, as opposed to natural disasters, are no exception, although some argue that the extreme weather being experienced in the era of global warming is a natural punishment for a sinful, profligate, and energy-wasting civilization.

Rescues of banks, institutions, homeowners, or other people who get themselves into financial trouble because of their misjudgments or reckless behavior produce what economists call "moral hazard"—the idea that long-term adverse consequences can result from short-term protections from those consequences. Moral hazard holds that immoral or destructive behavior is encouraged when it is not punished, and that debts incurred must be repaid to discourage people from taking on irresponsible debts in the future. A corollary is that lenders must on occasion accept less than the full value of their loans to discourage reckless *lending* in the future. Debts thus become a symbol of moral values, which is one reason why the outsized scale of US deficits and debts during the financial crisis also took on a morally pejorative aspect in the eyes of critics.

The term *moral hazard* appears to derive from the insurance industry in the mid-19th century and the question of whether insuring against risk encourages risky behavior. Just as one might ask whether fire insurance encourages someone to be careless about fire, does health insurance encourage risky behavior or even hypochondria—or does unemployment insurance discourage people from looking for jobs?[20] In a larger sense, moral hazard implies that well-intentioned efforts to help can actually backfire. For example, a famous study of this paradox by Sam Peltzman, a University of Chicago economist, asserted that laws requiring seat belts in cars appeared to have produced a larger number of accidents because drivers felt they could drive more carelessly knowing they were protected by safety belts (the study also showed that seat belts did reduce the number of fatalities, however).[21]

Behind the idea of moral hazard is a rich history of philosophical and religious meditation on charity and welfare assistance for the needy—and whether extending such benefits encourages dependence, laziness, and antisocial behavior. In addition, in contemporary American discourse concern about moral hazard extends to criticism by many conservatives of open-ended social safety net programs—welfare, health assistance, and unemployment insurance, for example—that may help people in the short run but encourage dependence or loss of initiative in the long run. A powerful example of this view was voiced by House Speaker Paul Ryan, the 2012 Republican vice presidential candidate who declared in 2011 that unchecked spending on Medicare and other government programs "will transform our social safety net into a hammock, which lulls able-bodied people into lives of complacency and dependency."[22]

The ancient fundamental beliefs about "moral hazard" can be found in how modern economics is discussed in the era of globalization.

Role of Virtue in the Economic Sphere

Liberty and justice are abstract principles that can guide or motivate an individual or a whole society. Virtue, by contrast, implies an aspirational code of conduct for an individual, community, or nation. Throughout much of history, including that of the United States, laws requiring certain "virtuous" codes of behavior in private were not challenged. It was commonplace in the United States, for example, to require salutes to the flag, prayers in school, sexual abstinence outside marriage, and heterosexual conduct only. Over the last few decades, attitudes toward such practices have changed. Except for certain segments of social conservatism, it is presumed that the goal of the state is not to require virtuous private behavior but rather to let people determine their own codes of social conduct. The acceptance of gay marriage by a majority of Americans, and by the US Supreme Court in June 2015, exemplifies this evolution of attitudes.

In the economic sphere, however, encouraging virtuous behavior is where liberals, social conservatives, and even libertarians meet. A consensus among these disparate groups accepts the notion that capitalism and prosperity can succeed only when practitioners adhere to certain upstanding modes of behavior. What are these codes of conduct? Essentially, they hold that social and economic cohesion depends on individuals becoming self-sufficient and self-disciplined, avoiding dependency on others, engaging in hard work, and displaying industriousness, reliability, honesty, thrift, and behavior worthy of trust. In the business world, one would add the importance of innovation, creativity, and ingenuity, and, when risk is necessary, that it be bold but prudent. Parallel to this set of behaviors is the belief that such behaviors, while worthy in themselves, are also deserving of reward—what philosophers call "moral desert."

Whether these codes of virtuous conduct are honored in the breach or in the observance, they have been a long-standing feature of thinking about human behavior. However, a peculiar progression has arisen with the advent of modern capitalism, particularly on a global scale. For example, in his book *The Moral Consequences of Economic Growth* (2006) Benjamin Friedman, an economist at Harvard, argues that capitalism fosters a healthy reciprocity between moral behavior and prosperity, in that virtuous conduct—"hard work, diligence, patience, discipline, and a sense of obligation to fulfill our commitments clearly"—produces economic growth. The resultant rising living standards in turn "make our society more open, tolerant and democratic."[23] Martin Wolf of the *Financial Times* has also contended that success in a market economy requires "trustworthiness, reliability, effort, civility, self-reliance and self-restraint," enabling those not motivated by material gain—such as doctors, teachers, policemen, or anticapitalist activists—to flourish.[24]

The earliest political philosopher to discern the importance of virtue as an ingredient in capitalism was no doubt the German philosopher and political economist Max Weber. In his seminal work *The Protestant Ethic and the Spirit of Capitalism*, Weber argued that the very origins and success of the market system derived from an inflection point as religious tenets moved away from their historic rejection of striving for material gain and into the spirit of achieving prosperity through commerce and markets by adhering to the dignity of work and the ability to measure that hard work by the amount of wealth it achieved.[25] Weber cited Benjamin Franklin, with his many proverbs about work, thrift, trustworthiness, and saving, as an example of this emerging ethic.

Weber's analysis has been widely challenged. Marcus Noland of the Peterson Institute for International Economics has noted that Weber mischaracterized not only Protestant theology but also Catholicism and many other religious traditions while too easily dismissing other factors nurturing capitalism in Protestant northern Europe.[26] In addition, with the rise of economic powers in Asia, many scholars have challenged Weber's implicit suggestion that hierarchical cultures and religious traditions cannot encourage the hard work, discipline, and other so-called Protestant virtues that make capitalism work in their non-Protestant societies. Confucian and Hindu societies such as China, Japan, and India have certainly done well with their brands of market economies, these scholars note, demonstrating that "Protestant" values are not essential to hard work, discipline, and the achievement of economic success. Indeed, Japan's postwar success is one of many such examples.[27] So, too, is the spirit of entrepreneurship in authoritarian China, unleashed in the late 1970s by the supreme leader Deng Xiaoping, who turned away from communism and revised Confucianism with the notorious slogan, "To be rich is glorious."[28]

One of the most interesting rebuttals of Weber's Protestant-oriented thesis has been mounted by conservative, free market–oriented Catholics. Their critique of Weber derives from a long-running debate among Catholic intellectuals around whether capitalism depends on selfish or virtuous impulses. One side of this debate was articulated by Pope Leo XIII in his 1891 encyclical *Rerum Novarum* (On Capital and Labor), which condemned the selfish drives and depredations of unfettered capitalism and called for worker rights and social welfare programs amounting to a welfare state.[29] Another exponent of this point of view was Pope Paul VI, whose 1967 encyclical, *Populorum Progressio* (Progressive Development of Peoples), raised such pointed questions about the value of free markets that some critics blamed the encyclical for encouraging violent revolution in Latin America and elsewhere. On the other side of the spectrum was the landmark 1991 encyclical of Pope John Paul II, *Centesimus Annus* (Hundredth Year), which was intended to be a modern response to Leo's socialist-leaning pronouncements of a century earlier. In his encyclical, John Paul, the anticommunist prelate from Poland, spoke positively of "the fundamental and positive role of business, the market, private property, and the resulting responsibility for the means of production, as well as free human creativity in the economic sector."[30] Pope Benedict and Pope Francis are more in the tradition of Leo XIII and Paul VI.

The author Michael Novak in his 1993 book *The Catholic Ethic and the Spirit of Capitalism*—a title consciously evoking Weber—saw *Centesimus Annus* of Pope John Paul II as a lodestar for Catholic market-oriented conservatives. "The complex of attitudes that Weber identified as Protestant actually was shared by many others besides Calvinists," Novak wrote.[31] "Capitalism is not a set of neutral economic techniques amorally oriented toward efficiency. Its practice imposes certain moral and cultural attitudes, requirements, and demands. Cultures that fail to develop the required habits cannot expect to eat broadly of capitalism's fruits."[32] Those economically conservative Catholics in agreement with Novak on this score include Reverend Richard John Neuhaus, a Lutheran pastor turned Catholic priest and author of several books on religion in the

United States, and George Weigel, a Catholic theologian and scholar at the Ethics and Public Policy Center in Washington. By contrast, these market-oriented writers have been disappointed with Pope Francis's view of the world, especially his rejection of the idea that economic self-interest can produce progress. "Francis doesn't seem to have practical strategies for a fallen world," wrote the *New York Times* columnist David Brooks. "He neglects the obvious truth that the qualities that do harm can often, when carefully directed, do enormous good."[33]

Few would dispute that success in a market economy also flows from extraneous factors that have nothing to do with moral behavior. Luck, access to natural resources, and monopolistic or oligopolistic advantages (what economists call rent-seeking) have a big role to play in determining one's success in a market economy. A landowner fortunate enough to be sitting on oil reserves or able to impose a toll on a road going through his property does not win praise for his industriousness or hard work. The idea that one "deserves" the consequences of behavior, good or bad, underpins Robert Nozick's critique of Rawls (see chapter 4). To recapitulate that argument, Nozick asserts that a morally based economic or political system should permit a person to be rewarded for his or her industriousness, whereas Rawls's emphasis was on ensuring a just distribution of arbitrarily earned wealth, especially for those at the bottom.[34] Part of Rawls's argument was that in the real world no one fully "deserves" unique credit for his or her success. Luck and other factors make the distribution of gifts to individuals haphazard and capricious.

But for all of the disagreements that continue over "moral desert," Weber's idea that capitalism rests on virtuous and industrious behavior has penetrated consciously and unconsciously the way in which many Americans think about their economic system. This attitude has survived as a mainstream tenet despite critics on the left complaining about the excesses of consumer society, notably John Kenneth Galbraith (*The Affluent Society,* 1958), the Marxist scholar Herbert Marcuse, and Christopher Lasch (*The Culture of Narcissism,* 1979). Their well-known critiques of the consumer culture helped inspire those young dissidents in the 1960s and 1970s who disdained materialist goals. These "New Left" intellectuals proclaimed a different kind of spiritual fulfillment characteristic of the musical, artistic, and drug culture of the era.

What is interesting about the left-of-center critique, however, is that it has been echoed by critics on the right warning that materialism and hedonism have *undermined* capitalism and the virtues that it supposedly encourages. Daniel Bell (1919–2011), a Harvard sociologist, self-described socialist, and latter-day neoconservative, was one such critic. Invoking Weber, Bell argued in *The Cultural Contradictions of Capitalism* (1976) that although virtuous behavior had contributed to the success of capitalism and to the establishment of a successful bourgeois society, the hedonism of the so-called counterculture and obsessive consumerism of the present day was bringing about the downfall of capitalism by undermining its distinctive culture of self-control.[35]

Bell's book served as an influential jeremiad against the self-indulgence of the 1960s and 1970s that he believed was undermining the cohesion of American society and culture. Capitalism, in other words, had become so materialist that it was destroying itself at a time of maximum peril, the battle against communism. Its adherents, he feared, had become obsessed with social liberty bordering on licentiousness, on the one hand, and reliance on government to impose equality, on the other. Capitalism, he maintained, could still serve as a basis of freedom, rising living standards, and even the defeat of poverty, but its "cultural, if not moral, justification" had been lost, replaced by "state-directed economies" and "state-managed societies."[36] Gone was a public willing to sacrifice for the common good. In short, capitalism may rest on virtuous behavior, but its excesses had led to the abandonment of virtue.

The writings by Bell and other so-called neoconservatives of the 1970s may seem dated by today's standards. The decline of the business ethic at the hands of hedonism does not seem to be at hand. But the idea of the culturally negative repercussions of market economics persists in other guises. For example, a novel theory that capitalism causes dangerous resentment in developing economies has been proposed by Amy Chua, a law professor at Yale. Chua, perhaps best known for her popular (and controversial) parenting memoir, *Battle Hymn of the Tiger Mother* (2011), has studied a range of ethnically diverse market economies, concluding that free markets aggravate sectarian hatreds within them. The system, she asserts, causes enmity to be directed at wealthy "market-dominant minorities," who are begrudged by others because of their success and perceived selfishness rather than any sort of virtuous model of behavior. This provocative thesis derives from the author's personal experience growing up in a family of ethnic Chinese who migrated to the Philippines and became wealthy, acquiring a large estate and many servants. In 1994 Chua's aunt was murdered by her chauffeur, an ethnic Filipino. Although the murderer stole money and jewels, the police listed the motive as revenge. Based on her study, Chua links market economics to past and present hatred of ethnic Chinese in Southeast Asia, Jews in Europe and the Middle East, ethnic Tamils in Sri Lanka, ethnic Tutsis in East Africa, and whites in South Africa and Zimbabwe. "Market-dominated minorities are the Achilles' heel of free market democracy," she asserts, adding "that the global spread of markets and democracy is a principal, aggravating cause of group hatred and ethnic violence throughout the non-Western world."[37]

Until this point, all of these reflections about the virtues of capitalism have been discussed in a vacuum in which public policy has been conspicuously absent. That raises a question: What is the role of government in ensuring that incentives for virtuous behavior are preserved?

The history of the United States suggests that a strong strand of belief has long existed around the idea that government must foster virtuous behavior or at least allow virtuous behavior—such as hard work, frugality, and discipline— to be rewarded without interference by government. The philosophy professor Michael Sandel has found that the role of government in promoting "virtuous" behavior has given way considerably in the social sphere. Laws that used to govern private conduct in the workplace, the public square, and the bedroom have been decreed by the Supreme Court to have unconstitutionally interfered with the way people seek to live their lives. Thus laws requiring school prayer and saluting the flag and prohibitions on abortion, birth control, homosexuality, and other "private" behaviors have been gradually erased or eased over the years. The tension over government's role "points to one of the great questions of political philosophy," Sandel wrote. "Does a just society seek to promote the virtue of its citizens? Or should law be neutral toward competing conceptions of virtue, so that citizens can be free to choose for themselves the best way to live?"[38] Sandel labels the efforts by conservatives to use government to support religion, sexual propriety, family coherence, and gun rights "the recrudescence of virtue," with obvious disapproval.[39] The advocates of government supporting such steps include conservative intellectuals such as the columnist George Will, the former education secretary William Bennett, and the columnist and editor William Kristol, son of the author and columnist Irving Kristol, one of the godfathers of the so-called neoconservative movement. Many of these conservatives, including most Republican candidates for the presidential nomination in 2016, have extended their battle to enacting laws that would permit American businesses to discriminate against gay married couples.

In the economic sphere, however, the desire for government to promote virtuous behavior is alive and well and widespread. It is part of a long tradition going back to the vision of the Founders. To understand the wellsprings of moral hazard, it is also thus important to trace the origins of these sentiments because they parallel the growth of the United States as a global player economically. That discussion is picked up in the next chapter.

6

Government and Just Deserts:
A Brief US History

Virtue and simplicity of manners are indispensably necessary in a republic among all orders and degrees of men.
—John Adams (1776)

I want every man to have the chance—and I believe a black man is entitled to it—in which he can better his condition—when he may look forward and hope to be a hired laborer this year and the next work for himself afterward, and finally to hire men to work for him! That is the true system.
—Abraham Lincoln (1860)

Campaigning for reelection in 2012, President Barack Obama had one of those defining moments in American politics. He contended that although the United States depended on successful businesses, businesses required the participation of others to succeed, including the help of government. "If you've been successful, you didn't get there on your own," he declared in Roanoke, Virginia. "Somebody along the line gave you some help. There was a great teacher somewhere in your life. Somebody helped to create this unbelievable American system that we have that allowed you to thrive. Somebody invested in roads and bridges. If you've got a business—you didn't build that. Somebody else made that happen."[1] A tsunami of conservative condemnation engulfed the president after those comments. The *Wall Street Journal* declared that Obama was undermining a basic belief in the United States in the value of self-made men.[2] Governor Mitt Romney, Obama's rival in the election, accused the president of undermining the entire moral scaffolding supporting American individualism, liberty, and capitalism. What infuriated Obama's critics was the implication that government, in seeking to equalize the benefits of capitalism, was denigrating the importance of entrepreneurial drive and individual success in the US story.

These arguments for and against the idea that governments must not interfere with the rewards of virtuous economic conduct have deep roots in US history. This chapter traces how the notion of the interdependence of civic virtue and market economics is embedded in the American DNA. It also seeks to explain how the power of this notion has shaped contemporary US politics and political debates.

The Early Days

The Founders of the United States, as products of the Age of Enlightenment, often addressed in their writings the challenge of maintaining and achieving a virtuous society in their newly established country. After the American Revolution, one of their earliest explicit concerns was how to build a virtuous society with a sense of national purpose that transcended its selfish quarreling and factionalism along sectional, regional, economic, and philosophical lines. They worried whether their rough-hewn, self-seeking, bumptious fellow citizens had enough strength of character to build such a nation. "Virtue and simplicity of manners are indispensably necessary in a republic among all orders and degrees of men," John Adams wrote in a letter in 1776. "But there is so much rascality, so much venality and corruption, so much avarice and ambition, such a rage for profit and commerce among all ranks and degrees of men even in America, that I sometimes doubt whether there is public virtue enough to support a republic."[3] (Adams could, of course, be describing the United States today.) Another Founder, Benjamin Franklin, famous for homilies about human conduct—but also famous for enjoying life's pleasures—listed temperance, frugality, industry, moderation, and humility among his famous "thirteen virtues."[4]

The US Constitution, superseding the dysfunctional Articles of Confederation in 1787, was an attempt to centralize the previously fractured government without compromising individual rights—that is, to tame factions and forge a Republic that enhanced the role of civic virtue and compromise. James Madison and the other drafters, realizing they could not banish or outlaw factions, chose instead to institutionalize them and make the system work productively through a balance of power while protecting minorities from the tyranny of the majority. They divided the government into three branches that would be subject to checks and balances against each other: a president, an independent judiciary, and a Congress with two chambers (a House of Representatives elected by the people by district and a Senate, originally appointed by state legislatures).

Quickly, however, a historic division opened up between Alexander Hamilton and Thomas Jefferson over issues of a strong central government versus the rights of states and of peoples, a disagreement that reverberates today. Hamilton, on one side, never disguised his patrician impulses and admiration of the British system of government, and Jefferson never disguised his disdain for aristocracy and his devotion to the farmers and shopkeepers of the working classes. Their divergent views derived from differing definitions of civic virtue. For Hamilton, virtue could flow from and contribute to entrepreneurship. He thus favored development of a strong business and manufacturing sector, not simply to accumulate wealth but also to instill discipline and work. For Jefferson, virtue sprang not from industry but from the yeoman farmer and the soil. Toiling in dark workshops to produce consumer goods made people subservient, dependent, and inclined to moral corruption, urban vices, luxuries, and even mob rule, Jefferson believed. "Those who labor in the earth are the chosen people of God," he proclaimed. "While we have land to labor then, let us never wish to see our citizens occupied at a workbench, or twirling a distaff. . . . For the general operations of manufacture, let our workshops remain in Europe."[5]

Rapid economic change in the young Republic's earliest decades, driven by westward expansion and the proliferation of railroads, canals, and roads, challenged the Founders' fixed ideas. New technologies and discoveries such as the telegraph and advances in chemistry, medicine, and machinery hastened the onset of an industrial revolution, just as Hamilton had hoped and envisioned. Contributing to that success was what became known as the "American system of manufactures," incorporating interchangeable and standardized parts, first in armaments and then in other goods. Meanwhile, foreign investment and expanding markets at home and abroad enriched new sectors of the population, while an expanding labor force of immigrants, African Americans (enslaved in the South, free in the North), and women added to the urbanized workforce in what had been an agrarian nation at its birth. These changes also stirred concerns about the preservation of American values, encouraging political and intellectual ferment with the emergence of political parties, religious revivals, and even new religions themselves. These developments were accompanied by utopian experiments, expanding educational opportunities, and reform movements to establish women's rights, abolish slavery, outlaw alcohol, and undertake many other minor crusades.

Many of these threads came together, however, with a common purpose that could be found in the writings and speeches of American leaders. That purpose was to ensure that citizens of the newly independent states had the ability to engage in self-government. By the middle of the 19th century, the proliferation of reform movements reflected what one historian has described as "a diffuse yet deeply felt commitment to improve the character of ordinary Americans, to make them more upstanding, God-fearing, and literate."[6] One might say, more virtuous.

The Hamiltonian approach to organizing the economy had clearly won the economic if not the moral debate. But the idea of what the literary historian R. W. B. Lewis called a virtuous, enterprising, and perhaps innocent "American Adam" persisted in the culture.[7] It was fostered as well by the powerful individualism at the heart of the Transcendental movement of Ralph Waldo Emerson and his followers such as Walt Whitman. Business and capitalism transformed the nature of civic virtue, from the yeoman farmer to the enterprising businessman laboring in factories and offices as well as on farms. The "American System" of Henry Clay, Hamilton's heir and a renowned early 19th-century statesman and senator, rested on government, however. Government was mobilized to foster a three-part economic system consisting of high tariff walls to protect domestic industry; a strong central bank that would backstop the financial system; and federal subsidies for "internal improvements," including infrastructure such as canals, roads, and railways, all geared to increasing production and the transit of goods, especially exports.

These programs were designed in many ways for the United States to take advantage of an increasingly globalized economy in which American factories and mills were in competition with others in Europe. The Whig Party, led by Clay, believed their output needed to be protected from foreign competition. Representing business, banking, and fledgling industry interests, the Whigs evolved in 1854 into the Republican Party, which became the country's dominant political force from the Civil War through the end of the 19th century.

But however idealistic these underpinnings were, growing industrialization did breed problems as crowded, grimy, and unsanitary factories, often filled with child labor, spread and began forming the base of the American economy, soon to employ the first waves of immigrants—another sign of globalization—from Ireland and Germany. Andrew Jackson, hero of the War of 1812, was the first president of the Democratic Party in the first American decades of the early 19th century. In contrast with the Whigs, the Democrats embraced the agrarian virtues they inherited from Jefferson, as well as distrust of finance and industry and the doctrines of laissez-faire, lower tariffs, less public spending, and opposition to the establishment of a central bank.

The toxic, emotional, and violent issue of slavery was one aspect of early American thinking about work and virtue. The Whigs held that free labor in a free market system bred the upstanding moral code required for citizenship. Democrats, representing slave states, defended slavery and derided factory workers as "wage slaves." Nonetheless, the Whig point of view was fed by a powerful truth elevated into a powerful mythology: that the artisans, craftsmen, and mechanics who were the backbone of manufacturing in the early part of the century were independent entrepreneurs who had acquired the skills and capital to form their own businesses and prosper, embodying capitalist virtues that contributed in turn to the good of society at large. Just as Adam Smith had described slavery as economically unviable and inefficient, so the Whigs argued that slavery ran counter to the philosophy of work being good for the soul and good for the country as well.

That uplifting view of work was expounded many times by Abraham Lincoln, a Whig who helped establish the Republican Party in 1854. Lincoln spoke often of the virtuous conduct of "free labor" at the core of his opposition to slavery. He argued that slavery was evil not only because it was immoral but also because it denied the black man the rewards of the virtues of self-discipline and industriousness enjoyed by the white man.[8] In 1859 Lincoln told the Wisconsin State Agricultural Society that under free labor, as opposed to slavery, a man can "better his condition" because "there is no such thing as a freeman being fatally fixed for life, in the condition of a hired laborer."[9]

While running for president in 1860, Lincoln described his own life experience and related it to slavery. "I am not ashamed to confess, that twenty-five years ago I was a hired laborer, mauling rails, at work on a flat-boat—just what might happen to any poor man's son," he declared, explaining that white and black men should be able to take advantage of the opportunity to lift themselves up by means of hard work.[10] As a smart politician, he was also making the point that his own hard work justified his rise from humble beginnings to become a successful corporate lawyer, representing railroads and other wealthy interests—he was no longer the rail splitter and flat-boat operator of his storied youth. Lincoln was one of the first American politicians to make his political biography part of his campaign for higher office. He and his ethos are still echoed, especially in what political leaders say today about the importance of hard work, small business, and enterprise as the source not only of prosperity in American life but, even more important, of worthy values in American culture.

Later in the 19th century, as Americans increasingly saw themselves as employees in a behemoth-like capitalist system, many of these values eroded and gave way to organizations that sought to balance the rights of workers against those of entrepreneurs. But the idea of the overriding goal of civic virtue was never very far from such activities. In its earliest decades, the labor movement involved itself in a "quest for moral and civic improvement" in the form of education, lectures, sports, journals, and other forms of uplift, as Michael Sandel has noted. Labor also promoted decent wages and an eight-hour workday on the grounds that their adoption "would improve the moral and civic character of workers."[11] The demand for worker advancement coincided with rising middle-class consciousness, which was alarmed by the astonishing wealth of the Gilded Age residing in the mansions of the big cities of the north.

The Progressive Era, with its emphasis on consumer and product safety, antitrust actions, lower tariffs, and labor rights, was also built on the idea of fostering a virtuous citizenry. An important Progressive Era writer, Herbert David Croly, a founder of the *New Republic* magazine, argued in *The Promise of American Life* (1909) that the objective of democratic reforms was to enlarge the civic spirit of Americans and broaden their sympathies. "The principle of democracy is virtue," he said, quoting the philosophers George Santayana and Montesquieu.[12] Theodore Roosevelt, the first Progressive Era president, was a tireless champion of civic virtue, self-reliance, sacrifice, bravery, and hard work even as he railed against wealthy business combines. "Americanism means the virtues of courage, honor, justice, truth, sincerity, and hardihood— the virtues that made America," he declared in 1917, five years after leaving the White House. "The things that will destroy America are prosperity-at-any-price, peace-at-any-price, safety-first instead of duty-first, the love of soft living and the get-rich-quick theory of life."[13]

It took some time for the idea to develop in the United States that government itself could destroy virtue.

From Virtue to Charity: The Deserving and Undeserving Poor

The issue of welfare is the issue of dependency....That is not to say that dependent people are not brave, resourceful, and admirable, but simply that their situation is never enviable, and rarely admired. It is an incomplete state of life: normal in a child, abnormal in an adult.

—Daniel Patrick Moynihan (1973)

In US history, the cult of free enterprise and individual virtue has been juxtaposed against a latent and sometimes explicit concern that charity for the needy, and government assistance more specifically, is suspect and a threat to the habits of virtue. While the Industrial Revolution was producing slums and unemployment in the 19th century, civic organizations were launching social programs that helped the poor or unemployed. Others in society, however, were expressing the view that relief was potentially dangerous to self-reliance. This tradition was perhaps as old as the idea of charity itself. Here the rival to "moral desert" was "moral hazard"—the developing notion that assisting those in need would encourage the bad behavior that might have led to the neediness in the first place.

As earlier noted, in scripture and practice, charity—often carried out by the church—has until the modern era been seen as something closer to mercy, a tempering of justice, than as a tenet of social justice itself. The purpose of the first Poor Law in the era of Queen Elizabeth in 1601 was not so much to help those who should help themselves, but to protect the poor from forces beyond their control such as war, disease, and famine. Indeed, it included penalties for able-bodied people trying to avoid work. The objective of the Poor Law was not simply humanitarian; it was also intended to minimize political discontent at a time when peasant uprisings were not uncommon (one of these uprisings was chronicled by Shakespeare in his history plays, beginning with the downfall in 1381 of the hapless Richard II, caused in part by the Black Death, the high taxes imposed to pay for the Hundred Years' War, and, of course, the scheming of Henry of Bolingbroke, later Henry IV).[14]

English statutes after the Poor Law continued in the church tradition of distinguishing between the "deserving" and the "undeserving" poor.[15] In the 18th century, a number of influential writers also voiced the belief that poverty was an inevitable and even necessary aspect of existence. Reverand Thomas Malthus, the originator of the theory that humankind was doomed to living on a precipice because of population growth and the limited supply of food, believed that poverty served as an incentive for people to accept low wages in return for job security. "To make the society happy, and people easy under the meanest circumstances, it is requisite that great numbers of them should be Ignorant as well as Poor," declared Bernard Mandeville, the mordant social commentator of the 18th century, underscoring perhaps ironically the Malthusian doctrine.[16] David Ricardo, pioneer of the theories of comparative advantage, argued in 1821 that Poor Laws encouraged laziness, discouraged saving, and created incentives for people to have children for whom they could not care. "Instead of making the poor rich, they are calculated to make the rich poor," he said. Helping the poor merely encouraged them to enter into "early and improvident marriages," whereas they should instead be taught "the value of independence" and to "look not to systematic or casual charity, but to their own exertions for support."[17]

In the United States in the 19th century, the great economic downturns brought appeals for government assistance, but these were rebuffed as dangerous paternalism. In the face of massive unemployment and requests for relief by hard-hit workers and farmers in the Panic of 1893, President Grover Cleveland warned that aid for the needy "undermines the self-reliance of our people and substitutes in its place dependence upon Government favoritism."[18] Such attitudes persisted even when programs to help the poor were introduced. President Franklin Roosevelt sought to strike a moral and political balance by insisting that government relief programs must not become a permanent substitute for work. "To dole out relief in this way is to administer a narcotic, a subtle destroyer of the human spirit," Roosevelt declared in 1935. "It is inimical to the dictates of sound policy. It is in violation of the traditions of America. Work must be found for able-bodied but destitute workers."[19]

Perhaps the best-known scholarly work on the dangers of dependence was advanced by Daniel Patrick Moynihan, whose report on welfare in the Johnson administration held that welfare dependency among poor people contributed to the breakup of poor families. He noted that welfare was cut off if the father stayed with the family and had a job, creating a perverse incentive for fathers not to work or to abandon their families. What became known as the Moynihan Report in 1965 was a milestone in a growing new consensus, even among liberals, that government programs could hurt, not help, supposed beneficiaries. "The steady expansion of this welfare program, as of public assistance programs in general, can be taken as a measure of the steady disintegration of the Negro family structure over the past generation in the United States," the Moynihan Report concluded.[20] Subsequently, Moynihan criticized antipoverty programs of the Great Society as boondoggles that did little to supplement the incomes of poor working families. In the Nixon administration starting in 1969, Moynihan helped to develop the ill-fated Family Assistance Plan, which again was designed to maintain incentives for the poor to work. It was based in part on a conservative idea—the "negative income tax" proposed by the economist Milton Friedman—and endorsed by liberals such as James Tobin, the Keynesian economist who served on President John F. Kennedy's Council of Economic Advisers.

The Family Assistance Plan died in Congress, opposed by conservatives who disapproved of what they saw as an expanded government giveaway and by liberals who said the funding was inadequate. But its concept survived. The negative income tax has actually become a central part of US income tax policy toward the working poor, but with a different name. Starting in 1975, Congress enacted increasingly expansive versions of the so-called earned income tax credit (EITC) in which the working poor receive a cash rebate designed to supplement their incomes without punishing them for continuing to work. (The "rebate" is supposedly a return on the taxes that low-income earners pay for Social Security and Medicare.) Many conservatives still oppose the EITC as a government giveaway, but it has been a feature of tax cuts enacted in the 1980s, 1990s, and 2000s under different presidents.

Moynihan died in 2003 after a career of persistent criticism of dependence, including in the US foreign aid program. He claimed that the program produced more resentment than gratitude among aid recipients such as India, where he served as ambassador from 1973 to 1975. He lamented, "The more we do for them, the more they will hate us."[21] Neoconservative writers have expanded the argument. In *Losing Ground: American Social Policy 1950–1980* (1984), Charles Murray argued that inducing dependency among the lower classes was actually the intention of the elite white upper classes that created the welfare programs of the 1930s. Gradually, this view became widely accepted and was a factor in President Bill Clinton and a Republican Congress ending the New Deal–era welfare program Aid to Families with Dependent Children in 1996. "Today, we are ending welfare as we know it," Clinton declared. "But I hope this day will be remembered not for what it ended, but for what it began."[22] Murray, however, continued to bemoan the establishment's failure to inculcate struggling blacks and whites with the moral values of hard work and discipline.[23]

The debate over dependency played a major role in the 2012 presidential campaign. The Republican candidate, former Massachusetts governor Mitt Romney, was secretly videotaped complaining about the 47 percent of Americans "who believe that they are victims, who believe the government has a responsibility to care for them, who believe that they are entitled to health care, to food, to housing, to you name it." He added that "these are people who pay no income tax" and "I'll never convince them they should take personal responsibility and care for their lives."[24] In his statement of facts if not his moral reasoning, Romney was not wrong. He was evidently drawing on a study by the Urban Institute and Brookings Tax Policy Center that estimated that 46.4 percent of households pay no federal income tax.[25] Their status was ironically a gift of the earned income tax credit, and what he failed to point out was that this program was actually in many cases sponsored or endorsed by Republicans over the years, in part in return for Democratic support for tax cuts for high-end earners.

The characterization that some people believe themselves to be "entitled" to housing, food, health care, and so forth was analyzed in less incendiary fashion in 2012 by Nicholas Eberstadt of the American Enterprise Institute in his book *A Nation of Takers: America's Entitlement Epidemic.*[26] He includes in the "taker" category the beneficiaries of not simply the major programs such as Social Security, Medicare, and Medicaid but also other income transfer programs, including child nutrition and health care delivery, unemployment insurance, and food stamps. The Congressional Budget Office cites these very programs in demonstrating that the actual incomes of the poorest Americans have been lifted by 50 percent since the 1970s, as discussed earlier in the context of Thomas Piketty's analysis of inequality (see chapter 4).

Going further, in a 2014 essay written on the occasion of the 50th anniversary of the Great Society, Eberstadt gave perhaps surprising credit to the War on Poverty of the Johnson presidency for dramatically raising the standard of living of poor people. The Great Society legacy, he said, did not reduce the percentage of poor people in the United States, but it "all but eliminated the sort of material deprivation that tens of millions of Americans in the early 1960s still suffered." He cited that change as a major achievement. But he also asserted that the cost was the creation of a welfare state breeding dependency and discouraging work.[27] "What is monumentally new about the American society today is the vast and colossal empire of entitlement payments that it protects, manages and finances," Eberstadt declares in A Nation of Takers.[28] Indeed, he points out that the Commerce Department has found that income transfers are being delivered through more than 50 separate programs, accounting for 18 percent of personal income in the United States. Moreover, from 1960 to 2010 US government transfers grew by a multiple of nearly 100. Their future growth, particularly in retirement and health care programs for the elderly, is widely viewed today as threatening to overwhelm the federal budget in the coming decades.

Although mobilized by the Romney campaign to make a partisan point, Eberstadt's argument is based at least in part on inarguable facts. The Congressional Budget Office reported in 2013, for example, that in a survey of federal spending in 2006 (the most recent year for which data were available in 2013), more than half of federal spending (outside interest payments) was on individual benefits and health care, most of which went to the elderly through Social Security and Medicare.[29] Ezra Klein, in a 2011 column for the Washington Post, noted that two of every five US government dollars go to Social Security, Medicare, or Medicaid, while a little bit more than one dollar goes to the military. "Calvin Coolidge once said that the business of America is business," observed Klein. "Well, the business of the American government is insurance. Literally. If you look at how the federal government spends our money, it's an insurance conglomerate protected by a large, standing army."[30]

But in ethical terms, the point of Eberstadt's argument is that these programs have led to atrophy of civic virtue: the "proud self-reliance" of Americans has become a collective "declaration of dependence."[31] Fraud in entitlement programs, he contends, has become a way of life for millions on such programs—as if fraud were unknown in business or other walks of life.[32] In the heated 2012 presidential campaign, conservatives took aim at a much-discussed television advertisement for President Obama that portrayed an imaginary American named "Julia." Julia was grateful for government help with her children's schooling, child care, student loans, health care, and retirement. Hailed by Democrats as an example of putting government on the side of the average American, the ad was deplored by Republicans as touting a kind of bribery for voters. "The voters, many of them feel that the economic system is stacked against them, and they want stuff," said the Fox News television commentator Bill O'Reilly. "People feel that they are entitled to things, and which candidate, between the two, is going to give them things?"[33] A Republican Senate candidate noted that while the federal government distributes free meals and food stamps to millions of people, the National Park Service asks visitors not to feed the animals in parks lest they grow dependent on handouts.[34]

Ironically, and impressively, Eberstadt's thesis was challenged in a persuasive rejoinder by the political scientist William Galston, which Eberstadt included in his own book. Far from coddling the poor, Galston said, the federal government actually provides more "entitlement" benefits to the privileged classes. For example, wealthy homeowners benefit from the mortgage tax deduction, and upper-income families get tax breaks for certain health care spending through employer-based programs. Moreover, he argued, entitlement programs for the middle class have grown, unlike those for the poor and near-poor, without any noticeable loss of *their* middle-class work and family ethics.[35] A related question is, as a society ages and as its elderly require more health care, does it not make sense for this responsibility to be borne by government rather than individual families? "When Moynihan worried about dependence, he was not thinking about individuals who have worked hard all their lives in low-wage jobs but whose payroll taxes do not suffice to fund what society regards as a dignified retirement," Galston noted.[36] He went on to point out that Eberstadt provides no convincing evidence that the growth of the federal government had sapped Americans' moral fiber.[37] In an odd way, Galston's rebuttal of Eberstadt is an implicit rebuttal of the argument made by Piketty that people who live off their own retirement savings are part of the "rent-seeking" class.

The economist Bradford DeLong, a former Treasury official in the Clinton administration, has written in the same vein, justifying the help that middle-class Americans receive at the end of their working lives. "The recipients of these social-insurance benefits do not think of themselves as moochers," he notes. "They paid into these systems. They believe that they earned those benefits—and in large part they did." Blaming them as undeserving, he says, reeks of "the pre-Enlightenment or non-Enlightenment river of thought that the late Albert Hirschman [1915–2012] called 'the rhetoric of reaction'—the idea that those who have should hold on to what they have, because any shift in the distribution of wealth away from present inequality will turn out to be destructive."[38]

Not surprisingly, the debate over dependence is highly political. For example, in a 2014 Pew Research Center poll 86 percent of conservatives said that government aid to the poor does them more harm than good. Indeed, three-quarters of conservative Americans agree that "poor people have it easy because they can get government benefits without doing anything." Only 7 percent of this group said that the poor "have hard lives."[39] Earlier, Romney's running mate in 2012, House Speaker Paul Ryan, while serving as chairman of the House Budget Committee, had proposed cutbacks in spending on Medicaid, Medicare, and other programs and warned that the social safety net "lulls able-bodied people into lives of complacency and dependency, which drains them of their very will and incentive to make the most of their lives. It's demeaning."[40]

Ryan's moralism ran into a different kind of rebuttal, however, from the Catholic Church, whose leaders in the United States rebuked him on this issue, despite their agreement with the Republican leadership on abortion and contraceptives. The United States Conference of Catholic Bishops expressed concern about "the moral and human dimensions" of Republican spending cuts, saying they hurt "the least of these" (quoting Matthew 25) and were contrary to various papal encyclicals.[41] In 2012 several dozen Catholic scholars at Georgetown University, a Jesuit institution, charged that Ryan was more driven by the teachings of Ayn Rand and her libertarian philosophy than by the Gospels.[42] Ryan was sufficiently stung by the criticism to accept an invitation to speak at Georgetown, where he contended that a "preferential option for the poor" does not mean that the poor become "dependent on the government so they stay stuck at their station in life."[43] As for Ayn Rand, Ryan said he admired her libertarianism but had long since rejected her philosophy of objectivism as "atheist."[44] He also said he believed Medicaid and other programs would be more efficient if they were consolidated into block grants to state governments. Georgetown faculty members, countering with the argument that block grants are more vulnerable to budget cuts, were not convinced.[45]

In a striking reversal two years after running for vice president, Ryan declared he had been wrong to talk about "makers" and "takers" in such a simplistic way. "The phrase gave insult where none was intended," he said, noting that his own family had benefited from some government programs such as the GI Bill. "People struggling and striving to get ahead—that's what our country is all about. On that journey, they're not 'takers'; they're trying to make something of themselves. We shouldn't disparage that. Of course, the phrase wasn't just insensitive; it was also ineffective." But he still embraced his goal of cutting back Medicare and other programs, consolidating them into block grants for states, and generally reducing the role of the federal government in health care and social welfare.[46]

If, in the view of conservatives, government programs punish virtuous behavior, what about the taxes imposed to pay for them?

Taxes are a special focus of the moral debate in the United States, perhaps more than in any other country in the developed world. The poet laureate of the antitax movement was the former Hollywood actor and television host Ronald Reagan. Reagan achieved success as a politician by eloquently assuring Americans that they were heroes if they earned their money—and that it was patriotic for them to want to keep it. In his inaugural address in 1981, Reagan declared that the tax system stifles hard work and civic virtue and "penalizes successful achievement and keeps us from maintaining full productivity."[47]

Reagan's tax cut theory was grounded in the so-called supply-side theories of conservative economists such as Arthur Laffer in the 1970s. But Reagan always insisted that his view that taxes discourage work was not rooted in theory. Rather, he said it was derived from his experience as an actor on contract with Warner Brothers after World War II, when his tax bracket was 94 percent. "The IRS took such a big chunk of my earnings that after a while I began asking myself whether it was worth it to keep on taking work," Reagan wrote in his memoirs. "Something was wrong with a system like that: When you have to give up such a large percentage of your income in taxes, incentive to work goes down. You don't say, 'I've got to do more pictures,' you say, 'I'm not gonna work for six cents on the dollar.' If I decided to do one less picture, that meant other people at the studio in lower tax brackets wouldn't work as much either; the effect filtered down, and there were fewer total jobs available. . . . The same principle that affected my thinking applied to people in all tax brackets: The more government takes in taxes, the less incentive people have to work."[48]

Leaving aside Reagan's contention that if he did not work on a picture, the studio could not find someone else, his assertion that lower taxes increase the incentive to work, in the process spurring economic growth, is not easy to prove or disprove. On the one hand, economic expansion in the United States was at a peak in the 1950s, when tax rates were at historic highs. On the other hand, the tax cuts signed into law by Presidents John F. Kennedy and Reagan were indeed followed by additional growth. Yet the tax *increases* signed into law by Presidents George H. W. Bush, Bill Clinton, and Barack Obama were also followed by economic expansion.[†] Independent studies come to no firm conclusion about whether tax cuts encourage work and growth. But the nonpartisan Congressional Research Service reported in 2012 that, for upper-income taxpayers at least, cutting taxes has had "little association with saving, investment, or productivity growth."[49] (The report was revised somewhat after Republicans attacked it, but its basic conclusion remained unchanged.)

Most economists agree that there is indeed a threshold at which taxes become confiscatory, an incentive to cheat, and a disincentive to work. David Lipton, the first deputy managing director of the International Monetary Fund, has acknowledged in the Fund's study of inequality and fiscal policy that if taxes are too high "taxpayers will find ways to avoid or evade the tax and a higher rate may no longer raise extra revenue."[50] In arguing for an 80 percent marginal tax rate, Piketty maintains in his book that his own studies show that a rate that high does not have a negative effect of the sort described by Lipton. According to a survey by the *Washington Post*, Democratic-leaning econ-

---

† Some critics charged that it would have been moral for President George W. Bush to have asked for tax *increases*, not cuts, while sending Americans to war in Iraq and Afghanistan. President Kennedy, who had memorably asked Americans to "ask not what your country can do for you—ask what you can do for your country," reputedly had some difficulty in proposing tax cuts because of fear that such a proposal would undercut his appeal for sacrifice in the battle against communism (Ezra Klein, "Larry Summers: 'I Think Keynes Mistitled His Book,'" *Washington Post*, July 26, 2011).

omists tend to say a rate that discourages work is closer to 60 percent, whereas Republican-leaning economists tend to say that the rate is about where it has been recently—in the mid- or upper 30s.[51]

Most of the arguments reviewed in this chapter relate to the reward for hard work, industriousness, and other positive values, and the concern that government programs and tax policies could discourage such virtuous behavior. But what if people engage in reckless conduct and get themselves into real trouble because of high indebtedness? And what if such conduct is carried out not simply by homeowners and mortgage holders but also by major financial institutions that are "too big to fail" and by governments that by definition cannot fail but can be subject to political backlash? That is the subject of the next chapter.

7

Bubbles, Panics, Crashes, and Bailouts:

Moral Hazard in the Marketplace

The ultimate result of shielding man from the effects of folly is to people the world with fools.
—Herbert Spencer, English philosopher (1891)

I'm not a believer in the Old Testament theory of business cycles. I think that if we can help people, we need to help people.
—Ben S. Bernanke, chairman, Federal Reserve (2011)

Everything looked great for Mexico's economy in the early 1990s, until it didn't. In January 1995, a little more than a year after the historic trade agreement that Mexico had signed with the United States and Canada, President Bill Clinton held a small ceremony in the Oval Office for the swearing-in of Robert Rubin as the 70th US secretary of the Treasury. But Rubin, a former cochairman of Goldman Sachs, had little time to savor the moment. Immediately after the ceremony, Rubin and his aides rushed to an emergency meeting with Clinton on a spreading financial crisis in Mexico. They tried to avoid words such as *panic* and *meltdown* when briefing the president, but the situation was urgent. Mexico, after years of current account deficits and borrowing, much of it short term, faced an imminent inability to meet payments on debts coming due. Rubin explained that letting Mexico default would cause the peso to collapse, followed by inflation and a recession, with grave consequences for the United States and indeed the world economy. Even worse, the economic reform efforts under way in other developing countries in Latin America might be reversed, unleashing a flood of unwanted immigrants into the United States.

Because the availability of resources from the International Monetary Fund (IMF) was limited by the size of Mexico's quota, the United States was the only possible additional rescuer. But Rubin and his top international deputy, Lawrence Summers, who later became Rubin's successor as Treasury secretary, told Clinton that although action was necessary, there were legitimate arguments against it. Not only might the rescue not work, it also would be "massively unpopular" and viewed as bailing out "wealthy American and European investors who had speculated on developing markets."[1] Congress, which had just turned Republican in a calamitous mid-term defeat of Clinton and the Democrats, would almost certainly be reluctant to approve a loan guarantee program for Mexico, and investors might continue their reckless and irresponsible behavior in the expectation of future bailouts.[2]

As Rubin feared, the proposed Mexican rescue package was reviled—even by the Clinton administration's allies. Liberals saw the Mexico bailout as a rescue of Wall Street, and critics of the North American Free Trade Agreement (NAFTA), which had lowered tariffs in the United States, Canada, and Mexico the year before and had drawn fire for ostensibly wiping out US jobs, felt vindicated in their criticism. Rubin and others wanted to warn these critics of the dire consequences of failure to act, but they feared that if they did, the markets would panic and make matters worse. After the initial plan failed to attract sufficient support in Congress, Clinton, in desperation, found an alternative to a congressional vote; he arranged for a loan (technically a swap arrangement) from the Exchange Stabilization Fund (ESF), which was used for currency interventions. Many in Congress were relieved that the administration had averted a worse crisis without making them complicit. Still, Congress passed legislation making it harder to tap the stabilization fund in the immediate future.

The Mexico crisis was a foretaste of what Rubin and others began to call a new era of peril arising from globalization. The United States was only then beginning to come to grips with an economically interdependent world, he noted, adding, "In 1995, the notion that a poor country's macroeconomic miscalculations could affect the largest economy in the world simply didn't register with a lot of people. A few years later, when the Asian crisis took hold, it still didn't."[3]

The Mexican episode illustrates the point discussed in this chapter—how the tough decisions in the modern global economy are influenced by public policymakers' concerns that virtuous behavior be preserved as the underpinning of international capitalism. But the chapter also discusses how virtue has been tested by the existence of modern asset bubbles, crashes, and debt crises—and the origins of the sentiment that debt itself is dishonorable.

"By Every Possible Means" versus "Purging the Rottenness Out of the System"

> *We did save the economy, but we lost the country doing it.*
> —Timothy F. Geithner, former Treasury secretary (2014)

The Mexican peso crisis has been only one of many such episodes in the modern history of globalized capitalism. Even prosperous countries in Europe such as Sweden, Finland, and Iceland have succumbed (see figure 7.1). Indeed, the world economy has faced such eruptions over nearly four centuries. One of the first ever recorded occurred in the 1630s in the Netherlands, when the price of tulip bulbs soared to many times an average worker's salary, hurting large numbers of investors when the price collapsed. It has never been easy for

Figure 7.1 Financial crises create lasting pain: Increase in unemployment rate following precrisis peak, selected countries

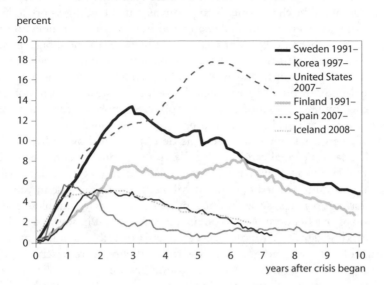

percent

Legend:
— Sweden 1991–
— Korea 1997–
— United States 2007–
— Finland 1991–
---- Spain 2007–
······ Iceland 2008–

years after crisis began

Source: Organization for Economic Cooperation and Development, Main Economic Indicators (database).

policymakers to devise ways of telling when a bubble poses a systemic danger and to determine what exactly must be done when that happens. Nor is it easy to assign blame when an asset bubble turns into a disaster, pitting the rescuer and the rescued against each other in an outbreak of recrimination.

Asset bubbles are invariably propelled by debt, as stakeholders borrow—often short term because it is cheaper—to finance their investments in something that looks like it will keep rising in value. The investment could be a commodity, part of the housing stock, or another country's debt. When the value of the investment peaks and starts to decline or even collapse—that is, when the music stops, in the memorable words of Charles Prince, a former CEO of Citigroup—panic selling sets in, wiping out the investor and rendering him or her unable to service the debts used to get rich. But it is warnings about the moral consequences of debt that give debt crises, even more than the issue of government assistance to the needy, an extraordinary ethical dimension. That dimension has sharpened during the crises that have erupted as globalization has speeded up over the last 25 years.

Financial crises were, of course, associated with fundamental values relating to virtuous conduct long before the last quarter-century. The economist Hyman Minsky argued in the 1960s and 1970s that "speculative euphoria" develops almost inevitably in modern industrial societies and that the "swings between robustness and fragility" are "an integral part of the process that generates business cycles."[4]

In his classic study *Manias, Panics, and Crashes: A History of Financial Crises* first published in 1978, the economic historian Charles Kindleberger defined the dilemma in exactly the way that the Clinton administration was to experience it. On one side, the instinct is to pump as much lending as possible into the economy to keep it from collapsing and hurting huge numbers of innocents. On the other side, concern arises about how not to encourage or enable bad behavior in the future, the definition of moral hazard in the context of debt relief. "Whether or not there should be a lender of last resort is a matter of some debate," Kindleberger wrote. "Those who oppose the function argue that it encourages speculation in the first place. Supporters worry more about the current crisis than about forestalling some future one."[5]

Kindleberger's study offers a classic description of how individual decisions that seem rational can lead to collective irrationality and a breakdown of acceptable norms. It may make sense to invest in or buy an asset that is increasing in value in the hope that it will continue to increase in value. But such behavior on a mass scale produces overvalued assets, or bubbles—the phenomenon of an asset becoming so inflated in value that it is destined to deflate. But a striking aspect of Kindleberger's analysis of bubbles is his invocation of terms of immoral and greedy excess from the literature describing them: "manias . . . insane land speculation . . . blind passion . . . financial orgies . . . frenzies . . . feverish speculation . . . epidemic desire to become rich quick . . . wishful thinking . . . intoxicated investors."[6] Adam Smith, in referring to the famous South Sea bubble of 1720 caused by the bust that resulted from the ill-fated investments of the South Sea Company in South America, spoke of the "folly, negligence and profusion" and "the knavery and extravagance of their stock-jobbing operations."[7] The South Sea bubble is sometimes called the first international financial crisis because the speculation had caught up investors in England, France, the Netherlands, Italy, and Germany. Another investor who improbably lost money in the company was Isaac Newton. "I can calculate the motions of the heavenly bodies, but not the madness of people," the founder of modern physics said.[8]

Of the many historical figures who have warned against sparing the perpetrators of reckless behavior from their own mistakes is the Social Darwinist Herbert Spencer, who coined the phrase "survival of the fittest" to justify letting the market sort out winners and losers without government interference. "The ultimate result of shielding man from the effects of folly is to people the world with fools," Spencer said.[9] The contrary course of action is to use whatever resources are available to rescue indebted financial institutions, individuals, and others from the consequences of their folly because failure to do so takes a huge toll on the innocent.

An elucidation of these issues helps to explain the reaction and counterreaction of those involved in stabilizing a number of modern economic calamities. On one side is the view enunciated by President Herbert Hoover's Treasury secretary, Andrew Mellon, a successful Pittsburgh financier before his appointment, whose advice to Hoover was to let the 1929 stock market crash wreak its havoc and run its course without government interference. "Mr. Mellon had only one formula: 'Liquidate labor, liquidate stocks, liquidate the farmers, liquidate real estate,'" wrote Hoover, adding that a purge of the system would make people "work harder" and "live a moral life."[10] On the other side of the argument is the defense of former Treasury secretary Timothy Geithner, who contends in his memoirs about his days in the Obama administration that, in effect, to have invoked moral hazard during the crisis of 2008–09 and let various vulnerable institutions fail would have produced a greater immorality—inflicting a new Great Depression on the entire world economy.

Many economists, historians, and commentators have agreed at different times on moral if not economic grounds with Treasury secretary Mellon's advice to Hoover. But most historians, including the conservative monetarists Milton Friedman and his coauthor Anna Schwartz, blame the Federal Reserve's stringent monetary policies in the face of panic for aggravating the Depression. Equally, many other critics say that the downturn was deepened because of the government's refusal to intervene to reverse the epidemic of bank failures that wiped out people's savings and sent the economy on a downward spiral. One such critic was a professor at Princeton, Ben Bernanke, whose academic career included a number of scholarly studies of how the Depression happened. (Bernanke has often said that, like historians specializing in the study of war, he was drawn to the study of the economic equivalent, the greatest nonwar disaster of the 20th century.) In 2013, in reviewing the century-long history of the Federal Reserve, Chairman Bernanke observed that "the so-called liquidationist view, that depressions perform a necessary cleansing function," was a "counterproductive doctrine."[11] Well before that comment, he referred to the Fed when he paid ironic tribute to Friedman on his 90th birthday in 2002, telling a dinner at the University of Chicago, "I would like to say to Milton and Anna: Regarding the Great Depression, you're right, we did it. We're very sorry. But thanks to you, we won't do it again."[12]

The classic defense of using the resources of government to rescue a banking system, heedless of the moral hazard consequences, was delivered by Walter Bagehot, essayist, journalist, and author in the late 19th century, who wrote in *Lombard Street: A Description of the Money Market* (1873) about crises facing the Bank of England. He describes the bank's response to the Panic of 1825, which occurred after the flush of victory in the Napoleonic Wars, when banks made a series of colossally bad investments in Latin America. Bagehot quotes the bank's governor as saying that it had no choice but to save the system by lending money "by every possible means and in modes we had never adopted before; we took in stock on security, we purchased Exchequer bills, we made advances on [those] bills, we not only discounted outright, but we made advances on the deposit of bills of exchange to an immense amount, in short, by every possible means consistent with the safety of the Bank."[13]

The very existence of a central bank's lending capacity as a backstop and the act of lending in a crisis automatically distort the incentives of the borrower and the lender, according to two specialists on crises, economists Nouriel

Roubini and Brad Setser. "Both creditors and debtors are susceptible to moral hazard," they wrote. "Creditor moral hazard is the risk of creditors' willingness to extend credit, which is influenced by the expectation that IMF (or G7) lending will assure payment. Debtor moral hazard is the risk of a debtor borrowing expecting either to default or to be able to borrow the funds needed to pay from an insurer and therefore failing to make the ongoing effort needed for payment."[14]

According to Roubini and Setser, moral hazard plays a role in the debate over how to respond to crises in two ways. First, there is the risk that a debtor will take out a loan that it has no intention of repaying. Second, there is the risk that a lender will make the loan not caring if it will be repaid, presumably because both the lender and debtor know that someone—the IMF in the case of countries—will step in. The IMF is in the background providing a kind of "insurance," much in the same way a person might theoretically be more careless about fire knowing that he has fire insurance. This "insurance" presumably encourages bad behavior, undermining the incentives toward virtue in capitalism itself.

But Roubini and Setser find that any assertion that the IMF is ipso facto a source of moral hazard is unfair—a bad rap. First, they note that IMF loans do have to be repaid. Second, the IMF usually imposes tough conditions on its loans that no country would willingly accept unless desperate.[15] Without international support, they point out, the costs of a financial collapse invariably hit ordinary citizens the hardest. Roubini and Setser offer many variations on the moral hazard theme, some surprising. For example, the existence of deposit insurance for depositors—an important innovation of the New Deal that prevented bank runs at the height of the crisis—can at least in theory encourage risky lending by bank owners because they know their depositors are protected. In addition, banks that are already insolvent but know their depositors are protected sometimes "have an incentive to 'gamble for redemption' by making risky loans." They might be hoping that if the loans pay off they win, and if the loans fail they do not lose much because the bank's capital is already gone.[16]

At the height of the 2007-09 financial crisis in the United States, both Bernanke and Treasury secretary Geithner evoked Hoover, disparaging the "liquidationist" view as an obsession with "Old Testament justice," whereas saving the system, and sparing the innocent, was the choice to be made. Geithner wrote in his memoir that this was particularly the case for what he called the five "financial bombs" threatening to blow up the economy in early 2009: the government housing agencies Fannie Mae and Freddie Mac, as well as AIG, Citigroup, and Bank of America, all of which had gotten into dire straits from investing in or insuring collateralized debt securities, or lending recklessly to homeowners unable to meet their mortgage obligations after the housing bubble burst in 2007. All received official backing or large infusions of government aid in 2008 to save them from failure, and all were in need of more aid to avoid a collapse at the start of the Obama term.[17]

"We needed to make sure they didn't explode," Geithner wrote of the five so-called bombs, "not to protect them from the consequences of their mistakes, but to prevent another messy failure from ravaging the rest of the economy." Like Rubin's warnings to Clinton over Mexico, Geithner's counsel to Obama (hardly necessary, of course) was that the politics would be abysmal. "People hated the idea of government bailouts for mismanaged financial behemoths," he acknowledged. "But if their creditors or the markets in general lost confidence that any of them could meet their obligations, we'd be looking at a worldwide financial meltdown, and a much deeper economic crisis."[18] Geithner acknowledged the moral hazard argument that "if you rescue pyromaniacs, you'll end up with more fires." But he rejected it, and he was equally against liquidating the creditors who lent these institutions money or even imposing costs on these creditors, known as "haircuts" in financial parlance, on the grounds that such costs would also panic the financial markets. "During a typical recession or even a limited crisis, firms should face the consequences of their mistakes, and so should the investors who lend them money," Geithner wrote. "But trying to mete out punishment to perpetrators during a genuinely systemic crisis—by letting major firms fail or forcing senior creditors to accept haircuts—can pour gasoline on the fire."[19]

From such logic came the notorious conclusion: the biggest US banks were "too big to fail." Indeed, of the 25 largest financial institutions in the United States at the start of 2008, 13 either failed (Lehman Brothers being the most dramatic case) or received government help to avoid failure (including Fannie Mae, Freddie Mac, AIG, Citigroup, and Bank of America) or, with government encouragement, merged to avoid failure (Countrywide, Bear Stearns, Merrill Lynch, and Wachovia) or transformed themselves (with government encouragement) into bank holding companies in order to take advantage of the federal lending lifeline (Morgan Stanley and Goldman Sachs).[20]

There is also a simple humanitarian argument supporting the need for government rescue programs, epitomized by President Franklin Roosevelt's stirring declaration in 1936, "Better the occasional faults of a Government that lives in a spirit of charity than the consistent omissions of a Government frozen in the ice of its own indifference."[21] Punishing ill-considered behavior, however satisfying morally, harms the innocent and guilty alike, this benevolent argument goes. In a famous example cited by, among others, Geithner and Chairman Bernanke of the Federal Reserve, one does not let a neighbor's house burn down, endangering an entire neighborhood, just because its occupant was smoking in bed.

Many Republicans, especially those allied with the Tea Party founded at the beginning of the Great Recession, were enraged over what they deplored as socialism and government paternalism. Indeed, the Tea Party itself was inspired specifically by the move to rescue homeowners, more even than banks. If there was one moment that produced and inspired the Tea Party more than any other, it was the February 2009 rant on CNBC by commentator Rick Santelli, speaking from the floor of the Chicago Board of Trade, as onlookers cheered and applauded his fiery denunciation of people being helped by government as "losers." ("The government is promoting bad behavior! This is America!") He was specifically referring to what he said was taxpayer-financed coddling of reckless citizens who borrowed too much money to buy houses or make home improvements they could not afford.[22]

But some of the toughest criticisms of Geithner's attitude toward "too big to fail" came from the Obama administration's own allies. Neil Barofsky, appointed in 2008 as the Treasury Department's special inspector general of the Troubled Asset Relief Program (TARP), the vehicle for providing capital to troubled banks, accused Geithner of excusing miscreants while "foaming the runway for the banks" as they headed for a potential crash.[23] Senator Elizabeth Warren, the sharply critical Democrat from Massachusetts and a former chair of the Congressional Oversight Panel for the government's rescue efforts, wrote in her own memoirs that "TARP sent truckloads of cash to the banks, but the banks gave virtually nothing in return—no haircuts for the creditors, no CEO firings, no promises to abandon risky trading. And that's when Too Big to Fail went on steroids—not just a bailout, but a pain-free bailout."[24] In meetings with Geithner during this period, she was shocked to find that in his view TARP was intended to help banks, not homeowners, and she was appalled that there were no "perp walks" or "mass indictments" of bankers.[25]

As Warren's comments suggest, especially galling to the critics of government intervention were the bonuses awarded to investment bankers whose miscalculations and speculations caused national misfortune. These bonuses were deeply offensive to taxpayers whose money was used to bail out the bankers in the most recent crisis, especially at AIG, which awarded the bonuses to the very unit that had speculated disastrously with derivatives. The furor over AIG's bonuses was an agonizing episode in the Obama administration, further undercutting support for its efforts to stabilize the system. But the administration concluded that it could not force the companies receiving government assistance to break compensation contracts with its employees, despite congressional demands for punishment of bank executives.

Meanwhile, the nation's leading bankers seemed to be thumbing their noses at the public, just as the nation's leading auto executives had done by taking private jets to Washington to plead for public funds.[26] It was infuriating and deemed immoral even to those who oversaw the bailouts. Henry Paulson, the Treasury secretary who implemented the first phase of the bailouts, said five years later that if the US government had restricted the bonuses as a price for the rescue, most banks would have refused to participate, and his priority at the time was to save the financial system with the widest possible program. "To say I was disappointed is an understatement," Paulson said of the lavish payouts to executives whose mistakes had led to the crisis. "My view has nothing to do with legality and everything to do with what was right, and everything to do with just a colossal lack of self-awareness as to how [the payouts] were viewed by the American public."[27]

Yet throughout the outrage, Geithner stuck to his policy of not wanting to punish creditors or executives in a fashion that he feared would deepen the panic in the markets at a time when the economy was heading toward the abyss. In his view, a "pain-free bailout" might have been morally repugnant, but a painful bailout would have defeated the purpose of the effort. In effect, Geithner was saying that invoking moral hazard during a crisis was . . . *immoral:* "Old Testament vengeance appeals to the populist fury of the moment, but the truly moral thing to do during a raging financial inferno is to put it out. The goal should be to protect the innocent, even if some of the arsonists escape their full measure of justice."[28]

Debt as a Morality Play: A Brief History

The moral logic of rescuing financial institutions could be a case study in utilitarianism. Associated with Jeremy Bentham and John Stuart Mill, this principle holds that one must act for the greatest good for the greatest number even if doing so imposes other costs or undermines other principles. This principle has some fairly obvious moral limits. For example, one would not enslave 10 percent of the population for the benefit of the other 90 percent.[29] When it comes to debt, history has shown that the issue is highly emotional. One reason seems to be that the metaphor of debt has been used since ancient times to apply to moral turpitude, and debt itself has played a role in many political upheavals. "For thousands of years, the struggle between rich and poor has largely taken the form of conflicts between creditors and debtors," wrote the anthropologist David Graeber. Stories from the ancient world are replete with accounts of popular insurrections motivated by demands that debts be canceled. Slavery has been a feature of history since ancient times, when slaves often became indentured because of their debts.[30]

Early Sanskrit hymns found in the Vedas, dating from the second millennium BCE, contain prayers pleading with the gods for liberation from commercial debts, although these debts were treated as synonymous with moral failings. According to some versions of the hymns, such debts can be repaid through virtuous behavior.[31] Warnings against debt can be found in various Greek and Roman writings as well. *Moralia,* a collection of essays by Plutarch, outlines codes of conduct such as the admonition that borrowing encourages sloth and erodes the character of lender and borrower alike.[32]

In Western scripture, the word for *debt* evolved in a meaningful way in ancient Mesopotamia. The earliest Hebrew writings of the Old Testament used a word for sin that employed the metaphor of a burden to be carried and relieved when forgiven. According to Leviticus, in the Jubilee year, coming every half-century, slaves and prisoners were to be freed and debts forgiven. But an important language change in this metaphor occurred after the Babylonian emperor Nebuchadnezzar conquered Judah and Jerusalem, destroying their temple and expelling the Jews in 587 and 586 BCE. Isaiah, Jeremiah, and other prophets who figure in Joshua, Judges, Samuel, and Kings—the so-called Deuteronomist books of the Bible because they expand on laws outlined in Deuteronomy— preached that the Jews were overrun first by the Assyrians and then by the

Babylonians as punishment by God for their sins, including worship of false gods. The people of Israel were described as having to work off these sins by hard toil in exile, effectively redeeming a debt incurred by wicked behavior.

After the Persian emperor Darius overran the Babylonians and permitted the Jews to return to their temple, Aramaic became the Persian empire's official language, and the Jews became bilingual (in Hebrew and Aramaic). It was then that the language of the Hebrew Bible adopted the Aramaic idiom of sin as debt in the sense of one person owing another in a commercial transaction. "One of the most striking developments in biblical religion comes in the wake of this shift in metaphors," wrote the biblical scholar Gary Anderson. "Once it becomes commonplace to think of sin as debt, the idea that virtuous activity generates a credit appears."[33] The book of Daniel, one of the later books of the Old Testament, contains a passage in which Daniel tells Nebuchadnezzar (the Babylonian conqueror) that he can redeem himself by giving alms to the poor. This teaching, Anderson says, stands "at the headwaters of one of the most important developments of early Judaism"—the idea that charity to the poor (*tsedaka* in Hebrew) enables one to alleviate one's sins, or debts, a concept that soon became part of early Christian teachings as well. In the Koran, the ban on usury is accompanied by a call for believers to give to charity (*sadaqa*). The Islamic obligation of alms via the state, also rooted in Koranic literature, is called *zakat*.[34] From such teachings come an ancient definition of virtue itself— the concept of *Imitatio Dei*—"imitate God" (in Hebrew *B'tselem Elohim*), referring to the divine ideal of showing generosity and compassion to one's fellow humans, just as God has graced humanity with mercy, especially the poorest and the most humble in society. Traditionally, this concept also invokes loyalty to one's family and community as well as to the neediest.

The two competing definitions of sin are reflected in the two versions of the Lord's Prayer contained in the Gospels. The version in Luke refers to the forgiveness of sins or trespasses. But the Gospel of Matthew's version is also well known and occasionally used in some denominations: "Forgive us our *debts* as we forgive our debtors." Moreover, in this Gospel Jesus tells the parable of the unmerciful servant, in which a king, checking the books on the accounts of one of his servants, orders the servant to repay a debt by selling himself, his wife, his children, and his property—that is, to become a "debt slave" or indentured servant. In the end, the king shows mercy and forgives the debt—until he finds out that the servant himself showed no mercy to another servant who owed *him* money, at which point the king orders his servant to be sent to jail until he can repay the original debt.[35]

The Gospels also pick up the theme of Daniel. "According to this teaching," wrote Anderson, "the money that one gives away was thought to be transferred to 'a bank account' in heaven. The hand of the poor man who begged for alms became a replacement for the altar, in that it provided an immediate conduit for goods from earth to heaven."[36] By the time of the Protestant Reformation, the importance of almsgiving as a means of forgiveness of sins had fallen by the wayside because Reformation writers believed that such charitable acts undercut the idea that salvation was due to grace alone. The Reformation raged over such debates—whether redemption, for example, is to be earned by good works or as "a gift graciously bestowed by God." The transcendent teaching of the Gospels is that this gracious gift is epitomized by Jesus' death on the cross, an act that redeems the debts, or sins, incurred by humankind, as an act of supreme sacrifice bestowed by God.[37]

Talmudic law, which became established in the first centuries of the Common Era, also addresses the issue of forgiving debts and the problem of moral hazard. Aaron Levine, professor of economics at Yeshiva University, has written in an unusual essay on the economic downturn of 2007–09 that rabbinic teachings place obligations on both borrowers and lenders. "Taking on debt obligations that an individual knows he will not, or even may not, meet violates Jewish law's 'good faith' imperative, which states that, if an individual makes a commitment, he must intend to fulfill it," Levine wrote.[38] Under Jewish law lenders must verify the borrower's income and resources in order to guarantee that the borrower can repay the loan. Avoiding that precaution, Levine says, is "illegal according to Jewish law because the borrower's 'good faith' imperative effectively imposes an underwriting standard on the lender."[39] In a comment with implications for mortgage lending and the responsibility that falls on the shoulders of lenders and borrowers alike, Levine explains that an "asset-based loan"—backed by the pledge to sell the asset the borrower is borrowing against—is unethical if the borrower knows that it might be difficult to sell the asset when necessary.[40]

In the Middle Ages, those who could not pay their debts were sent to debtors' prison, which was used extensively in Europe. Starting in the early 17th century, indentured servitude was a primary driver for migration to the British colonies. In Britain's colonies in North America and in Britain itself, debtors' prisons ensnared many a famous writer or public figure—among them, the novelist Daniel Defoe, the artist William Hogarth, the founder of the Quaker movement William Penn, and Robert Morris, a financier at the time of the American Revolution.[41] Charles Dickens's memories of his father's time in debtors' prison inspired works such as David Copperfield, in which Mr. Micawber was incarcerated through no fault of dishonesty. Such prisons were not abolished in Britain until the latter half of the 19th century, in part because of reform campaigns inspired by the searing descriptions of Dickens and the realization—now obvious—that punishing debtors by making it impossible for them to pay their debts was self-defeating. No one who has read Dickens's great work Little Dorrit can forget his vivid description of the hopelessness and corruption in notorious Marshalsea prison where his father served for a time during Dickens's youth. "Thirty years ago there stood, a few doors short of the church of Saint George, in the borough of Southwark, on the left-hand side of the way going southward, the Marshalsea Prison," Dickens wrote in that novel, which was published in 1855–57. "It had stood there many years before, and it remained there some years afterwards; but it is gone now, and the world is none the worse without it."[42]

In the United States, the debtors' prisons that were a feature during the colonial period and into the early years of the new nation were closed by the Bankruptcy Act of 1800, but only temporarily. Nonetheless, it was a "high-water mark for debtor relief in the eighteenth century," according to the historian Bruce Mann.[43] Objections to the law focused on its application to entrepreneurs but not ordinary citizens, and for this reason it was repealed in the era of Thomas Jefferson.

But in the 19th century something else changed. Society's view slowly evolved from viewing debt as a moral failure requiring punishment to viewing it as a normal reflection of the ups and downs of commerce that should be addressed in a practical rather than a moralistic way—that is, a problem to be solved by debtors and creditors in cooperation with each other. Promises to pay eventually became a kind of medium of exchange itself. Debt instruments could be traded, and debt became an integral part of commerce, requiring a practical approach. An important transition was under way. Debt went "from sin to risk," and insolvency was a condition that evolved "from moral failure to economic failures," Mann notes.[44] It was a harbinger of the way that debt would later be viewed in the international arena at a time of financial crises in Asia, Latin America, and Europe. For example, Argentina's most recent default in late 2001 involved negotiations with most creditors to accept less than full repayment of their debts and court battles with holdout creditors—including hedge funds that purchased the debt on the open market—demanding payment in full.

In 1898 bankruptcy became a permanent part of the US legal system. The notion of bankruptcy was destined to be overhauled from time to time, but it retained a stigma among many. "The fundamental dilemma of bankruptcy law has always been whether it is about death or rebirth," wrote Mann. "Is it a system for picking a debtor's bonds in a more orderly fashion? Or is it an economic and social safety net that allows debtors to return to the world? The fact that it is both has never slowed debate that it should be primarily one or the other."[45] Americans, as opposed to Europeans, began to see debt and bankruptcy as a political issue in the late 19th century during the series of economic "panics" that left farmers strangled by debt. The campaign for silver currency waged in the 1896 presidential campaign by William Jennings Bryan was based on the charge that debt-burdened farmers were being crucified on a "cross of gold," when they could more easily repay their debts with a more debased silver-backed currency. The debate between "hard money" and "soft money" politicians was thus essentially one of making it harder or easier to repay debts.

The unfairness of relieving some debts and not others remains at the heart of contemporary bailouts. The use of US government funds to shore up banks in 2008–09 provoked charges from many critics that banks and big lenders are protected in bankruptcy but that individuals who get over their heads in consumer debts are not. In Europe, there was criticism of the rescues that refinanced the debt held by creditors who should have been punished for making improvident loans.

Earlier, an acute confrontation over which creditors should be punished and which should be spared erupted over the 2005 overhaul of the US bankruptcy law, widely described at the time as a victory for the nation's largest banks, credit card companies, and retailers. The overhaul sought to make it more difficult for debtors to try to shelter their assets in bankruptcy proceedings. Civil rights groups, labor unions, and consumer organizations opposed the measure, saying many debtors had been victimized by misleading promotional campaigns by credit card companies. In fact, many of those groups cited the 2005 law when it was lenders who were rescued a few years later.[46]

Debt relief has also figured in the calculation of the obligation of the West to poor countries. Such obligations have been carried out in schemes such as those aimed at helping the so-called heavily indebted poor countries (HIPCs) through aid programs organized by institutions in the West and the World Bank, among others. Such schemes, like those that relieved Germany of its debts after World War II, circumvented reservations about "moral hazard" by tying aid to demands that poor countries reform their economies in ways that could spur growth, such as economic reform and openness to foreign trade and investment. Pressed by celebrities such as Bono and Bob Geldof, as well as a range of advocates around the world, British prime minister Tony Blair and President Bill Clinton agreed in 2000 to a major debt relief package for dozens of poor countries, many in Africa, although they were criticized again for allegedly encouraging the kinds of practices that would lead to more indebtedness.

One reason for the emotion surrounding this issue is that the public views government debts as different from personal debts. Traditionally, and certainly early in American history, public debts were tolerated only in times of emergencies, particularly war. Debts were incurred in the early years of the American Republic to expand territory—for example, the Louisiana Purchase—and to build infrastructure on the grounds that if borrowing was undertaken to build something that lasted into the future, it was acceptable to incur debts because future taxpayers would be receiving benefits. Debts were allowed to build up at times of conflict, especially the Civil War, World War I, and World War II, but each time they were retired in part because of the return of economic growth. Government debts were thus seen as a necessity in times of crisis—and as important to eliminate when crises eased.

It was only after the 1930s and the advent of John Maynard Keynes that debt took on a new legitimacy. Thus in the contemporary world, debt has become an economic policy tool. But it has never lost its moral dimension.

Who's Afraid of Debt?
Debt as a Public Policy Tool

> *I go on the principle that a public debt is a public curse,*
> *and in a Republican Government a greater than in any other.*
> —James Madison, letter to Henry Lee (1790)

> *Annual income twenty pounds, annual expenditure nineteen pounds nineteen and six,*
> *result happiness. Annual income twenty pounds, annual expenditure*
> *twenty pounds nought and six, result misery.*
> —Wilkins Micawber, in *David Copperfield* by Charles Dickens (1850)

President Franklin Roosevelt did not embrace Keynesian economics formally. Indeed, after his sole meeting with John Maynard Keynes in 1934, the president said he enjoyed the conversation but was confused by the great economist's "rigamarole" of numbers. Keynes came away disappointed with Roosevelt's lack of economic sophistication.[1]

Roosevelt was not troubled by deficits and debts as a political matter. He often said he understood that in times of crisis such as the Great Depression helping Americans to get back on their feet was a higher priority than reducing public deficits and debts. "To balance our budget in 1933 or 1934 or 1935 would have been a crime against the American people," FDR declared in 1936 in a speech in Pittsburgh. "To do so we should either have had to make a capital levy that would have been confiscatory, or we should have had to set our face against human suffering with callous indifference. When Americans suffered, we refused to pass by on the other side. Humanity came first. . . . We accepted the final responsibility of Government, after all else had failed, to spend money when no one else had money left to spend."[2]

Thus Roosevelt was a Keynesian in practice, though perhaps not one in theory. He had after all also campaigned against deficits and debts in 1932. In 1936–37, well into the New Deal, he sought to reduce the pileup of government debt, knowing how popular such steps would be and thinking that the danger zone in which debts could be tolerated had passed. His actions, however, had a calamitous effect. They contributed to a downturn sometimes known as the Second Great Depression.[3]

This chapter discusses how the view of debt as dishonorable, traced in the previous chapter, has evolved in a modern global economy that is dependent on debt and capital flows, which in turn have underscored the dangers of moral absolutism when it comes to punishing reckless behavior during crises. Like it or not, in the modern global arena policymakers have had to learn that forcing errant individuals, lenders, companies, and even countries to suffer the consequences of their mistakes must be balanced against concerns about protecting the innocent from economic calamities, especially those caused by elites. The travails of Greece in 2015, as discussed in chapter 5, well illustrate the moral hazard issue filtered through Keynesian economics.

Adherents of the Keynesian belief in deficit spending in times of economic downturn have criticized European policymakers for forcing Greece to adopt tough fiscal austerity in the form of tax increases and government spending cuts. Their argument is that such steps are self-defeating—that they reduce economic activity and thus make it even harder for Greece to meet its debt payments. But proponents of enforced austerity argue that any country is morally obligated to live within its means in order to give lenders confidence that it can meet its debt obligations and reduce its total debt burden over time. Even if lenders do not want to make such demands, the argument goes, the marketplace will force them to do so. Markets will drive up interest rates for countries deemed to be digging themselves deeper into debt even if more austerity worsens their economic outlook.

The Keynesian Revolution

Many economists have widely accepted the Keynesian revolution, which made it morally acceptable to incur debt to stimulate private sector growth—in theory strengthening the economy so that the debt could be more easily paid back. But it also has run counter to 200 years of economic norms and to the long-standing cultural antipathy in the West toward public debt. Whereas thriftiness has long generally been considered a virtue and a necessity in hard times, one of Keynes's most famous formulations alluded to the "paradox of thrift"—that is, widespread saving by individuals and companies, while commendable and understandable in normal times, can impede economic recovery in a downturn if it is not remedied by government spending to make up the difference.

But the acceptance of Keynesian economics has not overthrown other economic tenets. Economists also know that excessive debt and deficit spending can lead to public policy ills such as the "crowding out" of private investment. Debt also places a burden on future generations. It can raise interest rates, distort currency values, stoke inflation, undermine confidence in government, and generally promote extravagance or mismanagement. Reinforcing the strictures against debt is the relentless judgment of bond markets, which trade in debt and therefore regard it as an economic utility—a judgment that has not been kind to Spain, Italy, and Greece in recent years. They have learned the hard way that markets can force the price of debt to go up and down, depending on perceptions about the solvency of the governments and corporations that issue debts. This volatility has happened repeatedly during various global financial crises, and it is what many experts warn is the possible fate of the United States if it continues to pile up debt, especially the trillions owed to China and other countries.

In the modern world of globalization, when sovereign debt bonds can be bought and sold with a keystroke anywhere and everywhere, traders can make instant judgments about the conduct of governments, causing the price of debt to fluctuate dramatically. More than ever, these markets sit in judgment on countries—not simply their solvency but whether they are good for meeting their liabilities and whether they are trustworthy. In fact, some economists and market practitioners argue that Keynes's tolerance of debt was fashioned prior to the contemporary phenomenon of financial markets making rapid and radical judgments about the value and cost of that debt, punishing those countries that might dare to follow Keynes down the path to more debt and deficit spending.

If there was a turning point in *more* acceptance of Keynesian economics, it probably occurred in the 1950s and 1960s when a new consensus emerged that supported the concept that fiscal policy and deficits are more important in spurring economic growth than specific government programs that try to engage in social engineering or government programmatic intervention in an economy. A major figure in the legitimization of debts and deficits as a policy tool was the economist Paul Samuelson (see chapter 3).

The consensus among political leaders on Keynesian economics was also reflected in a collection of essays by Daniel Bell published in 1962. In *The End of Ideology: On the Exhaustion of Political Ideas in the Fifties*, Bell argued that the divisive overarching ideologies of conservatism and socialism or communism had exhausted themselves into irrelevance.[4] As if to echo this point, in 1962 President John F. Kennedy declared that the great challenges of the day were no longer over "basic clashes of philosophy or ideology" but rather over "the sophisticated and technical issues involved in keeping a great economic machinery moving ahead." Kennedy tried to defuse the old antagonisms by calling on both liberals and conservatives to abandon their ideological battles over liberty and efficiency versus social justice. "Today these old sweeping issues very largely have disappeared," Kennedy declared, no doubt with a measure of wishful thinking. "The central domestic issues of our time are more subtle and less simple. They relate not to basic clashes of philosophy or ideology but to ways and means of reaching common goals—to research for sophisticated solutions to complex and obstinate issues."[5]

Kennedy's economic advisers were apostles of Keynesianism. They had persuaded him to call for a tax cut to rekindle the sluggish economy when he took office in 1961, despite concerns about the deficit and inflation. By the end of 1965, two years after Kennedy's assassination, *Time* magazine was quoting the libertarian economist Milton Friedman as declaring, "We are all Keynesians now."[6] Even more strikingly, in 1971, after President Richard Nixon took the United States off the gold standard, he told a television interviewer, "I am now a Keynesian in economics."[7] After the global financial crisis of 2008–09, the United States won agreement from the leading economic powers in the Group of 20 (G-20) to accelerate deficit spending in order to avoid another Great Depression.

But the moral critique of deficits and debts, however defensible in times of crisis, has never gone away. Many economists believe the US federal debt not only threatens future recovery but also symbolizes a moral failing. One dimension of the morality or immorality of debts and deficits is that supposedly the profligate spending habits of the older generation today will have to be repaid by the children and grandchildren of tomorrow. In 2013 the economic historian Niall Ferguson, a vehement critic of deficit spending and the piling up of debt in the recent crisis, stirred a controversy by asserting that Keynes's famous observation ("In the long run we are all dead") implied that he was indifferent to the long-term costs of debt for the next generation because he had no children, which Ferguson attributed to Keynes being gay. (Under fire at Harvard, where he teaches, Ferguson later apologized.[8]) Nevertheless, the duties to the next generation have become a focus of debate over civic virtue because of the US fiscal and debt crises.

A series of authoritative studies have supported the moral dimension of this generational issue. The Congressional Budget Office projects that if current tax and spending policies continue, the US debt-to-GDP ratio will rise to 128 percent of GDP in 2030 and more than 200 percent of GDP in 2050, a level economists say will produce inflation, lower growth, unemployment, and possible financial crises.[9] Numerous other studies have shown that the mounting debts of the United States and other advanced economies tend to produce economic stagnation and crises. A particularly influential (though widely challenged) analysis by Carmen Reinhart and Kenneth Rogoff in 2010 held that when debt reaches a 90 percent debt-to-GDP ratio, economic growth sharply diminishes.[10] Even critics of the Reinhart-Rogoff study acknowledge that debts cannot continue to mount forever without taking an economic toll.

A separate ethical issue related to public debt is whether spending is directed too much at the elderly and not enough at the health and education of the young, who will have to take care of their parents in coming decades. In 2009, for example, a study by Julia Isaacs at the Center on Children and Families at the Brookings Institution found that the United States spends 2.4 times as much per capita on the elderly (including Social Security, Medicare, and Medicaid) as on children, with the ratio rising to 7:1 in the federal budget alone. According to the study, this ratio is similar to that in all member countries of the Organization for Economic Cooperation and Development (OECD), but the tilt toward the elderly is stronger in the United States. The study asserted that this imbalance is unfair to children by requiring the younger generation to bear the spending and tax burden of unfunded health and retirement benefits as they enter the workforce. The Brookings study also found that in 2004 the average public spending on a child (under 19) was $8,942, two-thirds of it by state and local governments. The same year, public spending on the elderly was $21,904 per person, or 2.4 times that amount.[11] These findings have driven many advocates to support cuts in entitlement programs for the elderly, which have run up debts that the next generation will have to bear.

Opponents of cutting Social Security and Medicare argue that they are social insurance programs whose benefits are "earned" by a lifetime of paying taxes into the programs' trust funds. In truth, however, what retirees receive from Social Security and Medicare is generally far more than what they put in. Benefits thus more resemble transfer payments from a younger generation to an older generation than an "insurance" program, even though that is how they are depicted. Medicaid is a Great Society program designed to provide health care for the poor, but much of its costs are driven by the needs of the elderly of modest means for nursing home care. Many young people are happy to have these programs help pay for the care of their parents, which makes it hard for Congress to cut spending on them. In fact, one can make the more general argument that public spending on the old does not take away money from the young—rather, it *helps* the young take care of the expensive long-term care and hospitalization needs of their parents.

What may be needed is what Isabel Sawhill and Emily Monea of Brookings called for in 2008: "a fundamental rethinking of the intergenerational con-tract, what the government provides to whom, and when in their lives the government provides it." They recommend that the growing elderly cohort do more to support itself on the grounds that the elderly are better able to work than in the past because of improved health and lifestyle. Meanwhile, the question is why only the elderly in the United States should be guaranteed universal, fee-for-service medical care when younger Americans have few such options.[12]

The prospect of the debt incurred by spending on the elderly, potentially sacrificing the welfare of the next generation, has produced moralistic argu-ments by leading commentators. For example, Thomas Friedman, the *New York Times* columnist, and Michael Mandelbaum of the School of Advanced International Studies (SAIS) at Johns Hopkins University argue that the United States has lost its way even more than it has lost its priorities. In their book *That Used to Be Us: How America Fell Behind in the World It Invented and How We Can Come Back* (2011), they all but characterize the United States as short-sighted, lazy, and complacent in failing to confront the problems of debts, deficits, globalization, technological advances, and climate change. Cuts in spending on the elderly are inevitable, they say, adding, "Anyone who says that these programs can continue exactly as they are is not being serious."[13]

But the United States is not alone in dealing with this problem of how to treat its elderly—a basic issue of whether a society should be considered virtu-ous or civic-minded. Aging populations and low fertility rates among the young are phenomena found in both developed and developing countries. According to some studies, by 2050, 1 billion working-age adults and 1.25 billion mem-bers of the 60-plus age groups will have been added to the world's population, but people younger than 25 will hold steady at 3 billion.[14] In East Asia, the aging population is driven by higher living standards, plummeting birth rates, and smaller families—trends that invite concern because these societies have yet to develop retirement systems to handle the coming problem. The expectation of the Confucian ethic in many parts of East Asia is that families will provide for their own elderly. A survey conducted in 2011 in China (including Hong Kong), Malaysia, Singapore, South Korea, and Taiwan found that between 35 and 65 percent of the elderly live in the household of one or more of their grown children. Yet surveys show a growing expectation in these same societies that grown children should not be expected to care for their elderly, that this should be the personal responsibility of the elderly themselves. Not surprisingly, Asian countries are looking to establish pension systems as they grow more affluent.[15]

Debt Morality Tale: How the East Asian Crisis Raised Doubts about Rescues

The moral issues engulfing the Mexico crisis of 1995 returned in the East Asian debt meltdown of the late 1990s, and then again in the US economic collapse after the bankruptcy of Lehman Brothers in 2008 and the euro area crisis that erupted in 2010. Each crisis saw a reversion to the pattern of rescuers struggling to find a balance between the moral obligation of punishing reckless behavior, in order to discourage its repetition in the future, and the equally strong moral obligation to protect the system from destroying the economic livelihoods of innocents. The fitful and tortured responses of various authorities involved in the rescues were testimony to the power of these conflicting ethical imperatives, one based on ensuring virtuous behavior by lenders and creditors, the other based on stabilizing a system on which the blameless depended.

The East Asian crisis started in Thailand in 1997. Its problems hardly came out of the blue. Many experts had warned that the "Asian miracle" of the "Asian tigers" was creating asset bubbles and "crony capitalism."[16] For years, Thailand's banks had borrowed easily and short term in foreign currencies, using this "hot money" to finance a boom in real estate and other investments that eventually turned sour. When the asset bubble first broke, banks were saddled with bad loans, and creditors began cutting back, pushing down the value of the Thai baht. The United States tried to work with the International Monetary Fund (IMF) to help with loans in return for economic reforms and interest rate increases, only to run into concerns about moral hazard and anger in Thailand that not enough was being done.

Contagion from Thailand soon spread to Indonesia in a similar pattern of overextended banks, plummeting currency values, and a corrupt government, led by the aging dictator Suharto, an archetypical "crony capitalist" whose family was connected to the financial institutions that were in trouble. In return for loans, the IMF called for the usual package of reforms, accompanied by demands that the government reduce the benefits it was handing out to industries controlled by various elites. As the crisis gripped Indonesia, South Korea soon succumbed, despite its successful record of economic growth. But South Korea, like its neighbors, had also borrowed short term in foreign currencies to invest long term in real estate and industry whose values suddenly went south. And so it, too, was soon knocking on the door of the IMF. US officials were especially concerned that if a success story like South Korea defaulted, the effects would be disastrous for many other emerging-market economies, and indeed financial crises did later consume Russia, Ukraine, Brazil, and Turkey.

For South Korea, the United States and the IMF stepped up their assistance to unprecedented levels to contain the crisis. One effect, however, was enabling foreign creditors who had recklessly pumped money into South Korea to escape unscathed. As they did so, South Korea's crisis worsened. Only after US and IMF officials joined with officials from other countries to persuade major foreign lenders to convert their short-term loans to longer-term loans did the situation stabilize. But the aftertaste of the perception that the United States, other creditor countries, and the IMF favored bailing out creditors while punishing ordinary citizens persisted for many years. Still, with outside assistance, Thailand, Indonesia, and South Korea quite promptly reversed their downward spirals. Indonesia, however, suffered greatly, both politically and economically. Reform measures—including an initial round of budget cuts, reduced subsidies for food and fuel, higher interest rates, and higher prices because of currency devaluations—caused riots and attacks on ethnic Chinese business owners, and Suharto—who was humiliated when photographed accepting IMF terms set forth by Michel Camdessus, managing director of the IMF—was later forced out of office after three decades in power.

In a separate outcome of the turmoil, Russia's devaluation and default in 1998 spooked investors around the world, bringing down a highly regarded but highly leveraged hedge fund, Long-Term Capital Management (LTCM), which had relied on a risk management strategy developed by two Nobel Laureate economists. The New York Fed encouraged several major Wall Street financial institutions to save the LTCM from collapse in an episode that would be replicated a decade later after the collapse of the housing boom in the United States. In the Asian crisis, Treasury secretary Robert Rubin acknowledged later that the reforms he and others demanded were perceived to be an arrogant imposition of the West's "free-market policy preferences" on hapless countries.[17] But, he said, there was no other choice except to observe a time-honored lesson: "Borrowers must bear the consequences of the debts they incur—and creditors of the lending they provide."[18] Rubin and his allies, including the Fed chairman, Alan Greenspan, and his deputy, Lawrence Summers, were rewarded with a *Time* magazine cover story in 1999, labeling them "The Committee to Save the World."

Many critics, however, believed what they had saved was a corrupt system and reckless behavior by lenders and borrowers, hurting ordinary people in between.[19] On the left, Joseph Stiglitz, former chief economist at the World Bank (1997–2000), accused the IMF of imposing its "ideology" of "market fundamentalism" and requiring what he insisted was unwarranted austerity as a kind of retribution for sins. "Suffering and pain became part of the process of redemption, evidence that a country was on the right track," he said.[20] Jeffrey Sachs, the economist who has advised Eastern European and developing economies on their transitions to market-based systems, said the IMF "threw together a Draconian program for Korea in just a few days, without deep knowledge of the country's financial system and without any subtlety as to how to approach the problems."[21]

Indeed, the criticism of the intrusion by the IMF and the United States was fierce. The argument that errant states should be left to their own devices even if the result is worse hardship and contagion of blameless countries was especially fervent after the crisis. It was morally repellant, said Paul O'Neill, the first Treasury secretary under President George W. Bush, to ask "plumbers and carpenters" in the United States to bail out wealthy creditors in the Mexican and Asian crises.[22] ("I liked Paul," Rubin said later. "But. . . I said to myself: *They say they won't intervene. But they will.*" He was right. The Bush team backed IMF rescues in Turkey, Uruguay, and Brazil.) These rescues set the pattern for the response to the euro crisis after 2010.[23]

As the Asian crisis receded, former Treasury secretary and secretary of state George Shultz joined with two other prominent conservatives—former Treasury secretary William Simon and Walter Wriston, former chairman of Citicorp—in labeling the IMF "ineffective, unnecessary, and obsolete." The Fund, they said, had lulled nations into complacency "by acting as the self-appointed lender of last resort, a function never contemplated by its founders."[24] Shultz later called on Congress to reject a new round of US funding for the IMF.[25]

The invocation of moral hazard continued through the US and European financial crises of the last decade, and the issue was always the same: Should rescues be undertaken even at the risk of not teaching bad actors a lesson? Should misconduct by lenders and borrowers be rewarded? As the author Paul Blustein put it in his book about the Asian crisis, "Should the world turn its back on a country in distress for the sake of deterring reckless behavior in the future? Wasn't that somehow analogous to denying medical treatment for a car-crash victim who has been driving too fast?"[26]

More mordantly, Michael Mussa, former chief economist of the IMF, commented, "If every time national default threatens, we say, 'Let's force it,' then we are not only going to get the creditors; we are also going to do a lot more damage to a lot of innocent victims. The objective is not to make a crisis as large and costly as possible so that we can discourage all risk taking. . . . Some amount of moral hazard is almost inevitably a consequence of international support packages. But the issue is a balancing one." In one of his famous sardonic formulations, Mussa theorized a case of moral hazard literally gone overboard: "If we hadn't rescued the 800 people we rescued from the *Titanic*, we would have taught an even more valuable lesson about people being careful about getting on ocean liners."[27]

Two separate issues are at play in these dramas. The first is whether the IMF or other sources should provide temporary funds in a crisis when markets shut down, in some cases simply to protect blameless countries from the contagion effects of the reckless. The moral dimension of that question is, again, whether such action encourages countries to misbehave in the future. The second question is whether such funds should be accompanied by adjustment—some sort of agreement setting up a tribunal to apportion or adjudicate costs between creditor banks and debtor countries, such as in a bankruptcy affecting individuals, businesses, or multinational corporations. Such a court would become a forum in which creditors and debtors could negotiate the apportionment of losses across national lines. Many agreements have been arranged between debtor countries and their creditors, but there have also been many controversies, especially when some creditors refused to go along. For example, Argentina, which defaulted on its debt in 2001, did not see eye to eye with its holdout creditors—some of which were so-called vulture funds that purchased Argentine debt for speculative purposes.

Following the financial crises of the late 1990s, the IMF and many of its constituent stakeholders began searching for ways out of the trap of rewarding bad behavior while still undertaking rescues to stabilize the global or regional economic and financial systems and spare those not guilty of recklessness. The purpose of the proposals and measures considered was to ensure a basic fairness when debts engulf countries—again, that lenders be punished along with borrowers, that they follow the rule of moral hazard, and that they be discouraged from behaving badly in the future. Yet the IMF remained concerned that in punishing creditors it should not spread turmoil in the markets, punishing other countries with sound finances.

One proposal was to set up a kind of international bankruptcy regime—that is, a kind of voluntary Chapter 11 for countries, to be called a sovereign debt restructuring mechanism, or SDRM, aimed at protecting the rights of creditors by encouraging countries with unsustainable debts to deal with them promptly.[28] It was not adopted, however. Another proposal was to incorporate "collective action clauses" in sovereign debt, allowing a supermajority of creditors to force sacrifice not only on themselves but also on recalcitrant lenders who oppose debt restructuring. In 2002 the IMF, concerned about criticism that it had lent too much too easily in the Asian crisis and did too much to let improvident lenders off the hook, established new criteria that would make it more likely that costs would be imposed on creditors in the interest of moral hazard. But this approach ran into a new problem in 2010 when Greece's economy collapsed.

In 2010, prodded by the United States, which feared a replay of the Lehman collapse two years earlier, European leaders and the IMF realized that they had to waive certain rules about collateral in loan programs in order to rescue Greece from default. Their action set in motion the establishment of new rescue and support funds in Europe out of fear that its economic system could not withstand the shock of a Greek financial collapse or its spread to other countries. It was the first time that major lenders indicated that their primary objective was to save the wider economic system rather than just the country that was in trouble. And yet the following October, President Nicolas Sarkozy of France and Chancellor Angela Merkel of Germany met in Deauville, France, and signaled that in the future the presumption would be that costs would have to be imposed on creditors. Their statement rattled the financial markets. As moral as they wanted to be, they ended up destabilizing markets and exacting costs on Spain and Italy, where interest rates rocketed up, forcing the two leaders to later back off from their hard line.

Strictly speaking, it has always been true that creditors have paid a price in many rescues. Debt restructuring, or "haircuts," has been a part of the IMF's toolkit in many crises. The prospect of such haircuts was again raised in the third Greek bailout package of 2015. But the specter of "private sector involvement"—as these write-downs are called—has made rescuers wary. To get around the problem in which the costs borne by creditors spook markets and threaten the stability of the system, in 2010 the US Congress passed the Dodd-Frank Wall Street Reform and Consumer Protection Act requiring major financial institutions to come up with "living wills" (plans for orderly "resolution" in the event of a collapse) ahead of time. The idea is to make it easier for banks to become insolvent without rattling markets across the board.[29] In Europe, there are also plans for a centralized banking authority and a "resolution" mechanism for insolvent banks, again imposing costs on the creditors and even bondholders of failing banks to ensure the perpetuation of "moral" behavior.[30]

After these steps, Europe had to take even more actions to stabilize the situation. In 2011 the European Central Bank (ECB) threatened to withdraw from its plan to purchase Italian government bonds—the aim was to keep interest rates from spiking and strangling Italy's economy—unless Italy took more austerity steps. Prime Minister Silvio Berlusconi had already lost the confidence of other European leaders because of his failure to do so, and he was forced out of office in November 2011. It was an extraordinary moment in European political history—an elected leader of one country being pressed to resign by other leaders in Europe through the mechanism of the ECB. The following July, the new ECB president, Mario Draghi, announced that the ECB would do "whatever it takes to preserve the euro." In response to his comment, markets stabilized throughout Europe, which nonetheless expected the troubled European economies to continue to rebalance their finances.

In 2013 IMF staff released an extraordinary mea culpa in the form of a report that criticized the Fund's own initial bailout program for Greece. (As a staff report, it did not reflect the views of either the Fund's management or board members, who were the ones responsible for its policies.) The report effectively said that the Fund had underestimated the seriousness of the economic problems Greece would face in carrying out IMF-demanded reforms in exchange for the initial rescue in 2010: "Market confidence was not restored, the banking system lost 30 percent of its deposits, and the economy encountered a much deeper-than-expected recession with exceptionally high unemployment." Accompanying their acknowledgment of error, IMF officials told the press that the Fund had also underestimated the difficulties that Greece's political leadership would have in responding effectively, and they acknowledged that they had overlooked Greece's problems in part because they feared that if help was not forthcoming, Greece would leave the eurozone, with disastrous consequences for the entire postwar European project.[31] In early 2015, Greek voters ousted the centrist government that had negotiated the rescue package with the group of rescuing entities known as the Troika (the ECB, European Commission, and IMF). The new radical left prime minister, Alexis Tsipras, sought to lift some of the harsh measures the previous government had accepted, only to be rebuffed by European creditors and the IMF. As discussed earlier, Tsipras was forced to go along with the pension and spending cuts, tax increases, privatizations, and eased regulations on business and labor in return for a new round of assistance. But he did get a judgment from the IMF that Greece's debt burdens were not sustainable without further debt relief, and the possibility of such relief was put on the agenda for further discussions once Greece implemented its initial steps.

What are the "moral" lessons to be learned from these crises? Looking back on the Mexican, East Asian, and other crises of the 1990s, Lawrence Summers observed in 2000 that crises inevitably produce moral hazard issues, but that they are exaggerated in an environment distorted by the vast speed and efficiency of the forces of globalization. This did not mean that globalization was a bad thing, he hastened to add. "The jet airplane made air travel more comfortable, more efficient, and more safe, though the accidents were more spectacular and for a time more numerous after the jet was invented," Summers pointed out. "In the same way, modern global financial markets carry with them enormous potential for benefit. Even if some of the accidents are that much more spectacular." As a veteran of various crises, Summers observed that the victims go through stages reminiscent of "the five stages of grief": denial that a crisis is taking place, the anger and blame of speculators and outside forces, a desperate search for "magic bullets" that may not help, despair leading to a call for outside help, and finally acceptance of a credible plan. Finally, like Rubin, Summers pointed out that moral hazard cannot be banished despite the dangers, declaring, "It is certain that a healthy financial system cannot be built on the expectation of bailouts."[32]

Christine Lagarde, managing director of the IMF, has tried to be philosophical about the conflicting demands of imposing costs on creditors to mitigate moral hazard and imposing costs on the citizens of countries even though they are not always the ones to directly blame for crises. "It is the fate of this organization to be criticized and to be seen as a negative force at the time it prescribes . . . reforms, fiscal consolidations [i.e., budget cuts and tax increases], in consideration for loans," Lagarde has observed. Harsh recriminations have been a fact of life for the Fund in all previous crises—Latin America and Asia before Europe. "We intervene at a time when no other tools, no other methods, no other political coalition has been able to restore the situation," said Lagarde. "We come in as the firefighter. We come in as the doctors, if you will. And the prescription we give is resented. That is very much part of our fate."[33]

Must Virtue Be Its Own Reward?

Dost thou think, because thou art virtuous, there shall be no more cakes and ale?
—Sir Toby Belch, Shakespeare's *Twelfth Night*, Act II, Scene 3

In recent crises and philosophical pronouncements since ancient times, the encouragement of virtuous behavior among citizens has long been praised and celebrated by writers as a goal of civil society. Political writers from Aristotle to John Adams and James Madison to contemporary figures such as Moynihan and Daniel Bell have maintained across the millennia that no society can succeed without the honest and upstanding conduct of its people (see chapter 7). These goals were the explicit objective of the Founders of the United States, many of whom worried that the new nation would fracture along sectional lines if its newly liberated citizens did not exercise self-discipline and sympathy, not to mention faithfulness to the law.

For most of the country's history, such standards have been commonly enforced through the law itself. Not until recent decades has it been considered unusual for US laws to require Americans to practice certain kinds of sexual behavior and to show their patriotism and religious faith through public prayer, saluting the flag, and even, in some cases, comporting themselves respectfully in public. Although these laws have largely given way to the principle that each citizen has the right to define his or her own personal code of conduct, within some limits, the inculcation of virtuous behavior is inextricably tied to the system of market economics prevailing in the era of globalization, where virtue remains front and center as a bedrock principle and goal accepted by most practitioners.

The tension between the goal of encouraging moral or virtuous behavior, on the one hand, and helping those who have made mistakes in order to prevent further damage to society, on the other, is not easy to resolve. The examples cited in this chapter demonstrate that virtue, too, presents challenging tradeoffs. Most everyone seems to want citizens to be self-sufficient and to practice the virtues of hard work, self-discipline, and even delayed gratification in order to make the market system work. Indeed, it has been argued here that capitalism would not have the support it commands if people did not think it was a system that, generally speaking but with some exceptions, rewards virtuous behavior.

Nonetheless, poverty, bad luck, and inequality have compelled society to indulge in charity and help those who need it, and the worry that such help will undermine the incentives for good behavior cannot be wished away. In the modern global arena, the pressure to force errant individuals, companies, and even countries to pay for their mistakes must be balanced against the pressure to protect the innocent from economic calamities, especially those caused by elites.

As the chapters in part II have shown, policymakers have sought to balance the tension between acting to avoid moral hazard and acting to avoid the immorality of economic calamities that harm the innocent. Just as in the case of liberty versus justice, it is not easy to navigate the tradeoff between encouraging correct behavior and saving the system. In fact, it is easier when practitioners recognize that no absolute truths are to be found, especially during crises.

But what about the issue of how to balance the demands of helping countries and citizens in far-off places at the risk of hurting one's own community? Is there a particular moral imperative to looking after one's own, even if it means ignoring others outside one's own sphere? This is a particularly urgent problem posed by the expanding world economy in the era of globalization. Part III discusses this problem.

III

THE CONFLICTS OVER LOYALTY

The decades-long decline of the US automobile industry is acutely reflected in the urban decay of Detroit, the city once lovingly referred to as Motor City, December 22, 2008.   © Timothy Fadek–Corbis

As man advances in civilisation, and small tribes are united into larger communities, the simplest reason would tell each individual that he ought to extend his social instincts and sympathies to all the members of the same nation, though personally unknown to him. This point being once reached, there is only an artificial barrier to prevent his sympathies extending to the men of all nations and races.
—Charles Darwin, *The Descent of Man* (1871)

Now and then it is possible to observe the moral life in process of revising itself, perhaps by reducing the emphasis it formerly placed upon one or another of its elements, perhaps by inventing and adding to itself a new element, some mode of conduct or of feeling which hitherto it had not regarded as essential to virtue.
—Lionel Trilling, *Sincerity and Authenticity* (1971)

9

The Moral Imperative of Loyalty

What, really, is the moral significance of national boundaries?
In terms of sheer need, the billion people around the world who live on less than
a dollar a day are worse off than our poor.
—Michael J. Sandel, *Justice: What's the Right Thing to Do?* (2009)

Moral imagination . . . the power that compels us to grant the highest possible reality and
the largest conceivable claim to a thought, action, or person that is not our own,
and not close to us in any obvious way.
—David Bromwich, *Moral Imagination* (2014)

In February 2011 President Barack Obama, faced with persistent high national unemployment, traveled to Silicon Valley to appeal to the leaders of several American companies to bring jobs back to the United States from their overseas operations. "Those jobs aren't coming back," Steve Jobs, founder and president of Apple, responded. In fact, he pointed out that the economic advantages of manufacturing and assembling parts for iMacs, iPads, iPods, and iPhones abroad were too powerful to resist and likely to continue. Like other high-tech companies, Apple went to China to take advantage of both cheaper labor and the flexibility of Chinese factories in adjusting work and production rules. What was once an obligation by American companies to embrace the label "Made in America" no longer applied. "Profits and efficiency have trumped generosity," a former Labor Department chief economist told the *New York Times*, which reported on Obama's visit.[1]

Obama later began to speak of "economic patriotism," a catch-all phrase encompassing his appeals to companies to keep jobs in the United States and refrain from moving operations offshore to escape US corporate taxes. But although Obama has tried to promote his brand of "patriotism" with proposals such as taxing corporate profits earned overseas, his advocacy of trade agreements with Asian and European trading partners has drawn fire from critics as economically disloyal. In the early phase of the 2016 election, leading candidates in both the Republican and Democratic parties have organized their campaigns around the charge that such trade deals cost US jobs because of imports and corporations transferring their production abroad.

The phrase "economic patriotism" is a by-product of another complex ethical and moral dilemma posed by globalization, in which the benefits and costs of economic growth have been unevenly distributed among and within countries, whether they are rich or poor. This uneven distribution poses difficult questions. To whom does a citizen owe loyalty—to his or her neighbors who might have lost jobs because of global competition, or to those in poor countries who have gained because of offshoring of jobs and investments? The role of multinational corporations makes this dilemma all the more complex, because most world trade in the globalization era is within and between their subdivisions or suppliers. It becomes nearly impossible to say who is "us" and who is "them" when thinking about products such as planes, autos, or iPods, all of which contain parts from dozens if not hundreds of different places. As for US-based multinational corporations, to whom should they be "loyal"—their workers, their investors, their home countries, or their customers, whether in the United States or distant countries?

Much of the opposition to trade and investment deals comes from organized labor. But employee solidarity becomes confused when workers are also investors—in the sense that their retirement funds are often invested in the same multinational companies that are offshoring operations or dependent on imports. Such workers may also benefit directly when their companies shift operations to tax havens such as Luxembourg or the Cayman Islands, lowering their costs so they can keep more of their employees on the job. Are people first and foremost citizens of their communities, of their countries, of their employers, or of the world as a whole? And what of the demands that people should keep faith with others of their race, nationality, gender, sexual orientation, income class, or labor union, irrespective of the countries in which they live?

This chapter explores the profound moral questions about the nature of citizenship, empathy, and loyalty or solidarity.

Three Categories of Loyalty

In the economic sphere, even the well-intentioned can be confused over the issue of loyalty. A striking example can be found in Pope Benedict's encyclical *Caritas in Veritate*. On the one hand, it calls on wealthy countries, as a matter of morality, to import more goods from poor countries. On the other hand, it laments the effects of imports by deploring the struggles of the working classes in rich countries whose jobs are displaced or whose wages are held down because of cheap imports from poor countries.[2]

Recent elections in the United States have partly turned on the same dilemmas over trade. Trade accords with Mexico and China and the establishment of a new World Trade Organization in the 1990s were also extremely divisive even as Congress approved such steps. Labor unions, environmental activists, and other antiglobalization groups opposed these deals, and more recently targeted the proposed Trans-Pacific Partnership (TPP) trade deal between the United States and 11 countries in Asia and the Western hemisphere, on the ground that US trading partners are stealing American jobs with their cheap labor and weak environmental and safety conditions. In part because of their campaigns, companies such as Foxconn Technology Group, whose Chinese operations supply parts and products for Apple and other companies, were forced to upgrade working conditions in the wake of bad publicity brought on by strikes, protests, and suicides (and the installation of suicide prevention nets at company dormitories).

President Obama was able to exploit the emotional quotient in these practices during his 2012 reelection campaign, when he attacked former Massachusetts governor Mitt Romney, the Republican presidential candidate and a former executive at Bain Capital, for Bain's stakes in companies that either moved their work overseas or helped other companies do so. Yet Obama's support of the TPP caused most Democrats in Congress to abandon him when he sought authorization to negotiate the pact in early 2015.

The fact is that lowering trade barriers has never been terribly popular in the United States, even during the heyday of trade deals going back to the Kennedy administration.[3] Trade in the early decades after World War II was not a big factor in the US economy, however, which meant that it was not a central issue of concern for Americans. In recent years, total trade as a share of the US economy has approached a quarter of US GDP, elevating its importance in any discussion of the economy (see figure 9.1). In addition, global exports have risen to new heights since 1960, reaching 30 percent of global GDP (see figure 9.2).

In the face of considerable skepticism in the 1990s, President Bill Clinton managed to convince majorities in Congress that the balance of benefits derived from trade and other aspects of globalization was positive, and that Congress had no choice but to embrace globalization because global trade and investment were not going away. Obama made the same argument but with less success, in part because the confidence of many Americans in trade deals has been shaken. Surveys show that although Americans seem to appreciate the benefits of opening new markets for American goods and services abroad, and are happy to buy less expensive imported electronic gadgets, toys, shoes, and clothes, they also think that globalization—combined with advances in labor-saving technologies in the workplace—has contributed to wage stagnation and unemployment at home and enriched corporations and the wealthy at the expense of the middle class.

Basic economic theory holds that trade and financial flows maximize efficiency and productivity to the benefit of producers and consumers alike through the theory of comparative advantage. But changes in the trade and flow of goods, services, and investments, while eliminating inefficiencies and building new competitive sectors, also do so in line with what the economist Joseph Schumpeter called in 1942 "creative destruction." If one country specializes in producing clothing and another in food, for example, and they concentrate in their areas of comparative advantage, each country is in theory better off than if they do not trade, but the less efficient clothing workers and farmers in each country may lose out. Offshoring jobs to other countries, in theory, also works to the advantage of workers in both countries, most econo-

Figure 9.1   Trade's share of the US economy is increasing

trade (exports and imports) as a percent of GDP

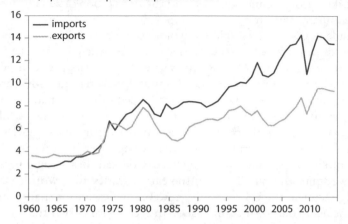

Sources: Trade data: US Census Bureau, Foreign Trade, Historical series; GDP data: US Bureau of Economic Analysis.

Figure 9.2   Global trade has reached new highs

global exports as percent of global GDP

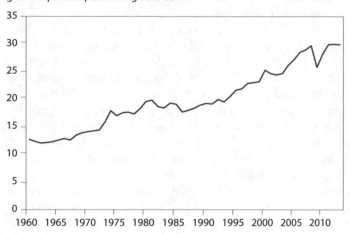

Source: World Bank, *World Development Indicators* Database, December 19, 2014.

mists would agree, but that does not mean the adjustment is painless. "Trade can make everyone better off," the economist Gregory Mankiw wrote in his classic economics textbook *Principles of Economics.* "But *will* trade make everyone better off? Probably not."[4]

The *moral* issue comes down to evaluating gains and losses in terms of one's own fellow citizens versus the less affluent citizens of the world. Martin Wolf of the *Financial Times* has written, for example, that it is "immoral for rich countries to deprive the poor of the world of so large an opportunity for betterment merely because they [the rich countries] are unable to handle sensibly and justly the distribution of the internal costs of a change certain to be highly beneficial overall."[5] In a similar vein, Thomas Nagel, professor of moral philosophy and law at New York University, finds it is "indecent" for wealthy nations to subsidize their own farmers and in the process cripple the ability of poor countries to export food.[6]

Critics of free trade and investment assert that such agreements are immoral because they hurt the working middle class, especially unskilled labor, and enrich the investor class and those fortunate enough to have the skills to take advantage of the new economic rules. But even these critics seem to have a threshold when it comes to some trade agreements that benefit poor countries. For example, while Congress struggled over legislation granting President Obama authority to negotiate trade deals in 2015, it overwhelmingly approved renewal of the African Growth and Opportunity Act (AGOA), which eliminates or lowers trade barriers for dozens of sub-Saharan African countries. AGOA has become a bipartisan moral imperative, generating tens of billions of dollars worth of exports to the United States from some of the poorest countries in the world, enabling them to lure foreign investments and increase employment, arguably at the expense of American domestic producers.[7]

Ethan Kapstein, professor of sustainable development at the graduate business school INSEAD, usefully divides advocates who disagree over these tradeoffs into three categories:[8]

1. *Economic communitarians. Communitarian* is the widely accepted term assigned to those primarily interested in the distributive impact of globalization on their own country or community. The United States advocated free trade after World War II, and in later decades it promoted programs to help those adversely affected. To the extent that critics oppose such steps on the grounds that they contribute to inequality, wage stagnation, and unemployment at home, they are economic communitarians. Some critics argue further that by weakening the US and European economies, globalization has reduced tax revenues and thus curbed the ability of governments to sustain social safety nets and train people for jobs. Communitarians may also focus on concerns about social and economic justice in communities defined by gender, religious, or local identities.

2. *Economic cosmopolitans. Cosmopolitan* is a term embraced by a group of modern philosophers who focus on the well-being of persons and groups around the world as a whole, especially the most poor and disadvantaged. They would invoke the Rawlsian "difference principle" (holding that a system is unjust if it hurts the least advantaged) on a global scale, which is something that John Rawls himself never did. Some cosmopolitan-leaning philosophers find fault with Rawls on these grounds. Rawls

argued that his principle was not necessarily applicable beyond a country's borders because each society has the right to adhere to its own norms. Cosmopolitans in this camp say that, on the contrary, rich countries owe something to the poor in other countries, although they disagree about whether globalization gives advantages to the poor in poor countries. Cosmopolitans would favor elimination of farm subsidies in rich countries and barriers on textiles and clothing produced in poor countries. To cosmopolitans, globalization is unjust to the degree that it hinders the opportunities of the world's most vulnerable citizens.

3. *Liberal internationalists.* These supporters of a global trading system advance the argument that such a structure creates a liberal international order that provides benefits well beyond the question of whether the rich or poor are better or worse served. Instead, their goal is to reduce the economic gap between rich and poor countries, irrespective perhaps of what happens within such countries, thereby strengthening the prospects for peace and political stability. The goal of liberal internationalists does not run counter to the goal of either cosmopolitans or communitarians. Instead, their primary objective is to fulfill the vision of the founders of the Bretton Woods system of world trade and development, achieving economic justice as a binding benefit of what Kapstein called the "society of states." A main concern of liberal internationalists is achieving greater cooperation among nations in order to pursue economic cooperation as well as justice. The overriding purpose is to accommodate disputes peacefully, achieve economic interdependence, and make war less likely. In their view, until there is more open trade, the international order falls short of the goal of economic justice (see chapter 12).

Who Is a Communitarian? The "Mystic Chords of Memory"

Neither human existence nor individual liberty can be sustained for long outside the interdependent and overlapping communities to which all of us belong.
—Manifesto of the Communitarian Network (established in 1993)

In theory, ethical norms are or ought to be universal, implying no double standards—for example, one for your family or community and another for those outside that circle. In the pantheon of moral tenets, the demands of loyalty are especially complicated because of the long tradition of fixed moral principles engraved in stone as they were thought to have been in the Ten Commandments. The literary critic Lionel Trilling, writing as moral absolutes were coming under attack in the 1960s and 1970s, has observed that the tradition of moral ideas fixed for all humanity began to undergo a change toward relativism in the 16th century and that in the modern era intellectuals understand morality to be defined differently in different eras and cultures, including the rules of family, tribe, and community.[9] Thus loyalty has become elevated as a virtue in modern times, even among philosophers trying to reconcile morality with the wellsprings of culture and history.

The *Wall Street Journal* op-ed contributor Eric Felten has called loyalty a "vexing" virtue because it does not seem to derive from a moral principle beyond helping friends and hurting enemies. He asks if such an evolving set of principles can be called moral. "We can't say that loyalty to principle always comes ahead of conflicting loyalties to people, nor the other way around," Felten has written. "We can't say that family always comes before country, nor the other way around. We can't say that our obligations to friends trump all. . . . For many, this is the irredeemable downfall of loyalty: How can we say it is a virtue when it works just as effectively in the cause of vice?"[10]

What exactly is this loyalty we feel? Michael Sandel, arguing that loyalty is indeed a fundamental moral trait, says it can derive from historic memory and narrative, mythology and art, religious faith, regional ties, ideological fealty, and other factors often evoked in history, narrative, legend, poetry, and song. An eloquent evocation of loyalty was delivered by Abraham Lincoln in his first inaugural address. He appealed to his listeners to save the Union based on "the mystic chords of memory, stretching from every battlefield and patriot grave to every living heart and hearthstone all over this broad land."[11]

Most everyone, however, is aware of examples in which loyalty compromises the ethical or even sensible thing to do. Anyone who has seen crowds cheering or booing umpires or referees in baseball or football games, and almost always siding with the home team, recognizes the irrationality driven by loyalty. When he placed loyalty to the South over his sworn allegiance to the Union and his misgivings about a war to defend slavery, General Robert E. Lee was considered a hero by many, a traitor by others. In another example of loyalty, two famous sets of brothers took different approaches to the issue of family loyalty. In 1995 William Bulger, a prominent Democratic Party political figure, lawmaker, and educator in Massachusetts, had contact with his brother, James Joseph (Whitey) Bulger Jr.—the Boston mobster who was wanted for murder and was a fugitive from justice—without informing the police. For that, he made no apology. Family loyalty trumped duty to society, he acknowledged. But the brother of Ted Kaczynski, the notorious "Unabomber" responsible for multiple murders and injuries, turned his sibling in to authorities—on the condition that the death penalty not be imposed.[12]

It is beyond dispute that the building blocks of society depend on loyalty to one's community, justifying the elevation of its importance over other ethical demands. But there are many ways in which tribal loyalties can blind members of that community to the goal of overarching welfare for all communities. In game theory, the "prisoner's dilemma" sets up a situation in which it would be rational for two criminal gang prisoners held separately to confess to a crime, but the prisoners nonetheless remain silent out of loyalty, even though both will be worse off. In his classic study of an impoverished southern Italian town in the 1950s, the sociologist Edward Banfield found, based on interviews with its inhabitants, that there was no loyalty to the larger community at all. Rather, the town was a tangled nest of rivalries and hatreds driven by the loyalty that families felt only to themselves. Banfield applied a revealing term to this phenomenon, "amoral familism," because tribal and family loyalties blocked the chances of cooperation that would yield progress for all.[13]

Displays of one's love of country are familiar in political culture, especially in times of war or conflict. The terrorist attack of September 11, 2001, on New York City and the Boston Marathon bombings on April 15, 2013, unleashed an outpouring of love among the citizens of those cities. Countries under attack—whether Britain during the Blitz in World War II, or Iran under siege today by global sanctions, or Israel faced with terrorist attacks and global condemnation of its policies, or Jordan when one of its soldiers is burned alive by the Islamic State—tend to rally around their leadership, sometimes to the exclusion of other moral considerations. Jonathan Haidt, professor of psychology at the University of Virginia and author of *The Righteous Mind: Why Good People Are Divided by Politics and Religion* (2012), argues that these ties override basic economic axioms, such as the assumption that people behave rationally to maximize self-interest. "Despite what you might have learned in Economics 101, people aren't always selfish," he wrote. "In politics, they're more often groupish. When people feel that a group they value—be it racial, religious, regional or ideological—is under attack, they rally to its defense, even at some cost to themselves. We evolved to be tribal, and politics is a competition among coalitions of tribes. . . . People who worship the same idol can trust one another, work as a team and prevail over less cohesive groups. So if you want to understand politics, and especially our divisive culture wars, you must follow the sacredness."[14]

The rise of the nation-state in the 17th century and the loyalty that new nations commanded were a modern phenomenon. Indeed, nations are a modern phenomenon. A nation that has broken off from empires is defined by its common factors of language, culture, history, and obviously territory, all of which command loyalty. In his book tracing the history of the idea of world government, the author and diplomat Strobe Talbott argues that national identity has fallen into varying camps. One camp of "primordialists" consists of people who see their identity founded on ancient and natural origins. Japan is a good example of this category. Another is India. Talbott notes that Jawaharlal Nehru, in his book *The Discovery of India*, written while he was imprisoned by the British, sought to define such a unified ancient civilization out of a country of disparate factions that he would lead as its first prime minister when it became independent in the late 1940s. Another camp cited by Talbott, the "perennialists," derives its national identity from ethnic and sectarian communities, some of them connected to particular myths (he cites Greeks, Turks, and the English). Finally, the "modernists" and "constructivists" tend to see nations as phenomena without deep roots but founded on practical necessity such as the desire for security. Many countries in the Middle East with arbitrary borders might fall into this category.[15]

But modern evolutionary biologists and others have found that cooperation and altruism among humans—and, by extension, loyalty—have evolved via the natural selection theorized by Charles Darwin. Scientists studying the willingness of ants or other insects to sacrifice themselves for the greater good of their "societies" have suggested that this altruistic behavior applies to human conduct as well. Edward Wilson, a pioneer in the field of sociobiology, has explained how evolution rewarded the moral sentiments of loyalty to one's own community because such behavior contributed to survival and more offspring.[16] Richard Dawkins, the evolutionary biologist (and later famous as an avowed atheist), coined the term *selfish gene* to describe the factor in evolution that causes humans to behave selflessly toward those to whom they are genetically related. His use of the word "selfish" caused some misunderstanding. He did not mean selfishness, he claimed, but rather the genetic impulse to preserve one's self or species in an evolutionary sense.[17] Other experts such as Christopher Boehm, a biological anthropologist at the University of Southern California, and Steven Pinker, author of books on psychology and cognitive science, have also explored the importance of human evolution in creating altruism, empathy, and a sense of justice among communities.[†]

Yet altruism, empathy, and justice do not appear to have evolved beyond the loyalty that one owes to one's community, according to some experts. Social scientists have labeled the negative impact from the conflict between loyalty to one's own people and to strangers in other communities of the world as the "tragedy of the commons." The "tragedy" lies in the danger arising from one community's commonsense pursuit of its own self-interest harming the community at large. A well-known example is the overgrazing of a common pasture by rival groups that either spoils the pasture for both or causes a fight because rival camps are blind to the benefits of cooperation.

The psychology professor Joshua Greene notes that Charles Darwin was an early pioneer in trying to use social psychology to answer the question: Where does morality come from? "We now have an answer," Greene claims. "Morality evolved as a solution to the problem of cooperation, as a way of averting the Tragedy of the Commons." But he clarifies that, "Morality evolved to enable cooperation, but this conclusion comes with an important caveat. Biologically speaking, humans were designed for cooperation, *but only with some people.* Our moral brains evolved for cooperation *within groups*, and perhaps only within the context of personal relationships. Our moral brains did not evolve for cooperation *between groups* (at least not *all* groups)." Universal cooperation, he concludes, is simply inconsistent with the principles that govern evolution by natural selection.[18]

---

† Not that altruism as a product of evolution is accepted by everyone. Free market libertarians have gone so far as to disdain the whole concept of altruism. "As to altruism—it has never been alive," Ayn Rand wrote. "It is the poison of death in the blood of Western civilization, and men survived it only to the extent to which they neither believed nor practiced it. . . . If any civilization is to survive, it is the morality of altruism that men have to reject." Ayn Rand, "Faith and Force: The Destroyers of the Modern World," lectures at Yale University on February 17, 1960, Brooklyn College on April 4, 1960, and Columbia University on May 5, 1960.

The "communitarian" school encompasses this set of philosophical views, upholding the moral justification of loyalty and altruism. Besides Sandel, this school of thought includes historians, academics, and social thinkers such as Robert Putnam (author of *Bowling Alone: The Collapse and Revival of American Community*), Michael Walzer, William Galston, and Amitai Etzioni (who helped found the Communitarian Network in the early 1990s). Putnam cites globalization as a particular challenge to communitarianism. Describing the fracturing of his hometown of Port Clinton, Ohio, he laments "the radically shriveled sense of 'we,'" undone by technology, globalization, and the resulting loss of an "egalitarian ethos" in which society's members once cared for one another as they did in the 1950s.[19]

The "we" of whom Putnam speaks are members of his own community or hometown, and his nostalgia for a cohesive local community is no doubt compelling. Recent history suggests, however, that breaking up nations into new, more manageable communitarian units is hardly an unmixed blessing. It can lead to a new "tragedy of commonsense morality," as Greene might put it, undermining the moral imperatives owed to larger states or to the world community.

Perhaps the greatest proponent of world government of modern times, Woodrow Wilson, underpinned his belief with the conviction that "self-determination" for the myriad sectarian and ethnic groups in Europe and elsewhere could help avert future conflicts and contribute to global order. Indeed, he and his victorious allies from Britain and France pored over maps and tried to create new boundaries to permit such a thing to happen. "Self-determination is not a mere phrase," Wilson told Congress in 1918. "It is an imperative principle of action which statesmen will henceforth ignore at their peril."[20] But whereas Wilson believed that self-determination and the loyalty it would engender would lead to global stability, many others thought differently. Prophetically, Wilson's own secretary of state, Robert Lansing, warned of the dangers of promoting self-determination. "The phrase is simply loaded with dynamite," Lansing wrote in his diary. "It will raise hopes which can never be realized. It will, I fear, cost thousands of lives. In the end, it is bound to be discredited, to be called the dream of an idealist who failed to realize the danger until too late to check those who attempt to put the principle into force. What a calamity that the phrase was ever uttered! What misery it will cause! Think of the feelings of the author when he counts the dead who died because he uttered a phrase!"[21]

The concept of self-determination returned to the forefront after the collapse of communism and the Soviet empire and its satellites in the early 1990s, especially in the wake of the breakup of Yugoslavia and the eruption of the Balkan Wars. Supporting self-determination, the communitarian Michael Walzer wrote in 1992 of a "new tribalism" asserting itself in nation-states around the world as communities yearned to find meaning in their own identities, a trend he said should be encouraged or at least not necessarily opposed.[22] That call for greater tolerance of separatist movements was later widely criticized by liberals such as the literary scholar David Bromwich, who pointed out in 2014 how such movements had devolved into nasty religious and sectarian wars everywhere, particularly in Yugoslavia. Events in the two decades since the early 1990s have proven that criticism worth taking seriously because sectarian and ethnic rivalries erupted in scores of countries, especially in the Middle East but also in Europe, where restive or rebellious Scots, Basques, Catalonians, Corsicans, and most recently Russian-speaking eastern Ukrainians have pressed for their independence.[23]

In its manifesto, the Communitarian Network declared itself skeptical of social engineering, the elevation of individual rights over the health of a community, and attempts to change the basic social structures of other societies. "Neither human existence nor individual liberty can be sustained for long outside the interdependent and overlapping communities to which all of us belong," the manifesto states. "A communitarian perspective does not dictate particular policies; rather it mandates attention to what is often ignored in contemporary policy debates: the social side of human nature; the responsibilities that must be borne by citizens, individually and collectively, in a regime of rights; the fragile ecology of families and their supporting communities; and the ripple effects and long-term consequences of present decisions."[24]

Communitarians do not disavow social justice. Indeed, it is a defining element of their moral imperative. Their emphasis, however, is on seeking fulfilling and just social connections through groups rather than the nation-state. They embrace what sociologists and political scientists call the group theory of politics, which holds that the state in a pluralist society mediates among interest groups—for example, business corporations and labor unions—or engages in a cooperative arrangement with them. Beyond interest groups, however, loyalty is commanded by what the sociologist Herbert Gans has called micro societies—family, neighborhood, local schools, voluntary associations, and the workplace. "These micro societies are elements, though not the totality of what is now being called civil society," William Galston wrote, citing Gans. "They require special kinds of bonds of intimacy, continuity, and stability. Their characteristic language is a language of commitment, responsibility, duty, virtue, memory, solidarity, and even love rather than the discourse, valuable in its own right, of choice, rights, personal freedom, and individualism." Galston asserts that these bonds and connections are under assault by economic growth and change, "collectivized" social norms, and the legacy of condescension harbored by liberal elites toward the working class that peaked in the United States in the 1970s. While favoring the buildup of communities, however, Galston makes clear his opposition to barriers placed in the way of the free flow of goods, capital, and people.[25]

Rawls is not associated with the term *communitarian* (the term came into greater vogue after his death in 2002). But a much-debated element of his 1971 work *Theory of Justice* is that his principle of requiring that a society's actions not hurt the least well-off of its citizens applies mainly to one's own community or nation. Rawls maintains that each society is self-contained with understood norms, values, and traditions.[26] In *The Law of Peoples* (1999), he explains that—beyond a minimal obligation to combat famine, disease, slavery, and genocide in other countries—one society does not necessarily have an obligation or even a right to impose its moral principles on another. To insist that other nations follow one's own morals would be impractical and even coercive, he suggests.

Citing a hypothetical example, Rawls notes that some countries may choose policies that have the effect of keeping them poor, and such choices should be respected by outsiders. "I believe that the causes of the wealth of a people and the forms it takes lie in their political culture and in the religious, philosophical, and moral traditions that support the basic structure of their political and social institutions, as well as in the industriousness and cooperative talents of its members," he wrote. A nation's economic policies derive from factors particular to that country, such as an abundance or an absence of natural resources or choices made by its peoples democratically. The problem is practical as well as moral, he explains, adding that although there remains a "duty of assistance" to poor countries by rich countries, "merely dispensing funds will not suffice" in some circumstances because of their inability to use such assistance effectively.[27]

Correct or not, Rawls did not cite any particular examples of countries that have made these choices. But many in the West would argue that developing countries that hewed to socialism and maintained tight government regulation or ownership of business and natural resources stymied the growth of their economies for years. Often, these policies were adopted because these countries wanted to break from the rule of the economic and political elites inherited from colonial years. Throughout the Cold War, Western countries urged and even pressured poor countries to turn away from socialism, arguing that it was for their own good and for the good of their poor, but these arguments frequently fell on deaf ears. India, for example, was a mostly socialist economy after its independence in 1947. Its founders argued that socialism helped to ensure democracy and ease sectarian and ethnic divisions that could have worsened with the emergence of a wealthy class of economic overlords manipulating the political system and producing instability. Some Westerners were resigned to that choice. "If I have any opinion about this country at all, it is that it has been a moderate economic failure, but a distinct political success," Daniel Patrick Moynihan, ambassador to India in the 1970s, wrote to President Richard Nixon in 1973. Moynihan suggested that India willingly accepted slow growth as the price for political cohesiveness: "There is a sense in which India, not wholly unwitting, has taken vows of poverty."[28] Despite India's appalling poverty, Rawls might well have understood that tradeoff.

Thomas Nagel has noted that Rawls's view in some ways descends from that of Thomas Hobbes, the 17th-century political philosopher, who, Nagel explains, maintained that justice cannot be achieved except within a sovereign state. If Rawls is correct, Nagel says, the goal of justice must be achieved through "a world of internally just states" that do not impose their views on one another. But if Hobbes is right that justice can be guaranteed only by a strong sovereign, "the idea of *global* justice without a *world government* is a chimera."[29] Chimera or not, a yearning for world consciousness has become a major factor in the debate over globalization in recent decades.

Who Is a Cosmopolitan? "I Am a Citizen of the World"

In his account of the death of Socrates, Plutarch argued that the charge that Socrates was a traitor and threat to his community was buttressed by the philosopher proclaiming himself not an Athenian or a Greek but "a citizen of the world." The phrase has also been attributed to the Greek philosopher Diogenes of Sinope.[30]

Other examples dating from antiquity note the higher calling of loyalty to those beyond one's own border. In his book on global government, for example, Strobe Talbott applies the cosmopolitan principle to the spread of Christianity, as promoted by the apostle Paul, and later embodied in the Nicene Creed of the Roman emperor Constantine. "When I learned to recite this basic part of the Christian liturgy in Sunday school in the 1950s, I remember thinking that it sounded like the pledge of allegiance that began each day in the elementary school I attended during the week," Talbott wrote.[31]

In the 13th century, Dante Alighieri was an early supporter of the idea of a global government, but in his vision such a government was to be established on the principles of the Roman Empire, which supposedly imposed its peace, *Pax Romana*, on warring European nations.[32] Still another cosmopolitan in the pantheon is Immanuel Kant, who "considered himself first and foremost not a Prussian but a citizen of the world," according to one biographer.[33] Kant's essay "An Idea for a Universal History with a Cosmopolitan Purpose" prophesied an end to monarchy and imperialism, and, Talbott argues, "anticipates some of the major, if still unfulfilled, features of the United Nations system" of international law, nonintervention and nonaggression, self-determination, human rights, and democracy.[34]

But the originators of cosmopolitanism spoke little or not at all of the *economic* sphere, where the issues of justice raised by Rawls's "difference principle" take on a particular salience. Whereas Rawls argued, not unpersuasively, against the dangers of applying his principle to other societies, cosmopolitans contend that the citizens of rich countries have multiple obligations to pursue policies that help (or at least do no harm to) the poor in other countries, especially in those poor countries dominated by rich elites.

The international economic system makes citizens of rich countries feel connected to the destitute abroad. "My relation of co-membership in the system of international trade with the Brazilian who grows my coffee or the Philippine worker who assembles my computer is weaker than my relation of co-membership in US society with the Californian who picks my lettuce or the New Yorker who irons my shirts," observed Nagel. "But doesn't the first pair of relations as well as the second justify concern about the moral arbitrariness of the inequalities that arise through our joint participation in this system?"[35] Going further, some cosmopolitans direct their sympathies to particular ethnic, religious, racial, or gender groups deemed to suffer more than others. Such sympathizers are sometimes called "prioritarian" cosmopolitans. Among them is Martha Nussbaum, professor of law and ethics at the University of Chicago, who has argued that women deserve special consideration in a world that is tilted against them.[36]

For all the logic of global justice and the pronouncements going back to antiquity, the postulating of any kind of universal moral precepts that ought to govern relations between rich and poor countries—indeed, between all countries—is a modern phenomenon. Most philosophical and political writings since ancient times have presumed that nations or their antecedents, such as the city-states of antiquity, are justified in pursuing their economic, political, and strategic interests, letting others fend for themselves. Accordingly, it is also presumed that the rulers of countries or nation-states should put the stability and welfare of their own state above universal moral values. As Niccolo Machiavelli wrote in *The Prince*, "It must be understood that a prince, and especially a new prince, cannot observe all those things which are considered good in men, being often obliged, in order to maintain the state, to act against faith, against charity, against humanity, and against religion."[37]

Self-interest, properly contained, was a building block of stability in the 1648 treaties known as the Peace of Westphalia that ended the Thirty Years' War, fought among empires, nation-states, and religions. The new political order on the European continent established by the treaties was to be based on state sovereignty, self-determination, and noninterference. Yet it hardly challenged—indeed, it reinforced—the assumption that nation-states relentlessly pursue their self-interest in a perpetual state of competition and hostility.[38] Thomas Hobbes, in *Leviathan* (1651), viewed the state of nature among nations, as among men, to be inherently in conflict over basic pursuits of self-interest. He wrote, "In all times kings and persons of sovereign authority, because of their independency, are in continual jealousies, and in the state and posture of gladiators, having their weapons pointing, and their eyes fixed on one another, that is, their forts, garrisons, and guns upon the frontiers of their kingdoms, and continual spies upon their neighbours, which is a posture of war."[39]

In the era of diplomacy after World War II, in which US national interest in combatting communism was accompanied by a moral fervor, the heirs to the Hobbesian view were those "realists" who argued that self-interest, including the pursuit of compacts with distasteful regimes, had to take precedence over moral issues such as universal human rights. According to Stanley Hoffman of Harvard, among the most prominent contemporary heirs of this "realist" approach to foreign policy in the postwar era were Hans Morgenthau, George F. Kennan, and former secretary of state Henry Kissinger, who, with President Richard Nixon, overcame decades of moral opposition to Chinese communism to open relations with Communist China.[40] The higher purpose of the China opening was to counter Soviet hegemony and negotiate an end to the Vietnam War, in the process seeking a new equilibrium of national interests to secure world stability. Kennan is renowned for proposing a policy of containment directed at the Soviet Union, but the policy was based on self-interest, not on morals. "Morality as the foundation of civic virtue, and accordingly as a condition precedent to successful democracy—yes," he wrote in the 1960s. "Morality in governmental method, as a matter of conscience and preference on the part of our people—yes. But morality as a general criterion for the determination of the behavior of different states—no. Here other criteria, sadder, more limited, more practical, must be allowed to prevail."[41]

In recent decades, however, realists have had to share influence with a more idealistic approach to international relations, emphasizing human rights, economic justice, and protections of health and the environment. This more idealistic approach has also called for cooperation and enforcement of agreed-on rules through international organizations such as the United Nations, International Monetary Fund (IMF), World Bank, and World Trade Organization (WTO). The emergence of morality-based foreign policy has come and gone in the decades since the end of the Cold War, in part because of the fading communist threat. Human rights, democracy, peacekeeping, protection of the environment, limits on greenhouse gases, and efforts to stop the proliferation of nuclear, biological, and chemical weapons are all features of the US post–Cold War objectives, heading in the direction of cosmopolitanism. The supposed universal yearning for democracy and liberty, for example, has been a centerpiece of US dealings—not always honored as much as proclaimed—with authoritarian countries in the Arab world. As for alleviating poverty, the Cold War itself was filled with declarations by the United States that it wished to help the economically disadvantaged masses of the developing world, and yet it was manifestly in the self-interest of the United States to compete with the Soviet Union for allies and client states among poor countries. Helping them with foreign assistance would lift their peoples from poverty and in theory stabilize their political environments, but the self-serving parallel objective was to earn credit, loyalty, and security alliances with the West.

Theories of international justice in the economic sphere focusing on trade, investment, and aid relationships are a phenomenon of recent decades. Samuel Scheffler, professor of philosophy and law at New York University, argued recently that the concept of "global justice" has emerged only in the last three decades. "New books and articles about global justice appear almost daily," he wrote. "It has been the topic of numerous academic conferences and symposia, and outside of academia the idea has become a focal point for political activism across a broad front. There are global justice centers, global justice programs, global justice projects, and a global justice movement. An *Encyclopedia of Global Justice* was published in 2011. Yet the phrase hardly appeared in the philosophical literature at all prior to 1980, nor did it figure much in non-academic discourse."[42]

Rawls's emphasis on justice as applicable to one's own society has sparked a counterargument that his theories are too limited. Peter Singer, professor of bioethics at the University Center for Human Values at Princeton, takes Rawls to task on the issue of immigration, which Rawls said was not an obligation for a rich country. This view, said Singer, effectively dispenses justice depending on which side of a national border one happens to live.‡ Singer compares Rawls's view of justice as confined to one's own society as comparable to that of President George W. Bush, who in 2001 told German chancellor Gerhard Schröder that he would not sacrifice domestic economic growth to the cause of curbing climate change. Singer claims that the heedless emissions of carbon dioxide from the exhausts of gas-guzzling sports utility vehicles of the United States are no less an assault on global humanity than the terrorist attacks on the World Trade Center on September 11, 2001.[43]

Two other leading cosmopolitan theorists and advocates of international economic justice have also taken on Rawls: Charles Beitz, professor of politics at Princeton, and Thomas Pogge, professor of law and philosophy at Yale. More than three decades ago, Beitz's book *Political Theory and International Relations* (1979) broke ground on the issue by arguing for the relevance of economic justice on a global scale. In it, he claims that worldwide economic integration since Rawls has increased the urgency of combating global poverty, food and energy shortages, and exploitation of natural resources. Beitz also contends that Rawls took a blinkered approach, overlooking the importance of a changed global economy and the rise of supranational political authorities that can help set or enforce the rules. These organizations include the World Bank, the IMF, the WTO (and its forerunner the General Agreement on Tariffs and Trade, GATT), and many other organizations under the United Nations umbrella that Beitz maintains deepen rather than alleviate the world's economic injustices. Global economic interdependence, Beitz asserts, "widens the gap between rich and poor countries even though it produces absolute gains for almost all of them," and foreign investment by multinational corporations—which have created jobs for many in poor countries—"appears in some instances to exacerbate international inequality."[44] In his view, corporations that move profits and investments to escape taxation, seek friendly political environments, and pay low wages have subverted self-governance in poor societies, although he does not cite any examples. "International interdependence involves a complex and substantial pattern of social interaction, which produces benefits and burdens that would not exist if national economies were autarkic," says Beitz. "In view of these considerations, Rawls's passing concern for the law of nations seems to miss the point of international justice altogether."[45]

Beitz acknowledges the validity of Rawls's point that "different cultures might have radically different conceptions of what morality is" and that the

---

‡ Singer is perhaps best known for his advocacy of animal rights and the view that it is unacceptable for people of means to allow poverty to exist in the world. He also calls on people to aim for "effective altruism," giving a third of their income to charities for the poor and focusing on where the money does the most good.

West cannot be confident of the correctness of its concepts. But despite an understandable concern about "intellectual imperialism," minimal standards of justice are universally accepted as rational, he says.[46] A "broadly cosmopolitan" approach might reasonably be constrained by "one's responsibilities to one's own compatriots," Beitz concedes, but that this is not persuasive because it is obvious that one's own self-interest does not trump the morality of seeking equality in the society in which one lives.[47]

Pogge, who studied under Rawls at Harvard, argues that his mentor's view of justice as limited to one's own society would be justified only "if modern states were indeed closed schemes."[48] His argument is different from that of Singer. Whereas Singer calls on the wealthy to compromise their lifestyles and directly help the poor—the "duty-to-help" argument—Pogge argues that charity alone cannot substitute for changing an immoral system. Singer's argument is that one would no more refuse to rescue a child because of concern over dirtying one's new suit than one should refuse to give a portion of one's income in order to save a starving child on the other side of the interdependent world. Pogge says, "I see a violation not in the mere fact that people don't have enough to eat and that they are very vulnerable, but I see it in the fact that the economic institutional order of the world is associated with this very persistent poverty and that different institutional arrangements at the supranational level could stop and even reverse the slide towards ever-greater income disparities."[49] It happens that many economists share one change Pogge advocates—ending curbs on the transfer of intellectual property in pharmaceuticals to poor countries. Instead of innovators reaping profits from their discoveries, Pogge says drug companies should receive government subsidies if they innovate.[50]

Another student of these issues, Kwame Anthony Appiah, professor of philosophy at New York University, weighs the tradeoffs between cosmopolitanism and communitarianism in a different way. In Cosmopolitanism: Ethics in a World of Strangers (2006), he invokes the "splendidly philosophical" question raised by Adam Smith himself: Would a civilized European sacrifice his comfort to help victims of an earthquake in China? (According to Smith, this "man of humanity in Europe" would express his sorrow and misfortune for the Chinese, then reflect on the effects of commerce in Europe, and then return to his own affairs "with the same ease and tranquility as if no such accident had occurred."[51]) Appiah points out that "cosmopolitan moral judgment requires us to feel about everyone in the world what we feel about our literal neighbors," but this does not mean that distant sufferers have "the same grip on our sympathies as our nearest and dearest." Indeed, he adds, "we'd better start with the recognition that they don't."[52] Continuing in this vein, Appiah reflects, "Whatever my basic obligations are to the poor far away, they cannot be enough, I believe, to trump my concerns for my family, my friends, my country; nor can an argument that every life matters require me to be indifferent to the fact that one of those lives is mine."[53]

Reconciling the demands of communitarian and cosmopolitan principles becomes all the more difficult when the abstract is translated into the concrete realities of the global economy, the subject of the next chapter.

10

Grappling with the Communitarian-Cosmopolitan Tradeoff

I do not share in the apprehension held by many as to the danger of governments becoming weakened and destroyed by reason of their extension of territory. Commerce, education, and rapid transit of thought and matter by telegraph and steam have changed all this. Rather do I believe that our Great Maker is preparing the world, in His own good time, to become one nation, speaking one language.

—Ulysses S. Grant, second inaugural address (1873)

Among the leading American economists wrestling with the issue of inequality in recent years was the Federal Reserve Chairman, Ben Bernanke. In a speech that was part of the Fed's outreach campaign in 2007, Bernanke traveled to the American heartland to lay down some caveats. Americans, he said, "strive to provide equality of economic opportunity" but not to guarantee "equality of economic outcomes." Nevertheless, he added, "we also believe that no one should be allowed to slip too far down the economic ladder, especially for reasons beyond his or her control." Significantly for a Republican appointee, Bernanke told the Greater Omaha Chamber of Commerce that the "long-term trend toward greater inequality" in the United States was troubling, but it was hard to assess exactly why the trend had taken place. Among the factors, the Fed chairman acknowledged, was "the variety of economic forces grouped under the heading of 'globalization. . .even as these forces have provided a major stimulus to economic growth and to living standards overall."[1]

One can read through many dense and learned pages of discussions by contemporary moral philosophers about the obligations to the poor without finding much favorable about the markets and capitalism that are at the heart of globalization. Indeed, communitarians and cosmopolitans seem to share one common assumption: the worldwide economic system favors the wealthy over the poor as well as the upper classes over the middle class. But the proposition that globalization, or indeed capitalism, has favored the rich and hurt the poor is not as easy to prove or disprove as the noneconomist moral philosophers on both sides assert. As noted in the earlier discussion of inequality, the preponderance of evidence indicates that the overall raising of standards of living of poor people around the world, especially in Asia, has *lowered* inequality among nations and their people on a global scale. On the other hand, globalization appears to have contributed to greater inequality within the United States, as Bernanke suggested in 2007. The problem is defining the extent to which globalization has been a factor.

In 2012 the journalist Timothy Noah surveyed a range of studies of the effects of globalization on the US economy by many economists and concluded that trade and investment with poor countries were "responsible for 12 to 13 percent of the Great Divergence, and perhaps more," using the term for the phenomenon of growing inequality of US incomes.[2]

One reason for the difficulty in quantifying the benefits or costs of more open trade is that it is problematic if not impossible to prove the counterfactual of what sort of equalities and inequalities would have resulted *without* global trade and investment. For example, one counterfactual exercise about the benefits of global trade and investment, a benchmark study by the Peterson Institute for International Economics, concluded in 2005 that incomes in the United States are $1 trillion higher as a result of the increased integration with the world economy since 1945 and that the costs associated with workers losing their jobs and suffering adversely are about $50 billion a year.[3]

Still harder is to disaggregate factors such as globalization and technology, both of which have upended the status quo, especially in the last few decades. Take, for example, manufacturing. Since World War II, employment in the US manufacturing sector has declined dramatically. Indeed, employment in that sector went from nearly 20 million Americans in the late 1970s to fewer than 12 million after the Great Recession.[4] But many factors besides the outsourcing of manufacturing jobs to overseas factories help explain the decline. For one thing, American consumers nowadays spend less of their income on manufactured goods and more on services. More important, technology has allowed American factories to become more productive—to achieve the same output with fewer workers. For example, the United States employed 2.4 million textile and apparel workers in 1973 and 1.3 million in 2005. The Bureau of Labor Statistics attributes that loss not simply to foreign competition but to new technologies, mergers undertaken to reduce costs, and other efforts to increase productivity.[5] Other studies have found that export powerhouses such as Germany and Japan have also streamlined their manufacturing sectors with the use of technologies and that their job losses are similar to those in the United States.[6]

Offshoring and Reshoring

Economic theory holds that when goods move easily around the world, the loss of low-skilled jobs in advanced countries becomes inevitable when the low-skilled labor that can fill such jobs is available in large quantities in poor countries. According to the Hecksher-Ohlin theory—put forward first by the economist Eli Filip Hecksher in 1919 and later in collaboration with Bertil Ohlin in 1933—countries produce goods based on the factors of production they enjoy in relative abundance. The evidence for the theory is mixed, but it has helped to explain why the United States specializes in exports of capital-intensive, high-technology goods and loses out on unskilled labor to developing countries exploiting their advantage in that area. In the simplest terms, the United States keeps "good jobs" with good wages and sends "bad jobs" with low wages overseas under free trade, though the gains of their prosperous coworkers—not to mention the gains of unskilled factory workers in China, Mexico, and Vietnam—are hardly any solace to the millions of Americans who lose these so-called bad jobs.

As illustrated by President Barack Obama's encounter with Apple's Steve Jobs (described in chapter 9), manufacturers invest in factories in poor countries not only because labor is cheap but also because technology allows manufacturers to rely more heavily on unskilled labor than in the past. According to the Stolper-Samuelson theory advanced in 1941 by economists Wolfgang Stolper and Paul Samuelson, a nation that manufactures goods with inexpensive labor and sells them to a rich nation with higher wages will raise the wages of its own workforce but lower the wages of the unskilled workers in the wealthier nation. This theory would then support the observed evidence that unskilled wages in the United States are stagnating at least in part because of expanding trade.

In recent years, however, there is some evidence that the trend is being reversed. Some "reshoring" has been under way as companies have discovered advantages in the United States stemming from its lower energy costs, the opportunity to avoid high shipping costs, and even competitive wages in some cases. Meanwhile, wages have gone up in formerly low-wage countries such as China. According to the *Economist*, the Boston Consulting Group surveyed US manufacturing companies in April 2012 and found that 37 percent were "planning or actively considering" shifting their production from China to the United States. Similar findings were reported by the Massachusetts Institute of Technology and the Hackett Group, a consulting company in Florida. The *Economist* article claimed, however, that the trend is still in favor of more offshoring, and many companies are trumpeting their "reshoring" simply because it is good publicity.[7]

Although relocating production may seem to be a contemporary business practice, the process is as old as the Industrial Revolution. In the 1880s, textile mills—once a dominant industry in New England and upstate New York—began moving South, and the trend accelerated after World War II. Likewise, in more recent decades the automobile industry has declined in Detroit and transplanted itself to the South. Meanwhile, factories and offices in big cities moved to the suburbs and rural office parks in distant locations in the 1950s, 1960s, and 1970s, dampening the employment prospects for largely unskilled blacks in inner cities. All these moves in the United States were accompanied by complaints about job losses, obsolete communities, and prophecies of doom. In 1964, for example, a panel of experts, including the chemist Linus Pauling, the economist Gunnar Myrdal, and Gerard Piel, publisher of

Scientific American, warned President Lyndon Johnson that massive unemployment would result from replacing millions of blue-collar and clerical jobs with machines that keep tabs on records at banks, handle executive schedules and appointments, process loan applications, and do the myriad tasks that used to be done by people who, although they did not get rich, at least functioned well with a high school education. The prophets of disaster failed to foresee, however, that these old jobs would be replaced by new jobs—managers, engineers, teachers, technicians, financiers—requiring the education and skills needed to exploit technology and improve productivity.[8] Still, the alarms continue to ring about technology as well as globalization, the theme of a more recent scholarly study of the issue, *The Second Machine Age: Work, Progress, and Prosperity in a Time of Brilliant Technologies* by Erik Brynjolfsson and Andrew McAfee.[9] The challenge in the face of that alarm, however, can be addressed more by education and training than by stopping the clock on technological change. In their book *The Race between Education and Technology*, economists Claudia Goldin and Lawrence Katz argue that the US education system, which used to be the envy of the world, has not prepared Americans for the newly competitive global economy.[10]

Trade and Globalization: Lifting All Boats or Only Yachts?

Because of the recent economic difficulties of the United States, the dominant voices on these issues today are probably those of the leading nonprofit organizations who view the rise of globalization and trade as hurting the poor in the United States and in other countries and who oppose additional agreements to lower trade and investment barriers with other countries, especially poor countries. The International Forum on Globalization represents a diverse group of unions, farmers, peasants in poor countries, women's and youth organizations, consumer advocates, environmentalists, AIDS and health activists, intellectuals, and others. It maintains that the benefits of globalization have "gone to the few at the exclusion of many." Rather than a rising tide lifting all boats, as trade proponents like to say of growth resulting from trade, the forum claims that globalization instead lifts "only yachts."[11] The forum has even suggested that the United States should grow its own food and produce its own necessities to maintain domestic livelihoods, a throwback to the days before the repeal of the Corn Laws in Britain in the 1840s, which marked the beginning of the era of freer trade in the 19th century.[12]

Many critics of globalization may be able to cite correctly the undeniable disadvantages that trade poses for lower-skilled workers, but they engage in some fallacious thinking. For example, antitrade groups routinely say that high trade deficits lead to higher unemployment in the United States, arguing that because Americans are buying more goods from overseas they should in theory be buying the same goods made domestically. But the cheap electronic gadgets, clothing, shoes, toys, and components imported by the United States are in many cases no longer made at home anyway. In addition, it is an established fact that the trade deficit increases at times of higher domestic *prosperity* because Americans are buying more goods generally, including more foreign-made goods that are not being made at home. For example, during one of the biggest periods of economic expansion, from 1992 to 2000, US imports increased nearly 240 percent. During the same period total US employment also grew at a nearly unprecedented rate, by 22 million jobs, and the unemployment rate fell from 7.5 to 4 percent, the lowest rate in more than 30 years.[13]

Balanced against job losses from globalization are what many would argue are gains to consumers from being able to buy less expensive imported goods. In 1994 Gary Clyde Hufbauer and Kimberly Ann Elliott of the Institute for International Economics (IIE) found that tariffs and quotas on imports in 1990 cost American consumers about $70 billion, or more than 1 percent of GDP, especially in higher prices for textiles and apparel.[14] (Many of these restrictions on clothing and textile imports were subsequently eased in the Uruguay Round of the General Agreement on Tariffs and Trade.) Still, the *Washington Post* pointed out in 2013 that Americans were paying more than $10 billion in tariffs on clothing in 2011, raising the cost of a pair of jeans made of Chinese cotton by 16 percent.[15] Another IIE study in 1997 by William Cline concluded that "a balanced reading of existing literature" shows that only about a tenth of the gap between skilled and unskilled wages could be explained by trade and immigration. But Cline also said that the increased supply of *skilled* labor probably caused wages to *fall* for these workers, contributing to greater wage equality.[16]

Some recent dramatic and powerful studies have illustrated the intuitive idea that trade has led to prosperity in China and problems in the United States. In 2013 David Autor, David Dorn, and Gordon Hanson, surveying 722 local US markets (or "commuting zones"), found that Chinese manufacturing imports between 1990 and 2007 cost the United States 1.4 million manufacturing jobs, reduced US wages, and increased the costs of government benefits for the unemployed, disabled, and retired. It was during this period that US imports from China increased 11.5 times.[17] A similar study by Peter Schott of the Yale School of Management and Justin Pierce of the Federal Reserve in 2012 found that the "sharp drop" in US manufacturing employment after 2001 resulted in part from a surge in imports from China and an increasing number of US companies offshoring their production to China, which had just been granted a phase-in of normal trading status with the United States.[18] A paper by Avraham Ebenstein, Ann Harrison, and Margaret McMillan published in 2015 by the National Bureau of Economic Research examined why Americans are getting poorer, as the authors put it. They found "significant effects of globalization, with offshoring to low-wage countries and imports both associated with wage declines of US workers." Globalization, they said, "has led to the reallocation of workers away from high-wage manufacturing jobs into other sectors and other occupations, with large declines in wages among workers who switch, explaining the large differences between industry and occupational analyses." Yet they also said that "other factors such as increasing computer use and substitution of capital for labor are significantly more important determinants of US employment rates across occupations."[19]

The number of American workers who lose jobs varies over time, and it is not easy to say which factors cause their "displacement." In 2014 the Labor Department reported that from January 2011 through December 2013, 4.3 million workers were involuntarily "displaced" from jobs they had held for at least three years, a number that was down from 6.1 million workers from the previous survey over a similar period of time (during the depth of the global financial crisis). By January 2014, 61 percent of these workers were reemployed, though only half at jobs with pay levels equivalent to or greater than what they had been earning. A little more than a third of those displaced lost their jobs because of plants or companies closing or relocating. Nearly one out of five of the total who lost those jobs were in manufacturing.[20] In a 2001 study, Lori Kletzer estimated that about 100,000 US workers lose their jobs each year because of the increase in imports, and in their replacement jobs they undergo pay cuts of 30 percent or more. However, about twice this number lose jobs but are able to find new employment at pay equal to or greater than what they were earning previously. Kletzer also found that from 1979 to 1999, 6.4 million workers were displaced from an import-competing industry out of 17 million workers displaced in manufacturing generally. All these workers tended to find new jobs at less pay, though not all were forced into lower-paying service jobs. Women were especially likely to be the victims in the apparel, footwear, and knitting industries.[21]

A 2013 study by Michael Elsby of the University of Edinburgh, Bart Hobjin of the Federal Reserve Bank of San Francisco, and Aysegul Sahin of the Federal Reserve Bank of New York concluded that the decline in the US labor share of the economy over the previous quarter-century was driven in large part by the rise in imports and the offshoring of labor-intensive components of the US supply chain. Their study dismissed technology and even the decline in unionization as factors in this phenomenon, which they said had been under way since before the 1980s. "Based on this suggestive evidence," they reasoned, "if globalization continues during the next decades, the labor share will continue to decline, especially in sectors that face the largest increases in foreign competition."[22]

Many of the concerns about globalization have focused on the loss of manufacturing jobs; however, more recent concerns have centered on the loss of jobs in the services sector, where the United States has long been more competitive. For example, in a study of the effects of offshoring as opposed to trade, Alan Blinder, professor of economics at Princeton and former vice chairman of the Federal Reserve, raised concerns in 2007 that more than a quarter of US jobs in services—"tens of millions" of them—were vulnerable to being shipped overseas, from medical records technicians to customer complaint call centers. Later, Blinder estimated that 22–29 percent of the US services workforce was "potentially offshorable."[23] Nobel Laureate economist Michael

Spence and Sandile Hlatshwayo, a researcher at the New York University Stern School of Business, have also warned that higher-paying jobs in all sectors are on their way to leaving the United States, potentially aggravating inequality and unequal distribution of wealth.[24]

Finally, in its 2012 report *State of Working America*, the pro–labor movement Economic Policy Institute (EPI) claimed that 6.5 percent of US employment is "highly offshorable," and another 15.1 percent is "offshorable." It was suggesting, then, that 31.6 million jobs are vulnerable to being sent overseas, a figure that it said was invoked by employers in order to suppress wage growth.[25] "Globalization might be a minority player behind the rise in inequality, but it's not a minor one," wrote Josh Bivens of the EPI. He concludes that it was a factor of between 10 and 40 percent in the past, and more so in recent years.[26]

The arc of the thinking of the economist Paul Krugman illustrates the ambivalence of many about globalization and its effects on inequality. Since his earliest years as a trade economist, Krugman has until recently championed liberalized trade. The evolution of his views is instructive. In the 1990s, Krugman said trade was not significantly responsible for the declining real wages of less educated workers. Raising trade barriers, he asserted, would "destroy the most promising aspect of today's world economy: the beginning of widespread economic development, of hopes for a decent living standard for hundreds of millions, even billions, of human beings."[27] A decade and a half later, Krugman shifted his views somewhat, saying the contributions to inequality of the influx of goods from low-wage manufacturing countries (principally China) "may well be considerably larger now than they were in the early 1990s."[28] Nonetheless, he continued to argue that exports offered poor countries "their best hope of moving up the income ladder."[29] In 2015 Krugman, a proponent of the benefits of the North American Free Trade Agreement (NAFTA), emerged as a major skeptic about the advantages of the Trans-Pacific Partnership.[30]

Proponents of open US trade policies, acknowledging that they have adverse effects on some Americans, favor programs to help those that are harmed. Successive Congresses since the Kennedy years have authorized the Trade Adjustment Assistance (TAA) program to help farmers, workers, businesses, and communities cope with the damage caused by imports. President John Kennedy put it this way in a special message to Congress in 1962: "When considerations of national policy make it desirable to avoid higher tariffs, those injured by that competition should not be required to bear the full brunt of the impact. Rather, the burden of economic adjustment should be borne in part by the Federal Government."[31]

TAA has been a constant in US trade policy, renewed many times over the years. However, in part because of budget constraints in recent years, it has not kept up with the problem of helping workers, businesses, and communities adjust to the impacts of trade. Over the years, it has disbursed roughly $1 billion annually and yet has assisted only some of the many workers affected by job displacement.

In 2015 Congress reauthorized the TAA to spend $450 million a year through 2021 as part of congressional approval of President Obama's trade negotiation authority. Many advocates of trade have argued for expanded efforts by the US government to help those who have lost their jobs from both trade and technology, but these efforts have fallen short of advocates' hopes.[32] The TAA reauthorization in 2015 was considered a major victory by such proponents, however, because the program was extended for seven years and the number of people eligible was expanded.[33]

Case Study of Loyalty: Divided over NAFTA

Few examples illustrate the deeply mixed feelings among Americans over trade better than the debate in the United States in the early 1990s over the North American Free Trade Agreement, which opened up nothing less than a new epoch in the world of trade relations. After decades of globally organized efforts to lower trade and investment barriers with a multitude of nations starting in the 1960s, NAFTA was the first trade pact between the United States, which was joined by Canada in the deal, and a major poorer, lower-wage country. Policymakers in the administrations of George H. W. Bush and Bill Clinton aimed not simply to boost exports to Mexico, which had higher barriers for US goods than the United States had for Mexican goods. They and other backers of NAFTA also hoped to lift a struggling and impoverished neighboring country by mobilizing foreign trade and investment to stimulate Mexico's political and economic reforms, stabilize a country that was veering close to the status of a failed state, and in the process discourage its citizens from flooding illegally across the border to the United States. The debate served as a template for future discussions, including the arguments over the Trans-Pacific Partnership (TPP) and other trade accords in 2015.

NAFTA committed the United States and Mexico to eliminating all tariffs over a 10-year period, except for some agricultural products that were to be phased out after 15 years. The loss of jobs was a major part of the debate, as was the opportunity to turn globalization to US advantage, but there was also some discussion about the moral issue of helping lift economic opportunity among Mexicans and stabilizing it as a country with problems that had caused immigration to the United States to increase. Also important in the debate was the simple question of whether either side was being honest in assessing the gains and losses to be obtained from opening trade with a poor neighboring country. Lawmakers, not surprisingly, shied away from dealing with the issues in abstract moral terms. Instead they addressed the needs of their own constituents. The axiom that all politics are local was writ large with NAFTA.

The NAFTA story began with the opening of Ronald Reagan's candidacy for president in 1979. His announcement included a little-noticed proposal for an economic cooperation agreement with Canada and Mexico. A former governor of California, Reagan carefully avoided the words "trade agreement." Part of his aim appeared to be to wean Mexico off its socialist ideology and hostility to imports and foreign investment. But Mexico was not ready to do so.[34] Reagan's successor, the first president Bush, revived the proposal in the late 1980s, promising to sweeten the deal by opening debt relief discussions with Mexico, according to Mexican president Carlos Salinas de Gortari. Salinas initially rejected this second approach, but then realized that the world had changed since the fall of the Berlin Wall, the collapse of the Soviet Union, and the growing economic integration of Europe. Mexico, he reasoned, needed to keep pace with these developments. "Globalization became an inevitable force," Salinas later said. "We had to confront this new political and economic reality."[35]

In the 1992 presidential campaign, most Democrats voiced concerns about trade deals they feared would hurt American workers and growers. Clinton, then the Democratic nominee and governor of Arkansas, claimed he could have negotiated a better deal. Once in the White House, he persuaded Mexico to accept several "side agreements" to ensure better enforcement of its labor and environmental laws, a step aimed at ensuring that Mexico's cheap imports did not exact a social cost for Mexicans—and also ensuring that imported goods would be a bit more expensive and less competitive with US goods. On the eve of the vote in Congress in late 1993, Clinton brought Presidents Gerald Ford, George Bush, and Jimmy Carter to the White House to support ratification, framing the issue in terms of its benefits to Americans rather than Mexicans. "NAFTA means jobs, American jobs and good-paying American jobs," he said. "If I didn't believe that, I wouldn't support this agreement."[36]

But the obstacles to approval in 1993 were formidable. In April of that year, *Businessweek* magazine called NAFTA "an unprecedented, politically explosive First World–Third World marriage" in which the United States would face competition posed by 10 million "skilled and semiskilled workers" at plants producing autos, TVs, computers, and other goods.[37] The *Wall Street Journal* reported that 455 executives said in a poll that they were "inclined to move some manufacturing to Mexico in the next few years" and that "more than one third of US companies" think the accord "will be at least somewhat unfavorable for American workers."[38]

The most memorable episode of the disputes occurred on CNN's *Larry King Live* show on November 9, 1993, in a debate between Vice President Al Gore and billionaire businessman H. Ross Perot. Perot had warned the previous year that NAFTA would produce a "giant sucking sound" of jobs lost, specifically claiming that 5.9 million jobs might disappear under the agreement. Put differently, he warned that half of US manufacturing jobs would be moving to Mexico. In the debate, Perot claimed that NAFTA, far from helping Mexican workers, would perpetuate their mistreatment. "Livestock in this country, and animals, have a better life than good, decent, hardworking Mexicans working for major US companies," he declared. Gore responded by accusing Perot of embracing the philosophy of the Smoot-Hawley Tariff of 1930, which economic historians say helped deepen the Great Depression by raising trade barriers. He showed a picture of Senator Reed Smoot and Representative Willis C. Hawley and sarcastically said Perot should hang it on his wall. When Gore declared that NAFTA was a "good deal" that would lead to more jobs, Perot shot back: "And there is a tooth fairy and there is an Easter Bunny."[39]

A significant aspect of Perot's arguments was that they went far beyond Mexico into making the case for economic autonomy of the kind reminiscent of the Corn Laws in Britain in the early 19th century. Perot claimed that after World War II the United States had been hoodwinked into importing from countries it had defeated out of a misguided attempt to help them get back on their feet. It was dangerous, he said, to import steel from Europe and Asia, aluminum from Russia, oil from the Middle East, and integrated circuits from Asia, where Toyota hired a "war criminal" to run one of its plants in Japan. In the 1992 presidential campaign, Perot, who ran as an independent, even suggested that the United States had been short-sighted in building up Germany and Japan after World War II, turning them into economic competitors.[40] It was a bold assertion, but Perot was suggesting that it had not been worth it to turn onetime enemies into prosperous allies at the cost of American jobs. In effect, he was attacking the entire postwar rationale for freer trade and investment aimed at building a stable new world order based on economic integration and shared prosperity.

Clinton's arguments rested on the theme that the United States should not wish away the challenges posed by global interdependence. "Nothing we do, nothing we do in this great capital can change the fact that factories or information can flash across the world, that people can move money around in the blink of an eye," he declared. "Nothing can change the fact that technology can be adopted, once created, by people across the world and then rapidly adapted in new and different ways by people who have a little different take on the way the technology works. For two decades, the winds of global competition have made these things clear to any American with eyes to see."[41] But the key to his NAFTA advocacy was that it would create 200,000 jobs in its first two years and a million jobs in its first five years.

To back up his numbers, Clinton cited what he said were 19 studies "by liberals and conservatives alike," and he claimed that 18 of them had concluded "there will be no job loss" resulting from approving the trade pact.[42] If he was referring to a report by the Congressional Research Service (CRS) the previous April 1993 estimating that "at least 20 studies have concluded that NAFTA will have little overall or net effect on US employment and wages," he left something out. The CRS also said that any gains and losses would be small and would "essentially balance each other out."[43] Basic economic theory holds that trade, in a full employment environment, does not "create" or "destroy" the total number of jobs but that it alters the composition of the workforce, with different kinds of jobs created to balance out those lost.[44] Winners might equal losers, but that did not mean that the losers would get the jobs created for winners. The CRS said that among the "winners" from NAFTA would be some US farmers and producers of textiles, apparel, chemicals, machinery, electronics, and auto parts. Financial, legal, accounting, insurance, and technology services would also gain. But many farm producers, including growers of fresh fruits and vegetables, would be hurt, along with manufacturers in some of the same sectors that would gain, including textiles, apparel, appliances, consumer electronics, autos and auto parts, and furniture because Mexican goods in these areas would be more competitively priced. "Which side is right—those who view NAFTA as an opportunity or those who view it as a threat?" the CRS asked. "Arguably, both are."[45]

Thus the arguments made by the president and NAFTA's critics came down to jobs at home versus jobs abroad, jobs for middle-class Americans versus jobs for poor Mexicans, jobs for some parts of the country versus job losses for other parts. The US Commerce Department estimated that every $1 billion in exports generated 19,000 jobs. (Because of gains in productivity since the early 1990s, in 2012 the department lowered its estimate of jobs created directly and indirectly by $1 billion in exports to a little more than 5,000 jobs.[46]) But at one congressional hearing, Senator Carl Levin, a Michigan Democrat, dismissed Clinton's claim that NAFTA would create 200,000 new jobs during its first two years as "not credible" because it failed to count the jobs displaced by imports and plants shifting to Mexico.[47] He demanded that the Commerce official giving testimony calculate the number of jobs that might be lost to balance those to be gained. "We haven't done that calculation," responded the official, adding that such an exercise would be "just very difficult to do." Levin asked whether the official would concede that NAFTA would produce at least some job losses. "I would concede that," the official replied, asserting that, on the other hand, many of these losses would have occurred anyway because of competition by other low-wage trading partners in Asia.[48]

During the congressional debate, a New York Times economics reporter said that Clinton's support of NAFTA "represents one of the most courageous acts of his young presidency" because lost jobs were always felt more acutely than jobs created, and many of these losses would occur in Democratic voting districts. "No congressman would vote for a measure that lost 10,000 jobs in his district," Senator Bill Bradley, the New Jersey Democrat (and a NAFTA supporter), said. "What you lose is always more vivid than what you gain."[49] Indeed, an analysis of congressional voting patterns published in 2006 unsurprisingly found that lawmakers' votes were determined by the "expected job gains/losses" in each district as well as the influence of organized labor.[50]

A common theme of the congressional debate was the excruciating nature of the dilemma it posed. Lawmakers confessed that they were torn by loyalties to their own communities versus the larger good of the country, if not that of a neighboring poor country. "NAFTA has got to be one of the most difficult decisions I have ever made since I came to Congress," said Representative Marty Martinez of California, who ended up voting "no."[51] The entire debate amounted to combat by anecdote. Sad stories and success stories competed with each other. The stories of loss tended to be the most compelling. An Arizona Democrat lamented that a yogurt manufacturer in his district would be moving to Mexico. A Georgia congressman said his state's peanut farmers would be wiped out. A lawmaker cited the decision by Green Giant to shut down a plant employing 800 in Watsonville, California, and move all the jobs to Gigante Verde in Mexico.[52]

Some lawmakers were frank enough to say that even if there were net gains from NAFTA, they were not worth losses among those hurt. "Nobody knows exactly how many jobs we will wind up winning or losing net," said Representative David Obey of Wisconsin. "But we do know, even the administration admits, that there will be at least 200,000 people who will lose their jobs. And what are we giving to them? Table scraps."[53]

NAFTA proponents came armed with job numbers from their constituents and local chambers of commerce. An Arizona Republican said 14,000 new jobs had been created in the previous year because of trade with Mexico. An Indiana congressman spoke of 95,000 "Hoosier jobs" to be created in auto parts, agribusiness, and steel. Others cited jobs to be created at Kodak, Xerox, General Motors, Bausch and Lomb, and various chemical, telecommunications, and high-tech businesses.[54] A wave of emotion engulfed the House as it voted. Representative Marcy Kaptur of Ohio wept openly as the votes were cast in favor, 234–200. As predicted, most Republicans voted yes and most Democrats no, despite Clinton's advocacy.[55]

The Senate debate, by contrast, was an anticlimax, but the same arguments were heard, with some additional rhetorical flourishes suggesting that gains outweighing losses did not matter to those who suffered from jobs going elsewhere. Senator Edward Kennedy of Massachusetts derided the concept of a "net gain"—a "little word with big implications—net." Warming to the tortured pun, he said, "That word slips easily off economists' tongues. But it has a devastating impact on all those who are caught in the net and whose jobs and livelihoods are at risk."[56] In the end, however, Kennedy voted yes, as did 60 of his Senate colleagues; the vote was 61–38. Clinton, welcoming the vote, repeated his job claims but acknowledged there would be some losses. "This is the world we face," he said. "We cannot stop global change. We cannot repeal the international economic competition that is everywhere."[57]

The Continuing Trade Debate

The debate over NAFTA has never gone away. It has shadowed every free trade agreement since its enactment, and it was cited repeatedly in Congress in the first decade of the 21st century by opponents of trade agreements with Colombia and South Korea. NAFTA cast its shadow over the debate in Congress on whether to authorize President Barack Obama to negotiate trade agreements between the United States and Europe—the Transatlantic Trade and Investment Partnership (TTIP)—and between the United States and 11 Asia-Pacific nations—the Trans-Pacific Partnership. In fact, the TPP was specifically and routinely derided by critics as "NAFTA on steroids."[58] It was, they said, an accord that would kill American jobs, contribute to inequality and wage stagnation, encourage sweatshops in Asia and Latin America, weaken environmental and food safety protections in the United States and its trading partners, protect the patents of pharmaceutical companies, and create an extrajudicial body that would allow multinational organizations to sue governments over regulations they consider harmful to profits.

The Obama administration argued that the TPP would make it easier to sell American-made products overseas, impose strong and enforceable labor and environmental standards on trading partners, and expand jobs in the small business sector by enabling these businesses to export to fast-growing parts of Asia and Latin America. Echoing some of the arguments on NAFTA, Michael Froman, the administration's special trade envoy, argued that exports were currently supporting nearly 12 million US jobs, and that these jobs were 18 percent higher-paying than jobs outside the export sector. With the TPP and TTIP in place, Froman said, "American workers, farmers, ranchers, and businesses of all sizes will have access to nearly two-thirds of the global economy."[59] As with NAFTA, geostrategic arguments were among the most powerful advanced by Obama and his team. The president contended that a TPP would enable the United States, not China, to write the rules on investment, trade, intellectual property protection, and environment and labor standards as trade and investment expand. The accord was advertised as achieving two contradictory aims: setting up an economic alliance that could challenge China's dominance of East Asia and setting up a regime that China could join in the future if it adopted the TPP's standards.

Republicans in Congress overwhelmingly supported the TPP, but Obama was unable to get more than a small minority of members of his own party to back him. Democrats were more persuaded by critics that the TPP would cost jobs and reinforce the problems facing the US working class. The AFL-CIO waged an expensive campaign of advertising and lobbying in the districts of wavering Democratic lawmakers, and the trade authorization legislation barely squeaked through Congress in mid-2015. It remained to be seen whether the final agreement of TPP, reached in October 2015, would be approved by Congress.

A striking truism about NAFTA, the TPP, and all recent trade debates is their illustration of what the psychologist Daniel Kahneman, Nobel Laureate in economics, calls "loss aversion"—the phenomenon that the fear of loss is a much more intense emotion for most people than the hope of gaining something, even if the potential gain outweighs the loss. Kahneman is one of the pioneers in economics who has jettisoned the longtime concept embraced by economists that human behavior in the economic sphere is rational. Instead, he has advanced a "prospect theory" that humans apply to real-life situations in which they weigh hopes, fears, and other emotions in a less than fully logical manner.[60] Along with his colleague Amos Tversky, Kahneman has written that "loss aversion" tends to favor the status quo over change in any case.[61]

The claims of 1993 about NAFTA remain instructive for all trade debates. Both Clinton's claim of 200,000 jobs created in two years and Perot's claim that 5.9 million US jobs would disappear turned out to be overblown. The prediction of many experts supporting NAFTA that the United States would export more to Mexico than it imported proved to be completely erroneous, largely because of the peso crisis later in 1994, resulting in a devaluation that scared away investors and reduced imports. As described in chapter 7, only a US-orchestrated rescue of Mexico in 1995 staved off an even worse disaster.

But by nearly every measure, the United States, Canada, and Mexico are far more economically interdependent today, and perhaps more prosperous, than they were before NAFTA. Some would argue that NAFTA has stabilized their relationship politically as well—no small consideration considering the vexing issue of immigration over the heavily guarded border. US exports to Mexico are now more than the combined total of its merchandise exports to Germany, France, the United Kingdom, and the Netherlands. Since 1993, US trade with Mexico has quintupled in nominal terms, compared with three times with the rest of the world.[62] But the Congressional Research Service concluded in 2012 that only "some" of the increase in US-Mexico trade since the 1990s was attributable to NAFTA, and that this increase had little impact on the US economy because trade with Mexico amounted to less than 3 percent of US GDP. According to the CRS, a sharp rise in US investment in Mexico resulted primarily from Mexico's unilateral steps to liberalize restrictions on investment rather than from NAFTA itself, although the possibility of increasing exports under NAFTA encouraged investments to flow into the country.[63] Meanwhile, in 2005 Gary Clyde Hufbauer and Jeffrey Schott of the Peterson Institute for International Economics concluded that their earlier estimate of 170,000 jobs added "over several years" was "statistically insignificant" in any case considering the tens of millions of jobs gained and lost each year in the labor market. They said it was "impossible to say whether the plants moved because of NAFTA or would have left in search of lower labor costs regardless."[64]

Yet the uneasiness of critics in the labor movement continues. In 2003, for example, the Economic Policy Institute said that NAFTA had "caused the displacement of production that supported 879,280 jobs," a figure derived from how many more jobs there would be if the US trade deficit with Canada and Mexico had not grown since 1993. The analysis assumed, dubiously, that anything imported from Mexico would have been made in the United States if NAFTA had not been enacted—and therefore that anything imported from Mexico potentially cost US jobs.[65] But as previously stated, trade deficits tend to go up at the same time that employment and growth also expand in the United States, not the other way around. Indeed, despite rising trade deficits with Mexico, the prediction of many that NAFTA would unleash a new wave of unemployment faded in the 1990s. In the seven-year period after NAFTA, the United States added nearly 17 million jobs, and unemployment dropped from 6.9 to 4 percent.[66] As for Mexico, from 1993 to 2013 its exports expanded 640 percent, and its real GDP per capita grew 31 percent—not as well as in some other Latin American countries such as Chile but enough to vault Mexico into the category of the world's major emerging-market countries.[67]

Facts, by themselves, will never definitely resolve the arguments over the effects of trade and investment on inequality or economic justice in general. Globalization, and indeed the full array of political conflicts in the modern era, must be resolved by men and women, not idealized concepts and truths. Moreover, citizens of the world must address these conflicts through political or representative institutions, imperfect as they must be—the subject of the next chapter.

11

Loyalties in Conflict:

Jobs, Communities, and Multinational Corporations

Sympathy, we shall allow, is much fainter than our concern for ourselves, and sympathy with persons remote from us, much fainter than with persons near and contiguous.
—David Hume, *An Inquiry Concerning the Principles of Morals* (1751)

It should also be remembered that, in the economic sphere, the principal form of assistance needed by developing countries is that of allowing and encouraging the gradual penetration of their products into international markets, thus making it possible for these countries to participate fully in international economic life.
—Pope Benedict XVI, *Caritas in Veritate* (2009)

In 2001, barely two months after the airliner hijackings and attacks on the World Trade Center in New York City and the Pentagon in Washington, the world's trade ministers embarked on a new global trade agenda with a priority unlike that of any previous trade rounds. The objective, the ministers said in Doha, the capital of Qatar, was specifically to "ensure that developing countries, and especially the least-developed among them, secure a share in the growth of world trade commensurate with the needs of their economic development" and achieve "enhanced market access" for their goods in richer nations. "We are committed to addressing the marginalization of least-developed countries in international trade and to improving their effective participation in the multilateral trading system," the ministers declared.[1]

As the Doha Round talks foundered in 2005, however, Pascal Lamy, the beleaguered director-general of the World Trade Organization (WTO), betrayed his own frustration when he called yet again for rich and poor countries alike to be more open about lowering their barriers. Poor countries were eager to export farm products, cotton, and other commodities not only to rich countries but also to other poor countries, he noted. However, many of these other poor countries opposed opening up their markets to foreign goods, citing the loss of jobs in their own farm sectors. Lamy said the Doha Round would not work unless all countries opened their borders to more imports: "I should add that market access interests lie not only in developed country markets, but also in other developing country markets and improved opportunities in South-South trade."[2]

In 2008, however, the Doha Round fell apart because the United States and European countries (and Japan) refused to lower their barriers unless the wealthier emerging-market countries—China, Brazil, India, and other countries in Africa and Latin America—did the same for their agricultural and manufactured goods and for services. But these emerging-market countries did not see it as their obligation to help the poorest countries of the world compete against them. An analogous situation arises at least theoretically over the obligations that cosmopolitans say should be felt by the United States toward poor countries. As William Galston has pointed out, from the standpoint of "pure cosmopolitanism," in which every citizen of the world counts the same morally, one would have to note that the poorest Americans are roughly 20 times better off than the poorest people around the world. Do the poor in the United States owe something to the global poor? He said that would be "an interesting argument" to make in the United States—perhaps almost as futile trying to convince "emerging" countries with huge amounts of poverty within their borders that they owe something to the most destitute countries of the world in Asia and Africa.[3]

The general obligation that rich countries have to poor countries has been a subject of debate since at least the end of World War II when the collapse of colonial empires began to give birth to struggling new nation-states in Asia and Africa. During the Cold War, the Soviet Union and the West competed for the loyalty of these new countries, seeing them as ideological battlegrounds and places where various theories of development could be tested. The new countries, understandably, sought to navigate and exploit these rivalries for their own advantage. To strengthen their leverage against the rich countries of East and West, the new countries formed alliances such as the Nonaligned Movement, founded in 1961; the Group of 77, established in 1964; and the Organization of Petroleum Exporting Countries (OPEC), the oil-producing cartel that was founded in 1960 but did not exercise its muscle until the 1970s.

President John F. Kennedy pledged in his inaugural address in 1961 to "break the bonds of mass misery" for the world's poor—"not because the Communists may be doing it, not because we seek their votes, but because it is right."[4] But foreign aid aimed at elevating the poor of the developing world obviously also advanced the foreign policy interests of the donor countries in the West. Richard Cooper, a policymaker, economist, and adviser in the Kennedy, Carter, and Clinton administrations, has written that this tension between idealism and realpolitik underscores the importance in the West of "distributive justice" on a global scale and within the countries that are recipients of aid. He and others argue that the mere transfer of wealth from rich to poor countries is an inadequate response if the poorest of the poor in those countries are not helped. As Cooper said in 1976, "If we are to justify resource transfers on ethical grounds, then, it must be on the basis of knowledge that via one mechanism or another the transferred resources will benefit those residents of the recipient countries who are clearly worse off than the worst-off 'taxed' (including taxes levied implicitly through commodity prices) residents of the donor countries."[5]

The argument that foreign aid must try to achieve social justice in the recipient country leads back to the dilemma raised by John Rawls and his critics and defenders: how to channel wealth from rich to poor societies and ensure it is going to those most in need without dictating to other governments how to spend their money and intruding in national sovereignty. There is also concern among rich countries that foreign aid be productive and that it not lead to excessive reliance on aid in perpetuity, as discussed earlier in this book about the encouragement of virtuous behavior. In supporting foreign aid, for example, Pope Benedict XVI said in his 2009 encyclical that "such aid, whatever the donors' intentions, can sometimes lock people into a state of dependence and even foster situations of localized oppression and exploitation in the receiving country."[6] Advocates of foreign aid, echoing Cooper, cite a practical aspect: For donor countries, foreign aid must be seen as worthwhile to the hard-working taxpayers supporting aid programs. Meanwhile, donors run the risk of trampling on local prerogatives when they set performance criteria and political goals for their aid. Such intrusions rankle the recipients. As Jagdish Bhagwati, professor of economics and law at Columbia, has argued, setting aid criteria for poor countries is an arrogant violation of these countries' prerogatives and inimical to their insistence on independence in a postcolonial world.[7]

The United Nations has for years called on wealthy countries that are members of the Organization for Economic Cooperation and Development (OECD) to deliver "official development assistance" at a level of 0.7 percent of GDP to the poorest countries. The United States is consistently at the bottom of what these countries do in percentage terms, with a level of 0.21 percent. (US officials argue that if nongovernmental aid, encouraged and facilitated by tax breaks, were counted, the US ranking would be much higher.) Moreover, much if not most American foreign assistance has gone recently to Iraq, Afghanistan, and Pakistan for reconstruction related to the war effort, and to Israel and Egypt. Private actors in the United States, including nongovernmental organizations (NGOs), make up some of the difference.[8]

Aid is not the only economic program subject to policies by which wealthy countries can help poor countries but at some possible cost to themselves. But trade with poor countries can involve a sacrifice of a different sort: not by taxpayers but by farmers and low-skilled workers who might lose their jobs and livelihoods from an influx of imports, or from the ability of corporations to move US operations to poor countries to take advantage of cheap labor or lax worker and environmental safety laws. In rich countries, widespread use of government subsidies and price supports work to the disadvantage of poor countries by enabling the rich countries to compete with cheaper foreign food imports. For James Wolfensohn, former head of the World Bank (1995–2005), such government programs are a moral issue. "European cows get a subsidy of $2.50 a day," he said in 2003. "We have 3 billion people in the world who live on under $2 a day. Japanese cows get $7.50 a day subsidy."[9] (The subsidy has gone down since Wolfensohn's claim, but his point remains a powerful one especially when one considers that these sums are the equivalent of the daily income in the poorest countries of Africa and Asia.)

The World Bank has estimated that abolishing tariffs, subsidies, and domestic support programs throughout the world would "boost global welfare by nearly $300 billion year," mostly in the agriculture area, with 45 percent of these gains accruing to poor countries. But because these poor countries account for a smaller share of global wealth, their gains would be "disproportionately large, amounting to more than twice their share of global gross domestic product." According to the Bank, cotton-producing countries in Africa have suffered especially hard because of US domestic price supports for cotton, backed by powerful cotton-growing interests in Congress.[10] (In 2014 the United States reached a deal with Brazil to reduce US cotton subsidies and to pay Brazil money for its cotton farmers.[11])

Lower trade barriers in the West have been opposed by special interests, including farmers' and workers' groups, to be sure. Also objecting, however, are environmentalists and those ideologically opposed to the allegedly arbitrary rulings by the WTO and other international institutions on intellectual property, the environment, and safety rules. Many of these groups endorsed the purpose of the antiglobalization protests in Seattle in 1999. That the protesters said they were demonstrating in favor of helping the world's poor was dismissed by many leaders of struggling countries, including President Ernesto Zedillo of Mexico. In the name of helping the poor, Zedillo and others said, these antiglobalization protesters were preventing them from achieving "prosperity and social justice."[12]

The common theme of the antiglobalization movements is that the distribution of globalization's benefits is unbalanced, undemocratic, and illegitimate. Their critique is pitched as a defense of the rights of communities to protect their own economic well-being, safety, and environment—a manifestation of solidarity with one's own kind in a bewildering world.[13] These themes culminated in Seattle in 1999. But the contrary view—that these critics' concerns about the poor are misplaced, and that it is immoral for them to deny the poor of the world the gains promised from economic development—also arose after Seattle. Zedillo, now director of the Yale Center for the Study of Globalization, called the protesters in Seattle "globaphobic" and chastised them for opposing the very steps—lower trade barriers—that would help poorer countries like his own.[14]

The Special Case of Immigration

Any discussion of the obligations of rich countries to poor countries should not overlook the effects of immigration. Immigration is not a major focus of this book, but the issue does raise the conflict between "loyalty" to one's own country versus "loyalty" to those outside the country. In mid-2015, immigration was an agonizing issue in Europe and the United States as hundreds of thousands of economic refugees and asylum seekers from Africa and the war-torn Middle East, especially Syria, traveled by overcrowded boats, railroad cars, and even on foot, prompting a painful moral debate between those who opposed their entry and those who insisted that Europe was obliged to welcome them. The early phase of the 2016 presidential election in the United States featured the leading Republican candidate, Donald Trump, demanding not only that a wall be built to keep out immigrants from Mexico but that 11 million undocumented immigrants be deported. His tough approach was an echo of the 2012 Republican presidential candidate Mitt Romney's call for "self-deportation" by immigrants. In his visit to the United States in September 2015, Pope Francis appealed to Congress to ease restrictions on immigrants from Latin America as a matter of utmost moral urgency.

A major concern in Europe and the United States is that immigrants take jobs away from citizens and are paid wages that are lower than those paid to comparable native-born workers. In the United States, these concerns are focused on workers who fill low-skilled *and* high-skilled jobs (for example, highly educated foreigners working in Silicon Valley). Indeed, an irony flowing from this phenomenon is the attitude of the AFL-CIO toward immigration. In the early decades of the 20th century, organized labor advocated restrictive immigration laws, partly out of fear that immigrants would lower wages for American workers. Today labor favors lower barriers to immigrant workers despite evidence that wage growth suffers as a result. But labor still opposes liberalizing trade and investment across countries on grounds that such actions suppress American wages. Although the evidence is mixed, most experts seem to agree that immigration does suppress US wage increases, even though immigrants fill jobs that might go unfilled without their willingness to take them. For example, in 2008 the Brookings Institution concluded that immigration was at least a factor contributing to widening income inequality in the United States.[15] Gordon Hanson, professor of economics at the University of California at San Diego, has concluded that immigrants taking low-paying jobs probably suppress the wages paid in those jobs, and that the same phenomenon occurs in higher-paying jobs. Ironically, because immigrants from Asia working in jobs at the higher end of the wage scale in the US technology and health industries are often paid less than the native-born Americans in these sectors, they contribute to *equality* by bringing down higher-end wages. Between 1980 and 2000, Hanson found, the wages of native workers without a high school degree fell by 9 percent as a result of immigration.[16] A study sponsored by the Federal Reserve Bank of San Francisco in 2007 drew on a county-by-county wage and income analysis across the United States, and concluded that immigration is a contributing factor in overall economic inequality.[17] And yet, despite such concerns, the American labor movement has continued to call for legal status for undocumented workers on the grounds that such a step will lead to increases in their wages.[18]

Immigration has been a fact of life since the dawn of humanity. After the invention of the steamship in 1803, 300,000 migrants a year were crossing the Atlantic from Europe, and by 1900 that number was 1.4 million. Despite concerns about inequality in the American economy, the overwhelming evidence is that immigrants contribute generally to US prosperity and to the well-being of the countries from which they emigrate. As of 2011, some 215 million people were living outside their countries of origin, an increase of 50 percent over two decades earlier, and today 13 percent of the US population is foreign-born. Michael Mandelbaum cites a 2005 World Bank study concluding that a 3 percent increase per year in immigration from poor to rich countries would deliver $300 billion annually in benefits to the low-wage countries and be worth $51 billion to the countries to which they emigrated.[19]

In 2013 George Borjas, an immigration expert at Harvard's John F. Kennedy School of Government, found that the presence of legal and illegal immigrant workers has made the US economy 11 percent bigger than it would otherwise be—a $1.6 trillion increase in GDP. Most of that extra income has accrued to the immigrants themselves, but some has benefited other workers, owners of firms, and users of the services provided by the immigrants. On the downside, Borjas agrees with other studies in concluding that the wages of the nonimmigrant Americans in competition for jobs with immigrants—primarily those with lower education levels—have been hurt by an estimated $402 billion a year. Immigrants who entered the country from 1990 to 2010, Borjas's study notes, reduced the average annual earnings of American workers by $1,396, and most of this loss was concentrated again among low-skilled workers and high school dropouts.[20]

Most studies do indeed say that immigration benefits both the person moving to a new opportunity and the country providing it. The money sent back home in 2005 by poor immigrants from developing countries (remittances) was estimated to be $160 billion, a huge jump from $5 billion in 1975. "Globally, remittances sent through official channels are today second only to foreign direct investment (FDI) as a source of hard currency for developing countries," wrote Ian Goldin in a study sponsored by the World Bank.[21] Yet poor countries also suffer when some of their most talented workers leave, the so-called brain drain. In addition, immigrants competing for jobs in their new countries use government-funded social services, incurring costs for those countries. As Goldin points out, citing the studies showing that immigration contributes to lower wages for both low-end and highly skilled workers—while draining public resources in social services and schools—the influx of immigrants also contributes tax revenue to support the retirement costs for older Americans: "By allowing more immigrants of working age to enter, aging developed countries can push the declining worker-retiree ratio back upward."[22]

Many liberals are uneasy about immigration because of moral and political opposition to the supposedly lower wages it produces. Many libertarians (at places such as the Cato Institute) favor more immigration as helpful to the tax base and as a symbol of their belief in freedom of movement.[23]

The Special Case of Multinational Corporations

As the issues of trade, investment, and globalization heated up in the early 1990s, the *Harvard Business Review* explored the dilemmas in two widely discussed articles about the growing phenomenon of US companies shifting operations abroad and of foreign companies establishing a presence in the United States. The articles by Robert Reich, who later would become labor secretary in the Clinton administration, explored the varying definitions of mutual loyalty between big corporations and American citizens or workers. The articles had provocative titles: "Who Is Us?" (1990) and "Who Is Them?" (1991). The question he posed was simple: Which is the true "American company"? Is it the one owned by American investors but with most of its employees overseas, or is it the one owned by foreigners but with a workforce largely of Americans?

Reich's conclusion was that American workers should start realizing that it was in their interest to support foreign investment as a generator of jobs, and he called on the US government to "promote human capital in this country rather than assuming that American corporations will invest on 'our' behalf."[24] The old myth of the "company town" dominated by a gigantic vertically integrated corporation has disappeared, he said. Companies like IBM and Whirlpool had long since transplanted manufacturing overseas, while foreign-owned companies were now employing 10 percent of the nation's manufacturing workers, creating more new jobs in that sector than American-owned companies. The global economy, Reich declared, is now ruled by "a purer form of capitalism, practiced globally by managers who are more distant, more economically driven—in essence, more coldly rational in their decisions, having shed the old affiliations with people and place."[25]

What was true in the 1990s when Reich made these observations is even truer in the second decade of the 21st century, a time of global supply chains and the multiplication of "tasks" in dozens of different countries contributing to the production of one consumer or industrial item, whether a smartphone, automobile, or airplane. As US companies have invested heavily overseas, they have depended on the United States to keep its own doors open to a considerable amount of foreign direct investment in the country itself. By the end of 2009, US firms had amassed $3.5 trillion in direct investment abroad, compared with $2.3 trillion in foreign investment in the United States.[26]

Corporations themselves are, in fact, answerable to a variety of constituents, and those constituents in turn depend on the corporations. Such constituents are not just workers but also investors (which may include union pension funds), communities, consumers, taxpayers (who pay for roads and other infrastructure for corporations), and other stakeholders. Adding to the complexity, today most trade takes place between and among multinational corporations and their affiliates or through networks with suppliers and other providers. Corporations frequently invest overseas in order to serve markets overseas, and these investments are sometimes associated with job gains in their home countries as well as job losses.[27] In addition, the US economy is increasingly reliant on investment from overseas, which is made possible because of reciprocal arrangements that permit US firms to invest abroad. Thus if the United States tried to bar companies from investing overseas, it could have the effect of curtailing foreign investment in the United States. The fact that the United States benefits from such investments puts a different cast on President Obama's charge that companies investing overseas to gain tax or resource advantages or exploit low-cost labor may be unpatriotic.

Distrust of the "loyalty" of corporations to the countries where they are located is hardly new. In 1814, Thomas Jefferson declared, "Merchants have no country. The mere spot they stand on does not constitute so strong an attachment as that from which they draw their gains."[28] Large parts of the American public and workforce today remain adamantly unreconciled to the new realities of divided loyalties posed by multinational corporations. Richard Trumka, president of the AFL-CIO, and other labor leaders assail corporations for putting profits ahead of paying American taxes and hiring American workers. "For a generation, we've made the mistake of orienting our international economic policies around the profitability of US corporations abroad rather than the quality and quantity of jobs at home, or sustainable and democratic development around the world, and the results are in," Trumka declared in 2011. "Large US-based multinational corporations have thrived as global enterprises, but the United States is suffering from massive job loss, unsustainable trade deficits masked by one ruinous bubble after another."[29] In 2004 Martin Wolf of the *Financial Times* cited an anonymous comment from a union leader: "We don't give a damn about workers in the Third World—we just want to protect our members' interests."[30]

It is hardly surprising that a debate over gains won—and losses inflicted—by globalization would focus on multinational corporations, the primary movers of capital and goods in the modern world. The question of loyalty is complicated because US citizens play three separate roles in these corporations: worker, consumer, and stakeholder. Indeed, the role of consumer is further muddied by the fact that, although Americans may enjoy cheaper prices of imported goods, they also become outraged by disclosures of the alleged indifference of multinational corporations to appalling working conditions at subsidiaries and suppliers overseas. Many Americans say they oppose multinational corporations sending jobs offshore. But many of these same people are likely themselves dependent on retirement savings, pension plans, 401(k)s, and the like, all of which are invested in companies making tough decisions about maximizing profits, minimizing tax liabilities, and moving offshore or participating in global supply chains to gain efficiencies. Indeed, the solvency of many union pension systems depends on the high returns delivered by multinational corporations.

A little more than half of American families are invested personally in the stock market, either through 401(k)s, individual retirement accounts (IRAs), mutual funds, or individual stocks, down from 65 percent before the recent financial crisis but possibly heading back up.[31] Beyond these holdings, most pension funds—including public employee and other labor union pension funds—are heavily invested in multinational corporations that engage in foreign investment. These investments are handled by the leading asset managers, from Goldman Sachs and Morgan Stanley to Carlyle and BlackRock. These pension funds depend on their managers to maximize the very profits that are reviled in the debate over offshoring.

According to the US census, in 2010, 34.8 percent ($930 billion) of public employee pension assets were invested in corporate stocks, and 50.7 percent ($1.355 trillion) of these assets were invested in both corporate stocks and bonds. More than 15 percent of the assets of public employee pension systems are invested in foreign and international securities. For the assets of private pension plans (both defined benefit and defined contribution plans, including 401(k)s), the percentages are similar: 31 percent (nearly $1.9 trillion) are invested in corporate equities, and 39.4 percent ($2.4 trillion) are invested in corporate equities and bonds issued in the United States and foreign countries by American corporations.[32] Back in the days of the debate over the North American Free Trade Agreement (NAFTA), Ross Perot, who opposed the accord, ridiculed the short-sightedness of workers dependent on just such activities by multinational corporations. "Can you believe the working people's pension fund managers will put money into these deals?" Perot asked at a Senate hearing in 1993. "That's a paradox. For those who have retirement, they may live better, but the guys who used to have a job will never get to retirement. You see what I mean?"[33]

Indeed, if there is pressure on corporations to focus on the bottom line and outsource their operations to cut costs, it comes heavily from the managers of the very pension funds who are effective slaves to their own performance targets. "Among the voices demanding that companies make bold cost-cutting moves are the managers of large charitable foundations, retirement funds of university teachers, and union pension funds," Robert Reich asserted in a 2007 book. "If a portfolio manager in charge of my teachers' retirement fund doesn't get the best possible return on my savings, I'll switch funds. I can switch more easily now than ever before. . . . So indirectly I'm pushing CEOs to squeeze wages and benefits. I may even be pressuring CEOs to fight their unions."[34]

In an ironic twist related to the dilemma over corporate citizenship, Reich noted that the California Public Employees' Retirement System, or CalPERS, which provides benefits to more than 1.6 million public employees and retirees, sold its shares in the French telecommunications giant Alcatel because of disappointing profits. The ailing telecom giant then let 12,000 employees go in 2001. The sale of shares prompted a role reversal, in which French protesters led President Jacques Chirac to blame "California retirees" for the layoffs.[35] Edward Luce, the US-based columnist of the *Financial Times*, makes the same point, noting that few constituents are more in favor of labor rights than teachers, except when their retirements are at stake. "It makes no difference whether you manage the private wealth of the world's most avaricious tycoon or whether, like CalPERS, you take care of the retirement savings of the state's granola-crunching liberal class," wrote Luce. "Fund managers will always chase the higher returns."[36]

Despite protests from union leaders, there is scant evidence of any unions using their pension systems to stop the companies in which they invest from pursuing corporate strategies to escape taxes or lower labor costs. In 2014 the *New York Times* columnist Andrew Ross Sorkin interviewed several public employee pension fund managers about whether to disinvest in such companies. Most declined to say they would act. "If you're in my seat, you're thinking about it not only as an investor, but you're thinking about it as a fiduciary, which sort of walls out a lot of the political considerations that might otherwise be there," said a chief investment officer of the Florida State Board of Administration.[37]

On the other hand, on occasion some unions have discovered that they can influence politics through the use of their pension funds, at least on the margin. In 2013 the California Teachers pension fund responded to the fatal shooting of schoolchildren and adults in Newtown, Connecticut, by reconsidering its $750 million investment in Cerberus Capital Management, which was an investor in the Freedom Group, the manufacturer of the rifle used in the shootings.[38]

Concerns about the conduct—and loyalty—of multinationals have a long and sometimes contradictory history, especially in the post–World War II era. In the 1960s, President Lyndon Johnson, alarmed about the effect of capital outflows on the US balance of payments, called for "voluntary restraints" on US-based corporations investing overseas. But by the mid-1970s, those restraints had faded away.[39] At the same time, expanding American investment overseas caused anxiety in some parts of Europe concerned about loss of sovereignty and the influence of American culture. By 1973, 5 of the top 10 American corporations—including Ford, Chrysler, ITT, and IBM—were making 80 percent or more of their profits abroad.[40]

European anxieties about US domination were epitomized in the 1967 book *The American Challenge* by the French intellectual journalist and political figure Jean-Jacques Servan-Schreiber, who feared a kind of US corporate takeover of European culture.[41] Servan-Schreiber's concerns are alive and well under the current socialist French president, François Holland, whose former minister for industrial relations, Arnaud Montebourg, warned (before he was dismissed in 2014) about foreign takeovers of French national champions in the fields of energy, water, transport, telecommunications, and public health. In 2014 he attempted to block General Electric's takeover of Alstom, a French electricity and transmission company.

Meanwhile, back in the 1970s multinationals were blamed by the left in the United States, Europe, and many other parts of the developed world not for transferring investments abroad but for doing so in a way that allegedly exploited foreign workers. Criticism was also directed at corporations for their alleged involvement in coups in the Middle East and Latin America. Political pressure on multinationals helped persuade many of them to withdraw from South Africa in the 1980s and early 1990s to protest its apartheid policy.

An early student of the phenomenon of global corporations and author of many books on international affairs, Raymond Vernon predicted in the 1960s and 1970s that multinationals would present enormous opportunities while posing a subtle threat to national sovereignty, policy objectives, and loyalties. In 1971 Vernon, also a member of the US team that developed the Marshall Plan and the Bretton Woods institutions, predicted that labor-intensive work on standardized products would increasingly flow overseas.[42] "The regime of nation-states is built fundamentally on the principle that the people in any national jurisdiction have a right to try to maximize their well-being, as they define it, within that jurisdiction," he wrote in 1998. "The multinational enterprise, on the other hand, is bent on maximizing the well-being of its stakeholders from global operations, without accepting any direct responsibility for the consequences of its actions in individual national jurisdictions."[43] Vernon's view can be summarized by the simple maxim that capital is mobile and labor is not, a basic theme of Thomas Piketty in describing the $r > g$ phenomenon in 2014. Vernon noted, however, that two major forces can counter both the nation-state and the multinational corporation. The first is unions, and the second is NGOs, which have established global campaigns for environmental protection, worker safety, and protection of endangered species, all of which they see as threatened by rampant capitalism.[44]

In a 1978 study of the global corporation phenomenon, Fred Bergsten, Thomas Horst, and Theodore Moran were struck by a lack of consensus on the role of such corporations. "Claims are made that foreign direct investment creates jobs and that it exports jobs, that it helps the balance of payments and that it hurts it, that it promotes US foreign policy, that it subverts US foreign policy, that it fosters economic development, and that it depresses economic development," they wrote.[45] In the contemporary world, some deplore what they see as multinational corporations anointing themselves super citizens, more powerful than countries and loyal (and accountable) to no one but their investors. David Rothkopf, an author, business consultant, and publisher of *Foreign Policy* magazine, has calculated that throughout the world as many as 1 to 2 billion people in 2000 were "dependent on these multinationals" in some way, and that "the top three hundred companies control over a quarter of the earth's productive capacity."[46]

Indeed, from 2000 to 2012 the total stock of US direct investment abroad rose from $1.32 trillion to $4.45 trillion. In the other direction, according to the International Monetary Fund's Coordinated Direct Investment Survey, the stock of foreign direct investment in the United States reached $2.65 trillion in 2012, an increase of more than $350 billion over the previous two years, most of it from other advanced countries.[47] Meanwhile, the world's financial assets grew from $12 trillion in 1980 to $225 trillion in 2013. Cross-border capital flows—which include lending, foreign direct investment, and purchases of equities and bonds—rose from half a trillion dollars in 1980 to $11.8 trillion in 2007, before dropping back to $4.6 trillion in 2012 as a result of the recent financial crises.[48]

Whether foreign investment by US-based corporations helps or hurts jobs at home is not easy to answer. The Congressional Research Service has concluded that "there appears to be no distinct pattern between the creation or loss of jobs within US multinational companies and a commensurate loss or creation of jobs among the foreign affiliates of those companies."[49] But there can be little doubt that at least some US manufacturing jobs have shifted overseas because of the decisions of multinational corporations. In 2011, in a survey of 2,347 large US-based multinational companies, the Bureau of Economic Analysis of the Commerce Department found that these corporations cut their workforces in the United States by 864,000 between 2000 and 2009 and added 2.9 million workers abroad. The survey also found that US multinational companies slowed in their growth during the first decade of the 21st century compared with the previous decade, but that their growth came substantially from foreign affiliates, which grew at a rate of 7 percent compared with that of their US parents of 1.7 percent. This growth was spurred by growing activities in China, Brazil, India, Eastern Europe, and other emerging markets, where the survey found that expanded production was aimed primarily at selling to local customers rather than reducing labor costs for goods and services destined for the United States and wealthy areas. On the other hand, during this period there was "relatively rapid growth in research and development" expenditures by multinationals, which could suggest that this benefited the United States. Still, the US operations of US-based multinationals accounted for more than two-thirds of their combined value, and foreign affiliates accounted for less than a third of that value.[50]

Many economists, however, point out that the Commerce Department's analysis overlooks countervailing trends. For example, in this same period some of the job losses at home could be explained by companies taking hits in the recent economic hard times rather than simply choosing to shift jobs overseas. Defenders of the practices of multinational corporations say those corporations should be regarded as a basic American success story and driver of US prosperity, not a cause of economic decline. In 2010 the McKinsey Global Institute concluded that relative to their size, US multinational companies contribute disproportionately to private sector real GDP growth (or value added) and labor productivity. McKinsey challenged the idea that multinational companies that invest in job creation overseas do so at the expense of jobs at home. For example, it estimated that although multinationals represent only 1 percent of American companies, they accounted for 11 percent of American private sector employment growth (31 percent of the overall growth in private sector GDP) from 1990 to 2007. Moreover, in 2007 multinationals accounted for 19 percent of the private sector workforce, 25 percent of private sector wages paid, and 25 percent of the share of total private sector gross profits. In addition, these companies accounted for 41 percent of the gains in labor productivity from 1990 to 2007, a figure that was higher during periods of economic expansion. Their role in trade is even more striking and not necessarily consistent with the view that they ship jobs overseas, McKinsey said, estimating that although multinationals account for 37 percent of imports, they have been responsible for 48 percent of total exports over the 1990–2007 time period. Finally, multinationals also account for 74 percent of the share of the nation's private sector research and development spending—a major source of employment and growth—and 90 percent of the "intermediate inputs" purchased from other US-based firms.[51]

A comparable study reaching a similar conclusion was produced by the Peterson Institute for International Economics in 2013. It found that US multinationals employ 20 percent of the country's civilian workforce, they pay higher wages than purely domestic firms, and they account for nearly 30 percent of US private sector investment and nearly three-quarters of private sector research and development. Like the McKinsey study, the Peterson Institute study found that the same companies that invest overseas are both large exporters and large purchasers of goods and services in the US domestic market. Indeed, it found that the more these companies employed people and sold goods abroad, the more they also employed workers, sold goods, and undertook capital expenditures and research and development in the United States. "Across all fronts, an increase in FDI [foreign direct investment] by a US MNC [multinational corporation] is associated with an increase in domestic US activities by that same firm," the authors said. "When a US firm increases the employment at its foreign affiliates by 10 percent, employment by that same firm in the United States goes up by an average of 4 percent."[52]

Role of US Consumers?

What about Americans' role as consumers? Do they owe loyalty to country and community by buying "American" products? Many do like to buy products "Made in the USA." But even selective consumer behavior of this nature becomes difficult in the modern globalization environment of elaborate global supply chains and of myriad "American" products that result from American ingenuity but depend on components made abroad. Since the enactment of the Buy American Act in the 1930s, laws have been passed favoring US products for federal government procurement. In 1996, however, the United States and many other countries signed on to the so-called Government Procurement Agreement, or GPA, which was negotiated during the Uruguay Round trade negotiations that decade. The agreement requires open competition in government procurement for signatories to the agreement. It does not apply to private companies.

The rallying cry of "Buy American" continues to have appeal. In early 2013, the American retailer Wal-Mart pledged to buy an additional $50 billion in US-made goods over the next decade in areas such as sporting goods and high-end appliances as part of its effort to boost US economic growth.[53] But suppose one wants to "Buy American" on one's own? It is a challenge. For example, a 2007 study sponsored by the Sloan Foundation of the enormously popular iPod traced its 451 parts to companies, factories, and assembly operations spread throughout Japan, China, the Philippines, and elsewhere in Asia. But the study estimated that $163 of the iPod's $299 retail value was captured by American companies and workers, making it valid to assert that the iPod is indeed an American product that can even be purchased by an advocate of the "Buy American" campaign.[54] Beyond such products sold by Apple, it has also become true that cars, computers, and many other products are increasingly produced by global supply chains.

Consumer boycotts have had more success when directed at corporate practices, at least by mobilizing publicity about workers' conditions. Stories about worker exploitation and unsafe conditions, in which factory employees are forced to work six days a week and up to 12 hours a day and live in cramped barracks while earning barely enough to support their families, have drawn cries of outrage and in some cases action.[55] Foxconn Technology, one of the companies accused of abuses, assembles 40 percent of the world's consumer electronics for companies such as Apple, Amazon, Dell, Hewlett-Packard, Motorola, Nintendo, Nokia, Samsung, and Sony.[56] Media accounts of abuses have reported suicides (and the installation of "suicide nets" outside dormitory windows), plant explosions, abusive overtime, child labor violations, and other problems at factories making products for Apple and other big companies in the West.[57]

In June 2013, the Obama administration announced plans to suspend trade privileges for Bangladesh because of safety concerns and labor rights abuses in its garment industry. Labor unions and others had pressed the administration to act after two horrifying accidents: a fire at the Tazreen Fashions factory that killed 112 workers the previous November and the collapse of the eight-story Rana Plaza factory building in April, killing 1,129 workers. The two disasters provoked demonstrations and political pressure throughout much of the West, with rising demands that big retailers such as Wal-Mart, Disney, and Sears, all of which market clothes made in Bangladesh, do more to ensure worker safety at such factories. The *New York Times* cited a study showing that more than 1,000 workers died in hundreds of factory fires or accidents in Bangladesh from 1990 to 2012, and that no factory owner had been charged with a crime.[58]

Various NGOs have mobilized to demand that Wal-Mart, the Gap, H&M, and other companies that sell garments made in Bangladesh demand higher standards and upgrades at their factories, which they say would add only pennies to the cost of t-shirts, jeans, and the other clothing produced. Among these groups are the Worker Rights Consortium, which was founded by university-based organizations protesting the conditions of factories that make athletic wear and other goods with university insignias, and the Institute for Global Labour and Human Rights, which charges that free trade agreements between the United States and developing countries have led to lax worker and safety standards. Responding to public pressure about conditions at Foxconn, the company—its official name is Hon Hai Precision Industry Co., based in Taiwan—joined with Apple to try to improve its record, including opening some factories to Western media and a pledge to cooperate with an audit by the Fair Labor Association.

In late 2012 Foxconn and Apple agreed to a series of reforms, including curtailing workers' hours and increasing their wages and installing safety equipment. Apple has tripled its corporate social responsibility staff and asked competitors to work with it to curb excessive overtime. It also has reached out to advocacy groups with which it once refused to work (including the Fair Labor Association). Executives with more than a dozen electronics manufacturers, including Hewlett-Packard and Intel, were reportedly overhauling how they interact with foreign plants and workers to avoid bad publicity. "The days of easy globalization are done," an anonymous Apple executive was quoted as claiming. "We know that we have to get into the muck now."[59] Yet it has been difficult to document the amount of progress achieved.

Search for Corporate Tax Havens

The issue of companies going abroad to take advantage of lower taxes is equally emotional and no less complicated. American companies have shifted not only their manufacturing but also their profits abroad—that is, out of high-tax countries and into low-tax or "tax haven" countries such as Bermuda, Ireland, Luxembourg, the Netherlands, and Switzerland. According to the Congressional Research Service, American companies earned $938 billion in profits overseas in 2008. It found that 43 percent of these profits were earned in these five tax havens, while only 4 percent of these companies' foreign workforce and 7 percent of their foreign investments were in those low-tax economies. For example, multinationals are allowed to register trademarks in foreign countries and record all profits from trademark usage there, avoiding US taxes. The Congressional Research Service found that profits recorded in Bermuda by American multinationals rose from 260 percent of Bermuda's GDP in 1999 to more than 1,000 percent in 2008. Profits in Luxembourg went from 19 percent of Luxembourg's GDP in 1999 to 208 percent in 2008.[60]

News organizations such as the *New York Times*,[61] *Washington Post*,[62] and Bloomberg[63] have had a field day citing anecdotal evidence of companies moving their headquarters or other operations abroad for tax reasons. Stories about Procter & Gamble, Apple, Cisco, Facebook, Google, and Microsoft have described how they use elaborate tax planning methods to lower their US tax burdens in this way. In Britain, Prime Minister David Cameron, a Conservative who is generally favorable to business, has assailed companies such as Google and Starbucks for allegedly shifting profits from their UK operations to low-tax havens. Both the German finance minister Wolfgang Schäuble and British chancellor of the exchequer George Osborne have called on the G-20 countries to work together to minimize profit shifting by multinational companies because of the loss of revenues. "Britain and Germany want competitive corporate tax systems that attract global companies to our countries, but also want global companies to pay those taxes," Schäuble and Osborne declared. "That is best achieved through international action in the G20 and other relevant international fora to ensure strong standards."[64] In response to the attacks, Starbucks, Apple, and other companies have hired high-powered public relations firms to improve their images. In 2014 Starbucks moved its regional headquarters from Amsterdam to London to quell some of the criticism.[65]

A separate spate of negative news stories have appeared about multinationals finding a loophole in US tax law and undertaking foreign mergers known as "inversions" to reduce their tax liability. Using this technique, US-based corporations have over the years found foreign partners to act as the "parent" element of their corporate structure even though the change involves hardly any shift in the location of their economic activity. Bermuda and the Cayman Islands, where there is no corporate income tax, have long been favorite locations of the newly created parent corporations of many companies. In 2004 the America Jobs Creation Act sought to end the practice, but it left open ways to carry out "inversions" that in recent years have been used by leading pharmaceutical companies, including Pfizer.[66]

In 2014 the *Wall Street Journal* reported that about 50 US firms had used "inversions" since 2008.[67] *Fortune*, a magazine usually devoted to celebrating corporate success, carried this telling headline in 2014: "Positively Un-American Tax Dodges: Bigtime Companies are Moving Their 'Headquarters' Overseas to Dodge Billions in Taxes . . . That Means the Rest of Us Pay Their Share." The article projected a loss of $19.5 billion in US tax revenue from future inversions if the trend continues to 2024.[68] These articles led President Obama and lawmakers to call for a ban on inversions through new statutes or executive action. Treasury secretary Jacob Lew said the steps to thwart various corporate moves were a short-term solution; the longer-term remedy, he said, was to reduce US corporate taxes to lower the incentives of companies to go overseas. But so-called tax reform has also not gone anywhere.

Cutting the corporate tax rate has won bipartisan consensus, but it is debatable how big of an effect such a cut would have. At present, the statutory rate is 35 percent—39.2 percent if one adds state and local tax rates—making the US rate the highest in the world. But the "effective" tax rate, after companies use provisions in the law (such as definitions of the tax base) to lower their tax liability, is 27.6 percent, according to a study by the Congressional Research Service.[69] A 2013 study by the Peterson Institute found that the average tax liability of all OECD economies is 18.3 percent (more than 10 percent lower than that of the United States) and that a lower tax rate might actually yield more revenue, especially if it is accompanied by a broadening of the corporate tax base.[70] In addition, the National Commission on Fiscal Responsibility and Reform created by President Obama in 2010 (also known as the Simpson-Bowles commission) found that the high tax rate was putting US corporations "at a competitive disadvantage against foreign competitors" and called for the same thing.[71]

The economist Martin Feldstein argues similarly: "The difference between the US corporate tax rate and the lower rates abroad encourages US firms to locate production in foreign countries and discourages foreign firms from producing in the US unless absolutely necessary."[72] On the other hand, the Congressional Research Service has found that the effective tax rate for US corporations is about the same as the effective tax rate for competing countries when they are averaged and weighted according to the size of their economies.[73]

The revenues generated by taxes on US corporations are by some measures low—only 1.9 percent of GDP compared with an average of 2.8 percent for other advanced countries—in part because so many corporations are now limited partnerships or other types of entities not subject to the corporate tax. Only half of US business income is now subject to the tax compared with 80 percent in 1980.[74]

Generally speaking, corporate executives defend their tactics. In 2012 Ursula Burns, chair and CEO of Xerox, was asked if Xerox, with half of its employees operating outside the United States, has an obligation to provide jobs for Americans. Companies must sell their products where their customers are, she said. "Xerox, as an American company, has a responsibility to have jobs in the US," she replied. "But we also have a huge business in the U.K.; I have a responsibility to have jobs in the U.K. I have a growing business in India; I have a responsibility to have jobs in India. I have a big business in the Soviet—in Russia, etc., etc. So, I don't look at it as myopically or as single-focused as providing jobs in the US only. . . . We bring jobs into the United States, as long as the US can continue to be competitive."[75]

Clearly, then, multinational corporations make their own rules on where to locate, whom to hire, which taxes to pay, and what safety practices to adhere to. By employing huge numbers of people all over the world, they command a unique blend of cross-border loyalty. However, other organizations also command cross-border loyalty: nongovernmental organizations, which embody what may be the ultimate cosmopolitan spirit. They have sprung up over the decades in the cosmopolitan spirit of liberal internationalism, embracing the moral demands of global citizenship but mediated through international governmental organizations. These partnerships may be the only way to resolve the tensions outlined in this book surrounding equality versus justice and the conflicting versions of instilling virtue. Illuminating that path is the goal of the next chapter.

12

Who Governs?
The Role of Liberal Internationalism

Out of the crooked timber of humanity, no straight thing was ever made.
—Immanuel Kant, *Idea for a Universal History with a Cosmopolitan Purpose* (1784)

Hundreds of diplomats, bankers, businessmen, and treasury officials from more than three dozen countries descended on Bretton Woods, New Hampshire, in July 1944, prepared for everything but the weather. The conference they were attending, organized to establish a post–World War II economic order, began in a midsummer cold snap, and US Treasury secretary Henry Morgenthau Jr. for one, wished he had brought along woollen socks.[1] The scene was the once grand but now fading Mount Washington Hotel, built by a railroad magnate in 1902 to evoke a Spanish Renaissance castle in the White Mountains. Yet as delegates arrived, the hotel was not exactly ready for its moment in history. Painters, plumbers, carpenters, and repairmen were still frantically readying the premises as army buses brought guests and their bags from the train station. Inside the hotel, the delegates faced shortages of beds, hot water, and other amenities.[2] Lydia Lopokova, the Russian ballerina married to John Maynard Keynes, complained of leaky water taps, windows that did not close, and a "madhouse" atmosphere. The Morgenthaus were ensconced next door to the Keyneses, and the Treasury secretary's wife carped about being kept awake in the evening by Baroness Keynes's calisthenics.[3]

In contrast to the madcap setting, the proposals to be discussed at Bretton Woods had been carefully planned and refined. The first outlines of the world economic superstructure to accompany the international entity—later called the United Nations—envisioned after the war had been circulated at the State Department and the Council on Foreign Relations as early as 1939. More serious planning got under way a few years later, guided by Keynes and by Morgenthau's top international economic adviser at Treasury, Harry Dexter White. Before the Bretton Woods session started, emissaries had already agreed to set up commissions to establish the two major institutions of the postwar era: an international monetary fund and a bank for reconstruction and development to help the countries of Europe get back on their feet.

The larger goal was to figure out ways to curb the chaotic and destructive currency and trade wars that were widely viewed as having deepened the Great Depression. White and Keynes had competing plans. Keynes wanted a new international central bank based on a common reserve asset. But the United States prevailed on most issues, establishing the dollar as the de facto basis of the new order—recognition that Washington controlled the resources and wielded the economic power to have its way in a world devastated by war. With its gold reserves, the United States would be the guarantor of stability, not simply because of the safety of its currency but also because of its willingness to open its markets to exports from other countries in a new free trading system.[4]

What they established were the formidable institutions of what might be called the liberal internationalist economic order: the International Monetary Fund (IMF), World Bank, and plans for what later became the General Agreement on Tariffs and Trade (GATT), which evolved in the 1990s into the World Trade Organization (WTO).

The Bretton Woods conference concluded on July 22, 1944. On the evening of July 19, word spread that the 61-year-old Keynes was ailing after struggling day and night to work out compromises. Although he lost some of the great battles at Bretton Woods, Keynes stood at its moral center, revered for his farsighted understanding of the causes of the Great Depression. On the last evening, the man who had spearheaded a revolution in economic thinking in the first half of the 20th century moved slowly toward the main table in the banquet hall, looking pale and exhausted. The guests stood silently. In the end, it was Keynes who moved that the final act be adopted. "If we can so continue, this nightmare, in which most of us present have spent too much of our lives, will be over," he said. "The brotherhood of man will have become more than a phrase." The delegates applauded, and, as Keynes left, an emotional chorus of "For He's a Jolly Good Fellow" rang throughout the hall.

Mediating Moral Principles in the Era of Globalization

The role of each of the Bretton Woods institutions has evolved since their birth in the postwar years, and each has assumed a distinctive role. The World Bank, conceived as a project to reconstruct war-ravaged Europe, has grown into a role of providing resources and helping middle-income and poor countries build their capacity for development. The GATT, which evolved into the WTO, set in motion eight trade agreements between 1947 and 1995, expanding trade in the process but never succeeding in eliminating the barriers in agriculture that were the most unfair to poor countries. "GATT's purpose was never to maximize free trade," the economist Dani Rodrik wrote. "It was to achieve the maximum amount of trade compatible with different nations doing their own thing. In that respect the institution proved spectacularly successful."[5]

The IMF began with the primary objective of stabilizing the international financial system, particularly exchange rates. But it was not the IMF that put Europe back on its feet after World War II. Rather, it was the Marshall Plan proposed by President Harry Truman's secretary of state, George Marshall. The plan called for sending $13.5 billion to Europe and another $500 million to Japan. The successor organization to the one that oversaw the Marshall Plan is another important international grouping, the Organization for Economic Cooperation and Development (OECD).[6]

Since then, the IMF has become a kind of firefighter, financed by a pool of funds contributed by members through a quota system and by borrowing facilities to access additional funds. It enables countries faced by balance-of-payment crises to borrow and stabilize their economies. More recently, though with mixed success, it has also conducted "surveillance" of each country's economic performance to ensure that countries do not engage in conduct detrimental to the economic system as a whole.

The IMF's firefighting role has drawn much criticism in recent years, especially from conspiracy theorists who view it as a cabal of bankers and politicians seeking to establish a secret world government.[7] Its lending has ebbed and flowed, reaching a peak of $30 billion in the mid-1980s and then further surging to $50 billion in the late 1990s. It reached $200 billion in 2014.[8] The countries getting into trouble have changed as well. Britain and Italy availed themselves of the IMF's help in the 1970s, Latin American countries in the 1980s, eastern European countries newly freed from the Soviet yoke in the 1990s, along with East Asian countries in the 1990s, and then, of course, Greece, Portugal, and Ireland after the European economic crisis in recent years.[9]

The other pillar of US policy after the war was to support the plans advanced by Jean Monnet and Robert Schuman to unify the shattered economic power of Europe as well as cement it to the Atlantic alliance. European cooperation began with the decision by France and Germany to establish the European Coal and Steel Community in 1951. In 1957–58, the Treaty of Rome created the European Economic Community, which lowered trade barriers to goods within Europe and paved the way for the advent of the European Union and its common currency, the euro, in the 1990s. To Japan, US policy brought the same mixture of idealism and self-interest. Americans agreed to open their markets to the Japanese so they too could stand up to the forces of communism, which seized control of China in 1949 and soon thereafter threatened the stability of the Korean Peninsula.

Since the end of the Cold War especially, governments around the world have come to see the management of their economies as their most important function, perhaps even more than providing security. Their post–Cold War goal has generally been to enhance their power through economic growth rather than the acquisition of territory, recognizing that there is little choice but to pursue that goal through participation in the international system of free markets.[10] Russia's aggressive military action in seizing pieces of the old Soviet empire in Ukraine, Georgia, and Moldova—reflecting President Vladimir

Putin's dream of a "Greater Russia"—is severely testing the post–Cold War balance of power. But if Russian aggression is to be constrained, one significant factor is likely to be the web of economic and energy ties that Russia has with the West.

The idea of some kind of an international organization devoted to keeping peace and stability in the world is traced by some scholars to the writings of Immanuel Kant. He produced the essay "Perpetual Peace: A Philosophical Sketch" in 1795 proposing a "league of nations" or a "league of peace" that would try to prevent wars. "This league does not tend to any dominion over the power of the state but only to the maintenance and security of the freedom of the state itself and of other states in league with it, without there being any need for them to submit to civil laws and their compulsion, as men in a state of nature must submit," Kant wrote.[11] In his book about the evolution of world governance, Strobe Talbott argues that Kant's original concept anticipated both the United Nations system and the European Union.[12] Yet Kant also accepted the imperfectability of humanity and its institutions, summarized by his famous quotation that "out of the crooked timber of humanity, no straight thing was ever made." (The quote was a favorite of Isaiah Berlin, another skeptic of perfect choices, and became part of the title of one of his books of essays.[13])

A forerunner of such international governance organizations was the new order created by the Congress of Vienna at the beginning of the 19th century, at which the victors over Napoleon established what came to be known as the Concert of Europe. It was intended to prevent more wars by establishing a balance of power. That system succeeded in preventing war in Europe until everything collapsed in World War I, a conflict between two major blocs of countries, the Allies and the Central Powers. Out of the ashes of World War I, the delegates at the 1919 Paris Peace Conference put forward a genuine League of Nations, adopting the language of Kant. The first Geneva Convention was established around the turn of the 20th century to establish humanitarian relief for victims of war, and it became a precursor of later conventions aimed at setting up rules of warfare banning torture and genocide.

It was commonplace after the end of the Cold War to proclaim a "new world order" of stability, self-determination, justice, and economic interdependence, as President George H. W. Bush declared at the time.[14] The skeptics on the left saw that order as cementing the supremacy of capitalism. The Marxist historian Eric Hobsbawm said derisively, "Bush's new world order is a new world disorder, and for the time being, no restoration of stability is visible or even conceivable." He suggested that the disorder was breeding its own counterreaction in which a new "supranationalism" or "transnationalism" would dominate "an increasingly integrated world economy or, more generally, a world whose problems cannot effectively be tackled let alone solved within the borders of nation states."[15]

If there is a new world order of cosmopolitan consciousness in the age of globalization, it surely is unrealistic to think of anything like a world government serving to mediate its conflicts. In recent times, attitudes in the United States toward the United Nations and institutions such as the IMF, International Court of Justice, and WTO reveal a deep skepticism of adjusting US policies to conform with institutions that purport to represent global rules or norms, especially if such enforcement takes the form of a global governance system.

Global governance, such as it is, can be divided into three categories: (1) government (international organizations, national governments, and to some extent local governments that interacted with the outside world); (2) the private sector (multinational corporations and firms at the national and local levels, among other things); and (3) the independent sector (nongovernmental organizations, or NGOs, at the international, national, and local levels). Because a global government does not exist, it has fallen to global quasi-governmental organizations to supply normative principles for the world economy.[16] The norm, for better or worse, is for states to give up some of their unilateral ability to act in their own interests and according to their own sovereignty in order to achieve a greater and more "just" global good.

There are many instances of countries and business firms accepting international standards on things such as accounting, banking regulations, technology, and the internet. Regional organizations also set up such standards. Then there is what some call the "club model of multilateral cooperation": the OECD, the voluntary group of 34 advanced economies. The Bank for International Settlements, an organization of central bankers, was established in 1930 to handle World War I reparations. Today, it is the venue for those setting rules to maintain the stability of the world banking system. In the 1970s, the leading industrial democracies established the Group of Seven (G-7) nations to handle economic coordination. To accommodate Russia, it became the G-8 after the fall of communism in the early 1990s. An expanded group of 20 nations began meeting at the level of finance ministers and central bank governors in the late 1990s, and in November 2008 this group was transformed into a summit meeting of leaders, so that the G-20 is now the largest steering committee for the world economy. It is, however, still an exclusive club resented by some of those on the outside. As these organizations have become more powerful, they have run into demands for them to be more accountable and transparent, especially because the internet now makes it more possible for the world to become privy to their activities.

But one of the ironies of modern international politics is that many critics of the supposed abuses of national sovereignty are also distrustful of the role of international institutions, including the WTO and the IMF, that are the supposed agents of reducing national sovereignty to conform to global norms. For example, Peter Singer argues that national sovereignty should override the authority of the WTO, especially when a nation's right to enforce its own laws is challenged. As he sees it, both the WTO and the IMF are not an attempt to achieve cosmopolitan norms. Rather, they are coercive agents of powerful corporate interests doing damage to the poor and to the environment of individual countries. On the other hand, Singer has written at length about the vital importance of the planet and the rights of all species of animals (see chapter 9). Humankind, he has written, is obligated to ensure social and economic justice on a planetary basis.[17] Yet how are these norms to be applied to governments and businesses if not through international organizations?

Enter the NGOs

NGOs have an incoherent approach, and it is no wonder they are a diverse and preachy lot. Their issues range from land mines to religion. Some are so amorphous as to be clearer in their ideals than in what precisely they want to achieve. For example, the Faith Foundation established by former prime minister Tony Blair of Britain seeks a unified code of ethical and religious behavior to transcend the "old boundaries of culture, identity and even nationhood," but no such code is offered.[18]

The US State Department estimates that 1.5 million NGOs operate in the United States alone, advocating on behalf of foreign policy issues, free elections, the environment, health care and mental health, women's rights, poverty alleviation, and economic development. They draw their funding from private individuals, private sector companies, philanthropic foundations, and grants from federal, state, and local governments.[19] Most of these groups espouse the central goals of the cosmopolitans, contending that moral responsibility for the globe must be embraced by individuals as well as societies, nations, and peoples, and that morality governs the treatment of all individuals by other individuals.

The Center for Global Development (CGD) argues that a "citizen-based civil society" and "global citizens" have played an indispensable role in the post–World War II era of globalization in matters such as eliminating land mines, fighting AIDS, spurring environmental movements, preserving biodiversity, supporting efforts to curb global warming, and encouraging the role of the Internet to help the poor. "It is global citizens who started the microfinance movement, are fighting to find new ways to finance rapid social and economic progress in poor countries via a currency transactions tax, and are creating Internet-based programs for direct citizen to citizen giving after natural disasters," Nancy Birdsall, president of the CGD, has said.[20] Such citizens are elites in one sense because they attend exclusive parleys such as the Davos World Economic Forum meetings; form exclusive and establishment groups such as the Clinton Global Initiative, the Bill and Melinda Gates Foundation, and the Rockefeller Foundation; and wield enormous sums of money. As elites, they direct much of their distrust toward one another.

The number of international NGOs grew from 6,000 to 26,000 in the 1990s alone, at which point they were providing more development assistance than the official organizations of the United Nations system.[21] Women's groups press government on health issues for women, and Transparency International monitors the openness of government. Other groups demand fair worker safety standards in factories in China and Mexico. After business and government,

NGOs "act as a third key set of players in value creation and governance around the world," wrote Hildy Teegen, Jonathan Doh, and Sushil Vachani, business school scholars, in 2004. They credit NGOs with spurring the global human rights movement and with serving as lobbyists, advisers to decision makers, researchers, and sponsors of conferences—and, of course, with protests. Recognition has come to them in the form of Nobel Prizes awarded to Amnesty International, the International Campaign to Ban Landmines, and Doctors without Borders. NGOs thus "challenge state sovereignty in important ways," the authors say, noting that while they protest globalization, their success results from the world's interconnectedness and speed of communications.[22]

NGOs have even won a place at the table in trade negotiations,[23] although that role has also brought contradictions. On the one hand, NGOs critical of globalization want the World Trade Organization to lift restrictions on intellectual property rights, enabling poor countries to produce generic drugs despite copyrights by pharmaceutical companies. They also want to give countries greater freedom to enforce their own consumer protections, environmental rules, and sanitary (food) and phytosanitary (plants) protections if these are tougher than international standards. On the other hand, some of the same critics also want the WTO to do *more* and to impose *tougher* enforcement of labor standards, global tax evasion measures, protection of species and their habitats, and protections against global warming.

Similarly, they want the IMF and the World Bank to impose *fewer* conditions and less austerity in return for their loans to poor countries—but *more* restrictions on those loans to protect the poor and the environment, as well as more restrictions on financial market participants and the ability of banks to demand repayment of heavy debt burdens. Sovereignty and autonomy are worthy goals, the critics say, unless they conflict with the global goals embraced by the environmentalists themselves.[24]

Similar contradictions surrounding sovereignty have arisen over the issue of worker safety and rights. Since its establishment in 1919, the International Labour Organization (ILO)—the only surviving organization from the Versailles Treaty negotiations after World War I—has adopted 189 "conventions" barring practices such as slave labor and child labor. The ILO has 185 member countries that work on updating labor standards, which have tended to be at the center of every trade agreement since the North American Free Trade Agreement (NAFTA) in the early 1990s.[25] The conventions must be approved by two-thirds of ILO members, but they are binding only for those countries that ratify them. The United States has ratified only 14 conventions, including two that ban forced labor and certain forms of child labor, but not including certain rights to organize that have become a part of demands by US trade negotiators.[26] "The disempowering of the nation-state in relation to the global economy may be one source of the discontent that afflicts not only American politics but other democracies in the world," the Harvard philosophy professor Michael Sandel wrote in 1996.[27] Lawrence Summers, the former Treasury secretary, has termed this a negative reaction to the elite parleys such as the World Economic Forum in Davos, which draws thousands of business, government, and NGO participants each year. "There's a concern within countries that business leaders are more citizens of Davos than citizens of their particular country," he has said. "To win support, global integration is going to require more credible demonstration that globalization doesn't mean local disintegration."[28]

Yet advocates of greater governance are hardly ready to give up on the vision of a negotiated global authority. Kemal Dervis, principal architect of Turkey's economic recovery program in the early 2000s and former head of the United Nations Development Program, has proposed the creation of a United Nations Economic and Social Security Council as a twin to the UN Security Council. It would supplant the United Nations Economic and Social Council, which was established in 1946 as a kind of debating forum for economic, environmental, and social issues. Members of the new council would operate in a system in which votes are weighted according to their portion of the world population and their contributions to the UN "global goods" budget. (Dervis would also change voting weights at the IMF to reflect economic clout differently.) Under his vision, the new council would set up a system of global taxation to support eradication of poverty and disease, overseen by a special policy board of 20-25 senior members, a quarter of whom would be policymakers in the poorest countries and another quarter "eminent personalities" from those countries. Other members would come from middle- and upper-income countries and from international NGOs and academic institutions.[29] Yet it is hard to see how such a system would not run up against the widespread objections to the supposed elitism of the international governing system.

The proliferation of nongovernmental activities is not entirely new. In the 19th century, various civil society groups—labor unions, women's suffrage groups, temperance societies, and the like—played important advocacy roles in Europe. Indeed, between the Congress of Vienna after the Napoleonic Wars and World War I a century later, there were nearly 3,000 international gatherings involving 450 private and nongovernmental organizations. After the turn of the century, the role of the corporate philanthropic player became more prominent, starting with the Rockefeller Foundation in 1913. It funded a large portion of the League of Nations Health Office between World Wars I and II. As for the environment, international cooperation began with the help of NGOs in the 1960s and 1970s, pushing for hundreds of environmental treaties in the 1970s, 1980s, and 1990s, including a ban on chlorofluorocarbons (CFCs) to protect the ozone layer. The latter-day activists on behalf of climate change are the legatees of those efforts.[30]

Some important standards governing corporate behavior were set in the 1970s. In 1976 governments belonging to the OECD adopted a policy "to provide an open and transparent environment for international investment and to encourage the positive contribution multinational enterprises can make to economic and social progress." It has been amended five times since then, most recently in 2011, when governments pledged to accord foreign investors the same treatment under law as their own national investors.[31] Another important precedent was set in the same decade with the promulgation of the Sullivan Principles, which were corporate codes of conduct developed by Reverand Leon Sullivan to oppose the apartheid policy in South Africa. Sullivan, a Baptist minister and civil rights champion, served on the General Motors board while GM was a major employer in South Africa. His campaign for divestment of businesses viewed as supportive of apartheid was adopted by more than 100 companies, but the campaign achieved only mixed success for many years. Nonetheless, the principles were later adopted and expanded at the United Nations under the leadership of Secretary General Kofi Annan and John Ruggie, who served as Annan's special representative for business and human rights (and later as a professor of human rights and international law at Harvard). Ruggie helped the UN adopt its Principles on Business and Human Rights in 2011. These principles were later adopted by the OECD, International Standards Organization, International Finance Corporation, and European Union. Guidelines on fair treatment of workers and human rights have since been become part of the United Nations Universal Declaration of Human Rights and the International Labour Organization, again in part because of the advocacy of NGOs such as the Business and Human Rights Resource Centre, based in Britain.

Other examples of nongovernmental activities are the Corporate Social Responsibility (CSR) Initiative begun at Harvard in 2004 and the Initiative for Responsible Investment, which was launched at Harvard's John F. Kennedy School of Government to undertake research and explore ways to challenge companies and pension funds to aspire to global citizenship standards. Another group in London called Principles for Responsible Investment (PRI) claims to have more than 1,000 signatories managing more than $30 trillion in assets, with the goal of adhering to environmental, social, and corporate governance issues. The Bangladesh factory disasters have highlighted NGO campaigns for worker safety and health. Among the groups at the forefront are the Clean Clothes Campaign, Institute for Global Labour and Human Rights, Bangladesh Center for Worker Solidarity, Fair Labor Association, Worker Support Center (a Mexican NGO), Worker Rights Consortium, Social Accountability International, Ethical Trading Initiative, and Worldwide Responsible Apparel Production (WRAP). The Fair Labor Association has reported on its efforts to protect worker health, safety, and wages at factories in Mexico, Thailand, El Salvador, Vietnam, and Bangladesh.[32]

NGO-government cooperation is evident in the so-called extractive industries, from diamonds to oil. Proceeds from the sale of diamonds have financed militias that have engaged in human rights abuses and war atrocities in Angola, Sierra Leone, and Liberia. They have even been used to support al Qaeda. Because diamonds are consumed by upper classes in advanced countries, it was perhaps easier to mobilize elites to back the campaign by NGOs that led to the establishment of the Kimberley Process, a nonbinding international accord initiated in 2003 that was aimed at eradicating "conflict diamonds." The accord was followed by the Diamond Development Initiative in 2005, a collaborative effort of the World Bank, the diamond company De Beers, the NGO Global Witness, and government aid agencies. Progress has been limited but not insignificant.[33] Similar pressure from NGOs directed at challenging the reputation of giant energy companies led to the establishment of the Extractive Industries Transparency Initiative (EITI) in 2002. The initiative's two objectives are to disclose the role of corruption and bribery in oil- and gas-producing countries and to establish an independent business-government-NGO group to set up standards and enforce accountability to meet them. The EITI has expanded its concerns to a broader range of commodities and has apparently achieved mixed success. Even so, both the Kimberley Process and the EITI are outstanding examples of NGO activism achieving action among governments, businesses, and other nonstate actors.[34]

Arrayed against these NGO efforts are the concerns of asset managers of retirement and pension systems seeking ever higher returns despite what might be the political aims of individuals invested with them (see chapter 11). Some NGO activities and pressure are also divisive in other ways. A controversial example of a successful NGO political activity, for example, has been the anti-Israel campaign carried out by various groups supporting the cause of a Palestinian state. In 2005 these groups launched the Boycott, Divestment and Sanctions (BDS) campaign against Israel. The BDS has organized Israel Apartheid Week forums on hundreds of campuses around the world and claims to have engineered the liquidation of a major Israeli exporter of agricultural produce. Campaigns in Britain have urged boycotts against supermarkets selling Israeli food. Ahava, the Israeli cosmetics company, closed a flagship store in London because of the boycott, it claimed. In 2014 the Presbyterian Church in the United States moved to withdraw investments in three major companies: Caterpillar, which it said sold the bulldozers used to destroy Palestinian homes; Hewlett-Packard, which was accused of providing logistics and technology to help enforce the naval blockade of Gaza; and Motorola Solutions, which was said to provide military surveillance systems. The BDS campaign has been assailed by Israel and its supporters, who note that human rights violations, including persecution of religious minorities in other neighboring countries, have not drawn its concern.[35]

How, finally, to resolve the demands of all these institutions and competing economic demands and moral imperatives will be a never-ending challenge in the global economy. The concluding chapter reprises the theme of the inevitability of moral tradeoffs, the Great Tradeoff.

13

Pulling Together the Threads

The public will arrive in the middle of the third act and will leave before the last curtain, having stayed just long enough perhaps to decide who is the hero and who is the villain of the piece.
—Walter Lippmann, *The Phantom Public* (1925)

When I first went into philosophy, I was looking for first principles. I thought that if you could get the right principles, everything else would fall into place. I was wrong. . . . We need a list of First Projects—of laws that will remedy gaping inequalities—much more than we need agreement on First Principles.
—Richard Rorty (1997)

Politics: A strife of interests masquerading as a contest of principles. The conduct of public affairs for private advantage.
—Ambrose Bierce, *The Devil's Dictionary* (1911)

This book has outlined three basic tensions between conflicting moral imperatives and has sought to trace their evolution in the hope of applying them to the rules of the world economy. Part I dealt with reconciling liberty and justice in a market economy in an era of globalization. As the three chapters in that part revealed, they are rooted in a contradiction that cannot be reconciled— and it is futile and even dangerous to try to do so. Justice and greater economic equality may be ideal, but in a democratic society people believe liberty should be exercised on a reasonably fair basis, leading to a compromised version of social justice.

The global economy raises questions, however, about what constitutes social justice. The question pondered in part I was whether efforts should be concentrated on elevating the lives of the poorest or on reducing inequality between rich and poor. Some of the answer depends on how one measures inequality. A nation can succeed in promoting economic growth that lifts up the welfare of the poor but that also increases inequality by enriching those at the top. A second question is whether inequality is necessary for growth. The IMF argues that more equal societies achieve greater economic growth, but that some steps to achieve the goal of greater equality can hamper such growth. If one invokes the principle of John Rawls, a first priority is to help the poorest, even if one must overlook inequality. But if inequality confers excessive power on the well-to-do, those at the bottom might enjoy greater economic benefits, but at the expense of being marginalized in a democracy. There is no easy answer. On balance, the argument that improving the condition of the poorest—which has actually occurred in the global economy of the last quarter-century—ought to be the highest priority.

Part II looked at the conflicts created by fostering virtuous behavior and a virtuous society while maintaining a system of social insurance and ensuring that people, institutions, and governments are not punished in a destructive way when they behave recklessly or suffer reversals from bad luck. Without question, it is morally repugnant to bail out miscreants, whether they are governments, banks and financial institutions, or individuals, particularly homeowners. When people or businesses know that a lifeline is available, their conduct is affected accordingly. But in the global crisis of the last seven years, as in previous financial crises going back to the Great Depression, the record shows that to punish the perpetrators of bad behavior in an economic contest will harm too many innocent people. There must be a way to punish wrongdoers in the aftermath of crises but not during them.

Part III assessed the costs and benefits of global economic engagement. It also took a closer look at the distribution of these gains and losses at home versus how they affect US interests, and more specifically how they affect the poorest countries and the poorest people for whom many Americans have a proud tradition of caring. Again, there is no easy answer. But in an increasingly interdependent world of globalization, the system of market economics can be brutal in punishing the inefficient and rewarding those that bring comparative advantages to bear. The global economy is far from perfect in its distribution of costs and rewards. But in the last 25 years it has elevated the lives of more poor people than in the history of the world. Indeed, it may even be fair to say it has transformed the lives of most of those participating in it, from workers to businesses to consumers. Meanwhile, it is up to political institutions and governments, not the workings of the economy, to protect those hurt by the modern economic system.

These tenets bring us to a larger truth. Accommodating conflicting moral imperatives, even more than accommodating conflicting interests and desires, must be a participatory political exercise after decision makers are given an opportunity to consider the practical ramifications of the values at stake. To reconcile moral principles perfectly may be impossible. But the overriding moral imperative for the world's citizens, countries, and organizations is to undertake such an accommodation in a peaceful manner and in a manner that promotes economic progress and stability in a spirit of social justice. As hard as it is to reconcile these conflicting impulses, governments, institutions, and citizens have no choice but to try.

John Maynard Keynes and most of the other participants at Bretton Woods were principled guardians of reason in an era of unreason. They were pragmatists—followers of the late 19th-century school of thought holding that the big philosophical questions are best understood in terms of their practical applications and whether these applications achieve a successful outcome.

Thus the Bretton Woods generation sought a system that would produce the greatest benefits for the greatest number of countries and people in a world destroyed by war and depression. But they had more than an economic goal in mind. Their overriding goal was to bring about shared prosperity, liberalized trade, and economic interdependence, which they believed would lessen the chances of future wars. "A world open for commerce would be a world at peace," summarized I. M. Destler.[1] The means to achieving global well-being and international cooperation was to be a new system of institutions, rules, norms, and organizations that would not always be democratic but at least would be representative of the major powers after the war.

These institutions, which have been buffeted by the events of modern history, embody the principle of liberal internationalism. This principle honors the existence of nation-states, but it holds that destructive competition among them can be mediated by cooperation, negotiation, and rules. Just as government and political forces within a nation-state are mediated through politics, representation, and mediation, so international rivalries, interests, and moral views, according to this vision, can be mediated through institutions for the greater good.

The record of these institutions in delivering on this vision is mixed at best. The International Monetary Fund (IMF) and World Bank remain dominated by the United States and Europe, though under pressure from China and other emerging economic powerhouses they have been forced to evolve in their representativeness. Efforts to rectify their governance have been endorsed by leaders of the major countries, but so far the US Congress has not approved legislation (as of mid-2015) to make the change effective. Nonetheless, these institutions continue to be a major factor in stabilizing the world economy, promoting fairness, and providing a forum for complaints that can be adjudicated through negotiations. In the long history of nationalist versus global impulses, they represent the first attempts of the postwar era to set up mechanisms to mediate *economic conflicts* through actions other than war and the sheer force of economic power.

Meanwhile, regional organizations and associations have sought to foster norms and rules to overcome conflicts of loyalties. These include a variety of economic blocs that have come and gone since World War II. The preeminent regional organization is the European Union; attempts to forge an alliance of Brazil, Russia, India, China, and South Africa—the so-called BRICS countries— have achieved uneven results. During the crisis of 2008–09, the Group of 20 leading industrial nations (G-20) became a de facto steering committee for the global economy. Its influence has faded but it convenes every year and has effectively taken over from the Group of 7 (G-7) nations established in the 1970s.

Finally, yet another set of organizations is participating in the liberal internationalist order, making decision making more complicated but no doubt better informed. These are the thousands of nongovernmental organizations that have tried to complement nation-states, the role of multinational corporations, and even the authority of the Bretton Woods international institutions, which many regard as unrepresentative and overly subject to the wealthy and powerful nations and to corporate interests.

The "Comfortable Beds of Dogma"—Sorting Out Liberty, Justice, Virtue, and Loyalty

Moral principles should ideally be of help in clarifying choices and making those choices rise above mere self-interest. As Isaiah Berlin has written, the central core of the intellectual tradition in the West has rested on three basic dogmas inherited from antiquity: that all questions have one true answer, that this answer is knowable, and that true answers to different questions cannot clash with one another. However, these dogmas no longer apply in the 21st century, least of all to the modern global economy.[2] Yet despite the emergence of moral relativism in the 18th and 19th centuries, the contemporary debates over the moral underpinnings of economics still seem rooted in dogma. This book has argued that framing debates in terms of moral absolutes has not always clarified one's understanding of those underpinnings. Ethical absolutes illuminate, but they also distort. They help people think through the dilemmas, but they also impede solutions and make assessments of tradeoffs difficult.

As stated at the beginning of this book, the system of market economics—globalization—is characterized by clashes of economic interests, whether of labor, capital, businesses, or countries. The system is rife with clashes of moral and ethical values as well. Humans are moral creatures. They have a habit of debating economics in moral terms. They have done so throughout modern history, and the moral aspects of the debates are important. They illuminate the choices that individuals and governments face. But any effort to adhere to absolute moral principles is dangerous and unrealistic. In an era in which public policy is focused on achieving a new inclusive capitalism or an inclusive prosperity, moral goals are, however, essential. The global economic system should be one in which opportunities are more equal, the distribution of awards is fairer, and the preservation of communities is more respected. This book has explored history, philosophy, politics, economics, and social anthropology in order to illuminate the complexities of reaching that goal. Yet as stated at the outset of this book, the only moral outcome in a conflict of moral principles is compromise—a tradeoff, the Great Tradeoff.

Just as no society can succeed in resolving differences except through its political systems, it is not possible to resolve such differences on a global scale except through negotiations and discussions, fostered if possible by international institutions, with a recognition that all players, including multinational corporations and nongovernment organizations, have a role to play. The success of political systems derives from the confidence of the citizenry that those systems faithfully represent individual interests and beliefs even when the result is a compromise of both. International institutions command little such respect, however. This book has tried to show that these institutions, when supplemented by other actors, including those in the private and non-governmental volunteer sectors, can at least be made more representative or responsive. There must, finally, be a recognition that in the fast-paced world of modern communication, technology, and information transfers, the idea of solidarity with one's own community, country, and fellow citizens around the world is being dramatically redefined.

This book began by claiming that there is a moral case to be made for globalization. But that case must rest on the recognition that each principle discussed in this book has a piece of the truth but leaves out the truth of the other pieces. The world is characterized by imperfect balances of laudable moral values. To choose among those values is to be human. To call on institutions to mediate these choices, however imperfectly, is to realize that in an interdependent global economy, everyone is a citizen, not simply of his or her own country, but of one economically interdependent world.

Notes

Chapter 1: What We Talk about When We Talk about Globalization (pages 1–15)

1. Isaiah Berlin, The Pursuit of the Ideal (1988), in *The Crooked Timber of Humanity: Chapters in the History of Ideas,* 2d ed., ed. Henry Hardy (Princeton, NJ: Princeton University Press, 2013).

2. Nayan Chanda, *Bound Together: How Traders, Preachers, Adventurers, and Warriors Shaped Globalization* (New Haven, CT: Yale University Press, 2007).

3. Brad DeLong, *Notes and Finger Exercises on Thomas Piketty's "Capital in the Twenty First Century"* (Washington Center for Equitable Growth, April 19, 2014).

4. Daniel Yergin and Joseph Stanislaw, *The Commanding Heights: The Battle for the World Economy* (New York: Touchstone, 2002).

5. Ibid., 408.

6. Trade and American Jobs—The Impact of Trade on U.S. and State-Level Employment: An Update, paper prepared for the Business Roundtable, July 2010.

7. World Trade Organization, *World Trade Report 2012: World Trade in 2011* (Geneva: WTO, 2012).

8. Charles Roxburgh, Susan Lund, and John Piotrowski, *Mapping Global Capital Markets 2011* (McKinsey Global Institute, August 2011).

9. Morrison, Wayne M., Mary Jane Bolle, James K. Jackson, Vivian C. Jones, M. Angeles Villarreal, and Candy Meza, *U.S. Trade Concepts, Performance, and Policy: Frequently Asked Questions.* CRS Report RL33944 (Washington: Congressional Research Service, August 3, 2015).

10. Jim Young Kim, "Global Development at a Pivotal Time," speech at Brookings Institution, July 19, 2012.

11. Mohammad Nejatullah Siddiqi, *Riba, Bank Interest and the Rationale of Its Prohibition* (Jeddah, Saudi Arabia: Islamic Development Bank and Islamic Research and Training Institute, 2004), 13, 41, 45.

12. Pew Research Center for the People and the Press, *Public Sees U.S. Power Declining as Support for Global Engagement Slips,* December 3, 2013.

13. *NBC News/Wall Street Journal* poll conducted by polling organization of Peter Hart (D) and Bill McInturff (R), September 22–26, 2010, of sample of 1,000 adults nationwide, www.pollingreport.com/trade.htm.

14. International Forum on Globalization mission statement at its website, http://ifg.org.

15. Bill Clinton, *My Life* (New York: Knopf, 2004), 550.

16. Thomas L. Friedman, *The World Is Flat: A Brief History of the Twenty-First Century* (New York: Farrar, Straus and Giroux, 2005).

17. Benedict XVI, *Encyclical Letter* Caritas in Veritate *of the Supreme Pontiff Benedict XVI to the Bishops, Priests and Deacons, Men and Women Religious, the Lay Faithful and All People of Good Will on Integral Human Development in Charity and Truth,* June 29, 2009.

18. Ibid.

19. Francis, *Encyclical Letter* Laudato Si' *of the Holy Father Francis on Care for Our Common Home,* May 24, 2015, sec. IV, para. 190.

20. Ibid., para. 171.

21. Reuters, "Unbridled Capitalism Is the 'Dung of the Devil', Says Pope Francis," *Guardian,* July 9, 2015.

22. Peter Baker and Jim Yardley, "Pope, in Congress, Pleads for Unity on World's Woes," *New York Times,* September 25, 2015.

23. Francis, *Encyclical Letter* Laudato Si'.

24. Rowan Williams, keynote address at TUC Economics Conference, Congress House, London, November 16, 2009.

25. Alan S. Blinder, "What's the Matter with Economics?" *New York Review of Books,* December 18, 2014.

26. Arthur M. Okun, *Equality and Efficiency: The Big Tradeoff* (Washington: Brookings Institution Press, 1975), 119.

27. Adam Smith, *The Theory of Moral Sentiments* (London: A. Millar, 1759).

28. John Maynard Keynes, Liberalism and Labour, in *Essays in Persuasion* (1931, repr., New York: Classic House Books, 2009).

29. Okun, *Equality and Efficiency.*

30. Ibid., 91.

31. See Jonathan D. Ostry, Andrew Berg, and Charalambos G. Tsangarides, *Redistribution, Inequality, and Growth,* IMF Staff Discussion Note, Research Department (Washington: International Monetary Fund, April 2014).

32. Milton Friedman, *Capitalism and Freedom: Fortieth Anniversary Edition.* (Chicago: University of Chicago Press, 2002), chap. 1.

33. John Rawls, *A Theory of Justice* (Cambridge, MA: Harvard University Press, 1971).

34. James Madison, *The Papers of James Madison,* ed. William T. Hutchinson and William M. E. Rachal. (Chicago: University of Chicago Press, 1962–77), vol. 1, chap. 13, doc. 36.

35. Theodore H. Moran, *Foreign Investment and Supply Chains in Emerging Markets: Recurring Problems and Demonstrated Solutions,* Working Paper WP 14-12 (Washington: Peterson Institute for International Economics, December 2014).

36. Stephen Carmel, Globalization, Security, and Economic Well-Being, *Naval War College Review* 66, no. 1 (winter 2013): 41–55.

37. Hal R. Varian, "An iPod Has Global Value: Ask the (Many) Countries That Make It," *New York Times,* June 28, 2007.

38. Ethan B. Kapstein, *Economic Justice in an Unfair World: Toward a Level Playing Field* (Princeton, NJ: Princeton University Press, 2006), xv.

39. Michael Mandelbaum, *The Road to Global Prosperity* (New York: Simon and Schuster, 2014).

40. Joshua Greene, *Moral Tribes: Emotion, Reason, and the Gap Between Us and Them* (New York: Penguin Press, 2013), 117.

Chapter 1 (pages 1–15)

41. John Keats, *The Complete Poetical Works and Letters of John Keats*, Cambridge ed. (Boston: Houghton Mifflin, 1899), 277.

42. F. Scott Fitzgerald, "The Crack-Up," *Esquire*, February 1936.

43. David Herbert Donald, *Lincoln* (New York: Simon and Schuster, 1995).

44. Berlin, The Pursuit of the Ideal (1988), 13–14.

45. Louis Menand, An Introduction to Pragmatism, in *Pragmatism: A Reader* (New York: Random House, 1997), xi.

46. Ibid., xiii.

47. William James, What Pragmatism Means, in *Pragmatism: A Reader* (New York: Random House, 1997), 97.

48. Oliver Wendell Holmes Jr., speech at Harvard Law School, 1886, on the 250th anniversary of the founding of Harvard, in *The Essential Holmes: Selections from the Letters, Speeches, Judicial Opinions, and Other Writings of Oliver Wendell Holmes Jr.*, ed. Richard A. Posner (Chicago: University of Chicago Press, 1992).

Chapter 2: Economic Liberty: From Freedom of the Seas to Freedom of Capital (pages 19–32)

1.   Richard Tuck, *Natural Rights Theories: Their Origin and Development* (New York: Cambridge University Press, 1979).

2.   Richard Tuck, *The Rights of War and Peace: Political Thought and the International Order from Grotius to Kant* (New York: Oxford University Press, 1999), 80. See also Martine Julia van Ittersum, *Profit and Principle: Hugo Grotius, Natural Rights Theories and the Rise of Dutch Power in the East Indies (1595–1615)* (Leiden, The Netherlands: Brill Academic Publishers, 2006). My thanks go to Stephen Darwall, professor of philosophy at Yale, for pointing out the role of Grotius and explaining its significance.

3.   Hugo Grotius, *The Freedom of the Seas: The Right Which Belongs to the Dutch to Take Part in the East Indian Trade* (1608; repr., New York: Oxford University Press, 1916), 7 (Googlebooks, accessed on April 16, 2014).

4.   Douglas A. Irwin, *Against the Tide: An Intellectual History of Free Trade* (Princeton, NJ: Princeton University Press, 1996).

5.   Plato, *The Republic*, trans. Benjamin Jowett, Mineola, NY: Dover, 2000.

6.   Aristotle, *Nicomachean Ethics*, trans. W. D. Ross, http://classics.mit.edu/Aristotle/nicoma-chean.html.

7.   Irwin, *Against the Tide*, 12–13.

8.   Jonathan Sacks, *The Dignity of Difference: How to Avoid the Clash of Civilizations*, 2d ed. (New York: Continuum, 2009), 91–99.

9.   Quoted in Irwin, *Against the Tide*, 15.

10. John 2:13–16, King James Version (KJV).

11. Samuel Fleischacker, *A Short History of Distributive Justice* (Cambridge, MA: Harvard University Press, 2004), 17.

12. David D. Friedman, The Just Price, in *The New Palgrave: A Dictionary of Economics*, 4 vols., ed. John Eatwell, Murray Milgate, and Peter Newman (New York: Macmillan, 1987).

13. Robert L. Heilbroner, *The Worldly Philosophers: The Lives, Times, and Ideas of the Great Economic Thinkers*, 7th ed. (New York: Touchstone, 1999); Irwin, *Against the Tide*; Fleischacker, *Short History of Distributive Justice*.

14. Irwin, *Against the Tide*.

15. John Plender, *Capitalism: Money, Morals and Markets* (London: Biteback Publishing, 2015), 3.

16. Bernard Bailyn, Robert Dallek, David Brion Davis, David Herbert Donald, John L. Thomas, and Gordon S. Wood, *The Great Republic: A History of the American People*, vol. 1, 3d ed. (Lexington, MA: D. C. Heath, 1985).

17. Mohammad Nejatullah Siddiqi, *Riba, Bank Interest and the Rationale of Its Prohibition* (Jeddah, Saudi Arabia: Islamic Development Bank and Islamic Research and Training Institute, 2004), 53–64.

18. Heilbroner, *Worldly Philosophers*, 30–33.

19. William R. Allen, Mercantilism, in *The New Palgrave: A Dictionary of Economics*, 4 vols., ed. John Eatwell, Murray Milgate, and Peter Newman (New York: Macmillan, 1987), 2:445.

20. Irwin, *Against the Tide*, 56–61.

21. Laura LaHaye, "Mercantilism," Library of Economics and Liberty, www.econlib.org/library/About.html.

22. Adam Smith, *The Theory Of Moral Sentiments* (London: A. Millar, 1759), part 4, chap. 1.

23. Adam Smith, *An Inquiry into the Nature and Causes of the Wealth of Nations*, ed. Edward Cannan (London: Methuen, 1776), book IV, chap. 2.

24. Ibid., book I, chap. 11.

25. Emma Rothschild, *Economic Sentiments: Adam Smith, Condorcet, and the Enlightenment* (Cambridge, MA: Harvard University Press, 2001), 69.

26. See Jeffry A. Frieden, *Global Capitalism: Its Fall and Rise in the Twentieth Century* (New York: Norton, 2006).

27. Niall Ferguson, *Empire: The Rise and Demise of the British World Order and the Lessons for Global Power* (New York: Basic Books, 2004), xxxi. Quoted by Dani Rodrik in *The Global Paradox: Democracy and the Future of the World Economy* (New York: Norton, 2011), 32.

28. Quoted in Thomas L. Friedman, *The World Is Flat: A Brief History of the Twenty-First Century* (New York: Farrar, Straus and Giroux, 2005), 515.

29. Liaquat Ahamed, *Lords of Finance: The Bankers Who Broke the World* (New York: Penguin Books, 2009).

30. I. M. Destler, *American Trade Politics*, 4th ed. (Washington: Institute for International Economics, 2005).

31. Daniel Yergin and Joseph Stanislaw, *The Commanding Heights: The Battle for the World Economy* (New York: Touchstone, 2002).

32. Ronald Reagan, Inaugural Address, Washington, January 20, 1981.

33. See Yergin and Stanislaw, *Commanding Heights*.

34. Robert Skidelsky, *Keynes: The Return of the Master: Why, Sixty Years after His Death, John Maynard Keynes Is the Most Important Economic Thinker for America* (New York: PublicAffairs, 2009), 162.

35. Quoted in Martin Wolf, *Why Globalization Works* (New Haven, CT: Yale University Press, 2004), 54–55.

36. See Carmen M. Reinhart and Kenneth S. Rogoff, *A Decade of Debt*, Policy Analyses in International Economics 95 (Washington: Peterson Institute for International Economics, September 2011).

37. Quoted in John Cassidy, "Pope Francis's Challenge to Global Capitalism," *New York Times*, December 4, 2013.

38. See Yergin and Stanislaw, *Commanding Heights*.

39. See John Williamson, *What Washington Means by Policy Reform* (Washington: Institute for International Economics, November 2002); John Williamson, ed., *Latin American Adjustment: How Much Has Happened?* (Washington: Institute for International Economics, April 1990). Williamson has spent years correcting the misimpression that he favors completely open capital flows—the kind that produce speculative floods and bubbles in good times and sudden stops and crises in bad times. He has also said repeatedly that he never meant to endorse the turn to the right on taxes and regulation associated with the eras of Reagan and Thatcher or the privatizations that enriched privileged elites in a host of countries.

40. Paul Blustein, *The Chastening: Inside the Crisis that Rocked the Global Financial System and Humbled the IMF* (New York: PublicAffairs, 2003), 45.

41. Rawi Abdelal, *Capital Rules: The Construction of Global Finance* (Cambridge, MA: Harvard University Press, 2007).

42. Blustein, *The Chastening*, 44.

43. Rudiger Dornbusch, Capital Controls: An Idea Whose Time Is Past, *Essays in International Finance* 207 (May 1998). Also see Stanley Fischer, Richard N. Cooper, Rudiger Dornbusch, Peter M. Garber, Carlos Massad, Jacques J. Polak, Dani Rodrik, and Savas S. Tarapore, Should the IMF Pursue Capital-Account Convertibility? *Essays in International Finance* 207 (May 1998).

44. Michel Camdessus, address to the Board of Governors of the [International Monetary] Fund, Hong Kong, China, September 23, 1997.

45. Barry Eichengreen, *Globalizing Capital: A History of the International Monetary System*, 2d ed. (Princeton, NJ: Princeton University Press, 2008), 185.

46. Wolf, *Why Globalization Works*, 280–284.

47. Jagdish Bhagwati, "The Capital Myth: The Difference between Trade in Widgets and Dollars," *Foreign Affairs* 77 (May/June 1998): 7–12.

48. Dani Rodrik and Arvind Subramanian, *Why Did Financial Globalization Disappoint?* IMF Staff Papers, vol. 56, no. 1 (Washington: International Monetary Fund, 2009).

49. Dani Rodrik, *The Globalization Paradox: Democracy and the Future of the World Economy* (New York: Norton, 2011), 110.

50. William R. Cline, prepared remarks at "The Globalization Paradox: Democracy and the Future of the World Economy," Peterson Institute for International Economics, Washington, May 4, 2011.

51. Joseph E. Stiglitz, *Globalization and Its Discontents* (New York: Norton, 2002).

52. Robert E. Rubin and Jacob Weisberg, *In an Uncertain World: Tough Choices from Wall Street to Washington* (New York: Random House, 2003).

53. *The IMF's Approach to Capital Account Liberalization,* report of the Independent Evaluation Office, International Monetary Fund (prepared by staff led by Shinji Takagi and Jeffrey Allen Chelsky) (Washington: IMF, 2005).

54. Abdelal, *Capital Rules*, 130.

55. Stanley Fischer, opening remarks at the IMF Conference on Economic Policy and Equity, International Monetary Fund, Washington, June 8, 1998.

56. Ibid.

57. Jonathan D. Ostry, Andrew Berg, and Charalambos G. Tsangarides, *Redistribution, Inequality, and Growth,* IMF Staff Discussion Note (Washington: International Monetary Fund, 2014); Andrew G. Berg and Jonathan D. Ostry, *Inequality and Unsustainable Growth: Two Sides of the Same Coin?* IMF Staff Discussion Note (Washington: International Monetary Fund, April 8, 2011).

58. International Monetary Fund, *Fiscal Policy and Income Inequality,* IMF Policy Paper (Washington: IMF, January 22, 2014).

59. Binyamin Appelbaum, "Nominee for Fed Vice Chairman Has Long History as Policy Leader," *New York Times*, March 13, 2014.

60. Eduardo Porter, "In New Tack, I.M.F. Aims at Income Inequality," *New York Times*, April 18, 2014.

Chapter 3: The Wolves and the Lambs: "Justice, Justice Shalt Thou Pursue" (pages 33–45)

1. Jeffrey Owen Jones and Peter Meyer, *The Pledge: A History of the Pledge of Allegiance* (New York: Thomas Dunne Books, 2010), 71–72.

2. Jean-Jacques Rousseau, *A Discourse on Political Economy*, 1755.

3. Noah Webster, 1802, "An Oration on the Anniversary of the Declaration of Independence," www.lexrex.com/enlightened/writings/webster_decl.htm.

4. Alexis de Tocqueville, *Democracy in America*, Book 2, *Influence of Democracy on the Feelings of Americans* (New York: Schocken Books, 1974), 117.

5. Pew Research Center, *The American–Western European Values Gap* (Washington: Pew Research Center, November 17, 2011).

6. Samuel Fleischacker, *A Short History of Distributive Justice* (Cambridge, MA: Harvard University Press, 2004), 2.

7. Robert L. Heilbroner, *The Worldly Philosophers: The Lives, Times, and Ideas of the Great Economic Thinkers*, 7th ed. (New York: Touchstone, 1999), 107.

8. See Lawrence Goodwyn, *Democratic Promise: The Populist Moment in America* (New York: Oxford University Press, 1976).

9. Steven R. Weisman, *The Great Tax Wars: Lincoln—Teddy Roosevelt—Wilson: How the Income Tax Transformed America* (New York: Simon and Schuster, 2002).

10. Ibid.

11. *Lochner v. New York*, 198 US 45 (1905). See https://supreme.justia.com/cases/federal/us/198/45/case.html for more information.

12. Ibid.

13. Michael J. Sandel, *Democracy's Discontent: America in Search of a Public Philosophy* (Cambridge, MA: Harvard University Press, 1996).

14. Owen M. Fiss, *Troubled Beginnings of the Modern State, 1888–1910*, Vol. 8, *The Oliver Wendell Holmes Devise: History of the Supreme Court of the United States*, ed. Stanley N. Katz (New York: Cambridge University Press, 2006), 10.

15. *Obergefell v. Hodges*, 576 U.S. __ (2015). See Joe Palazzolo, "Chief Justice Roberts Drops the L Word," *Wall Street Journal* Law Blog, June 26, 2015.

16. Franklin D. Roosevelt, Annual Message to Congress on the State of the Union, Washington, January 6, 1941.

17. See David M. Kennedy, *Over Here: The First World War and American Society* (New York: Oxford University Press, 2004); David M. Kennedy, *Freedom from Fear: The American People in Depression and War, 1929–1945* (New York: Oxford University Press, 1999).

18. Isaiah Berlin, Two Concepts of Liberty, in *Four Essays on Liberty* (New York: Oxford University Press, 1969).

19. Lyndon B. Johnson, "To Fulfill These Rights," commencement address at Howard University, Washington, June 4, 1965.

20. Daniel Patrick Moynihan, memorandum to Harry McPherson, assistant to President Lyndon B. Johnson, May 20, 1965, in *Daniel Patrick Moynihan: A Portrait in Letters of an American Visionary*, ed. Steven R. Weisman (New York: PublicAffairs, 2010), 103–104.

21. Matthew Luttig, "The Structure of Inequality and Americans' Attitudes toward Redistribution," *Public Opinion Quarterly* 77 (fall 2013): 811–21.

22. Frank Newport, "Majority Say Not Government Duty to Provide Healthcare for All," Gallup Organization, November 20, 2014.

23. See Paul A. Samuelson and William D. Nordhaus, *Economics*, 19th ed. (Boston: McGraw-Hill/Irwin, 2010).

24. Paul A. Samuelson and William D. Nordhaus, *Macroeconomics,* 16th ed. (Boston: McGraw-Hill/Irwin, 1998), xx–xxi.

25. Barack Obama, remarks at Osawatomie High School, Osawatomie, KS, December 6, 2011.

26. Jason Furman, "Global Lessons for Inclusive Growth," speech to the Institute of International and European Affairs, Dublin, Ireland, May 7, 2014.

27. Michael Mandelbaum, *The Road to Global Prosperity* (New York: Simon and Schuster, 2014).

28. Rebecca Blank, *Do Justice: Linking Christian Faith and Modern Economic Life* (Cleveland: United Church Press, 1992), 17–18.

29. Gary Dorrien, "Morality Should Not Be Priced in the Marketplace," debate, "God and Mammon," NYTimes.com, June 26, 2014.

30. Michael J. Sandel, *What Money Can't Buy: The Moral Limits of Markets* (New York: Farrar, Straus and Giroux, 2012), 6–11.

31. Felicia Sonmez, "Boehner on Obama Debt Plan: 'I Don't Think I Would Describe Class Warfare as Leadership,'" *Washington Post,* September 19, 2011.

32. Both quoted in Timothy Noah, *The Great Divergence: America's Growing Inequality Crisis and What We Can Do about It* (New York: Bloomsbury Press, 2012), 117, 124.

33. Finis Welch, "In Defense of Inequality," Richard T. Ely Lecture in American Economic Review, *American Economic Association Papers and Proceedings* (May 1999).

34. Thomas A. Garrett, *U.S. Income Inequality: It's Not So Bad* (St. Louis: Federal Reserve Bank of St. Louis, spring 2010).

35. Richard Epstein, interview by Paul Solman, "Does U.S. Economic Inequality Have a Good Side?" *PBS Newshour,* October 26, 2011.

36. Edward Conard, *Unintended Consequences: Why Everything You've Been Told about the Economy Is Wrong* (New York: Penguin Portfolio, 2012).

37. Holman W. Jenkins Jr., "Mulally vs. Piketty," *Wall Street Journal,* April 23, 2014.

38. Ronald Dworkin, *Justice for Hedgehogs* (Cambridge, MA: Harvard University Press, 2011), 2.

39. Americans' Views on Income Inequality and Workers' Rights, *New York Times*/CBS News Poll, June 3, 2015.

40. Central Intelligence Agency, *The World Factbook,* www.cia.gov/library/publications/the-world-factbook/rankorder/2172rank.html.

41. Emmanuel Saez, Striking It Richer: The Evolution of Top Incomes in the United States (Updated with 2009 and 2010 Estimates), University of California, Berkeley, March 2, 2012, photocopy.

42. Thomas Piketty, *Capital in the Twenty-First Century,* trans. Arthur Goldhammer (Cambridge, MA: Harvard University Press, 2014).

43. Thomas Piketty, *The Economics of Inequality,* trans. Arthur Goldhammer (Cambridge, MA: Harvard University Press, 2015).

44. Joseph E. Stiglitz, *The Price of Inequality: How Today's Divided Society Endangers Our Future* (New York: Norton, 2012); Paul Krugman, *End This Depression Now!* (New York: Norton, 2012). Also see Jacob S. Hacker and Paul Pierson, *Winner-Take-All Politics: How Washington Made the Rich Richer—and Turned Its Back on the Middle Class* (New York: Simon and Schuster, 2010); Lawrence Lessig, *Republic, Lost: How Money Corrupts Congress—and a Plan to Stop It* (New York: Twelve, 2011); Jeffrey D. Sachs, *The Price of Civilization: Reawakening American Virtue and Prosperity* (New York: Random House, 2011); Timothy Noah, *The Great Divergence: America's Growing Inequality Crisis and What We Can Do about It* (New York: Bloomsbury Press, 2012); Larry M. Bartels, *Unequal Democracy: The Political Economy of the New Gilded Age* (Princeton, NJ: Princeton University Press, 2008); Nolan McCarty, Keith T. Poole, and Howard Rosenthal, *Polarized America: The Dance of Ideology and Unequal Riches* (Cambridge, MA: MIT Press, 2006); Don Peck,

Pinched: How the Great Recession Has Narrowed Our Futures and What We Can Do about It (New York: Broadway, 2012); and Thomas B. Edsall, *The Age of Austerity: How Scarcity Will Remake American Politics* (New York: Doubleday, 2012).

45. Lawrence Mishel and Natalie Sabadish, *CEO Pay in 2012 Was Extraordinarily High Relative to Typical Workers and Other High Earners* (Washington: Economic Policy Institute, June 26, 2013). The EPI received some of its funding from the US labor movement.

46. Sam Pizzigati, "Alan Greenspan, Egalitarian?" TomPaine.com, November 7, 2005.

47. Martin Crutsinger, "Greenspan Talk Doesn't Roil Markets," *Washington Post*, March 13, 2007.

48. Sewell Chan, "In Interview, Bernanke Backs Tax Code Shift," *New York Times,* December 5, 2010.

49. Ben S. Bernanke, "The Level and Distribution of Economic Well-Being," remarks before the Greater Omaha Chamber of Commerce, February 6, 2007.

50. Ibid.

Chapter 4: Justice for All: Defining and Measuring Inequality (pages 47–65)

1. See Douglas Martin, "John Rawls, Theorist on Justice, Is Dead at 82," *New York Times*, November 26, 2002; and John Rawls (1921–2002), in *Internet Encyclopedia of Philosophy*, www. iep.utm.edu/rawls/#H1.

2. John Rawls, *A Theory of Justice* (Cambridge, MA: Harvard University Press, 1971); *Political Liberalism* (New York: Columbia University Press, 1993); *The Law of the Peoples* (Cambridge, MA: Harvard University Press, 1999).

3. Robert Nozick, *Anarchy, State and Utopia* (New York: Basic Books, 1974), 183.

4. Thomas Piketty, *Capital in the Twenty-First Century*, trans. Arthur Goldhammer (Cambridge, MA: Harvard University Press, 2014), 296.

5. Ibid., 1.

6. See Sylvia Nasar, *Grand Pursuit: The Story of Economic Genius* (New York: Simon and Schuster, 2011).

7. Karl Marx and Friedrich Engels, *Manifesto of the Communist Party* (1848), http://avalon.law. yale.edu/subject_menus/mancont.asp.

8. Chris Giles and Ferdinando Giugliano, "Thomas Piketty's Exhaustive Inequality Data Turn Out to Be Flawed," *Financial Times*, May 23, 2014.

9. Martin Feldstein, "Piketty's Numbers Don't Add Up," *Wall Street Journal*, May 15, 2014.

10. Gregory N. Mankiw, "Defending the One Percent," *Journal of Economic Perspectives* 27 (summer 2013): 21–34.

11. Robert M. Solow, "The Rich-Get-Richer Dynamic: The Actual Economics of Inequality," *New Republic*, May 12, 2014.

12. Lawrence H. Summers, "The Inequality Puzzle: Thomas Piketty's Tour de Force Analysis Doesn't Get Everything Right, but It's Certainly Gotten Us Pondering the Right Questions," *Democracy Journal* 32 (spring 2014).

13. Matthew Rognlie, "Deciphering the Fall and Rise in the Net Capital Share," conference draft for spring 2015 Brookings Panel on Economic Activity, Brookings Institution, Washington, March 2015. Also see Matthew Rognlie, "A Note on Piketty and Diminishing Returns to Capital," Massachusetts Institute of Technology, Cambridge, MA, June 15, 2014.

14. Gary Burtless, "Has Rising Inequality Brought Us Back to the 1920s? It Depends on How We Measure Income," Brookings Institution blog post, May 20, 2014.

15. Ron Haskins, "Means-Tested Programs, Work Incentives, and Block Grants," testimony to the House Budget Committee, Washington, April 17, 2012.

16. Piketty, *Capital in the Twenty-First Century*, 52.

17. Ibid., 423.

18. Ibid.

19. Ibid., 346–347.

20. Ibid., 115–116.

21. A US Census Bureau study found that between 2000 and 2011 US aggregate net worth increased from $28.9 trillion to $40.2 trillion, about a quarter of which could be attributed to homeownership and 30 percent to retirement accounts. Alfred Gottschalck, Marina Vornovytskyy, and Adam Smith, "Household Wealth in the U.S.: 2000 to 2011," US Bureau of the Census, Washington.

22. Daniel Schuchman, "To Have and Have Not" (book review), *Wall Street Journal*, April 22, 2014.

23. Clive Crook, "The Most Important Book Ever Is All Wrong," *BloombergView*, April 20, 2014.

Chapter 4 (pages 47–65)

24. Organization for Economic Cooperation and Development (OECD), Labour Losing to Capital: What Explains the Declining Labour Share? in *OECD Employment Outlook 2012* (Paris: OECD Publishing, 2012).

25. Organization for Economic Cooperation and Development (OECD), *Divided We Stand: Why Inequality Keeps Rising* (Paris: OECD Publishing, 2011).

26. Piketty, *Capital in the Twenty-First Century,* 15.

27. Branko Milanović, "The Real Winners and Losers of Globalization," *Globalist,* October 25, 2012.

28. Nancy Birdsall, "Inequality and Injustice in Our Global Economy," Wider Annual Lecture 9, UNU World Institute for Development Economics Research (UNU-Wider), Helsinki, Finland, 2006.

29. Thomas Pogge, "Are We Violating the Human Rights of the World's Poor?" *Yale Human Rights and Development Law Journal* 14, no. 2 (2011).

30. Caroline Freund (assisted by Sarah Oliver), *Rich People Poor Countries: The Rise of Emerging Market Tycoons and Their Mega Firms* (Washington: Peterson Institute for International Economics, 2015).

31. Andrew M. Cuomo, "Op-ed: Fast-Food Workers Deserve a Raise," *New York Times,* May 6, 2015.

32. Quoted in E. J. Dionne, "A Vision Obama Needs for the State of the Union," *Washington Post,* January 27, 2014.

33. Philip Rucker and Zachary A. Goldfarb, "Clintons Fight Back, Signaling New Phase in '16 Preparations," *Washington Post,* May 14, 2014.

34. Noam Scheiber, "The Upshot: To Fight Income Inequality, Lifting the Poor Isn't Enough," *New York Times,* July 7, 2015.

35. Sara J. Solnicka and David Hemenway, "Is More Always Better? A Survey on Positional Concerns," *Journal of Economic Behavior and Organization* 37 (1998): 373–383.

36. Ibid.

37. Richard H. Thaler, "Anomalies: The Ultimatum Game," *Journal of Economic Perspectives* 2, no. 4 (1988): 195–206.

38. International Comparison Program, World Bank, http://icp.worldbank.org.

39. Branko Milanović, Global Income Inequality in Numbers: In History and Now, *Global Policy* 4, no. 2 (May 2013). For a fuller explanation of Milanović's methodology, see Branko Milanović, *Worlds Apart: Measuring International and Global Inequality* (Princeton, NJ: Princeton University Press, 2005). Also see Christoph Lakner and Branko Milanović, *Global Income Distribution: From the Fall of the Berlin Wall to the Great Recession,* Policy Research Working Paper 6719 (Washington: World Bank, December 2013); Milanović, "The Real Winners and Losers of Globalization."

40. Tomas Hellebrandt and Paolo Mauro, *The Future of Worldwide Income Distribution,* Working Paper 15-7 (Washington: Peterson Institute for International Economics, April 2015).

41. Simon Kuznets, Economic Growth and Income Inequality, in *American Economic Review* 45 (March 1955). Article is drawn from the presidential address delivered at the Sixty-seventh Annual Meeting of the American Economic Association, Detroit, December 29, 1954.

42. World Bank, Regional Aggregation Using 2005 PPP and $1.25/Day Poverty Line, http://iresearch.worldbank.org/PovcalNet/index.htm?1 (accessed February 12, 2013).

43. International Labour Organization, *World of Work 2014: Developing with Jobs* (Geneva: ILO, 2014).

44. World Bank Group and International Monetary Fund, *Global Monitoring Report 2014/2015: Ending Poverty and Sharing Prosperity* (Washington: World Bank, 2015).

45. United Nations Development Program, *Human Development Report 2013—The Rise of the South: Human Progress in a Diverse World* (New York: UNDP, 2013).

46. Robert B. Zoellick, "Payoff from the World Trade Agenda," speech at Peterson Institute for International Economics, Washington, June 14, 2013.

47. United Nations, *The Millennium Development Goals Report* (New York: United Nations, July 6, 2015).

48. See Richard Dobbs, Jaana Remes, James Manyika, Charles Roxburgh, Sven Smit, and Fabian Schaer, *Urban World: Cities and the Rise of the Consuming Class* (McKinsey Global Institute, June 2012).

49. James Manyika, Jacques Bughin, Susan Lund, Olivia Nottebohm, David Poulter, Sebastian Jauch, and Sree Ramaswamy, *Global Flows in a Digital Age: How Trade, Finance, People, and Data Connect the World Economy* (McKinsey Global Institute, April 2014).

50. World Bank, "News: Migration and Remittances," 2013, http://go.worldbank.org/ RR8SDPEHO0 (accessed on February 9, 2013).

51. Milanović, "The Real Winners and Losers of Globalization."

52. See World Bank, "Poverty Overview," 2013, www.worldbank.org/en/topic/poverty/overview (accessed April 17, 2013).

53. Oxfam, *Working for the Few: Political Capture and Economic Inequality*, 178 Oxfam Briefing Paper—Summary (Oxford: Oxfam, January 20, 2014).

54. David Dollar, Tatjana Kleineberg, and Aart Kraay, *Growth Still Is Good for the Poor*, Policy Research Working Paper 6568, Macroeconomics and Growth Team, Development Research Group (Washington: World Bank, August 2013).

55. Ibid.

56. Adam S. Posen, "The 'World If' Debate: If the Rich World Aimed for Minimal Growth, Would It Be a Disaster or a Blessing?" *Economist*, August 1, 2015.

57. Meghan Purvis, "Treasurer Summers Met with Protest, Catcalls," *Oberlin Review*, December 8, 2000.

58. Lawrence Summers, interview, *Commanding Heights*, PBS, April 24, 2001.

59. Martin Feldstein, "Reducing Poverty, Not Inequality," *Public Interest* 137 (fall 1999).

60. Anne O. Krueger, "Supporting Globalization," remarks at the Eisenhower National Security Conference on "National Security for the 21st Century: Anticipating Challenges, Seizing Opportunities, Building Capabilities," Washington, September 26, 2002.

61. Andrew G. Berg and Jonathan D. Ostry, *Inequality and Unsustainable Growth: Two Sides of the Same Coin?* IMF Staff Discussion Note (Washington: International Monetary Fund, April 8, 2011), 3.

62. Ibid., 4.

63. Joseph E. Stiglitz, "Inequality Is Holding Back the Recovery," *New York Times*, January 19, 2013.

64. Raghuram Rajan, "How Inequality Fueled the Crisis," *Project Syndicate*, May 28, 2013. Also see Raghuram Rajan, *Fault Lines: How Hidden Fractures Still Threaten the World Economy* (Princeton, NJ: Princeton University Press, 2010).

65. Jonathan D. Ostry, Andrew Berg, and Charalambos G. Tsangarides, *Redistribution, Inequality, and Growth*, IMF Staff Discussion Note (Washington: International Monetary Fund, April 2014).

66. International Monetary Fund, *Staff Report on Fiscal Policy and Income Equality*, IMF Policy Paper (Washington: IMF, January 22, 2014).

Chapter 4 (pages 47–65)

67. Douglas Elmendorf, comments on IMF paper on fiscal policy and long-term growth, Peterson Institute for International Economics, June 30, 2015. Text provided by author.

68. Martin Wolf, "Capital in the Twenty-First Century, by Thomas Piketty" (book review), *Financial Times,* April 15, 2014.

69. Piketty, *Capital in the Twenty-First Century,* 512.

70. Branko Milanović, "Global Income Inequality: A Review," *World Economics* 7, no. 1 (January–March 2006).

Chapter 5: The Hazards of Moral Hazard (pages 69–80)

1. Nelson D. Schwartz and Katrin Bennhold, "European Leaders Vow to Fight Financial Crisis," *New York Times*, October 5, 2008.

2. Liz Alderman and Alison Smale, "Divisions Grow as a Downturn Rocks Europe," *New York Times*, August 29, 2014.

3. "Locust, Pocus," *Economist*, May 5, 2005.

4. Paul Krugman, "Debt, Guilt and America's Good Fortune," *Economist*, November 8, 2011.

5. Steven Ozment, "German Austerity's Lutheran Core," *New York Times*, August 11, 2012.

6. Adrian Chadi and Matthias Krapg, The Protestant Fiscal Ethic: Religious Confession and Euro Skepticism in Germany, German Socio-Economic Panel Study, Berlin, March 30, 2015.

7. Timothy F. Geithner, *Stress Test: Reflections on Financial Crises* (New York: Crown, 2014), 444.

8. Quoted in Peter Müller, "Opposition to the Euro Grows in Germany," *Der Spiegel*, December 27, 2010.

9. Geithner, *Stress Test*, 444.

10. Jacob Soll, "Op-ed: Germany's Destructive Anger," *New York Times*, July 15, 2015.

11. Anthony Faiola and Stephanie Kirchner, "Debt Crisis Revives the 'Cruel German,'" *Washington Post*, July 16, 2015.

12. See, for example, Robert Kuttner, *Debtor's Prison: The Politics of Austerity versus Possibility* (New York: Knopf, 2013), 95–97. Also see Eduardo Porter, "Germans Forget Postwar History Lessons on Debt Relief in Greece Crisis," *New York Times*, July 7, 2015.

13. Quoted in David Gordon Smith, "The World from Berlin: 'EU Has Not Yet Faced the Whole Sad Truth about Greece,'" *Der Spiegel*, February 22, 2012.

14. "Lessons from Cyprus: Euro Crisis Poses Grave Dangers to EU Unity," *Der Spiegel*, March 25, 2013.

15. "Jean-Claude Juncker Interview: 'The Demons Haven't Been Banished,'" *Der Spiegel*, March 11, 2013.

16. Helmut Schmidt, "Germany in and with and for Europe," speech given at Social Democratic Party (SDP) conference in Berlin, December 4, 2011.

17. See entries in the *Stanford Encyclopedia of Philosophy*, http://stanford.library.usyd.edu.au/index.html.

18. See Jerry Evensky, "Adam Smith's Essentials: On Trust, Faith, and Free Markets," *Journal of the History of Economic Thought* 33, no. 2 (June 2011).

19. Daniel Bell, *The Cultural Contradictions of Capitalism*, 20th anniversary edition. (New York: Basic Books, 1996), xii.

20. For a discussion of the term, see William Safire, "On Language: Moral Hazard," *New York Times*, April 6, 2008.

21. Sam Peltzman, "The Effects of Automobile Safety Regulation," *Journal of Political Economy* 83, no. 4 (August 1975): 677–726.

22. Rachel Weiner, "Paul Ryan Responds That Government Spending Needs to Stop," *Washington Post*, January 25, 2011.

23. Benjamin M. Friedman, *The Moral Consequences of Economic Growth* (New York: Random House, 2006), 17–18.

24. Martin Wolf, *Why Globalization Works* (New Haven, CT: Yale University Press, 2004), 55–56.

25. Max Weber, *The Protestant Ethic and the Spirit of Capitalism* (Sydney: Allen and Unwin, 1930).

26. Marcus Noland, *Religion, Culture, and Economic Performance*, Working Paper 03-8 (Washington: Institute for International Economics, September 2003).

27. See Francis Fukuyama, "Social Capital and the Global Economy: A Redrawn Map of the World," *Foreign Affairs* 74, no. 5 (September/October 1995): 89–103. Also see the writings of Chalmers A. Johnson, especially *MITI and the Japanese Miracle: The Growth of Industrial Policy, 1925–1975* (Stanford, CA: Stanford University Press, 1982); and Chalmers Johnson, Laura D'Andrea Tyson, and John Zysman, *Politics and Productivity: The Real Story of Why Japan Works* (Cambridge, MA: Ballinger, 1991).

28. Patrick E. Tyler, "Obituary: Deng Xiaoping: A Political Wizard Who Put China on the Capitalist Road," *New York Times,* February 20, 1997.

29. Leo XIII, *Rerum Novarum: Encyclical of Pope Leo XIII on Capital and Labor,* May 15, 1891.

30. John Paul II, Centesimus Annus: *Encyclical Letter to His Venerable Brother Bishops in the Episcopate, the Priests and Deacons, Families of Men and Women Religious, All the Christian Faithful, and to All Men and Women of Good Will on the Hundredth Anniversary of* Rerum Novarum, May 1, 1991.

31. Michael Novak, *The Catholic Ethic and the Spirit of Capitalism* (New York: Free Press, 1993), 6.

32. Ibid., 8.

33. David Brooks, "Fracking and the Franciscans," *New York Times,* June 23, 2015.

34. Robert Nozick, *Anarchy, State, and Utopia* (New York: Basic Books, 1974).

35. Bell, *Cultural Contradictions of Capitalism.*

36. Ibid., 21, 24.

37. Amy Chua, *World on Fire: How Exporting Free Market Democracy Breeds Ethnic Hatred and Global Instability* (New York: Doubleday, 2003), 9.

38. Michael Sandel, *Democracy's Discontent: America in Search of a Public Philosophy* (Cambridge, MA: The Belknap Press of the Harvard University Press, 1996), 7–9.

39. Ibid., 324.

Chapter 6: Government and Just Deserts: A Brief US History (pages 81–93)

1. See C-Span, July 13, 2012, www.c-span.org/video/?307056-2/president-obama-campaign-rally-roanoke.

2. "'You Didn't Build That'," *Wall Street Journal*, July 17, 2012.

3. John Adams to Mercy Warren, April 16, 1776, *Warren-Adams Letters*, ed. Worthington C. Ford (Boston: Massachusetts Historical Society, 1917), 1:222.

4. Benjamin Franklin, *The Autobiography of Benjamin Franklin*, www.ushistory.org/franklin/autobiography/page38.htm.

5. Thomas Jefferson, Notes on the State of Virginia, in *Jefferson: Writings: Autobiography, Notes on the State of Virginia, Public and Private Papers, Addresses, Letters,* ed. Merrill D. Peterson (1782; repr., New York: Library of America, 1984), 288–91.

6. David M. Kennedy, Lizabeth Cohen, and Thomas Bailey, *The American Pageant: A History of the American People,* 14th ed. (Boston: Wadsworth, Cengage Learning, 2010), 340.

7. R. W. B. Lewis, *The American Adam: Innocence, Tragedy, and Tradition in the Nineteenth Century* (Chicago: University of Chicago Press, 1955).

8. Abraham Lincoln, speech at New Haven, Connecticut, March 6, 1860, www.historyplace.com/lincoln/haven.htm (accessed on November 12, 2012).

9. Abraham Lincoln, Address before the Wisconsin State Agricultural Society, Milwaukee, September 30, 1859.

10. Lincoln, speech at New Haven.

11. Michael J. Sandel, *Democracy's Discontent: America in Search of a Public Philosophy* (Cambridge, MA: Harvard University Press, 1996), 191.

12. Herbert David Croly, *The Promise of American Life* (New York: Macmillan, 1909), www.gutenberg.org/files/14422/14422-h/14422-h.htm (accessed May 14, 2015).

13. Theodore Roosevelt, letter to S. Stanwood Menken, chairman, Committee on Congress of Constructive Patriotism, January 10, 1917. Quoted in Paul Dickson, *Words from the White House: Words and Phrases Coined or Popularized by America's Presidents* (New York: Walker Publishing, 2013).

14. See A. Picchio, Poor Law, in *The New Palgrave: A Dictionary of Economics,* 4 vols., ed. John Eatwell, Murray Milgate, and Peter Newman (New York: Macmillan, 1987), 3:912–914.

15. Samuel Fleischacker, *A Short History of Distributive Justice* (Cambridge, MA: Harvard University Press, 2004), 51.

16. Bernard Mandeville, *The Fable of the Bees; Or, Private Vices, Public Benefits, with an Essay on Charity and Charity Schools, and a Search into the Nature of Society* (London, 1795), 179.

17. David Ricardo, *On the Principles of Political Economy and Taxation* (London: John Murray, 1817), chap. 5, www.econlib.org/library/Ricardo/ricP2.html.

18. Steven R. Weisman, *The Great Tax Wars: Lincoln–Teddy Roosevelt–Wilson: How the Income Tax Transformed America* (New York: Simon and Schuster, 2002), 107.

19. Franklin D. Roosevelt, Annual Message to Congress, Washington, January 4, 1935, www.presidency.ucsb.edu/ws/?pid=14890 (accessed June 3, 2013).

20. US Department of Labor, Office of Policy Planning and Research, *The Negro Family: The Case for National Action* (Washington, March 1965). This became known as the Moynihan Report.

21. Steven R. Weisman, ed., *Daniel Patrick Moynihan: A Portrait in Letters of an American Visionary* (New York: PublicAffairs, 2010), 333.

22. Barbara Vobejda, "Clinton Signs Welfare Bill Amid Division," *Washington Post*, August 23, 1996.

23. See Charles Murray, *Losing Ground: American Social Policy, 1950–1980*, 10th anniversary ed. (New York: Basic Books, 1994); Charles Murray, *Coming Apart: The State of White America, 1960–2010* (New York: Crown Forum, 2012).

24. "Romney's Speech from Mother Jones Video," *New York Times,* September 19, 2012.

25. Tax Policy Center, "Who Doesn't Pay Federal Taxes?" Joint Project of the Urban Institute and Brookings Institution, 2012.

26. Nicholas Eberstadt, *A Nation of Takers: America's Entitlement Epidemic* (West Conshohocken, PA: Templeton Press, 2012).

27. Nicholas Eberstadt, "The Great Society at Fifty: What LBJ Wrought," *Weekly Standard*, May 19, 2014.

28. Eberstadt, *Nation of Takers,* 3.

29. Congressional Budget Office, *The Distribution of Federal Spending and Taxes in 2006* (Washington, November 7, 2013).

30. Ezra Klein, "The US Government: An Insurance Conglomerate Protected by a Large, Standing Army," *Washington Post*, February 14, 2011.

31. Eberstadt, *A Nation of Takers,* 24.

32. Ibid., 51.

33. Bill O'Reilly, Fox News, November 6, 2012, http://mediamatters.org/video/2012/11/06/foxs-oreilly-50-of-voters-will-support-obama-be/191188.

34. "GOP Senate Candidate Likens Food Stamp Recipients to Wild Animals," *Huffington Post*, May 1, 2014.

35. William A. Galston, "Have We Become a 'Nation of Takers?'" in *A Nation of Takers: America's Entitlement Epidemic*, Nicholas Eberstadt (West Conshohocken, PA: Templeton Press, 2012).

36. Ibid., 100.

37. Ibid., 105.

38. J. Bradford DeLong, "Shrugging Off Atlas: Exactly How Did Once-Respectable Conservative Economists Get Swept Up in 'Moocher Class' Mania?" *Democracy: A Journal of Ideas* (spring 2013): 92–100.

39. Pew Research Center: US Politics and Policy, "Section 3: Fairness of the Economic System, Views of the Poor and Social Safety Net," June 25, 2014.

40. Dana Milbank, "Paul Ryan's Budget Hurts the Poor," *Washington Post,* March 20, 2012.

41. Stephen E. Blaire and Richard E. Pates, United States Conference of Catholic Bishops letter to US House of Representatives, March 6, 2012.

42. Georgetown University, letter to Paul Ryan, April 24, 2012.

43. Jane Little, "Paul Ryan Defends Budget at Catholic University," BBC News, April 26, 2012.

44. Robert Costa, "Ryan Shrugged: Representative Paul Ryan Debunks an 'Urban Legend,'" *National Review*, April 26, 2012.

45. Little, "Paul Ryan Defends Budget at Catholic University."

46. Paul Ryan, "A Better Way Up from Poverty," *Wall Street Journal*, August 16–17, 2014.

47. Ronald Reagan, Inaugural Address, Washington, January 20, 1981.

48. Ronald Reagan, *An American Life* (New York: Simon and Schuster, 1990), 231.

49. Thomas L. Hungerford, *Taxes and the Economy: An Economic Analysis of the Top Tax Rates since 1945* (Washington: Congressional Research Service, September 14, 2012).

50. David Lipton, "Fiscal Policy and Income Inequality," remarks at the Peterson Institute for International Economics, Washington, March 13, 2014.

51. "Where Does the Laffer Curve Bend?" *Washington Post*, August 9, 2010.

Chapter 7: Bubbles, Panics, Crashes, and Bailouts: Moral Hazard in the Marketplace (pages 95–107)

1. Robert E. Rubin and Jacob Weisberg, *In an Uncertain World: Tough Choices from Wall Street to Washington* (New York: Random House, 2003), 5.

2. Ibid., 8.

3. Ibid., 15.

4. Hyman P. Minsky, "The Modeling of Financial Instability: An Introduction," paper presented at Fifth Annual Pittsburgh Conference on Modeling and Simulation, University of Pittsburgh, April 24–26, 1974.

5. Charles P. Kindleberger, *Manias, Panics, and Crashes: A History of Financial Crises,* 3rd ed. (New York: Wiley, 1996), 16.

6. Ibid., 22.

7. Adam Smith, *The Wealth of Nations* (1776; repr., New York: Random House, 1937), 703–704.

8. John Carswell, *The South Sea Bubble* (London: Cresset Press, 1960), 131, 199.

9. Herbert Spencer, *Essays: Scientific, Political, and Speculative,* 3 vols. (London: Williams and Norgate, 1891), 3:354.

10. Herbert Hoover, *The Memoirs of Herbert Hoover,* Vol. 2, *The Cabinet and the Presidency: 1920–1933* (New York: Macmillan, 1952), 30.

11. Ben S. Bernanke, "The First 100 Years of the Federal Reserve: The Policy Record, Lessons Learned, and Prospects for the Future," speech at a conference sponsored by the National Bureau of Economic Research, Cambridge, MA, July 10, 2013.

12. Ben S. Bernanke, "On Milton Friedman's Ninetieth Birthday," remarks at the Conference to Honor Milton Friedman, University of Chicago, November 8, 2002.

13. Walter Bagehot, *Lombard Street: A Description of the Money Market* (London: Henry S. King and Co., 1873), www.econlib.org/library/Bagehot/bagLom.html (accessed November 14, 2012).

14. Nouriel Roubini and Brad Setser, *Bailouts or Bail-Ins? Responding to Financial Crises in Emerging Economies* (Washington: Institute for International Economics, 2004), 411.

15. Ibid., 74–75.

16. Ibid., 74–75, 99–101.

17. Timothy F. Geithner, *Stress Test: Reflections on Financial Crises* (New York: Crown Publishers, 2014).

18. Ibid., 4–5.

19. Ibid., 9.

20. Ibid., 255–256.

21. Franklin D. Roosevelt, Acceptance Speech for the Renomination for the Presidency, Philadelphia, June 27, 1936.

22. For a video clip of the remarks, see www.youtube.com/watch?v=6XkjyKfLZTI, uploaded February 19, 2009 (accessed May 28, 2013).

23. Neil Barofsky, *Bailout: An Inside Account of How Washington Abandoned Main Street While Rescuing Wall Street* (New York: Free Press, 2012).

24. Elizabeth Warren, *A Fighting Chance* (New York: Henry Holt, 2014), 111.

25. Ibid., 121.

26. Michael J. Sandel, *Justice: What's the Right Thing to Do?* (New York: Farrar, Straus and Giroux, 2009), 7–9.

27. Andrew Ross Sorkin, "Five Years after TARP, Misgivings on Bonuses," *New York Times,* August 27, 2003.

28. Geithner, *Stress Test*, 9.

29. Joshua Greene, *Moral Tribes: Emotion, Reason, and the Gap Between Us and Them* (New York: Penguin Press, 2013).

30. David Graeber, *Debt: The First 5,000 Years* (New York: Melville House Publishing, 2011), 9.

31. Ibid., 56–59.

32. See Plutarch, Against Debt and Borrowing upon Usury, in *Plutarch's Morals*, ed. William W. Goodwin, with an Introduction by Ralph Waldo Emerson (Boston: Little, Brown, 1878).

33. Gary A. Anderson, *Sin: A History* (New Haven, CT: Yale University Press, 2009), 6.

34. Mohammad Nejatullah Siddiqi, *Riba, Bank Interest and the Rationale of Its Prohibition* (Jeddah, Saudi Arabia: Islamic Development Bank, Islamic Research and Training Institute, 2004), 48.

35. Anderson, *Sin: A History*, 6–9. The story of the master and servant is in Matthew 18:21–35.

36. Ibid., 12.

37. Ibid., 13–14.

38. Aaron Levine, The Global Recession of 2007–2009: The Moral Factor and Jewish Law, in *The Oxford Handbook of Judaism and Economics*, ed. Aaron Levine (Oxford: Oxford University Press, 2009), 405.

39. Ibid., 408–409.

40. Ibid.

41. Jason Zweig, "Are Debtors' Prisons Coming Back?" *Wall Street Journal*, August 28, 2012.

42. From the opening of book I, chapter 6, of *Little Dorrit* by Charles Dickens (1855–57).

43. Bruce H. Mann, *Republic of Debtors: Bankruptcy in the Age of American Independence* (Cambridge, MA: Harvard University Press, 2002), 2.

44. Ibid., 5.

45. Ibid., 265.

46. Robert Kuttner, *Debtor's Prison: The Politics of Austerity versus Possibility* (New York: Knopf, 2013), 7.

Chapter 8: Who's Afraid of Debt? Debt as a Public Policy Tool (pages 109–121)

1. This anecdote appears in *The Roosevelt I Knew*, originally published in 1946 by Frances Perkins, Roosevelt's secretary of labor (New York: Penguin Group, 2011); see the introduction by Adam Cohen.

2. Remarks made by President Roosevelt during a campaign speech in Pittsburgh in 1936. Quoted in "FDR: From Budget Balancer to Keynesian. A President's Evolving Approach to Fiscal Policy in Times of Crisis," Franklin D. Roosevelt Presidential Library and Museum.

3. See Alan Brinkley, *The End of Reform: New Deal Liberalism in Recession and War* (New York: Knopf, 1995); and David M. Kennedy, *Freedom from Fear: The American People in Depression and War, 1929–1945*, Vol. 9, *The Oxford History of the United States*, ed. C. Vann Woodward (New York: Oxford University Press, 1999).

4. Daniel Bell, *The End of Ideology: On the Exhaustion of Political Ideas in the Fifties* (Cambridge, MA: Harvard University Press, 1962).

5. John F. Kennedy, commencement address, Yale University, June 11, 1962.

6. "The Economy: We Are All Keynesians Now," *Time,* December 31, 1965. Friedman later objected to being quoted this way, saying it was taken out of context and that he merely meant that he and others employed Keynesian concepts to analyze economic phenomena. Also see Justin Fox, "The Comeback Keynes," *Time,* October 23, 2008.

7. Leonard S. Silk, "Nixon's Program—'I Am Now a Keynesian,'" *New York Times,* January 10, 1971.

8. Niall Ferguson, "An Open Letter to the Harvard Community," *Harvard Crimson*, May 7, 2013.

9. Congressional Budget Office, *The 2012 Long-Term Budget Outlook* (Washington, June 2012).

10. Carmen M. Reinhart and Kenneth S. Rogoff, Growth in a Time of Debt, *American Economic Review: Papers and Proceedings* 100, no. 2 (May 2010): 573–578. Also see Carmen M. Reinhart and Kenneth S. Rogoff, *This Time Is Different: Eight Centuries of Financial Folly* (Princeton, NJ: Princeton University Press, 2009); and *A Decade of Debt*, Policy Analyses in International Economics (Washington: Peterson Institute for International Economics, September 2011).

11. Julia B. Isaacs, *Spending on Children and the Elderly* (Washington: Brookings Institution Press, November 2009).

12. Isabel Sawhill and Emily Monea, "Old News," *Democracy* 9 (summer 2008): 20–31.

13. Thomas L. Friedman and Michael Mandelbaum, *That Used to Be Us: How America Fell Behind in the World It Invented and How We Can Come Back* (New York: Farrar, Straus and Giroux, 2011), 177.

14. Ronald Lee and Andrew Mason, "The Price of Maturity," *Finance and Development* 48, no. 2 (June): 7–11.

15. Richard Jackson, Neil Howe, and Tobias Peter, *Balancing Tradition and Modernity: The Future of Retirement in East Asia* (Washington: Center for Strategic and International Studies, 2012).

16. Paul Krugman, "The Myth of Asia's Miracle: A Cautionary Fable," *Foreign Affairs* 73, no. 6 (November/December 1994).

17. Robert E. Rubin and Jacob Weisberg, *In an Uncertain World: Tough Choices from Wall Street to Washington* (New York: Random House, 2003), 246.

18. Ibid., 251.

19. Also see Nouriel Roubini and Brad Setser, *Bailouts or Bail-Ins? Responding to Financial Crises in Emerging Economies* (Washington: Institute for International Economics, 2004), 2–3.

20. Joseph E. Stiglitz, *Globalization and Its Discontents* (New York: Norton, 2002), xi, 36–37.

21. Quoted in Paul Blustein, *The Chastening: Inside the Crisis that Rocked the Global Financial System and Humbled the IMF,* rev. and updated (New York: PublicAffairs, 2003), 152.

22. Ibid., 372.

Chapter 8 (pages 109–121)

23. Rubin and Weisberg, 297.

24. George P. Shultz, William E. Simon, and Walter B. Wriston, "Who Needs the IMF?" *Wall Street Journal,* February 2, 1998, A22.

25. Bob Davis, "Ex-Cabinet Secretary Shultz Testifies Against US Funding for IMF," *Dow Jones Business News,* May 5, 1998.

26. Blustein, *Chastening,* 173.

27. Agustin Carstens, *Opening Remarks by Agustin Carstens at IMF Conference in Honor of Michael Mussa,* IMF Staff Papers, vol. 52 (special issue, 2005).

28. Anne O. Krueger, *A New Approach to Sovereign Debt Restructuring* (Washington: International Monetary Fund, April 2002).

29. See Board of Governors of the Federal Reserve System, "Resolution Plans," www.federalreserve.gov/bankinforeg/resolution-plans.htm.

30. See European Commission, "Commission Proposes Single Resolution Mechanism for the Banking Union," July 10, 2013; and "Communication from the Commission on the Application from 1 August 2013 of State Aid Rules to Support Measures in Favour of Banks in the Context of the Financial Crisis."

31. See International Monetary Fund, *Greece: Ex Post Evaluation of Exceptional Access under the 2010 Stand-By Arrangement June 2013,* IMF Country Report No. 13/156 (Washington: IMF, 2013). Also see Annie Lowrey, "I.M.F. Concedes Major Missteps in Bailout of Greece," *New York Times,* June 5, 2013.

32. Lawrence Summers, "International Financial Crises: Causes, Preventions, and Cures," Richard T. Ely Lecture, *American Economic Review* 90, no. 2 (May 2000): 1–16.

33. Howard Schneider, Q & A with IMF director Christine Lagarde, *Washington Post,* June 29, 2013.

Chapter 9: The Moral Imperative of Loyalty (pages 125–141)

1. Charles Duhigg and Keith Bradsher, "The iEconomy: How the US Lost Out on iPhone Work," *New York Times,* January 21, 2012. In December 2012, Apple announced plans to bring some manufacturing jobs back to the United States, however. Timothy Cook, who took over as CEO after the death of Jobs in 2011, told *NBC News* that despite its offshoring, Apple had "created" 600,000 jobs in the United States. Ronnie Polidoro, "Apple CEO Tim Cook Announces Plans to Manufacture Mac Computers in USA," *NBC News: Rock Center,* December 6, 2012.

2. Benedict XVI, *Encyclical Letter* Caritas in Veritate *of the Supreme Pontiff Benedict XVI to the Bishops, Priests and Deacons, Men and Women Religious, the Lay Faithful and All People of Good Will on Integral Human Development in Charity and Truth,* June 29, 2009.

3. I. M. Destler, *American Trade Politics,* 4th ed. (Washington: Institute for International Economics, 2005).

4. N. Gregory Mankiw, *Principles of Economics,* 5th ed. (Mason, OH: South-Western Cengage Learning, 2009), 183.

5. Martin Wolf, *Why Globalization Works* (New Haven, CT: Yale University Press, 2004), 170.

6. Thomas Nagel, "The Problem of Global Justice," *Philosophy and Public Affairs* 33, no. 2 (spring 2005): 113–47.

7. Brock R. Williams, "African Growth and Opportunity Act (AGOA): Background and Reauthorization," report from the Congressional Research Service, April 22, 2015.

8. Ethan B. Kapstein, *Economic Justice in an Unfair World: Toward a Level Playing Field* (Princeton, NJ: Princeton University Press, 2006). Also see Ethan B. Kapstein, Models of International Economic Justice, *Ethics and International Affairs* 18, no. 2 (2004): 79–92.

9. Lionel Trilling, *Sincerity and Authenticity* (Cambridge, MA: Harvard University Press, 1971), 26, based on lectures in 1970 by the author as Charles Eliot Norton Professor at Harvard University.

10. Eric Felten, *Loyalty: The Vexing Virtue* (New York: Simon and Schuster, 2011), 9–11.

11. Abraham Lincoln, Inaugural Address, March 4, 1861.

12. Michael J. Sandel, *Democracy's Discontent: America in Search of a Public Philosophy* (Cambridge, MA: Harvard University Press, 1996).

13. Edward C. Banfield, *The Moral Basis of a Backward Society* (New York: Free Press, 1958).

14. Jonathan Haidt, "Forget the Money, Follow the Sacredness," op-ed in the *New York Times,* March 17, 2012.

15. Strobe Talbott, *The Great Experiment: The Story of Ancient Empires, Modern States, and the Quest for a Global Nation* (New York: Simon and Schuster, 2008), 23–24.

16. See, for example, Edward O. Wilson, *Sociobiology: The New Synthesis* (Cambridge, MA: Harvard University Press, 1975).

17. Richard Dawkins, *The Selfish Gene* (Oxford: Oxford University Press, 1976).

18. Joshua Greene, *Moral Tribes: Emotion, Reason, and the Gap Between Us and Them* (New York: Penguin Press, 2013), 23.

19. Robert D. Putnam, "Crumbling American Dreams," *New York Times,* August 3, 2013.

20. Karl E. Meyer, "Editorial Notebook: Woodrow Wilson's Dynamite," *New York Times,* August 14, 1991.

21. Robert Lansing, *The Peace Negotiations: A Personal Narrative* (Boston: Houghton Mifflin, 1921).

22. Michael Walzer, "A New Tribalism," *Dissent: A Quarterly of Politics and Culture* (spring 1992).

23. David Bromwich, *Moral Imagination: Essays* (Princeton, NJ: Princeton University Press, 2014).

24. Communitarian Network, "Responsive Communitarian Platform," Institute for Communitarian Policy Studies, Washington, www.gwu.edu/vccps/platformtext.html (accessed on June 10, 2015).

25. William A. Galston, "Progressive Politics and Communitarian Culture," in *Toward a Global Civil Society*, ed. Michael Walzer (Providence, RI: Berghahn Books, 1995), 109.

26. John Rawls, *A Theory of Justice* (Cambridge, MA: Harvard University Press, 1971)

27. John Rawls, *The Law of Peoples* (Cambridge, MA: Harvard University Press, 1999), 108–109.

28. See Steven R. Weisman, ed., *Daniel Patrick Moynihan: A Portrait in Letters of an American Visionary* (New York: PublicAffairs, 2010), 304.

29. Nagel, The Problem of Global Justice, 114–115 (emphasis added).

30. Cited in Talbott, *The Great Experiment*, 25.

31. Talbott, *Great Experiment*, 50.

32. Ibid., 76.

33. Manfred Kuehn, *Kant: A Biography* (Cambridge: Cambridge University Press, 2001), 385, quoted by ibid., 97.

34. Talbott, *Great Experiment*, 100.

35. Nagel, The Problem of Global Justice, 141.

36. See Martha C. Nussbaum, *Women and Human Development: The Capabilities Approach* (New York: Cambridge University Press, 2001); and Martha C. Nussbaum, "Duties of Justice, Duties of Material Aid: Cicero's Problematic Legacy," Symposium on Cosmopolitanism, *Journal of Political Philosophy* 8, no. 2 (2000): 176–206.

37. Niccolo Machiavelli, *The Prince*, trans. Luigi Ricci (1552, repr., New York: Signet Classic, 1999).

38. See Stanley Hoffman, "The Political Ethics of International Relations: Seventh Morgenthau Memorial Lecture on Ethics and Foreign Policy," Carnegie Council on Ethics and International Affairs, New York, 1988.

39. Thomas Hobbes, Chapter XIII; Of the Natural Condition of Mankind, as Concerning Their Felicity, and Misery, *Leviathan* (1651), History Guide: Lectures on Modern European History.

40. Hoffman, "Political Ethics of International Relations."

41. George F. Kennan, *Realities of American Foreign Policy* (New York: W. W. Norton & Company, 1966), 49.

42. Samuel Scheffler, "The Idea of Global Justice: A Progress Report," *Harvard Review of Philosophy* 20 (2014): 17–35.

43. Peter Singer, *One World: The Ethics of Globalization*, 2nd ed. (New Haven, CT: Yale University Press, 2004), 177.

44. Charles R. Beitz, *Political Theory and International Relations* (Princeton, NJ: Princeton University Press, 1979), 145–146.

45. Ibid., 149.

46. Ibid., 18.

47. Ibid., 87.

48. Thomas W. Pogge, *Realizing Rawls* (Ithaca, NY: Cornell University Press, 1989), 240.

49. Keane Bhatt, "Thomas Pogge on the Past, Present and Future of Global Poverty" (interview), *Truthout*, May 29, 2011.

50. Pogge, *Realizing Rawls*, 260.

51. Adam Smith, *The Theory of Moral Sentiments* (London: A. Millar, 1759).

52. Kwame Anthony Appiah, *Cosmopolitanism: Ethics in a World of Strangers* (New York: Norton, 2006), 157–158.

53. Ibid., 165.

Chapter 10: Grappling with the Communitarian-Cosmopolitan Tradeoff (pages 143–157)

1. Ben S. Bernanke, "The Level and Distribution of Economic Well-Being," remarks before the Greater Omaha Chamber of Commerce, Omaha, NE, February 6, 2007.

2. Timothy Noah, *The Great Divergence: America's Growing Inequality Crisis and What We Can Do about It* (New York: Bloomsbury Press, 2012), 106.

3. Scott C. Bradford, Paul L. E. Grieco, and Gary Clyde Hufbauer, The Payoff to America from Global Integration, in *The United States and the World Economy: Foreign Economic Policy for the Next Decade,* ed. C. Fred Bergsten and the Institute for International Economics (Washington: Institute for International Economics, 2005).

4. Megan M. Barker, Manufacturing Employment Hard Hit during the 2007–09 Recession, *Monthly Labor Review,* published by Bureau of Labor Statistics, US Department of Labor (April 2011).

5. Mark Mittelhauser, Employment Trends in Textiles and Apparel, 1973–2005, *Monthly Labor Review,* published by Bureau of Labor Statistics, US Department of Labor (August 1997).

6. Lawrence Edwards and Robert Z. Lawrence, *Rising Tide: Is Growth in Emerging Economies Good for the United States?* (Washington: Peterson Institute for International Economics, 2013).

7. *Economist,* "Special Report: Reshoring Manufacturing: Coming Home," January 19, 2013.

8. Frank Levy and Richard J. Murnane, *The New Division of Labor: How Computers Are Creating the Next Job Market* (Princeton, NJ: Princeton University Press, 2004).

9. Erik Brynjolfsson and Andrew McAfee, *The Second Machine Age: Work, Progress, and Prosperity in a Time of Brilliant Technologies* (New York: Norton, 2014).

10. Claudia Goldin and Lawrence Katz, *The Race between Education and Technology* (Cambridge, MA: Harvard University Press, 2008).

11. International Forum on Globalization, Position Statement, http://ifg.org/about/position-statement.

12. Kemal Dervis, in cooperation with Ceren Ozer, *A Better Globalization: Legitimacy, Governance and Reform* (Washington: Center for Global Development, 2005).

13. See J. F. Hornbeck, Mary Jane Bolle, William H. Cooper, Craig K. Elwell, James K. Jackson, Vivian C. Jones, and M. Angeles Villarreal, *Trade Primer: Qs and As on Trade Concepts, Performance, and Policy* (Washington: Congressional Research Service, January 18, 2013).

14. Gary Clyde Hufbauer and Kimberly Ann Elliott, *Measuring the Costs of Protection in the United States* (Washington: Institute for International Economics, 1994).

15. Lydia DePillis, "America's Strange Trade Policy Makes Your Jeans More Expensive than They Should Be," Wonkblog, *Washington Post,* October 9, 2013.

16. William R. Cline, *Trade and Income Distribution* (Washington: Institute for International Economics, 1997), 256–257.

17. David H. Autor, David Dorn, and Gordon H. Hanson, "The China Syndrome: Local Labor Market Effects of Import Competition in the United States," *American Economic Review* 103, no. 6 (2013): 2121–68.

18. Justin R. Pierce and Peter K. Schott, *The Surprisingly Swift Decline of U.S. Manufacturing Employment* (Washington: Division of Research and Statistics and Monetary Affairs, Federal Reserve Board, 2014).

19. Avraham Ebenstein, Ann Harrison, and Margaret McMillan, *Why Are American Workers Getting Poorer? China, Trade and Offshoring,* NBER Working Paper 21027 (Cambridge, MA: National Bureau of Economic Research, 2015), abstract.

20. Bureau of Labor Statistics, Displaced Workers Summary, US Department of Labor Economic News Release, August 26, 2014.

21. Lori G. Kletzer, *Job Loss from Imports: Measuring the Costs* (Washington: Institute for International Economics, 2001).

22. Michael Elsby, Bart Hobijn, and Aysegul Sahin, *The Decline of the U.S. Labor Share*, Brookings Papers on Economic Activities, BPEA Conference, spring 2015.

23. Alan S. Blinder, *Offshoring: Big Deal, or Business as Usual?* CEPS Working Paper No. 149 (Princeton, NJ: Princeton University, June 2007). Also see Alan S. Blinder, "Free Trade's Great, but Offshoring Rattles Me," *Washington Post,* May 6, 2007.

24. A. Michael Spence and Sandile Hlatshwayo, *The Evolving Structure of the American Economy and the Employment Challenge,* CFR Working Paper (New York: Council on Foreign Relations, 2011).

25. Economic Policy Institute, Characteristics of offshorable and nonoffshorable jobs, in *The State of Working America* (Washington: Economic Policy Institute, 2012).

26. Josh Bivens, *Everybody Wins, Except for Most of Us: What Economics Teaches about Globalization* (Washington: Economic Policy Institute, 2008), 4–6.

27. Paul Krugman, *Pop Internationalism* (Cambridge, MA: MIT Press, 1997), 67.

28. Paul Krugman, *Trade and Wages, Reconsidered,* Brookings Papers on Economic Activity (Washington: Brookings Institution, Spring 2008), 106.

29. Paul Krugman, "Trouble with Trade," *New York Times,* December 28, 2007.

30. Paul Krugman, "TPP Versus NAFTA," The Conscience of a Liberal (blog), *New York Times,* June 17, 2015.

31. John F. Kennedy, "Special Message to the Congress on Foreign Trade Policy," Washington, January 25, 1962.

32. Matthew J. Slaughter and Robert Z. Lawrence, "More Trade and More Aid," *New York Times,* June 8, 2011.

33. Cathleen Cimino-Isaacs, Gary Clyde Hufbauer, and Jeffrey J. Schott, "The New TAA Package Stands on Its Own Merits," Trade and Investment Policy Watch (blog), Peterson Institute for International Economics, June 22, 2015.

34. Ronald Reagan's announcement for presidential candidacy, November 13, 1979.

35. Carlos Salinas de Gortari, speech reprinted in *NAFTA at 10: Progress, Potential, and Precedents* (Washington: Woodrow Wilson International Center for Scholars, 2005), 60.

36. Bill Clinton, "Remarks at the Signing Ceremony for the Supplemental Agreements to the North American Free Trade Agreement," September 14, 1993.

37. "The Mexican Worker," *Businessweek,* April 18, 1993.

38. George Anders, "One America—Heading South: US Companies Plan Major Moves into Mexico," *Wall Street Journal,* September 24, 1992.

39. Larry King, interview with H. Ross Perot and Vice President Al Gore, *Larry King Live,* CNN, November 10, 1993.

40. Hearing before the Joint Committee on the Organization of Congress, 103rd Cong., lst sess., March 2, 1993 (statement of H. Ross Perot).

41. Clinton, "Remarks at the Signing Ceremony for the Supplemental Agreements to the North American Free Trade Agreement."

42. Ibid.

43. Mary Jane Bolle, *NAFTA: U.S. Employment and Wage Effects* (Washington: Congressional Research Service, 1993), 1.

44. See C. Fred Bergsten, comments to Daniel W. Drezner, Drezner/Bergsten—The Bootleg Tapes, *Foreign Policy,* June 21, 2012. Bergsten said that the Institute for International Economics had "big internal debates" about whether to satisfy the demands of Congress and come up with job numbers gained from NAFTA, finally deciding to project a gain of 170,000 jobs over five years even though as "good economists" they knew that trade agreements do not "create" or "destroy" jobs but simply shift the kinds of jobs that are in existence.

45. Federal Job Movement Data and the Implications for NAFTA: Hearings before the Subcommittee on Oversight of Government Management of the Committee on Governmental Affairs, US Senate, 103rd Cong., 1st sess., April 1, 1993–April 28, 1993.

46. Chris Rasmussen and Martin Johnson, *Jobs Supported by Exports, 1993–2011*, Manufacturing and Services Economics Brief (Washington: Office of Competition and Economic Analysis, International Trade Administration, US Department of Commerce, October 2012).

47. NAFTA Job Claims: Truth in Statistics, Hearing Before the Committee on Governmental Affairs, US Senate, 103rd Cong., lst sess., November 10, 1993.

48. Ibid.

49. David E. Rosenbaum, "Good Economics Meet Protective Politics," *New York Times,* September 19, 1993.

50. Leo H. Kahane, "Congressional Voting Patterns on NAFTA: An Empirical Analysis," *American Journal of Economics and Sociology* 55, no. 4 (October 1996): 395–409.

51. "Against NAFTA," Cong. Rec., House of Representatives, 103rd Cong., 1st sess., November 16, 1993.

52. "North American Free-Trade Agreement Implementation Act," Cong. Rec., House of Representatives, 103rd Cong., 1st sess., November 17, 1993.

53. "Providing for Consideration of H.R. 3450, North American Free-Trade Agreement Implementation Act," Cong. Rec., House of Representatives, 103rd Cong., 1st sess., November 17, 1993.

54. "North American Free-Trade Agreement Implementation Act."

55. Michael Wines, "The Free Trade Accord: Reporter's Notebook; After Marathon of a Debate, a 6-Minute Dash to Settle It," *New York Times,* November 18, 1993.

56. "North American Free-Trade Agreement Implementation Act," Cong. Rec., Senate, 103rd Cong., 1st Sess., November 20, 1993.

57. Bill Clinton, "Remarks on Signing the North American Free Trade Agreement Implementation Act," Washington, December 8, 1993.

58. Lori Wallach, "NAFTA on Steroids," *The Nation,* June 27, 2012.

59. Ambassador Michael Froman, testimony before the Senate Finance Committee on Congressional Trade Priorities, April 16, 2015.

60. Daniel Kahneman, *Thinking, Fast and Slow* (New York: Farrar, Straus and Giroux, 2011) 278–288.

61. Daniel Kahneman and Amos Tversky, "Choices, Values, and Frames," *American Psychologist* (April 1984).

62. See Gary Clyde Hufbauer, Cathleen Cimino, and Tyler Moran, *NAFTA at 20: Misleading Charges and Positive Achievements,* Policy Brief 14-13 (Washington: Peterson Institute for International Economics, May 2014).

63. M. Angeles Villarreal, *U.S.-Mexico Economic Relations: Trends, Issues, and Implications* (Washington: Congressional Research Service, August 9, 2012).

64. Gary Clyde Hufbauer and Jeffrey J. Schott, assisted by Paul L. E. Grieco and Yee Wong, *NAFTA Revisited: Achievements and Challenges* (Washington: Institute for International Economics, 2005), 36.

65. Robert E. Scott, *The High Price of "Free" Trade: NAFTA's Failure Has Cost the United States Jobs across the Nation* (Washington: Economic Policy Institute, 2003).

66. Hufbauer, Cimino, and Moran, *NAFTA at 20.*

67. Ibid.

Chapter 11: Loyalties in Conflict: Jobs, Communities, and Multinational Corporations (pages 159–175)

1. World Trade Organization, Ministerial Declaration, November 14, 2001.

2. Pascal Lamy, address to Committee on Trade and Development, World Trade Organization, November 28, 2005.

3. Steven R. Weisman, ed., *Ethics and Globalization: The Tradeoffs Underlying Our Policy Choices*, proceedings of conference held by the Peterson Institute for International Economics, Washington, January 7, 2013 (Washington: Peterson Institute for International Economics, 2013), 15–18.

4. John F. Kennedy, "Inaugural address," Washington, January 20, 1961.

5. Richard N. Cooper, Panel Discussion, in *The New International Economic Order: The North-South Debate*, ed. Jagdish N. Bhagwati (Boston: MIT Press, 1977).

6. Benedict XVI, *Encyclical Letter Caritas in Veritate of the Supreme Pontiff Benedict XVI to the Bishops, Priests and Deacons, Men and Women Religious, the Lay Faithful and All People of Good Will on Integral Human Development in Charity and Truth*, June 29, 2009.

7. Jagdish N. Bhagwati, ed., *The New International Economic Order: The North-South Debate* (Boston: MIT Press, 1977).

8. See Organization for Economic Cooperation and Development (OECD), "The 0.7% ODA/GNI Target—A History," OECD.org, July 1, 2013. Also see OECD, "Table 3. DAC Members' Commitments and Performance," OECD.org, April 2011.

9. David T. Cook, "James Wolfensohn: Excerpts from a Monitor Breakfast on Poverty and Globalization," *Christian Science Monitor*, June 13, 2003.

10. World Bank, "Tariff Reform Could Deliver Annual Global Gains of $300 Billion by 2015, Says World Bank Study," press release, World Bank, Washington, November 9, 2005.

11. Alan Bjerga, "U.S. Reaches Deal with Brazil Ending Cotton Dispute," Bloomberg News, October 1, 2014.

12. Ernesto Zedillo, speech at Kansas State University, May 3, 2001.

13. Kimberly Ann Elliott, Debayani Kar, and J. David Richardson, *Assessing Globalization's Critics: "Talkers Are No Good Doers???"* Working Paper 02-5 (Washington: Institute for International Economics, 2002). The authors note that the number of nongovernmental organizations mobilized against globalization ranges from 15,000 to 20,000. But they found that 100 coalitions, networks, and groups working on the issue seem to be the most influential.

14. Ernesto Zedillo, "Against Globaphobia," *New Perspectives Quarterly* 17, no. 2 (June 28, 2008).

15. Julia B. Isaacs, Isabel V. Sawhill, and Ron Haskins, *Getting Ahead or Losing Ground: Economic Mobility in America* (Washington: Brookings Institution Press, February 2008).

16. Gordon H. Hanson, Challenges for US Immigration Policy, in *The United States and the World Economy: Foreign Economic Policy for the Next Decade*, ed. C. Fred Bergsten (Washington: Institute for International Economics, 2005), 357–358.

17. Tali Regev and Daniel Wilson, *Changes in Income Inequality across the U.S.*, FRBSF Economic Letter, Number 2007-8 (San Francisco: Federal Reserve Bank of San Francisco, September 21, 2007).

18. See "Remarks by AFL-CIO President Richard L. Trumka, 2013 Immigration Campaign Launch Event, Chicago, Illinois," March 7, 2013.

19. Michael Mandelbaum, *The Road to Global Prosperity* (New York: Simon and Schuster, 2014), 64–66.

20. George Borjas, *Immigration and the American Worker: A Review of the Academic Worker* (Washington: Center for Immigration Studies, April 2013).

21. Ian Goldin, *Globalizing with Their Feet: The Opportunities and Costs of International Migration*, World Bank Global Issues Seminar Series (Washington: World Bank, 2006).

22. Ibid, 12.

23. See Alex Nowrasteh, "Immigration and Economic Inequality," Cato At Liberty blog post, April 21, 2015.

24. Robert B. Reich, "Who Is Us?" *Harvard Business Review* (January–February 1990): 54.

25. Robert B. Reich, "Who Is Them?" *Harvard Business Review* (March–April 1991): 77.

26. That is on a cumulative basis, however. Today, other countries are larger recipients of annual foreign investment than the United States, according to the Congressional Research Service; see James K. Jackson, *Outsourcing and Insourcing Jobs in the U.S. Economy: Evidence Based on Foreign Investment Data*, CRS Report (Washington: Congressional Research Service, May 10, 2012).

27. See Theodore H. Moran, *Foreign Investment and Supply Chains in Emerging Markets: Recurring Problems and Demonstrated Solutions,* Working Paper 14-12 (Washington: Peterson Institute for International Economics, 2014).

28. Jefferson, Thomas, Letter to Horatio G. Spafford. In *The Papers of Thomas Jefferson, Retirement Series: Volume 7: 28 November 1813 to 30 September 1814*, ed. J. Jefferson Looney (Princeton, NJ: Princeton University Press, 2011).

29. Richard Trumka, remarks at the Council on Foreign Relations event "A Conversation with Richard Trumka," March 18, 2011.

30. Martin Wolf, *Why Globalization Works* (New Haven, CT: Yale University Press, 2004), 185.

31. Catherine Rampell, "Stock Markets Rise, but Half of Americans Don't Benefit," Economix Online Column, *New York Times*, May 8, 2013.

32. Erika Becker-Medina, *Public-Employee Retirement Systems State- and Locally-Administered Pensions Summary Report: 2010,* Government Division Briefs (Washington: US Department of Commerce, US Census Bureau, 2012).

33. The Impact of the North American Free Trade Agreement on US Jobs and Wages: Hearing before the Committee on Banking, Housing, and Urban Affairs, Senate, 103rd Cong., lst sess., April 22, 1993.

34. Robert B. Reich, *Supercapitalism: The Transformation of Business, Democracy and Everyday Life* (New York: Knopf, 2007), 100–101.

35. Ibid., 122–123.

36. Edward Luce, *Time to Start Thinking: America in the Age of Descent* (New York: Atlantic Monthly Press, 2012), 261.

37. Antoine Gara, "Years After Sandy Hook Shooting, Pension Fund CalSTRS Exits Cerberus-Backed Remington," *Forbes,* June 8, 2015.

38. Cerberus Capital Management LP, "Cerberus Capital Management Statement Regarding Freedom Group, Inc.," PRNewswire, New York, December 18, 2012.

39. US Department of State, Office of the Historian, "Foreign Relations of the United States, 1964–1968, Vol. VIII, International Monetary and Trade Policy, Document 94," May 10, 1966.

40. Jeffry A. Frieden, *Global Capitalism: Its Fall and Rise in the Twentieth Century* (New York: Norton, 2006), 293.

41. Jean-Jacques Servan-Schreiber, *The American Challenge,* trans. Ronald Steel (London: Hamish Hamilton, 1968).

42. Raymond Vernon, *Sovereignty at Bay: The Multinational Spread of U.S. Enterprises* (New York: Basic Books, 1971).

43. Raymond Vernon, *In the Hurricane's Eye: The Troubled Prospects of Multinational Enterprises* (Cambridge, MA: Harvard University Press, 1998), 28.

44. Ibid.

45. C. Fred Bergsten, Thomas Horst, and Theodore H. Moran, *American Multinationals and American Interests* (Washington: Brookings Institution Press, 1978), 4.

46. David Rothkopf, *Power, Inc.: The Epic Rivalry Between Big Business and Government—and the Reckoning That Lies Ahead* (New York: Farrar, Straus and Giroux, 2012), 201.

47. International Monetary Fund, Coordinated Direct Investment Survey (CDIS), Washington.

48. McKinsey Global Institute, *Financial Globalization: Retreat or Reset?* New York, March 2013.

49. James K. Jackson, *Outsourcing and Insourcing Jobs in the U.S. Economy: Evidence Based on Foreign Investment Data* (Washington: Congressional Research Service, May 10, 2012), 7.

50. Kevin B. Barefoot and Raymond J. Mataloni Jr., *Operations of U.S. Multinational Companies in the United States and Abroad: Preliminary Results from the 2009 Benchmark Survey* (Washington: US Department of Commerce, Bureau of Economic Analysis, November 2011).

51. McKinsey Global Institute, *Growth and Competitiveness in the United States: The Role of Its Multinational Companies*, Washington, June 2010.

52. Gary Clyde Hufbauer, Theodore H. Moran, and Lindsay Oldenski, assisted by Martin Vieiro, *Outward Foreign Direct Investment and US Exports, Jobs, and R&D: Implications for US Policy* (Washington: Peterson Institute for International Economics, 2013), xix.

53. Jessica Wohl, "Wal-Mart Plans $50 Billion 'Buy American' Push," Reuters, January 15, 2013.

54. Hal R. Varian, "An iPod Has Global Value: Ask the (Many) Countries That Make It," *New York Times*, June 28, 2007.

55. Charles Duhigg and David Barboza, "In China, Human Costs Are Built into an iPad," *New York Times*, January 25, 2012. Also see David Barboza and Keith Bradsher, "Foxconn Plant Closed after Riot, Company Says," *New York Times*, September 24, 2012.

56. Charles Duhigg and Keith Bradsher, "How the US Lost Out on iPhone Work," *New York Times*, January 21, 2012.

57. David Barboza, "After Suicides, Scrutiny of China's Grim Factories," *New York Times*, June 6, 2010.

58. Jim Yardley, "Justice Still Elusive in Factory Disasters in Bangladesh," *New York Times*, June 29, 2013.

59. Keith Bradsher and Charles Duhigg, "Signs of Changes Taking Hold in Electronics Factories in China," *New York Times*, December 26, 2012.

60. Jane G. Gravelle, *Tax Havens: International Tax Avoidance and Evasion* (Washington: Congressional Research Service, January 23, 2013).

61. Charles Duhigg and David Kocieniewski, "How Apple Sidesteps Billions in Taxes," *New York Times*, April 28, 2012.

62. Jia Lynn Yang, "Post Analysis of Dow 30 Firms Shows Declining Tax Burden as a Share of Profits," *Washington Post*, March 26, 2013. Also see Jia Lynn Yang, "The Dow 30's Tax Burden: Behind the Washington Post's Analysis," *Washington Post*, March 27, 2013.

63. Jesse Drucker, "Google 2.4% Rate Shows How $60 Billion Lost to Tax Loopholes," Bloomberg, October 21, 2010.

64. George Osborne, Statement of the Exchequer, "Britain and Germany Call for International Action to Strengthen Tax Standards," Gov.uk, November 5, 2012.

65. Danny Hakim, "Europe Takes Aim at Deals Created to Escape Taxes," *New York Times*, November 15, 2014.

66. Donald J. Marples and Jane G. Gravelle, *Corporate Expatriation, Inversions, and Mergers: Tax Issues* (Washington: Congressional Research Service, May 27, 2014).

67. Liz Hoffman and Hester Plumridge, "Race to Cut Taxes Fuels Urge to Merge," *Wall Street Journal*, July 15, 2014.

68. Allan Sloan, "Positively Un-American Tax Dodges: Bigtime Companies Are Moving Their 'Headquarters' Overseas to Dodge Billions in Taxes . . . That Means the Rest of Us Pay Their Share," *Fortune*, July 21, 2014, 62–70.

69. Jane G. Gravelle, *International Corporate Tax Rate Comparisons and Policy Implications* (Washington: Congressional Research Service, December 28, 2012).

70. Gary Clyde Hufbauer and Martin Vieiro, *Corporate Taxation and US MNCs: Ensuring a Competitive Economy*, Policy Brief 13-9 (Washington: Peterson Institute for International Economics, April 2013).

71. National Commission on Fiscal Responsibility and Reform, *The Moment of Truth: Report of the National Commission on Fiscal Responsibility and Reform* (Washington: White House, December 1, 2010), 28.

72. Martin Feldstein, "Want to Boost the Economy? Lower Corporate Tax Rates: The Increased Flow of Capital to the US Would Result in Greater Productivity and Higher Real Wages," *Wall Street Journal*, February 15, 2011.

73. Jane G. Gravelle, *International Corporate Tax Rate Comparisons and Policy Implications* (Washington: Congressional Research Service, December 28, 2012).

74. Ibid.

75. Ursula Burns, interview by Renee Montagne, "Xerox CEO: 'If You Don't Transform, You're Stuck,'" *Morning Edition*, National Public Radio, May 23, 2012.

Chapter 12: Who Governs? The Role of Liberal Internationalism (pages 177–186)

1. John H. Crider, "Delegates Search for Warm Clothes," *New York Times*, July 2, 1944.

2. Benn Steill, *The Battle of Bretton Woods: John Maynard Keynes, Harry Dexter White, and the Making of a New World Order* (Princeton, NJ: Princeton University Press, 2013), 9.

3. Robert Skidelsky, ed. *John Maynard Keynes,* Vol. 3, *Fighting for Britain: 1937–1946* (New York: Viking, 2000), 347.

4. I. M. Destler, *American Trade Politics,* 4th ed. (Washington: Institute for International Economics, 2005).

5. Dani Rodrik, *The Globalization Paradox: Democracy and the Future of the World Economy* (New York: Norton, 2011), 71–74.

6. Jeffry A. Frieden, *Global Capitalism: Its Fall and Rise in the Twentieth Century* (New York: Norton, 2006), 267.

7. Liaquat Ahamed, *Money and Tough Love: On Tour with the IMF* (London: Visual Editions, 2014), 30.

8. Ibid., 31.

9. Ibid., 33–35.

10. Michael Mandelbaum, *The Road to Global Prosperity* (New York: Simon and Schuster, 2014).

11. Immanuel Kant, "Perpetual Peace: A Philosophical Sketch," 1795.

12. Strobe Talbott, *The Great Experiment: The Story of Ancient Empires, Modern States, and the Quest for a Global Nation* (New York: Simon and Schuster, 2008), 98–100.

13. Isaiah Berlin, The Pursuit of the Ideal (1988), in *The Crooked Timber of Humanity: Chapters in the History of Ideas,* 2d ed., ed. Henry Hardy (Princeton, NJ: Princeton University Press, 2013), 19.

14. George H. W. Bush, "Address Before a Joint Session of the Congress on the Persian Gulf Crisis and the Federal Budget Deficit," Washington, September 11, 1990, George Bush Presidential Library and Museum.

15. Eric Hobsbawm, Ethnicity, Migration, and the Validity of the Nation-State, in *Toward a Global Civil Society,* ed. Michael Walzer (New York: Berghahn Books, 1995), 236.

16. Samuel Scheffler, The Idea of Global Justice: A Progress Report. *Harvard Review of Philosophy* 20 (2012).

17. Peter Singer, *One World: The Ethics of Globalization,* 2nd ed. (New Haven, CT: Yale University Press, 2004).

18. Tony Blair, "Faith and Globalization," lecture at Westminster Cathedral, London (The Cardinals Lectures), April 4, 2008.

19. US Department of State, "Fact Sheet: Non-Governmental Organizations (NGOs) in the United States," 2012.

20. Nancy Birdsall, "Global Citizens and the Global Economy," essay adapted from a speech delivered to the UN General Assembly on September 10, 2010, for the United Nations' 66th General Assembly Development Dialogue (Washington: Center for Global Development, September 2012).

21. Robert O. Keohane and Joseph S. Nye Jr., introductory essay in Joseph S. Nye Jr. and John D. Donahue, eds., *Governance in a Globalizing World* (Washington: Brookings Institution Press, 2000), 22.

22. Hildy Teegen, Jonathan P. Doh, and Sushil Vachani, "The Importance of Nongovernmental Organizations (NGOs) in Global Governance and Value Creation: An International Business Research Agenda," *Journal of International Business Studies* 35, no. 6 (November 2004): 463–483.

23. Jonathan P. Doh and Barbara Kotschwar, Participation by Civil Society and Non-Governmental Organizations in Western Economic Integration, in *Research in Global Strategic Management,* Vol. 10, *North American Economic and Financial Integration,* ed. Alan M. Rugman (Oxford: Eslevier, 2004), 317–338.

24. Kimberly Ann Elliott, Debayani Kar, and J. David Richardson, *Assessing Globalization's Critics: Talkers Are No Good Doers???* Working Paper 2-5 (Washington: Institute for International Economics, 2002).

25. International Labour Organization, *Normlex: Information System on Labour Standards,* Geneva, 2012.

26. International Labour Organization, *Ratifications of All Conventions by Country,* Geneva, 2012.

27. Michael J. Sandel, *Democracy's Discontent: America in Search of a Public Philosophy* (Cambridge, MA: Harvard University Press, 1996), 339.

28. Larry Summers Exit Interview, *International Economy* (winter 2011): 8.

29. Kemal Dervis, with Ceren Ozer, *A Better Globalization: Legitimacy, Governance, and Reform* (Washington: Center for Global Development, 2005).

30. William D. Savedoff, *Global Government, Mixed Coalitions, and the Future of International Cooperation* (Washington: Center for Global Development, July 2012).

31. Organization for Economic Cooperation and Development, *OECD Guidelines for Multinational Enterprises* (Paris: OECD, 2011).

32. See Fair Labor Association, www.fairlabor.org.

33. Cullen S. Hendrix and Marcus Noland, *Confronting the Curse: The Economics and Geopolitics of Natural Resource Governance* (Washington: Peterson Institute for International Economics, 2014), 92–101.

34. Ibid., 101–119.

35. BDS Movement, www.bdsmovement.net.

Chapter 13: Pulling Together the Threads (pages 187–191)

1. I. M. Destler, *American Trade Politics,* 4th ed. (Washington: Institute for International Economics, 2005), 6.

2. Isaiah Berlin, The Apotheosis of the Romantic Will, in *The Crooked Timber of Humanity: Chapters in the History of Ideas*, 2d ed., ed. Henry Hardy (Princeton, NJ: Princeton University Press, 2013), 221.

Bibliography

Aaronson, Susan Ariel, and Jamie M. Zimmerman. *Trade Imbalance: The Struggle to Weigh Human Rights Concerns in Trade Policymaking*. New York: Cambridge University Press, 2008.

Abdelal, Rawi. *Capital Rules: The Construction of Global Finance*. Cambridge, MA: Harvard University Press, 2007.

Ahamed, Liaquat. *Lords of Finance: The Bankers Who Broke the World*. New York: Penguin Books, 2009.

Ahamed, Liaquat. *Money and Tough Love: On Tour with the IMF*. London: Visual Editions, 2014.

Altman, Daniel. *Outrageous Fortunes: The Twelve Surprising Trends That Will Reshape the Global Economy*. New York: Times Books, 2011.

Anderson, Gary A. *Sin: A History*. New Haven, CT: Yale University Press, 2009.

Appiah, Kwame Anthony. *Cosmopolitanism: Ethics in a World of Strangers*. New York: Norton, 2006.

Aristotle. *The Politics*, trans. Ernest Barker. Oxford: Clarendon Press, 1948 (first published 1946), book III, chap. ix.

Aristotle. *Nicomachean Ethics*, trans. W. D. Ross. Oxford University Press, revised edition, July 15, 2009.

Arvidsson, Adam, and Nicolai Peitersen. *The Ethical Economy: Rebuilding Value after the Crisis*. New York: Columbia University Press, 2013.

Autor, David H., David Dorn, and Gordon H. Hanson. The China Syndrome: Local Labor Market Effects of Import Competition in the United States. *American Economic Review* 103, no. 6 (October 2013): 2121–68.

Bagehot, Walter. *Lombard Street: A Description of the Money Market*. London: Henry S. King, 1873.

Bailyn, Bernard. *The Ideological Origins of the American Revolution*. Cambridge, MA: Harvard University Press, 1967.

Bailyn, Bernard, Robert Dallek, David Brion Davis, David Herbert Donald, John L. Thomas, and Gordon S. Wood. *The Great Republic: A History of the American People*, Vol. 1, 3rd ed. Lexington, MA: D. C. Heath, 1985.

Bailyn, Bernard, Robert Dallek, David Brion Davis, David Herbert Donald, John L. Thomas, and Gordon S. Wood. *The Great Republic: A History of the American People*, Vol. 2, 4th ed. Lexington, MA: D. C. Heath, 1992.

Banfield, Edward C. *The Moral Basis of a Backward Society*. New York: Free Press, 1958.

Barefoot, Kevin B., and Raymond J. Mataloni Jr. *Operations of US Multinational Companies in the United States and Abroad: Preliminary Results from the 2009 Benchmark Survey*. Washington: US Department of Commerce, Bureau of Economic Analysis, 2011.

Barofsky, Neil. *Bailout: An Inside Account of How Washington Abandoned Main Street While Rescuing Wall Street*. New York: Free Press, 2012.

Barker, Megan M. Manufacturing Employment Hard Hit during the 2007–09 Recession. *Monthly Labor Review*, Bureau of Labor Statistics, US Department of Labor, April 2011.

Bartels, Larry M. *Unequal Democracy: The Political Economy of the New Gilded Age*. Princeton, NJ: Princeton University Press, 2008.

Bastasin, Carlo. *Saving Europe: How National Politics Nearly Destroyed the Euro*. Washington: Brookings Institution Press, 2012.

Becker-Medina, Erika. *Public-Employee Retirement Systems State- and Locally-Administered Pensions Summary Report: 2010*. Washington: US Census Bureau, 2012.

Beitz, Charles R. Justice and International Relations. *Philosophy and Public Affairs* 4, no. 4 (summer 1975): 360–389.

Beitz, Charles R. *Political Theory and International Relations*. Princeton, NJ: Princeton University Press, 1979.

Bell, Daniel. *The End of Ideology: On the Exhaustion of Political Ideas in the Fifties*. Cambridge, MA: Harvard University Press, 1962.

Bell, Daniel. *The Cultural Contradictions of Capitalism*, 20th anniversary edition. New York: Basic Books, 1996.

Benedict XVI. *Encyclical Letter* Caritas in Veritate *of the Supreme Pontiff Benedict XVI to the Bishops, Priests and Deacons, Men and Women Religious, the Lay Faithful and All People of Good Will on Integral Human Development in Charity and Truth*, June 29, 2009.

Berg, Andrew G., and Jonathan D. Ostry. *Inequality and Unsustainable Growth: Two Sides of the Same Coin?* IMF Staff Discussion Note. Washington: International Monetary Fund, April 8, 2011.

Bergsten, C. Fred, ed. *The Long-Term International Economic Position of the United States*. Special Report 20. Washington: Peterson Institute for International Economics, 2009.

Bergsten, C. Fred, Thomas Horst, and Theodore H. Moran. *American Multinationals and American Interests*. Washington: Brookings Institution Press, 1978.

Bergsten, C. Fred, and Institute for International Economics. *The United States and the World Economy: Foreign Economic Policy for the Next Decade*. Washington: Institute for International Economics, 2005.

Berkman, Steve. *The World Bank and the Gods of Lending*. Sterling, VA: Kumarian Press, 2008.

Berlin, Isaiah. *Four Essays on Liberty*. New York: Oxford University Press, 1969.

Berlin, Isaiah. *The Crooked Timber of Humanity: Chapters in the History of Ideas*, 2d ed., ed. Henry Hardy. Princeton, NJ: Princeton University Press, 2013.

Bhagwati, Jagdish. The Capital Myth: The Difference between Trade in Widgets and Dollars. *Foreign Affairs* 77, no. 3 (May/June 1998): 7–12.

Bhagwati, Jagdish N. *In Defense of Globalization*. New York: Oxford University Press, 2004.

Bhagwati, Jagdish N., ed. *The New International Economic Order: The North-South Debate*. Panel Discussion. Boston: MIT Press, 1977.

Bhalla, Surjit. *Imagine There's No Country: Poverty, Inequality, and Growth in the Era of Globalization*. Washington: Institute for International Economics, 2002.

Bierce, Ambrose. *The Devil's Dictionary*. New York: Doubleday, Page, 1911.

Birdsall, Nancy. Inequality and Injustice in Our Global Economy. Wider Annual Lecture 9, UNU World Institute for Development Economics Research, Helsinki, Finland, 2006.

Bivens, Josh. *Everybody Wins, Except for Most of Us: What Economics Teaches about Globalization.* Washington: Economic Policy Institute, 2008.

Bivens, Josh. *Globalization and American Wages: Today and Tomorrow.* EPI Briefing Paper No. 196. Washington: Economic Policy Institute, 2007.

Blank, Rebecca. *Do Justice: Linking Christian Faith and Modern Economic Life.* Cleveland: Pilgrim Press, 1992.

Blank, Rebecca. *Economic Justice for All: A Pastoral Letter on Catholic Teaching and the US Economy.* Washington: United States Conference of Catholic Bishops, 1986.

Blanshard, Paul. *American Freedom and Catholic Power.* Boston: Beacon Press, 1958.

Blinder, Alan S. *After the Music Stopped: The Financial Crisis, the Response, and the Work Ahead.* New York: Penguin Press, 2013.

Blinder, Alan S. *How Many US Jobs Might Be Offshorable?* Center for Economic Policy Studies Working Paper No. 142. Princeton, NJ: Princeton University, March 2007.

Blinder, Alan S. *Offshoring: Big Deal, or Business as Usual?* Center for Economic Policy Studies Working Paper No. 149. Princeton, NJ: Princeton University, June 2007.

Blum, John M., Bruce Catton, Edmund Morgan, Arthur Schlesinger, Kenneth M. Stampp, and Vann Woodward. *The National Experience: A History of the United States.* New York: Harcourt, Brace and World, 1968.

Blustein, Paul. *And the Money Kept Rolling In (and Out): The World Bank, Wall Street, the IMF, and the Bankrupting of Argentina.* New York: PublicAffairs, 2005.

Blustein, Paul. *The Chastening: Inside the Crisis that Rocked the Global Financial System and Humbled the IMF* (revised and updated). New York: PublicAffairs, 2003.

Blustein, Paul. *Misadventures of the Most Favored Nations: Clashing Egos, Inflated Ambitions, and the Great Shambles of the World Trade System.* New York: PublicAffairs, 2009.

Blustein, Paul. *Off Balance: The Travails of Institutions That Govern the Global Financial System.* Waterloo, ON: Centre for International Governance Innovation, 2013.

Bolle, Mary Jane. *NAFTA: US Employment and Wage Effects.* Washington: Congressional Research Service, April 27, 1993.

Bookstaber, Richard. *A Demon of Our Own Design: Markets, Hedge Funds, and the Perils of Financial Innovation.* Hoboken, NJ: Wiley, 2007.

Borjas, George. *Immigration and the American Worker: A Review of the Academic Worker.* Washington: Center for Immigration Studies, April 2013.

Bradford, Scott C., Paul L. E. Grieco, and Gary Clyde Hufbauer. The Payoff to America from Global Integration. In *The United States and the World Economy: Foreign Economic Policy for the Next Decade,* ed. C. Fred Bergsten and Institute for International Economics. Washington: Institute for International Economics, 2005.

Brinkley, Alan. 1995. *The End of Reform: New Deal Liberalism in Recession and War.* New York: Knopf, 1995.

Bromwich, David. *Moral Imagination: Essays.* Princeton, NJ: Princeton University Press, 2014.

Brooks, Arthur C. *The Road to Freedom: How to Win the Fight for Free Enterprise.* New York: Basic Books, 2012.

Brynjolfsson, Erik, and Andrew McAfee. *The Second Machine Age: Work, Progress, and Prosperity in a Time of Brilliant Technologies.* New York: Norton, 2014.

Burns, R. Nicholas, and Jonathan Price, eds. *The Global Economic Crisis and Potential Implications for Foreign Policy and National Security.* Washington: Brookings Institution Press, 2009.

Bush, George H. W. Speech. In *NAFTA at 10: Yesterday, Today, and Tomorrow. Lessons Learned and Unmet Challenges.* Washington: Woodrow Wilson International Center for Scholars, 2005.

Camdessus, Michael. Address to the Board of Governors of the Fund, Hong Kong, China, September 23, 1997.

Carmel, Stephen. Globalization, Security, and Economic Well-Being. *Naval War College Review* 66, no. 1 (winter 2013): 41–55.

Carswell, John. *The South Sea Bubble.* London: Cresset Press, 1960.

Castelot, E. Laissez-Faire, Laissez-Passer, History of the Maxim. In *The New Palgrave: A Dictionary of Economics,* 4 vols., ed. John Eatwell, Murray Milgate, and Peter Newman. New York: Stockton Press, 1987.

Chace, James. *Acheson: The Secretary of State Who Created the American World.* New York: Simon and Schuster, 2008.

Chanda, Nayan. *Bound Together: How Traders, Preachers, Adventurers, and Warriors Shaped Globalization.* New Haven, CT: Yale University Press, 2007.

Chua, Amy. *World on Fire: How Exporting Free Market Democracy Breeds Ethnic Hatred and Global Instability.* New York: Doubleday, 2003.

Clausing, Kimberly. Multinational Firm Tax Avoidance and Tax Policy. *National Tax Journal* 62, no. 4 (December 2009).

Clausing, Kimberly. The Revenue Effects of Multinational Firm Income Shifting. *Tax Notes,* March 28, 2011.

Cline, William R. *Financial Globalization, Economic Growth, and the Crises of 2007–09.* Washington: Peterson Institute for International Economics, 2010.

Cline, William R. *Trade and Income Distribution.* Washington: Institute for International Economics, 1997.

Cline, William R. *The United States as a Debtor Nation.* Washington: Institute for International Economics and Center for Global Development, 2005.

Clinton, Bill. *Back to Work: Why We Need Smart Government for a Strong Economy.* New York: Knopf, 2011.

Clinton, Bill. *My Life.* New York: Knopf, 2004.

Conard, Edward. *Unintended Consequences: Why Everything You've Been Told about the Economy Is Wrong.* New York: Penguin Portfolio, 2012.

Congressional Budget Office. *The Distribution of Federal Spending and Taxes in 2006.* Washington, November 7, 2013.

Croly, Herbert David. *The Promise of American Life.* New York: Macmillan, 1909.

Cuomo Commission on Trade and Competitiveness. *The Cuomo Commission Report: A New American Formula for a Strong Economy.* New York: Touchstone, 1988.

Damrosch, Leo. *Jean-Jacques Rousseau: Restless Genius.* New York: Houghton Mifflin, 2005.

Darwin, Charles. *The Descent of Man.* 1871, repr., New York: Penguin Classics, 2004.

Dawkins, Richard. *The Selfish Gene.* Oxford: Oxford University Press, 1976.

DeLong, J. Bradford. Shrugging Off Atlas: Exactly How Did Once-Respectable Conservative Economists Get Swept Up in 'Moocher Class' Mania? *Democracy: A Journal of Ideas* (spring 2013): 92–100.

Dervis, Kemal, with Ceren Ozer. *A Better Globalization: Legitimacy, Governance, and Reform.* Washington: Center for Global Development, 2005.

DesLauriers, Jacqueline, and Barbara Kotschwar. After Seattle: How NGOs Are Transforming the Global Trade and Finance Agenda. In *How NGOs Are Transforming Corporate Strategy, Public Policy, and Business Government Relations,* ed. Jonathan P. Doh and Hildy Teegen. Westport, CT: Praeger, 2003.

Destler, I. M. *American Trade Politics,* 4th ed. Washington: Institute for International Economics, 2005.

de Tocqueville, Alexis. *Democracy in America,* trans. Henry Reeve. New York: Schocken Books, 1974.

Dickson, Paul. *Words from the White House: Words and Phrases Coined or Popularized by America's Presidents.* New York: Walker Publishing, 2013.

Dionne, E. J., Jr. *Souled Out: Reclaiming Faith and Politics after the Religious Right.* Princeton, NJ: Princeton University Press, 2008.

Dionne, E. J., Jr., William A. Galston, Korin Davis, and Ross Tilchin. *Faith in Equality: Economic Justice and the Future of Religious Progressives.* Governance Studies Program. Washington: Brookings Institution Press, 2014.

Dobbs, Richard, Jaana Remes, James Manyika, Charles Roxburgh, Sven Smit, and Fabian Schaer. *Urban World: Cities and the Rise of the Consuming Class.* McKinsey Global Institute, June 2012.

Doh, Jonathan P., and Barbara Kotschwar. Participation by Civil Society and Non-Governmental Organizations in Western Economic Integration. In *Research in Global Strategic Management,* Vol. 10, *North American Economic and Financial Integration,* ed. Alan M. Rugman. Oxford: Elsevier, 2004.

Doh, Jonathan P., and Hildy Teegen, eds. *Globalization and NGOs: Transforming Business, Government, and Society.* Westport, CT: Praeger, 2003.

Dollar, David, Tatjana Kleineberg, and Aart Kraay. *Growth Still Is Good for the Poor.* Policy Research Working Paper 6568. Macroeconomics and Growth Team, Development Research Group. Washington: World Bank, August 2013.

Donald, David Herbert. *Lincoln.* New York: Simon and Schuster, 1995.

Dornbusch, Rudiger. 1998. Capital Controls: An Idea Whose Time Is Past. In *Should the IMF Pursue Capital-Account Convertibility?* ed. Stanley Fischer et al. Essays in International Finance No. 207. Princeton, NJ: International Finance Section, Department of Economics, Princeton University, 1998.

Dworkin, Ronald. *Justice for Hedgehogs.* Cambridge, MA: Harvard University Press, 2011.

Ebenstein, Avraham, Ann Harrison, and Margaret McMillan. *Why Are American Workers Getting Poorer? China, Trade and Offshoring.* NBER Working Paper 21027. Cambridge, MA: National Bureau of Economic Research, 2015.

Eberstadt, Nicholas. The Great Society at Fifty: What LBJ Wrought. *Weekly Standard,* May 19, 2014.

Eberstadt, Nicholas. *A Nation of Takers: America's Entitlement Epidemic.* West Conshohocken, PA: Templeton Press, 2012.

Economic Policy Institute. *The State of Working America.* Washington, 2012.

Edsall, Thomas B. *The Age of Austerity: How Scarcity Will Remake American Politics.* New York: Doubleday, 2012.

Edwards, Lawrence, and Robert Z. Lawrence. *Rising Tide: Is Growth in Emerging Economies Good for the United States?* Washington: Peterson Institute for International Economics, 2013.

Eichengreen, Barry. *Globalizing Capital: A History of the International Monetary System.* 2nd ed. Princeton, NJ: Princeton University Press, 2008.

Eizenstat, Stuart E. *The Future of the Jews: How Global Forces Are Impacting the Jewish People, Israel, and Its Relationship with the United States.* Lanham, MD: Rowman and Littlefield, 2012.

Elliott, Kimberly Ann, Debayani Kar, and J. David Richardson. *Assessing Globalization's Critics: "Talkers Are No Good Doers???"* Washington: Institute for International Economics, 2002.

Elsby, Michael, Bart Hobijn, and Ayesegul Sahin. *The Decline of the U.S. Labor Share.* Brookings Papers on Economic Activities, Spring 2013 BPEA Conference. Washington: Brookings Institution Press, 2013.

Evensky, Jerry. Adam Smith's Essentials: On Trust, Faith, and Free Markets. *Journal of the History of Economic Thought* 33, no. 2 (June 2011).

Feldstein, Martin. Is Income Inequality Really a Problem? In *Income Inequality: Issues and Policy Options* (Federal Reserve Bank of Kansas City) (1998): 357–360.

Feldstein, Martin. Reducing Poverty, Not Inequality. *Public Interest* 137 (fall 1999).

Felten, Eric. *Loyalty: The Vexing Virtue*. New York: Simon and Schuster, 2011.

Felsenthal, Mark. "Bernanke keeps focus on jobs, warns on Europe." Reuters, November 10, 2011.

Ferguson, Niall. *Empire: The Rise and Demise of the British World Order and the Lessons for Global Power.* New York: Basic Books, 2044.

Fischer, Stanley. Capital Account Liberalization and the Role of the IMF. Paper presented at the IMF seminar on Asia and the IMF, Hong Kong, China, September 19, 1997.

Fischer, Stanley, Richard N. Cooper, Rudiger Dornbusch, Peter M. Garber, Carlos Massad, Jacques J. Polak, Dani Rodrik, and Savas S. Tarapore, Should the IMF Pursue Capital-Account Convertibility? *Essays in International Finance* 207 (May 1998).

Fiss, Owen M. *Troubled Beginnings of the Modern State, 1888–1910*, Vol. 8, *The Oliver Wendell Holmes Devise: History of the Supreme Court of the United States,* ed. Stanley N. Katz. New York: Cambridge University Press, 2006.

Fleischacker, Samuel. *A Short History of Distributive Justice*. Cambridge, MA: Harvard University Press, 2004.

Fletcher, Ian. *Free Trade Doesn't Work: What Should Replace It and Why*. Sheffield, MA: Coalition for a Prosperous America, 2011.

Fogel, Robert Williams. *The Fourth Great Awakening and the Future of Egalitarianism*. Chicago: University of Chicago Press, 2000.

Fox, Justin. *The Myth of the Rational Market: A History of Risk, Reward, and Delusion on Wall Street*. New York: Harper Business, 2011.

Pope Francis. *Apostolic Exhortation* Evangelii Gaudium *of the Holy Father Francis, to the Bishops, Clergy, Consecrated Persons and the Lay Faithful on the Proclamation of the Gospel in Today's World,* November 24, 2013.

Frank, Robert H., and Philip J. Cook. *The Winner-Take-All Society: Why the Few at the Top Get So Much More Than the Rest of Us*. New York: Penguin Books, 1996.

Freeland, Chrystia. *Plutocrats: The Rise of the New Global Super Rich and the Fall of Everyone Else*. New York: Penguin Press, 2012.

Freund, Caroline (assisted by Sarah Oliver). *Rich People Poor Countries: The Rise of Emerging Market Tycoons and Their Mega Firms*. Washington: Peterson Institute for International Economics, forthcoming 2016.

Frieden, Jeffry A. *Global Capitalism: Its Fall and Rise in the Twentieth Century*. New York: Norton, 2006.

Friedman, Benjamin M. *The Moral Consequences of Economic Growth*. New York: Vintage Books, 2006.

Friedman, David D. The Just Price. In *The New Palgrave: A Dictionary of Economics,* 4 vols., ed. John Eatwell, Murray Milgate, and Peter Newman. New York: Macmillan, 1987.

Friedman, Milton. *Capitalism and Freedom: Fortieth Anniversary Edition*. Chicago: University of Chicago Press, 2002.

Friedman, Thomas L. *The Lexus and the Olive Tree: Explaining Globalization*. New York: Farrar, Straus and Giroux, 1999.

Friedman, Thomas L. *The World Is Flat: A Brief History of the Twenty-First Century*. New York: Farrar, Straus and Giroux, 2005.

Friedman, Thomas L., and Michael Mandelbaum. *That Used to Be Us: How America Fell Behind in the World It Invented and How We Can Come Back*. New York: Farrar, Straus and Giroux, 2011.

Funabashi, Yuichi. *Managing the Dollar: From the Plaza to the Louvre*, 2nd ed. Washington: Institute for International Economics, 1989.

Fukuyama, Francis. Social Capital and the Global Economy: A Redrawn Map of the World. *Foreign Affairs* 74, no. 5 (September/October 1995).

Gagnon, Joseph E., with Marc Hinterschweiger. 2011. *The Global Outlook for Government Debt over the Next 25 Years: Implications for the Economy and Public Policy*. Policy Analyses in International Economics 94. Washington: Peterson Institute for International Economics, 2011.

Galbraith, John Kenneth. *The Affluent Society*. New York: Houghton Mifflin, 1958.

Galston, William A. *Liberal Purposes: Goods, Virtues, and Diversity in the Liberal State*. New York: Cambridge University Press, 1991.

Galston, William A. Progressive Politics and Communitarian Culture. In *Toward a Global Civil Society*, ed. Michael Walzer. Providence, RI: Berghahn Books, 1995.

Garrett, Thomas A. US Income Inequality: It's Not So Bad. *Inside the Vault* (Federal Reserve Bank, St. Louis) (spring 2010).

Geithner, Timothy F. *Stress Test: Reflections on Financial Crises*. New York: Crown Publishers, 2014.

Goldin, Ian. *Globalizing with Their Feet: The Opportunities and Costs of International Migration*. World Bank Global Issues Seminar Series. Washington: World Bank, 2006.

Goldin, Claudia, and Lawrence Katz. *The Race Between Education and Technology*. Cambridge, MA: Harvard University Press, 2008.

Goodman, Peter S. *Past Due: The End of Easy Money and the Renewal of the American Economy*. New York: Times Books, 2009.

Goodwyn, Lawrence. *Democratic Promise: The Populist Moment in America*. New York: Oxford University Press, 1976.

Graeber, David. *Debt: The First 5,000 Years*. New York: Melville House Publishing, 2011.

Graham, Edward M., and J. David Richardson. *Competition Policies for the Global Economy*. Washington: Institute for International Economics, 1997.

Gravelle, Jane G. *International Corporate Tax Rate Comparisons and Policy Implications*. CRS Report R41743. Washington: Congressional Research Service, December 28, 2012.

Gravelle, Jane G. *Tax Havens: International Tax Avoidance and Evasion*. CRS Report R40623. Washington: Congressional Research Service, January 23, 2013.

Greene, Joshua. *Moral Tribes: Emotion, Reason, and the Gap Between Us and Them*. New York: Penguin Press, 2013.

Greenspan, Alan. *The Age of Turbulence: Adventures in a New World*. New York: Penguin Press, 2007.

Grotius, Hugo. *The Freedom of the Seas: The Right Which Belongs to the Dutch to Take Part in the East Indian Trade*. 1608, repr., New York: Oxford University Press, 1916.

Grunwald, Michael. *The New Deal: The Hidden Story of Change in the Obama Era*. New York: Simon and Schuster, 2012.

Hacker, Jacob S., and Paul Pierson. *Winner-Take-All Politics: How Washington Made the Rich Richer—And Turned Its Back on the Middle Class*. New York: Simon and Schuster, 2010.

Haidt, Jonathan. *The Righteous Mind: Why Good People Are Divided by Politics and Religion*. New York: Pantheon Books, 2012.

Halm, George N. *International Monetary Cooperation*. Chapel Hill: University of North Carolina Press, 1945.

Hanson, Gordon H. Challenges for US Immigration Policy. In *The United States and the World Economy: Foreign Economic Policy for the Next Decade*, ed. C. Fred Bergsten. Washington: Institute for International Economics, 2005.

Haskins, Ron, and Isabel V. Sawhill. *Creating an Opportunity Society*. Washington: Brookings Institution Press, 2009.

Hayek, Friedrich. *The Road to Serfdom*. Chicago: University of Chicago Press, 1944.

Heilbroner, Robert L. *The Worldly Philosophers: The Lives, Times, and Ideas of the Great Economic Thinkers,* 7th ed. New York: Touchstone, 1999.

Hellebrandt, Tomas, and Paolo Mauro. *The Future of Worldwide Income Distribution.* Working Paper 15-7. Washington: Peterson Institute for International Economics, April 2015.

Hendrix, Cullen S., and Marcus Noland. *Confronting the Curse: The Economics and Geopolitics of Natural Resource Governance.* Washington: Peterson Institute for International Economics, 2014.

Hirsch, Michael. *Capital Offense: How Washington's Wise Men Turned America's Future over to Wall Street.* Hoboken, NJ: John Wiley, 2010.

Hobbes, Thomas. Chapter XIII; Of the Natural Condition of Mankind, as Concerning Their Felicity, and Misery, *Leviathan* (1651), History Guide: Lectures on Modern European History.

Hobsbawm, Eric. Ethnicity, Migration, and the Validity of the Nation-State. In *Toward a Global Civil Society,* ed. Michael Walzer. New York: Berghahn Books, 1995.

Hoffman, Stanley. *The Political Ethics of International Relations: Seventh Morgenthau Memorial Lecture on Ethics and Foreign Policy.* New York: Carnegie Council on Ethics and International Affairs, 1998.

Hofstadter, Richard. *The Age of Reform: From Bryan to FDR.* New York: Vintage Books, 1995.

Hoover, Herbert. *The Memoirs of Herbert Hoover.* New York: Macmillan, 1952.

Hufbauer, Gary Clyde, and Kimberly Ann Elliott. *Measuring the Costs of Protection in the United States.* Washington: Institute for International Economics, 1994.

Hufbauer, Gary Clyde, and Jeffrey J. Schott. *NAFTA: An Assessment,* rev. ed. Washington: Institute for International Economics, 1993.

Hufbauer, Gary Clyde, and Jeffrey J. Schott, assisted by Paul L. E. Grieco and Yee Wong. *NAFTA Revisited: Achievements and Challenges.* Washington: Institute for International Economics, 2005.

Hufbauer, Gary Clyde, and Martin Vieiro. *Corporate Taxation and US MNCs: Ensuring a Competitive Economy.* PIIE Policy Brief 13-9. Washington: Peterson Institute for International Economics, 2013.

Hufbauer, Gary Clyde, Theodore H. Moran, and Lindsay Oldenski, assisted by Martin Vieiro. *Outward Foreign Direct Investment and US Exports, Jobs, and R&D: Implications for US Policy.* Washington: Peterson Institute for International Economics, 2013.

Hufbauer, Gary Clyde, Cathleen Cimino, and Tyler Moran, *NAFTA at 20: Misleading Charges and Positive Achievements,* No. PB 14-13. Washington: Peterson Institute for International Economics, May 2014.

Hume, David, *An Enquiry Concerning the Principles of Morals,* ed. J.B. Schneewind (1751; repr., Indianapolis: Hackett, 1983), 49.

Hungerford, Thomas L. *Taxes and the Economy: An Economic Analysis of the Top Tax Rates since 1945.* Washington: Congressional Research Service, September 14, 2012.

Hutchinson, William T., and William M. E. Rachal, eds. *The Papers of James Madison,* 10 vols. Chicago: University of Chicago Press, 1962–77.

International Labor Organization. *World of Work 2014: Developing with Jobs.* Geneva, 2014.

International Monetary Fund. *Staff Report on Fiscal Policy and Income Equality.* IMF Policy Paper. Washington, January 22, 2014.

International Monetary Fund. *Fiscal Policy and Income Inequality.* IMF Policy Paper. Washington: IMF, January 23, 2014.

International Monetary Fund. *Special Issue: IMF Conference in Honor of Michael Mussa.* IMF Staff Paper, Vol. 52. Washington, 2005.

International Monetary Fund. *The IMF's Approach to Capital Account Liberalization.* Report of the Independent Evaluation Office, International Monetary Fund (prepared by staff led by Shinji Takagi and Jeffrey Allen Chelsky). Washington, 2005.

Ip, Po Keung. 2009. Is Confucianism Good for Business Ethics in China? *Journal of Business Ethics* 88 (2009): 463–476.

Irwin, Douglas A. 1996. *Against the Tide: An Intellectual History of Free Trade.* Princeton, NJ: Princeton University Press, 1996.

Isaacs, Julia B. *Spending on Children and the Elderly.* Washington: Brookings Institution Press, November 2009.

Isaacs, Julia B., Isabel V. Sawhill, and Ron Haskins. *Getting Ahead or Losing Ground: Economic Mobility in America.* Brookings Economic Mobility Project Report. Washington: Brookings Institution Press, February 2008.

Istrate, Emilia, and Nicholas Marchio. *Export Nation 2012: How US Metropolitan Areas Are Driving National Growth.* Brookings Metropolitan Policy Program Report. Washington: Brookings Institution Press, March 8, 2012.

Jackson, James K. *Foreign Direct Investment in the United States: An Economic Analysis.* CRS Report RS21857. Washington: Congressional Research Service, October 26, 2012.

Jackson, James K. *Outsourcing and Insourcing Jobs in the U.S. Economy: Evidence Based on Foreign Investment Data.* CRS Report RL32461. Washington: Congressional Research Service, May 10, 2012.

Jackson, James K. *US Direct Investment Abroad: Trends and Current Issues.* CRS Report RS21118. Washington: Congressional Research Service, October 26, 2012.

Jackson, Richard, Neil Howe, and Tobias Peter. *Balancing Tradition and Modernity: The Future of Retirement in East Asia.* Washington: Center for Strategic and International Studies, 2012.

James, Harold. *International Monetary Cooperation Since Bretton Woods.* Washington: International Monetary Fund, 1996.

James, William. What Pragmatism Means, in *Pragmatism: A Reader.* New York: Random House, 1997.

Jeanne, Olivier, Arvind Subramanian, and John Williamson. *Who Needs to Open the Capital Account?* Washington: Peterson Institute for International Economics, 2012.

Jefferson, Thomas. Letter to Horatio G. Spafford. In *The Papers of Thomas Jefferson, Retirement Series: Volume 7: November 1813 to September 1814,* ed. J. Jefferson Looney. Princeton, NJ: Princeton University Press, 2011.

Jefferson, Thomas. Notes on the State of Virginia. In *Jefferson: Writings: Autobiography, Notes on the State of Virginia, Public and Private Papers, Addresses, Letters,* ed. Merrill D. Peterson 1782, repr., New York: Library of America, 1984.

Jensen, J. Bradford. *Global Trade in Services: Fear, Facts, and Offshoring.* Washington: Peterson Institute for International Economics, 2011.

Jensen, J. Bradford, and Lori G. Kletzer. *Tradable Services: Understanding the Scope and Impact of Services Offshoring.* Working Paper 05-9. Washington: Peterson Institute for International Economics, September 2005.

John Paul II. Centesimus Annus: *Encyclical Letter to His Venerable Brother Bishops in the Episcopate, the Priests and Deacons, Families of Men and Women Religious, All the Christian Faithful, and to All Men and Women of Good Will on the Hundredth Anniversary of* Rerum Novarum. May 1, 1991.

Johnson, Chalmers A. *MITI and the Japanese Miracle: The Growth of Industrial Policy, 1925–1975.* Stanford, CA: Stanford University Press, 1982.

Johnson, Chalmers, Laura D'Andrea Tyson, and John Zysman. *Politics and Productivity: The Real Story of Why Japan Works.* Cambridge, MA: Ballinger, 1991.

Johnson, Simon, and James Kwak. *13 Bankers: The Wall Street Takeover and the Next Financial Meltdown.* New York: Pantheon Books, 2010.

Johnson, Simon, and James Kwak. *White House Burning: The Founding Fathers, Our National Debt, and Why It Matters to You*. New York: Pantheon Books, 2012.

Jomo K. S., and Jacques Baudot, eds. *Flat World, Big Gaps: Economic Liberalization, Globalization, Poverty and Inequality*. London: Zed Books, in association with the United Nations, 2007.

Jones, Jeffrey Owen, and Peter Meyer. *The Pledge: A History of the Pledge of Allegiance*. New York: Thomas Dunne Books, 2010.

Kahane, Leo H. Congressional Voting Patterns on NAFTA: An Empirical Analysis. *American Journal of Economics and Sociology* 55, no. 4 (October 1996): 395–409.

Kahneman, Daniel. *Thinking, Fast and Slow*. New York: Farrar, Straus and Giroux, 2011.

Kahneman, Daniel , and Amos Tversky. Choices, Values, and Frames. *American Psychologist* (April 1984).

Kaletsky, Anatole. *Capitalism 4.0: The Birth of a New Economy in the Aftermath of Crisis*. New York: PublicAffairs, 2010.

Kant, Immanuel. *Idea for a Universal History with a Cosmopolitan Purpose* (1784). Translation by Lewis White Beck. From Immanuel Kant, *On History*, Bobbs-Merrill Co., 1963.

Kant, Immanuel. *Lectures on Ethics*. 1775–1780, repr., Indianapolis, IN: Hackett Publishing Company, 1981.

Kant, Immanuel. *Perpetual Peace: A Philosophical Sketch*. 1795, repr., Indianapolis, IN: Hackett Publishing Company, 2003.

Kapstein, Ethan B. *Economic Justice in an Unfair World: Toward a Level Playing Field*. Princeton, NJ: Princeton University Press, 2006.

Kapstein, Ethan B. Models of International Economic Justice. *Ethics and International Affairs* (Carnegie Council on Ethics and International Affairs) 18, no. 2 (2004): 79–92.

Kazin, Michael. *A Godly Hero: The Life of William Jennings Bryan*. New York: Anchor Books, 2006.

Keats, John. *The Complete Poetical Works and Letters of John Keats*, Cambridge ed. Boston: Houghton Mifflin, 1899.

Keightley, Mark P., and Molly F. Sherlock. *The Corporate Income Tax System: Overview and Options for Reform*. CRS Report R42726. Washington: Congressional Research Service, September 13, 2012.

Kennan, George F. *Realities of American Foreign Policy*. New York: Norton, 1966.

Kennedy, David M. *Freedom from Fear: The American People in Depression and War, 1929–1945*. Vol. 9, *The Oxford History of the United States*, ed. C. Vann Woodward. New York: Oxford University Press, 1999.

Kennedy, David M. *Over Here: The First World War and American Society*. 1980, repr., New York: Oxford University Press, 2004.

Kennedy, David M., Lizabeth Cohen, and Thomas A. Bailey. *The American Pageant: A History of the American People*, 14th ed. Boston: Wadsworth, Cengage Learning, 2010.

Keynes, John Maynard. *Essays in Persuasion*. 1931, repr., New York: Classic House Books, 2009.

Keynes, John Maynard. *The General Theory of Employment Interest and Money*. http://cas.umkc.edu/ economics/people/facultypages/kregel/courses/econ645/winter2011/generaltheory.pdf.

Kindleberger, Charles P. *Manias, Panics, and Crashes: A History of Financial Crises*, 3rd ed. Hoboken, NJ: John Wiley, 1996.

Kletzer, Lori G. *Job Loss from Imports: Measuring the Costs*. Washington: Institute for International Economics, 2001.

Kletzer, Lori G., and Howard Rosen. Easing the Adjustment Burden on US Workers. In *The United States and the World Economy: Foreign Economic Policy for the Next Decade*, ed. C. Fred Bergsten and the Institute for International Economics. Washington: Institute for International Economics, 2005.

Koenig, Evan F., Robert Leeson, and George A. Kahn, eds. *The Taylor Rule and the Transformation of Monetary Policy*. Stanford, CA: Hoover Institute Press, 2012.

Krueger, Anne O. *A New Approach to Sovereign Debt Restructuring*. Washington: International Monetary Fund, April 2002.

Krueger, Anne O. Supporting Globalization. Remarks at the 2002 Eisenhower National Security Conference on National Security for the 21st Century: Anticipating Challenges, Seizing Opportunities, Building Capabilities, September 26, 2002.

Krugman, Paul. The Myth of Asia's Miracle: A Cautionary Fable. *Foreign Affairs* 73, no. 6 (November/December 1994).

Krugman, Paul. *Pop Internationalism*. Cambridge, MA: MIT Press, 1997.

Krugman, Paul. *The Conscience of a Liberal*. New York: Norton, 2007.

Krugman, Paul. *Trade and Wages, Reconsidered*. Brookings Papers on Economic Activity, Spring. Washington: Brookings Institution Press, 2008.

Krugman, Paul. Debt, Guilt and America's Good Fortune. *Economist*, November 8, 2011.

Krugman, Paul. *End This Depression Now!* New York: Norton, 2012.

Krugman, Paul, and Maurice Obstfeld. *International Economics Theory and Policy*, 2d ed. New York: HarperCollins, 1991.

Kuehn, Manfred. *Kant: A Biography*. Cambridge: Cambridge University Press, 2001.

Kuttner, Robert. *Debtor's Prison: The Politics of Austerity versus Possibility*. New York: Knopf, 2013.

Kuznets, Simon. Economic Growth and Income Inequality. In *The American Economic Review* 45, no. 1 (March 1955) (article drawn from presidential address delivered at the Sixty-seventh Annual Meeting of the American Economic Association, Detroit, Michigan, December 29, 1954).

Lakner, Christoph, and Branko Milanović. *Global Income Distribution: From the Fall of the Berlin Wall to the Great Recession*. Policy Research Working Paper 6719. Washington: World Bank, December 2013.

Lansing, Robert. *The Peace Negotiations: A Personal Narrative*. Boston: Houghton Mifflin, 1921.

Lasch, Christopher. *The Culture of Narcissism: American Life in An Age of Diminishing Expectations*. New York: Norton, 1979.

Lawrence, Robert Z. *Blue Collar Blues: Is Trade to Blame for Rising US Income Inequality?* Policy Analyses in International Economics 85. Washington: Peterson Institute for International Economics, January 2008.

Lawrence, Robert Z., and Lawrence Edwards. Shattering the Myths about US Trade Policy. *Harvard Business Review* (March 2012): 2901–05.

Lee, Ronald, and Andrew Mason. The Price of Maturity. *Finance and Development* 48, no. 2 (June 2011).

Leo XIII. Rerum Novarum: *Encyclical of Pope Leo XIII on Capital and Labor*. May 15, 1891.

Lessig, Lawrence. *Republic, Lost: How Money Corrupts Congress—and a Plan to Stop It*. New York: Twelve, 2011.

Levine, Aaron, ed. *The Oxford Handbook of Judaism and Economics*. New York: Oxford University Press, 2010.

Levy, Frank, and Richard J. Murnane. *The New Division of Labor: How Computers Are Creating the Next Job Market*. Princeton, NJ: Princeton University Press, 2004.

Lewis, Howard III, and J. David Richardson. *Why Global Commitment Really Matters*. Washington: Institute for International Economics, 2001.

Lewis, Michael. *Boomerang: Travels in the New Third World*. New York: Norton, 2011.

Lewis, R. W. B. *The American Adam: Innocence, Tragedy and Tradition in the Nineteenth Century*. Chicago: University of Chicago Press, 1955.

Lippmann, Walter. *The Phantom Public* (1925). Transaction Publishers, 1993.

Lipset, Seymour Martin. *American Exceptionalism: A Double-Edged Sword.* New York: Norton, 1996.

Looney, J. Jefferson, ed. *The Papers of Thomas Jefferson, Retirement Series: Volume 7: 28 November 1813 to 30 September 1814.* Princeton, NJ: Princeton University Press, 2011.

Lucas, Robert E. The Industrial Revolution: Past and Future. 2003 Annual Report Essay, Federal Reserve Bank of Minneapolis, May 1, 2004.

Luce, Edward. *Time to Start Thinking: America in the Age of Descent.* New York: Atlantic Monthly Press, 2012.

Lund, Susan, Toos Daruvala, Richard Dobbs, Philipp Härle, Ju-Hon Kwek, and Ricardo Falcon. *Financial Globalization: Retreat or Reset?* New York: McKinsey Global Institute, March 2013.

Luttig, Matthew. The Structure of Inequality and Americans' Attitudes toward Redistribution. *Public Opinion Quarterly* 77, no. 3 (fall 2013): 811–821.

Machiavelli, Niccolo. *The Prince,* trans. Luigi Ricci. 1552, repr., New York: Signet Classic, 1999.

Mandelbaum, Michael. *The Road to Global Prosperity.* New York: Simon and Schuster, 2014.

Mandeville, Bernard. *The Fable of the Bees; Or, Private Vices, Public Benefits, with an Essay on Charity and Charity Schools, and a Search into the Nature of Society.* London, 1795.

Mankiw, N. Gregory. Defending the One Percent. *Journal of Economic Perspectives* 27, no. 3 (summer 2013): 21–34.

Mankiw, N. Gregory. *Principles of Economics,* 5th ed. Mason, OH: South-Western, Cengage Learning, 2009.

Mann, Bruce H. *Republic of Debtors: Bankruptcy in the Age of American Independence.* Cambridge, MA: Harvard University Press, 2002.

Mann, Catherine L., with Jacob Funk Kirkegaard. *Accelerating the Globalization of America: The Role of Information Technology.* Washington: Peterson Institute for International Economics, 2006.

Manyika, James, Jacques Bughin, Susan Lund, Olivia Nottebohm, David Poulter, Sebastian Jauch, and Sree Ramaswamy. *Global Flows in a Digital Age: How Trade, Finance, People, and Data Connect the World Economy.* McKinsey Global Institute, April 2014.

Marke, Julius J., ed. *The Holmes Reader,* 2nd ed. Dobbs Ferry, NY: Oceana Publications, 1964.

Marples, Donald J., and Jane G. Gravelle. *Corporation Expatriation, Inversions, and Mergers: Tax Issues.* Washington: Congressional Research Service, May 27, 2014.

Martin, Rex, and David Reidy, eds. *Rawls's Law of Peoples: A Realistic Utopia?* Malden, MA: Blackwell Publishing, 2006.

McCarty, Nolan, Keith T. Poole, and Howard Rosenthal. *Polarized America: The Dance of Ideology and Unequal Riches.* Cambridge, MA: MIT Press, 2006.

McGreevy, John T. *Catholicism and American Freedom: A History.* New York: Norton, 2003.

McKinsey Global Institute. *Big Data: The Next Frontier for Innovation, Competition, and Productivity.* New York: McKinsey and Company, May 2011.

McKinsey Global Institute. *An Economy That Works: Job Creation and America's Future.* New York: McKinsey and Company, June 2011.

McKinsey Global Institute. *Growth and Competitiveness in the United States: The Role of Its Multinational Companies.* New York: McKinsey and Company, June 2010.

McNeill, William H. *The Pursuit of Power: Technology, Armed Force, and Society Since A.D. 1000.* Chicago: University of Chicago Press, 1984.

Menand, Louis, ed. *Pragmatism: A Reader.* New York: Random House, 1997.

Milanović, Branko. *Worlds Apart: Measuring International and Global Inequality.* Princeton, NJ: Princeton University Press, 2005.

Milanović, Branko. Global Income Inequality: A Review. *World Economics* 7, no. 1 (January–March 2006.

Milanović, Branko. *The Haves and the Have-Nots: A Brief and Idiosyncratic History of Global Inequality.* New York: Basic Books, 2011.

Milanović, Branko. The Real Winners and Losers of Globalization. *Globalist*, October 25, 2012.

Milanović, Branko. Global Income Inequality in Numbers: In History and Now. *Global Policy* 4, no. 2 (May 2013).

Minsky, Hyman P. The Modeling of Financial Instability: An Introduction, paper presented at Fifth Annual Pittsburgh Conference on Modeling and Simulation, University of Pittsburgh, April 24–26, 1974.

Mishel, Lawrence, and Natalie Sabadish. *CEO Pay in 2012 Was Extraordinarily High Relative to Typical Workers and Other High Earners.* Washington: Economic Policy Institute, June 26, 2013.

Mishel, Lawrence, Josh Bivens, Elise Gould, and Heidi Shierholz. *The State of Working America.* Economic Policy Institute. Ithaca, NY: Cornell University Press, 2012.

Mishkin, Frederic S. *The Next Great Globalization: How Disadvantaged Nations Can Harness Their Financial Systems to Get Rich.* Princeton, NJ: Princeton University Press, 2006.

Mittelhauser, Mark. Employment Trends in Textiles and Apparel, 1973–2005. *Monthly Labor Review,* Bureau of Labor Statistics, US Department of Labor, August 1997.

Moran, Theodore H. *American Multinationals and American Economic Interests: New Dimensions to an Old Debate.* Working Paper 09-3. Washington: Peterson Institute for International Economics, July 2009.

Moran, Theodore H. *Foreign Investment and Supply Chains in Emerging Markets: Recurring Problems and Demonstrated Solutions.* Working Paper WP 14-12. Washington: Peterson Institute for International Economics, 2014.

Morris, Charles S. *The Trillion Dollar Meltdown: Easy Money, High Rollers, and the Great Credit Crash,* rev. and updated. New York: PublicAffairs, 2008.

Montesquieu, Charles de. *Considerations on the Causes of the Greatness of the Romans and Their Decline* (1734). Hackett Publishing Company, Inc., 1999.

Morrison, Wayne M., Mary Jane Bolle, James K. Jackson, Vivian C. Jones, M. Angeles Villarreal, and Candy Meza, *U.S. Trade Concepts, Performance, and Policy: Frequently Asked Questions.* CRS Report RL33944. Washington: Congressional Research Service, August 3, 2015.

Moynihan, Daniel Patrick. *The Politics of a Guaranteed Income: The Nixon Administration and the Family Assistance Plan.* New York: Random House, 1973.

Moynihan, Daniel Patrick. *Pandaemonium: Ethnicity in International Politics.* New York: Oxford University Press, 1993.

Murray, Charles. *Coming Apart. The State of White America, 1960–2010.* New York: Crown Forum, 2012.

Murray, Charles. *Losing Ground: American Social Policy, 1950–1980,* 10th anniversary ed. New York: Basic Books, 1994.

Nagel, Thomas. The Problem of Global Justice. *Philosophy and Public Affairs* 33, no. 2 (March 2005): 113–147.

Nasar, Sylvia. *Grand Pursuit: The Story of Economic Genius.* New York: Simon and Schuster, 2011.

Nasr, Vali. *The Dispensable Nation: American Foreign Policy in Retreat.* New York: Doubleday, 2013.

National Commission on the Causes of the Financial and Economic Crisis in the United States. *The Financial Crisis Inquiry Report: Final Report of the National Commission on the Causes of the Financial and Economic Crises in the United States.* New York: PublicAffairs, 2011.

National Commission on Fiscal Responsibility and Reform. *The Moment of Truth: Report of the National Commission on Fiscal Responsibility and Reform.* Washington: White House, December 2010.

Nicholas, David A. *Eisenhower 1956: The President's Year of Crisis—Suez and the Brink of War*. New York: Simon and Schuster, 2012.

Niskanen, William A. Reshaping the Global Financial Architecture: Is There a Role for the IMF? *Cato Journal* 18, no. 3 (winter 1999): 331–334.

Noah, Timothy. *The Great Divergence: America's Growing Inequality Crisis and What We Can Do about It*. New York: Bloomsbury Press, 2012.

Noland, Marcus. *Religion, Culture, and Economic Performance*. Working Paper 03-8. Washington: Institute for International Economics, September 2003.

Novak, Michael. *The Catholic Ethic and the Spirit of Capitalism*. New York: Free Press, 1993.

Novak, Michael. *The Spirit of Democratic Capitalism*. Lanham, MD: Madison Books, 1982.

Nozick, Robert. *Anarchy, State, and Utopia*. New York: Basic Books, 1974.

Nussbaum, Martha C. Symposium on Cosmopolitanism. Duties of Justice, Duties of Material Aid: Cicero's Problematic Legacy. *Journal of Political Philosophy* 8, no. 2 (2000): 176–206.

Nussbaum, Martha C. *Women and Human Development: The Capabilities Approach*. New York: Cambridge University Press, 2001.

Nye, Joseph S., Jr., and John D. Donahue, eds. *Governance in a Globalizing World*. Washington: Brookings Institution Press, 2000.

Obey, David R. 1993. Potential Economic Impacts of NAFTA: An Assessment of the Debate: Staff Study. United Joint Economic Committee, US Congress, Washington.

Okun, Arthur M. *Equality and Efficiency: The Big Tradeoff*. Washington: Brookings Institution Press, 1975.

Organization for Economic Cooperation and Development. *OECD Guidelines for Multinational Enterprises*. Paris, 2011.

Organization for Economic Cooperation and Development. *Divided We Stand: Why Inequality Keeps Rising*. Paris, December 2011.

Organization for Economic Cooperation and Development. Labour Losing to Capital: What Explains the Declining Labour Share? In *OECD Employment Outlook 2012*. Paris: OECD Publishing, 2012.

Ostry, Jonathan D., Andrew Berg, and Charalambos G. Tsangarides. *Redistribution, Inequality, and Growth*. IMF Staff Discussion Note, Research Department. Washington: International Monetary Fund, April 2014.

Ottaviano, Gianmarco I. P., Giovanni Peri, and Greg C. Wright. *Immigration, Offshoring and American Jobs*. NBER Working Paper 16439. Cambridge, MA: National Bureau of Economic Research, October 2010.

Oxfam. *Working for the Few: Political Capture and Economic Inequality*. Oxfam Briefing Paper 178, Summary. Oxford, January 20, 2014.

Paul VI. *Populorum Progressio: Encyclical of Pope Paul VI on the Development of Peoples*. March 26, 1967.

Peck, Don. *Pinched: How the Great Recession Has Narrowed Our Futures and What We Can Do about It*. New York: Broadway, 2012.

Peil, Jan, and Irene van Staverson, eds. *Handbook of Economics and Ethics*. Northampton, MA: Edward Elgar, 2009.

Peltzman, Sam. The Effects of Automobile Safety Regulation. *Journal of Political Economy* 83, no. 4 (August 1975): 677–726.

Penn, Mark J., with E. Kinney Zalesne. *Microtrends: The Small Forces Behind Tomorrow's Big Changes*. New York: Twelve, 2008.

Pessen, Edward. *Riches, Class, and American Power: America Before the Civil War*. Lexington, MA: D. C. Heath, 1973.

Pew Research Center for the People and the Press. *The American-Western European Values Gap.* Washington, November 17, 2011.

Pew Research Center for the People and the Press. Public Sees U.S. Power Declining as Support for Global Engagement Slips. Washington, December 3, 2013.

Phillips, Kevin. *Bad Money: Reckless Finance, Failed Politics, and the Global Crisis of American Capitalism.* New York: Viking, 2008.

Pierce, Justin R., and Peter K. Schott. *The Surprisingly Swift Decline of U.S. Manufacturing Employment.* Washington: Division of Research and Statistics and Monetary Affairs, Federal Reserve Board, 2014.

Piketty, Thomas. *Capital in the Twenty-First Century,* trans. Arthur Goldhammer. Cambridge, MA: Harvard University Press, 2014.

Piketty, Thomas. *The Economics of Inequality,* trans. Arthur Goldhammer. Cambridge, MA: Harvard University Press, 2015.

Pisani-Ferry, Jean, André Sapir, and Guntram B. Wolff. *EU-IMF Assistance to Euro-Area Countries: An Early Assessment.* Bruegel Blueprint Series No. 19. Brussels: Bruegel, 2013.

Plato. *The Republic,* trans. Benjamin Jowett. Mineola, NY: Dover, 2000.

Plender, John. *Capitalism: Money, Morals and Markets.* London: Biteback Publishing, 2015.

Plutarch. Against Debt and Borrowing upon Usury. In *Plutarch's Morals,* ed. William W. Goodwin. Boston: Little, Brown, 1878.

Pogge, Thomas. Are We Violating the Human Rights of the World's Poor? *Yale Human Rights and Development Law Journal* 14, no. 2 (2011).

Pogge, Thomas W. Cosmopolitanism and Sovereignty. *Ethics* 103, no. 1 (October 1992): 48–75.

Pogge, Thomas W. *Realizing Rawls.* Ithaca, NY: Cornell University Press, 1989.

Pope, Alexander. *An Essay on Man* (1734). Scolar Press, 1969.

Posen, Adam S. "The 'World If' Debate: If the Rich World Aimed for Minimal Growth, Would It Be a Disaster or a Blessing?" *Economist,* August 1, 2015.

Posner, Richard A., ed. *The Essential Holmes: Selections from the Letters, Speeches, Judicial Opinions, and Other Writings of Oliver Wendell Holmes, Jr.* Chicago: University of Chicago Press, 1992.

Pringle, Robert. *The Money Trap: Escaping the Grip of Global Finance.* New York: Palgrave Macmillan, 2012.

Purvis, Meghan. Treasurer Summers Met with Protest, Catcalls. *Oberlin Review,* December 8, 2000.

Putnam, Robert D. *Bowling Alone: The Collapse and Revival of American Community.* New York: Simon and Schuster, 2000.

Rachman, Gideon. *Zero-Sum Future: American Power in the Age of Anxiety.* New York: Simon and Schuster, 2011.

Rajan, Raghuram G. *Fault Lines: How Hidden Fractures Still Threaten the World Economy.* Princeton, NJ: Princeton University Press, 2010.

Rasmussen, Chris, and Martin Johnson. *Jobs Supported by Exports, 1993–2011.* Manufacturing and Services Economics Brief. Washington: Office of Competition and Economic Analysis, International Trade Administration, US Department of Commerce, October 2012.

Rawls, John. *A Theory of Justice.* Cambridge, MA: Harvard University Press, 1971.

Rawls, John. *Political Liberalism.* New York: Columbia University Press, 1993.

Rawls, John. *The Law of the Peoples.* Cambridge, MA: Harvard University Press, 1999.

Reagan, Ronald. *An American Life.* New York: Simon and Schuster, 1990.

Regev, Tali, and Daniel Wilson, *Changes in Income Inequality across the U.S.* FRBSF Economic Letter, Number 2007-8. San Francisco: Federal Reserve Bank of San Francisco, September 21, 2007.

Reich, Robert B. *Supercapitalism: The Transformation of Business, Democracy, and Everyday Life*. New York: Knopf, 2007.

Reich, Robert B. Who Is Them? *Harvard Business Review* (March–April 1991).

Reich, Robert B. Who Is Us? *Harvard Business Review* (January–February 1990).

Reidy, David A. A Just Global Economy: In Defense of Rawls. *Journal of Ethics* 11, no. 2 (2007): 193–236.

Reinhart, Carmen M., and Kenneth S. Rogoff. *A Decade of Debt*. Policy Analyses in International Economics 95. Washington: Peterson Institute for International Economics, September 2011.

Reinhart, Carmen M., and Kenneth S. Rogoff. Growth in a Time of Debt. *American Economic Review: Papers and Proceedings* 100, no. 2 (May 2010).

Reinhart, Carmen M., and Kenneth S. Rogoff. *This Time Is Different: Eight Centuries of Financial Folly*. Princeton, NJ: Princeton University Press, 2009.

Ricardo, David. *On the Principles of Political Economy and Taxation*. London: John Murray, 1817.

Richardson, J. David, and Edward M. Graham, eds. *Global Competition Policy*. Washington: Institute for International Economics, 1997.

Rodrik, Dani. *The Globalization Paradox: Democracy and the Future of the World Economy*. New York: Norton, 2011.

Rodrik, Dani. *Has Globalization Gone Too Far?* Washington: Institute for International Economics, 1997.

Rodrik, Dani, and Arvind Subramanian. Why Did Financial Globalization Disappoint? *IMF Staff Papers* 56, no. 1 (January 2009): 112–138.

Rognlie, Matthew. Deciphering the Fall and Rise in the Net Capital Share. Conference draft for Spring 2015 Brookings Panel on Economic Activity, March 2015.

Rognlie, Matthew. A Note on Piketty and Diminishing Returns to Capital. Massachusetts Institute of Technology, photocopy, June 15, 2014.

Rorty, Richard. First Projects, Then Principles, *The Nation*, December 22, 1997, 18.

Rothkopf, David. *Power, Inc.: The Epic Rivalry Between Big Business and Government—and the Reckoning That Lies Ahead*. New York: Farrar, Straus and Giroux, 2012.

Rothkopf, David. *Superclass: The Global Power Elite and the World They Are Making*. New York: Farrar, Straus and Giroux, 2008.

Rothschild, Emma. *Economic Sentiments: Adam Smith, Condorcet, and the Enlightenment*. Cambridge, MA: Harvard University Press, 2001.

Roubini, Nouriel, and Stephen Mihm. *Crisis Economics: A Crash Course in the Future of Finance*. New York: Penguin Press, 2010.

Roubini, Nouriel, and Brad Setser. *Bailouts or Bail-Ins? Responding to Financial Crises in Emerging Economies*. Washington: Institute for International Economics, 2004.

Rousseau, Jean-Jacques. *A Discourse on Political Economy*, 1755.

Rousseau, Jean-Jacques. Considerations on the Government of Poland and on Its Proposed Reformation. Constitution Society, unpublished, 1772.

Rousseau, Jean-Jacques. *Social Contract and Discourses*. New York: Dutton, 1913.

Roxburgh, Charles, Susan Lund, and John Piotrowski. *Mapping Global Capital Markets 2011*. McKinsey Global Institute, August 2011.

Rubin, Robert E., and Jacob Weisberg. *In an Uncertain World: Tough Choices from Wall Street to Washington*. New York: Random House, 2003.

Sachs, Jeffrey D. *The Price of Civilization: Reawakening American Virtue and Prosperity*. New York: Random House, 2011.

Sacks, Jonathan. *The Dignity of Difference: How to Avoid the Clash of Civilizations*, 2d ed. New York: Continuum, 2009.

Saez, Emmanuel. *Striking It Richer: The Evolution of Top Incomes in the United States (Updated with 2009 and 2010 Estimates)*. Berkeley: University of California, Berkeley, 2012.

Salinas, Carlos. Remarks in *NAFTA at 10: Progress, Potential, and Precedents*, Vol. 2. Washington: Woodrow Wilson International Center for Scholars, 2005.

Samuelson, Paul A., and William D. Nordhaus. *Economics*, 19th ed. Boston: McGraw-Hill/Irwin, 2010.

Samuelson, Paul A., and William D. Nordhaus. *Macroeconomics*, 16th ed. Boston: McGraw-Hill/Irwin, 1998.

Sandel, Michael J. *Democracy's Discontent: America in Search of a Public Philosophy*. Cambridge, MA: The Belknap Press of the Harvard University Press, 1996.

Sandel, Michael J. *Justice: What's the Right Thing to Do?* New York: Farrar, Straus and Giroux, 2009.

Sandel, Michael J. *What Money Can't Buy: The Moral Limits of Markets*. New York: Farrar, Straus and Giroux, 2012.

Savedoff, William D. *Global Government, Mixed Coalitions, and the Future of International Cooperation*. Washington: Center for Global Development, July 2012.

Sawhill, Isabel, and Emily Monea. Old News. *Democracy* 9 (summer 2008).

Scheffler, Samuel. The Idea of Global Justice: A Progress Report. *Harvard Review of Philosophy* 20 (2014).

Scheiber, Noam. *The Escape Artists: How Obama's Team Fumbled the Recovery*. New York: Simon and Schuster, 2011.

Scheve, Kenneth F., and Matthew J. Slaughter. *Globalization and the Perception of American Workers*. Washington: Institute for International Economics, 2001.

Schott, Jeffrey J., and Cathleen Cimino. *Crafting a Transatlantic Trade and Investment Partnership: What Can Be Done*. PIIE Policy Brief 13-8. Washington: Peterson Institute for International Economics, March 2013.

Scott, Robert E. *The Burden of Outsourcing: US Non-oil Trade Deficit Costs More than 5 Million Jobs*. EPI Briefing Paper No. 222. Washington: Economic Policy Institute, October 2, 2008.

Scott, Robert E. *The High Price of "Free" Trade: NAFTA's Failure Has Cost the United States Jobs Across the Nation*. EPI Briefing Paper No. 147. Washington: Economic Policy Institute, November 17, 2003.

Seglow, Jonathan. Altruism. In *Handbook of Economics and Ethics*, ed. Jan Peil and Irene van Staveren. Northampton, MA: Edward Elgar, 2009.

Sen, Amartya. Justice. In *The New Palgrave: A Dictionary of Economics*, 4 vols., ed. John Eatwell, Murray Milgate, and Peter Newman. New York: Macmillan, 1987.

Servan-Schreiber, Jean-Jacques. *The American Challenge*, trans. Ronald Steel. London: Hamish Hamilton, 1968.

Shue, Henry. *Basic Rights: Subsistence, Affluence and US Foreign Policy*, 2d ed. Princeton, NJ: Princeton University Press, 1996.

Siddiqi, Mohammad Nejatullah. *Riba, Bank Interest and the Rationale of Its Prohibition*. Jeddah, Saudi Arabia: Islamic Development Bank, Islamic Research and Training Institute, 2004.

Simmons, N. E. Natural Law. In *The New Palgrave: A Dictionary of Economics*, 4 vols., ed. John Eatwell, Murray Milgate, and Peter Newman. New York: Macmillan, 1987.

Singer, Peter. *One World: The Ethics of Globalization (The Terry Lectures)*, 2nd ed. New Haven, CT: Yale University Press, 2004.

Skidelsky, Robert, ed. *John Maynard Keynes*, Vol. 3, *Fighting for Britain: 1937–1946*. New York: Viking, 2000.

Skidelsky, Robert. *Keynes: The Return of the Master: Why, Sixty Years after His Death, John Maynard Keynes Is the Most Important Economic Thinker for America.* New York: PublicAffairs, 2009.

Smith, Adam. *The Wealth of Nations,* 1776; repr., New York: Random House, 1937.

Smith, Adam. *An Inquiry into the Nature and Causes of the Wealth of Nations,* ed. Edward Cannan. London: Methuen, 1776.

Smith, Adam. *The Theory of Moral Sentiments.* London: A. Millar, 1759.

Solnicka, Sara J., and David Hemenway. Is More Always Better? A Survey on Positional Concerns. *Journal of Economic Behavior and Organization* 37 (1998): 373–383.

Sorkin, Andrew Ross. *Too Big to Fail.* New York: Viking, 2009.

Spence, A. Michael, and Sandile Hlatshwayo. *The Evolving Structure of the American Economy and the Employment Challenge.* CFR Working Paper. New York: Council on Foreign Relations, March 2011.

Spencer, Herbert. *Essays: Scientific, Political, and Speculative,* 3 vols. London: Williams and Norgate, 1891.

Stackhouse, Max L. *God and Globalization,* Vol. 4, *Globalization and Grace.* New York: Continuum, 2007.

Steill, Benn. *The Battle of Bretton Woods: John Maynard Keynes, Harry Dexter White, and the Making of a New World Order.* Princeton, NJ: Princeton University Press, 2013.

Stiglitz, Joseph E. *Freefall: America, Free Markets, and the Sinking of the World Economy.* New York: Norton, 2010.

Stiglitz, Joseph E. *Globalization and Its Discontents.* New York: Norton, 2002.

Stiglitz, Joseph E. *The Price of Inequality: How Today's Divided Society Endangers Our Future.* New York: Norton, 2012.

Summers, Lawrence. Larry Summers: Exit Interview. *International Economy* 25, no. 1 (winter 2011): 8–11, 67.

Talbott, Strobe. *The Great Experiment: The Story of Ancient Empires, Modern States, and the Quest for a Global Nation.* New York: Simon and Schuster, 2008.

Tanenhaus, Sam. *The Death of Conservatism: A Movement and Its Consequences.* New York: Random House, 2010.

Taylor, John B. *First Principles: Five Keys to Restoring America's Prosperity.* New York: Norton, 2012.

Taylor, John B. *Getting Off Track: How Government Actions and Interventions Caused, Prolonged, and Worsened the Financial Crisis.* Stanford, CA: Hoover Institution Press, 2009.

Taylor, Timothy. Economics and Morality. *Finance and Development* (June 2014).

Teegen, Hildy, Jonathan P. Doh, and Sushil Vachani. 2004. The Importance of Nongovernmental Organizations (NGOs) in Global Governance and Value Creation: An International Business Research Agenda. *Journal of International Business Studies* 35, no. 6 (November): 463–483.

Thaler, Richard H. Anomalies: The Ultimatum Game. *Journal of Economic Perspectives* 2, no. 4 (autumn 1988): 195–206.

Trilling, Lionel. *Sincerity and Authenticity.* Cambridge, MA: Harvard University Press, 1971.

Truman, Edwin M. *A Strategy for IMF Reform.* Policy Analysis for International Economics 77. Washington: Peterson Institute for International Economics, February 2006.

Truman, Edwin M., ed. *Reforming the IMF for the 21st Century.* Special Report 19. Washington: Peterson Institute for International Economics, April 2006.

Tuck, Richard. *Natural Rights Theories: Their Origin and Development.* New York: Cambridge University Press, 1979.

Tuck, Richard. *The Rights of War and Peace: Political Thought and the International Order from Grotius to Kant.* New York: Oxford University Press, 1999.

Tuck, Richard, and Michael Silverthorne, eds. *Hobbes: On the Citizen.* New York: Cambridge University Press, 2003.

Tyson, Laura D'Andrea. *Who's Bashing Whom? Trade Conflict in High-Technology Industries.* Washington: Institute for International Economics, 1992.

United Nations. *The Millennium Development Goals Report.* New York, July 6, 2015.

United Nations Development Program. *Human Development Report 2013—The Rise of the South: Human Progress in a Diverse World.* New York: UNDP, 2013.

United States Council of Catholic Bishops. *Economic Justice for All: Pastoral Letter on Catholic Teaching and the US Economy.* Washington: United States Conference of Catholic Bishops, 1986.

US Department of Labor, Office of Policy Planning and Research. *The Negro Family: The Case for National Action.* Washington, March 1965.

Van Agtmael, Antoine. *The Emerging Markets Century: How a New Breed of World-Class Companies Is Overtaking the World.* New York: Free Press, 2007.

van Ittersum, Martine Julia. *Profit and Principle: Hugo Grotius, Natural Rights Theories and the Rise of Dutch Power in the East Indies (1595–1615).* Leiden: Brill Academic Publishers, 2006.

van Staveren, Irene. Efficiency. In *Handbook of Economics and Ethics,* ed. Jan Peil and Irene van Staveren. Northampton, MA: Edward Elgar, 2009.

Vernon, Raymond. *In The Hurricane's Eye: The Troubled Prospects of Multinational Enterprises.* Cambridge, MA: Harvard University Press, 1998.

Vernon, Raymond. *Sovereignty at Bay: The Multinational Spread of U.S. Enterprises.* New York: Basic Books, 1971.

Vernon, Raymond. *Storm Over the Multinationals: The Real Issues.* Cambridge, MA: Harvard University Press, 1977.

Vernon, Raymond, and Debora L. Spar. *Beyond Globalism: Remaking American Foreign Economic Policy.* New York: Free Press, 1989.

Villarreal, M. Angeles. *US Mexico Economic Relations: Trends, Issues, and Implications.* CRS Report RL32934. Washington: Congressional Research Service, August 9, 2012.

Walzer, Michael. A New Tribalism. *Dissent: A Quarterly of Politics and Culture* (spring 1992).

Walzer, Michael, ed. *Toward a Global Civil Society.* Providence, RI: Berghahn Books, 1995.

Warren, Elizabeth . *A Fighting Chance.* New York: Henry Holt, 2014.

Weber, Max. *The Protestant Ethic and the Spirit of Capitalism.* Sydney: Allen and Unwin, 1930.

Welch, Finis. In Defense of Inequality. *American Economic Review* 89, no. 2 (May 1999): 1–17.

Michael M., Weinstein, ed. *Globalization: What's New?* New York: Columbia University Press, 2005.

Wessel, David. 2009. *In Fed We Trust: Ben Bernanke's War on the Great Panic.* New York: Crown Business.

Williamson, John, ed. *Latin American Adjustment: How Much Has Happened?* Washington: Institute for International Economics, April 1990.

Williamson, John, ed. *The Political Economy of Policy Reform.* Washington: Institute for International Economics, 1994.

Williamson, John. *What Washington Means by Policy Reform.* Washington: Institute for International Economics, November 2002.

Wilson, Edward O. *Sociobiology: The New Synthesis.* Cambridge, MA: Harvard University Press, 1975.

Wilson, James Q. *The Moral Sense.* New York: The Free Press, 1993.

Wolf, Martin. *Why Globalization Works.* New Haven, CT: Yale University Press, 2004.

Woodward, Bob. *Maestro: Greenspan's Fed and the American Boom.* New York: Simon and Schuster, 2000.

Woodward, Bob. *The Price of Politics*. New York: Simon & Schuster, 2012.

World Bank. *A Guide to the World Bank*. Washington: World Bank, 2004.

World Bank Group and International Monetary Fund. *Global Monitoring Report 2014/2015: Ending Poverty and Sharing Prosperity*. Washington, 2015.

World Trade Organization. *World Trade Report 2012: World Trade in 2011*. Geneva, 2012.

Wright, Robert. *The Moral Animal: Why We Are the Way We Are: The New Science of Evolutionary Psychology*. New York: Vintage Books, 1994.

Wright, Robert. *Nonzero: The Logic of Human Destiny*. New York: Vintage Books, 2001.

Yergin, Daniel, and Joseph Stanislaw. *The Commanding Heights: The Battle for the World Economy*. New York: Touchstone, 2002.

Zedillo, Ernest. Against Globaphobia. *New Perspectives Quarterly* 17, no. 2 (June 28, 2008).

Acknowledgments

This book began years ago at the Peterson Institute for International Economics with conversations among colleagues about morality and economics. Those talks evolved improbably into a sustained undertaking of research and thinking that drew on the help of many people, to whom I express thanks.

The project would not have been possible without the support of Adam Posen, president of the Peterson Institute, who honored me by expanding my responsibilities at PIIE even as he helped shepherd the manuscript through a long process of study group, peer review, and revision after revision. Marcus Noland was a strong supporter, adviser, and organizer of the review and editing process. Fred Bergsten, emeritus director of the Institute, encouraged me to try my hand at a book for the Institute. Howard Rosen came up with the idea of a book about this subject and recommended many of its approaches. I am grateful to the Stavros Niarchos Foundation for its generous assistance, and especially the backing of Stelios Vasilakis, director of programs and strategic initiatives.

In a book that stretches some normal boundaries of commentary and analysis, I had to rely on an unusual assortment of colleagues and friends. They are hardly responsible for its errors or misjudgments. Many colleagues were crucial in this study's preparation. At the Institute, Mia Adamowsky helped in the early stages with her research. Michael Jarand assisted me in exploring and documenting myriad details and locating data for the graphics. Several colleagues read some or all of the manuscript and made constructive suggestions. They include Bill Cline, Simon Johnson, Morris Goldstein, Caroline Freund, Anders Åslund, Joe Gagnon, Tomas Hellebrandt, Jacob Kirkegaard, Nicolas Véron, Gary Hufbauer, Jeff Schott, Randy Henning, Jan Zilinsky, and Arvind Subramanian. Ted Truman went above and beyond by reading it not once but twice and correcting many misunderstandings of history and economics. Before his death in 2012, Mike Mussa was a great teacher of economics and moral issues. Daniel Yergin has been a superb editor and source of ideas on organization, emphasis, and language, helping this book find its voice. Liaquat Ahamed also read the manuscript carefully and gave smart suggestions. Others who read and helped were Bill Galston, Kim Elliott, Jessica Einhorn, Nancy Birdsall, Strobe Talbott, Antoine van Agtmael, and Peter Fisher. Steve Darwall, professor of philosophy at Yale, and a friend since our undergraduate days there, guided me through Rawls, Grotius, Kant, Hobbes, Locke, and moral philosophy in general. He should not be held accountable for my mistakes and oversimplifications, of course. I thank Branko Milanović for his help with the section on equality and for permission to republish some of his figures. I.M. (Mac) Destler and an anonymous reviewer made extremely helpful suggestions in the final rewriting.

Several friends have patiently heard me out on this subject and helped shape my thinking. They include Robert Zoellick, Jonathan Lear, Rabbi Daniel Zemel, Sally Quinn, the Very Rev. Gary Hall, Derek Shearer, James Kugel, Ellen Chesler, Ken Auletta, Amanda Urban, Richard Boucher, E. J. Dionne, Michael Kinsley, Patty Stonesifer, Rick Hertzberg, Tim Noah, Ed Luce, Walter Isaacson, Leon Wieseltier, Michael Mandelbaum, and Steve Pearlstein. I especially thank Erica Brown—teacher, friend, and counselor—who brought a unique perspective to reading this book. Under her guidance, my brothers in Jewish studies have taught me about ethics and faith: David Brooks, Frank Foer, Jeff Goldberg, David Gregory, Martin Indyk, and Dan Silva.

The support of the publications and communications team at the Peterson Institute has been indispensable. I single out the friendship and support of Edward Tureen, former publications and marketing director at the Institute, who died tragically in 2013. He brought sensitivity, knowledge, and encouragement to my interest in religious and moral ethics, and I dedicate this book to his memory. Madona Devasahayam worked tirelessly in the editing and restructuring of this book, forcing me to rethink some of my assumptions and clarify parts that I mistakenly thought were already clear. Sabra Ledent did brilliant line editing, fact-checking, and organizational work and challenged sloppy thinking. Susann Luetjen expertly handled the challenging production and design problems. The professionalism and friendship of Helen Hillebrand, Molly Tilghman, Jeremey Tripp, Dan Housch, Brian Reil, and Eitan Urkowitz lightened my burdens in overseeing publications and communications at PIIE. Jeff Cordeau has also been a great source of strength and fellowship.

I conclude with an expression of special gratitude to my family. My children, Madeleine and Teddy, have patiently heard me out on these subjects. My brilliant and extraordinary wife, Elisabeth Bumiller, despite work and family demands, has been my greatest supporter, especially when I left daily journalism years ago to join the world of a great think tank, and more recently when I struggled with this unorthodox writing project. Her patience, honesty, humor, judgment, and love have made this book possible, and my life a joy.

Index

Adams, John, 82
Affordable Care Act (US), 41
African Growth and Opportunity Act (AGOA), 129
aging population, 112–14
Agriculture Adjustment Act (AAA), 38
Aid to Families with Dependent Children, 88
AIG, 102
Alcatel, 167
Alighieri, Dante, 137
Alstom, 168
altruism, 133–34
America Jobs Creation Act, 174
American Adam, 83
American System, 25, 83–84
American system of manufactures, 83
American values, 34, 40, 75, 78–79, 81
amoral familism, 132
Anderson, Gary, 104
Annan, Kofi, 185
antiglobalization movement, 5–8, 146–50, 162, 183
Appiah, Kwame Anthony, 141
Argentina, 106, 117
Aristotle, 20
asset bubbles, 36, 97–98
Augustine, St., 21

Bagehot, Walter, 99
bailouts
    moral hazard and, 95–107, 116–17
    virtuous behavior and, 11–12, 74–75

Bain Capital, 43, 127
Banfield, Edward, 131–32
Bangladesh garment industry, 172, 185
Bank for International Settlements, 181
Bank of England, 99
Bank of the United States, 35–36
bank rescues, 99–103, 106–107
bankruptcy, 106–107, 117
Bankruptcy Act of 1800 (US), 106
Barofsky, Neil, 102
Beitz, Charles, 140–41
Bell, Daniel, 74, 78–79, 111
Bellamy, Francis, 33
Benedict XVI, Pope, 7, 77, 126, 161
Bennett, William, 80
Bentham, Jeremy, 103
Berlin, Isaiah, 2, 14, 39, 180, 190
Berlusconi, Silvio, 69, 118
Bernanke, Ben, 45, 99, 100–101, 143–44
Bill and Melinda Gates Foundation, 182
Bill of Rights (US), 35, 39
Birdsall, Nancy, 54, 182
Blair, Tony, 107, 182
Blank, Rebecca, 42
Blinder, Alan, 29, 148
Blustein, Paul, 29, 116
Boehm, Christopher, 133
Boehner, John, 43
bond markets, 110–11
Boston Marathon bombings, 132
Boycott, Divestment and Sanctions (BDS) campaign, 186

Bradley, Bill, 153
Bretton Woods system, 25–26, 130, 169, 177–78, 188–89
BRICS countries, 189
Britain. *See* United Kingdom
Bromwich, David, 135
Brooks, David, 78
Brown, Gordon, 69
Bryan, William Jennings, 36, 37*n*, 106
bubbles, 36, 97–98
Bulger, James Joseph (Whitey), Jr., 131
Bulger, William, 131
Burns, Ursula, 175
Burtless, Gary, 51
Bush, George H. W., 29, 92, 150–51, 180
Bush, George W., 41, 92*n*, 116, 140
business cycles, 36, 97
Buy American Act, 171
"Buy American" obligation, 13, 171–73

California Public Employees' Retirement System (CalPERS), 167–68
California Teachers pension fund, 168
Camdessus, Michel, 30, 31, 115
Cameron, David, 173
capital
    cross-border flows of, 28–31, 169–70
    economic growth and, 50–54, 61–64
    human, 64
    return on, 50–53
    role of, 61–62, 64–65
capitalism
    cultural effects of, 43, 79–80
    effects of global financial crisis on, 28
    ethics and, 70
    inclusive, 2
    inequality and, 45
    patrimonial, 48–49
    religious doctrine on, 7–8, 76–78
    versus socialism, 26–27
    virtue in, 73–80, 120–21
Carmel, Stephen, 12–13
Carter, Jimmy, 41, 151
Carthaginian Peace, 72
Catholic doctrine
    capitalism, 7–8, 77–78
    global financial crisis, 7–8
    justice, 42
    loyalty, 126
    social welfare, 28, 91
Center for Global Development (CGD), 182
central banks, 99–100
Cerberus Capital Management, 168
charity, 86–93

China
    entrepreneurship in, 77
    inequality in, 54
    offshoring to, 145, 147
    US relations with, 138–39
Chirac, Jacques, 167
chlorofluorocarbons (CFCs), 184
Christian doctrine. *See also* Catholic doctrine
    cosmopolitanism, 137
    debt, 104–105
    justice, 35, 42
Chua, Amy, 79
citizen-based civil society, 182, 191
civil rights, 39
class warfare, 43, 79
Clay, Henry, 25, 83–84
Cleveland, Grover, 87
climate change, 140, 184
Clinton, Bill
    antiglobalization movement, 6
    capital liberalization, 30
    debt relief, 107
    Mexico crisis, 95–96
    social welfare programs, 41, 54–55, 88
    tax increases, 92
    trade agreements, 29, 127, 150–54
Clinton Global Initiative, 182
club model of multilateral cooperation, 181
Cobden, Richard, 25
Colbert, Jean-Baptiste, 22
Cold War
    economic goals since, 179–80
    European rift caused by, 70
    ideological battle during, 136–39, 160
communism
    collapse of, 28, 61, 77, 134–35
    justice and, 49
    liberty and, 39
    US foreign policy on, 138–39
communitarianism, 130–37
    overview, 12–13, 49, 129
    quantification of, 143–57
comparative advantage, 23, 78
compensation, executive, 43, 45, 50, 55
Conard, Edward, 43
Concert of Europe, 180
Congressional Budget Office, 51, 89, 112
Congress of Vienna, 180, 184
conservatism, 41
Constitution (US), 82
constructivists, 132
consumer culture, 78–79
consumers, role of, 171–73
contagion, 11

Coolidge, Calvin, 89
Cooper, Richard, 160
Corn Laws (UK), 24, 146, 152
Corporate Social Responsibility (CSR)
        Initiative, 185
corporate tax havens, 173–75
cosmopolitanism, 137–41
    overview, 12–13, 49, 129–30
    quantification of, 143–57
creative destruction, 127
creditor moral hazard, 100
Croly, Herbert David, 40, 85
Crook, Clive, 52
Cuomo, Andrew, 54
Cyprus, 73

Darwin, Charles, 37, 98, 133
Davos World Economic Forum, 182, 184
Dawkins, Richard, 133
debt
    as moral issue, 71–72, 75, 96–107, 112–19
    as public policy tool, 109–21
debt crises, 28–31, 107, 114–19
debtor moral hazard, 100
debtors' prisons, 105–106
Decker, Matthew, 23
DeLong, Bradford, 4, 90
democracy
    foreign policy based on, 139
    justice and, 48–49
    social, 35
    virtue in, 85
Democratic Party (US), 84
demonstrations, antiglobalization, 6, 162
Deng Xiaoping, 4, 27, 77
deontology, 73–74
deposit insurance, 100
deregulation of capital flows, 28–31
Dervis, Kemal, 184
Diamond Development Initiative, 185
Dickens, Charles, 105
difference principle, 47, 129–30, 137
Dodd-Frank Act (US), 41, 118
Doha Round, 159–60
Donald, David Herbert, 14
Dornbusch, Rudiger, 30
Dorrien, Gary, 42
Draghi, Mario, 69, 118
duty-to-help argument, 141
Dworkin, Ronald, 43

earned income tax credit (EITC), 88
East Asian crisis, 11, 28–31, 114–19
Eberstadt, Nicholas, 88–90

economic growth
    capital and, 50–54, 61–64
    inequality and, 187
    taxation and, 92–93
economic justice. See justice
economic liberty. See liberty
economic patriotism, 125–26, 171–73. See also
        loyalty
economics, moral principles in, 8–10
economic tradeoffs, 8. See also tradeoffs
education, 146
efficiency-equality tradeoff, 9–10
Elmendorf, Douglas, 64
emerging-market economies
    aid to, 88, 107, 114–16, 160–62
    in global economic system, 137–38, 141,
        160
    immigration from, 59, 84, 140, 162–64
    inequality in, 54, 143–44
    liberty and, 27, 29–30
    socialism in, 136
    trade agreements and, 129–30, 159–62
Emerson, Ralph Waldo, 83
empathy, 133
employment. See also labor
    in manufacturing sector, 144–49, 170
    offshoring, 5–6, 125–28, 144–48, 166
    pension assets, 166–68
    reshoring, 144–46
    trade agreements and, 150–57
    unemployment, 96, 97f, 125, 144–50
Engels, Friedrich, 49
entitlement programs, 88–90, 112–14
entrepreneurship, 77, 81
environmental treaties, 184
Epstein, Richard, 43
equality
    doctrine of, 33
    justice aligned with, 33–34, 38–40, 56–64,
        187–88
    lack of (See inequality)
    of opportunity versus rights, 39–40
    public opinion of, 6, 44, 55–56
    tradeoff between efficiency and, 9–10
ethics. See also morality
    capitalism and, 70
    of debt, 112–14
    inequality and, 45
    virtue, 74
Etzioni, Amitai, 134
Europe
    anxieties about US domination in, 168
    global financial crisis and, 7, 69–73, 117–19
    history of, 22–23, 179

immigration to, 59, 84, 140, 162–64
  inequality in, 44
  values in, 34, 40
European Central Bank (ECB), 118
European Coal and Steel Community, 26, 179
European Economic Community, 26, 179
European Union (EU), 26, 180, 189
evolution, 37, 98, 133
Exchange Stabilization Fund (ESF), 96
executive compensation, 43, 45, 50, 55
exports, global, 127, 128*f*
externalities, 8–9
Extractive Industries Transparency Initiative
  (EITI), 186

Fair Labor Association, 173, 185
faith foundation, 182
Family Assistance Plan, 87
Federal Reserve (US), 99
Feldstein, Martin, 50, 55, 63, 174
Felten, Eric, 131
Ferguson, Niall, 25, 112
financial crises. *See also specific crisis*
  moral hazard and, 99–103, 114–19
  unemployment following, 96, 97*f*
fiscal policy, 32, 70, 92
Fischer, Stanley, 31, 32
Fiss, Owen, 38
Fitzgerald, F. Scott, 14
Fleischacker, Samuel, 35
food imports, 161–62
Ford, Gerald, 151
foreign aid, 88, 107, 114–16, 160–62
foreign investment, 165–71
foreign policy, 138–39, 179
four freedoms, 39
Foxconn Technology Group, 127, 172–73
France, 22
Francis, Pope, 7–8, 28, 77–78, 163
Franklin, Benjamin, 76, 82
freedom, 38–39. *See also* liberty
Freedom Group, 168
free trade, loyalty and, 12
French Revolution, 12, 33
Friedman, Benjamin, 76
Friedman, Milton, 10, 27, 87, 99, 111
Friedman, Thomas, 113
Froman, Michael, 155
Fuller, Melville, 37–38

Galbraith, John Kenneth, 41, 78
Galston, William, 90, 134–35, 160
game theory, 55–56, 131
Gans, Herbert, 135

Garrett, Thomas, 43
gay marriage, 38, 76, 80
Geithner, Timothy, 99–103
General Agreement on Tariffs and Trade
  (GATT), 26, 29, 140, 178
generational issue, debt as, 112–14
Geneva Convention, 180
Germany, 70–73
Gini index, 56–57, 58*f*
global citizens, 182, 191
global financial crisis (2007-08)
  capitalism shaken by, 28
  debt and, 112
  depictions of, 1
  European fallout from, 7, 69–73, 117–19
  moral hazard in, 69–80, 100–103
  virtuous behavior and, 11–12
global governance, 13, 137–41, 178–82,
  189–91
globalization
  backlash against, 5–8, 146–50
  definition of, 3
  economic results of, 4–5, 58–64
  first era of, 25, 36
  history of, 3–5
  morally based, 1–3, 120–21, 178–82
global justice, 138–41
Golden Rule, 74
goods, free flow of. *See* liberty
Gore, Al, 151–52
government bailouts
  moral hazard and, 95–107, 116–17
  virtuous behavior and, 11–12, 74–75
Government Procurement Agreement (GPA),
  171
government role
  history of, 81–93
  in liberty and justice, 43
  in promoting virtuous behavior, 79–80,
    87–88
  in reducing inequality, 51, 54–55, 63–65,
    75, 87–88
Graeber, David, 103
Great Depression, 1, 25, 61, 99, 109, 178
Great Divergence, 144
Great Recession, 1, 44, 63
Great Society, 87, 89
Great Tradeoff, 3, 8–13. *See also* tradeoffs
Greece, 69–73, 110, 117–19
Greene, Joshua, 14, 133–34
Greenspan, Alan, 45, 115
Grotius, Hugo, 19–20
Group of 7 (G-7), 181, 189
Group of 20 (G-20), 112, 181, 189

Group of 77, 160
group theory of politics, 135
growth. *See* economic growth

Haidt, Jonathan, 132
haircuts, 71, 101, 118
Hamilton, Alexander, 25, 35, 40, 82–83
Harlow, Bryce, 43
Havel, Vaclav, 27–28
Hayek, Friedrich, 27
health insurance, 41
heavily indebted poor countries (HIPCs), 107
Hebrew doctrine, 20–21, 103–105
Hecksher-Olin theory, 144–45
hedonism, 78–79
Heilbroner, Robert, 35
Hirschman, Albert, 90
Hobbes, Thomas, 136–38
Hobsbawm, Eric, 180
Hochhuth, Rolf, 72
Hoffman, Stanley, 138
Holland, François, 168
Holmes, Oliver Wendell, Jr., 14–15, 37
Hon Hai Precision Industry Co., 172
Hoover, Herbert, 98–100
housing sector, 51
human capital, 64

immigration, 59, 84, 140, 162–64
imperialism, 22, 25
inclusive capitalism, 2
income
    global distribution of, 58–61, 60*f*
    inequality of (*See* inequality)
    labor share of, 53
income tax. *See* taxation
India, 136
individual rights versus justice, 38–40, 86–93
Indonesia, 114–15
Industrial Revolution, 4, 35, 57, 83–84, 86
inequality, 47–65
    categories of, 56–57
    class warfare raised by, 43, 79
    in Europe, 44
    IMF report on, 32
    liberty versus justice tradeoff, 10–11, 33–34,
        187–91 (*See also* justice; liberty)
    measurements of, 51, 56–64, 187–88
    as political issue, 39–40
    public opinion of, 6, 44, 55–56
    religious leaders on, 28
    as symbol of injustice, 56–64
    trend toward, 34, 44–45, 53–54, 58–60,
        143–50
    in United States, 44, 63, 143–44

inflation, 27
Initiative for Responsible Investment, 185
Institute for Global Labour and Human
        Rights, 172
intergenerational contract, 112–14
International Bank for Reconstruction and
        Development, 26
International Forum on Globalization, 6, 146
international institutions. *See also specific*
        institution
    creation of, 26, 178
    criticism of, 7
    NGO attitudes toward, 183
    role of, 13, 139–41, 178–82, 189–91
    US attitudes toward, 181
International Labour Organization (ILO),
        183, 185
International Monetary Fund (IMF)
    capital restrictions, 30, 31
    Coordinated Direct Investment Survey,
        169–70
    creation of, 26, 178
    criticism of, 7
    debt restructuring programs, 28, 95–96,
        117–19
    East Asian rescue, 11
    on economic growth, 63–64, 187
    on fiscal policy, 32, 92
    loans, 70–71, 100, 114–17, 179
    poverty statistics, 59
    role of, 139–41, 178–82, 189
    on social justice, 31–32
    wealth redistribution programs, 9–10, 64
international standards, 181
inversions, 174
investment
    debt and, 110
    free flow of (*See* liberty)
    in human capital, 64
    importance of, 51–52, 61–62
    multinational corporations and, 165–71
Islamic doctrine, 22, 104
Israel Apartheid Week, 186
Italy, 118

Jackson, Andrew, 36, 84
James, William, 14–15
Japan, 179
Jefferson, Thomas, 24, 35, 40, 82–83, 166
Jenkins, Holman, Jr., 43
Jim Yong Kim, 5
jobs. *See* employment
Jobs, Steve, 125, 145
John Paul II, Pope, 40*n*, 77

Johnson, Lyndon, 9, 39, 40, 87, 89, 146, 168
JP Morgan, 37
Juncker, Jean-Claude, 73
justice
    overview, 10–11, 33–34, 187–91
    appeal of, 44–45
    communitarianism and, 135
    definitions of, 49–56, 74
    equality aligned with, 33–34, 38–40, 56–64,
        187–88 (See also inequality)
    evolution of, 133
    global, 138–41
    history of, 35–43
    measures of, 48
    moral, 62–63
    principles of, 47
    in Washington Consensus, 29
just price, 21–22

Kaczynski, Ted, 131
Kant, Immanuel, 73, 137, 180
Kapstein, Ethan, 13, 129–30
Kaptur, Marcy, 154
Keats, John, 14
Kennan, George F., 138–39
Kennedy, Edward, 154
Kennedy, John F., 87, 92, 111, 149, 160
Keynes, John Maynard
    at Bretton Woods, 26, 177–78, 188
    on debt, 107, 110–14
    on Germany, 72
    on inequality, 61
    on moral values, 9–10
    Roosevelt's meeting with, 109
Keynesian revolution, 110–14
Kimberly Process, 185–86
Kindleberger, Charles, 98
Kissinger, Henry, 138
Klein, Ezra, 89
Kristol, Irving, 80
Kristol, William, 80
Krueger, Anne, 63
Krugman, Paul, 45, 149
Kuznets, Simon, 50, 57–58

labor. See also employment
    immigration and, 163
    income derived from, 53–54
    multinational corporations and, 166
    trade agreements and, 126–28, 156
    as virtuous behavior, 84–85
    working conditions, 172–73, 183–85
labor movement, 85, 172–73, 183–85
Laffer, Arthur, 92

Lagarde, Christine, 32, 119
Lamy, Pascal, 159
Lansing, Robert, 134
Lasch, Christopher, 78
Latin American debt crises, 28–29
League of Nations, 180, 184
leaky bucket idea, 9, 32, 63–64
Lee, Robert E., 131
Lee Kuan Yew, 4
Lehman Brothers, 69, 101, 114, 117
Leo XIII, Pope, 77
Levin, Carl, 153
Levine, Aaron, 105
Lewis, R. W. B., 83
Libanius, 21
liberal internationalism, 13, 130, 177–86, 189
liberalism, 24n, 40n, 40–41
libertarianism, 41, 133n, 164
liberty
    overview, 10–11, 19–20, 33–34, 187–91
    economic theory on, 9–10, 19–32
    foreign policy based on, 139
    forms of, 39
    modern crisis in, 28–32
    origins of, 20–24
    in United States, 24–28, 38–39
Lincoln, Abraham, 36, 84–85, 131
Lipton, David, 92
liquidationist view, 99, 100
living standards, 58–60, 143–44
Lochner v. New York, 37–38
Locke, John, 24
Long-Term Capital Management (LTCM), 115
Lopokova, Lydia, 177
loss aversion, 155
Louis XIV, King, 22
loyalty
    overview, 12–13, 125–26, 187–91
    case study of, 150–54
    categories of, 126–30
    to community (See communitarianism)
    conflicts involving, 159–75
        consumers' role, 171–73
        corporate tax havens, 173–75
        immigration, 162–64
        multinational corporations, 165–71
    to world (See cosmopolitanism)
Luce, Edward, 167–68
luck, 78

Maastricht Treaty, 26
Machiavelli, Niccolo, 138
Madison, James, 11, 35, 82
Malthus, Thomas, 49, 86

Mandelbaum, Michael, 42, 113, 164
Mandeville, Bernard, 23, 86
Mankiw, Gregory, 50, 128
Mann, Bruce, 106
manufacturing sector, 144–49, 170
Marcuse, Herbert, 78
market economy. *See also* capitalism
    cultural effects of, 43, 79–80
    moral hazard in, 95–107
    moral principles in, 42–43, 74, 78
Marshall Plan, 72, 169, 179
Martinez, Marty, 153
Martyn, Henry, 23
Marx, Karl, 35, 49
materialism, 78–79
McCarthy, Joseph, 41
McKinley, William, 36
Medicaid, 113
Medicare, 113
Mellon, Andrew, 98–99
Menand, Louis, 14
mercantilism, 22–23, 25
Merkel, Angela, 70–72, 118
metamorality, 14
Mexico
    debt crisis, 29, 95–96, 114
    immigration, 163
    US trade agreement with (*See* North
        American Free Trade Agreement)
micro societies, 135
Middle Ages, 21, 105
middle class
    effect of globalization on, 60–61, 144–50
    entitlement programs for, 90
Middle East, 27
Mill, John Stuart, 103
minimum wage, 54–55
Minsky, Hyman, 97
mixed economy, 9, 41
modernists, 132
Monnet, Jean, 26, 179
Montebourg, Arnaud, 168
moral absolutism, 14–15, 110, 130, 190
moral desert, 76, 78
moral hazard
    bailouts and, 95–107, 116–17
    creditor, 100
    debtor, 100
    definition of, 11–12, 74–75
    in global financial crisis, 69–80, 100–103
    sources of, 100
morality. *See also* loyalty; virtue
    basic dogmas, 190–91
    debt and, 71–72, 75, 96–107, 112–19

    in economics, 8–10
    evolution of, 133
    foreign policy based on, 138–39
    globalization, 1–3, 120–21, 178–82
    in market economy, 42–43, 74, 78
    as political exercise, 188
    rules of conduct, 73–74
moral justice, 62–63
moral tradeoffs, 9. *See also* tradeoffs
Morgenthau, Hans, 138
Morgenthau, Henry, Jr., 72, 177
Moynihan, Daniel Patrick
    on liberalism, 40n
    on liberty versus justice, 39–41
    on socialism, 136
    on welfare dependency, 87–88, 90
multilateral cooperation, 181
multinational corporations
    behavior standards, 184–85
    loyalty and, 12, 126, 165–71
    public opinion of, 6
    tax havens, 173–75
Muntefering, Franz, 71
Murray, Charles, 88
Mussa, Michael, 116

Nagel, Thomas, 129, 136–38
National Commission on Fiscal Responsibility
    and Reform, 174
National Recovery Administration (NRA), 38
nation-state, 22, 132, 183–84, 189
natural rights, 24, 27, 37
natural selection, 133
negative capability, 14
negative income tax, 87–88
negative liberty, 39
Nehru, Jawaharlal, 132
neoconservatism, 79, 88
Netherlands, 96
Neuhaus, John, 77–78
New Deal, 38, 39, 100, 109
New Lanark experiment, 35
New Left intellectuals, 78
Newton, Isaac, 98
Nixon, Richard
    monetary policy, 27, 111
    relations with China, 138
    relations with India, 136
    social welfare programs, 40–41, 87
Noah, Timothy, 144
Nonaligned Movement, 160
nongovernmental organizations (NGOs). *See
    also specific organization*
    antiglobalization movement, 6, 146–50, 183

Bangladesh garment industry, 172
  history of, 184–85
  role of, 13, 182–86, 189–90
North American Free Trade Agreement
    (NAFTA)
  continuing debate over, 154–57
  liberty and, 29
  loyalty and, 12, 150–54
  moral hazard and, 96
  multinational corporations and, 167
  public opinion of, 5, 150–54
Novak, Michael, 77
Nozick, Robert, 48–49, 78
Nussbaum, Martha, 138

Obama, Barack
  Bangladesh garment industry, 172
  election campaigns, 11, 81, 127
  global financial crisis, 72, 100–103
  government initiatives, 41–42, 89
  multinational corporations, 166, 174
  tax increases, 92
  trade agreements, 7, 127, 129, 154–55
  unemployment, 125, 145
Obergefell v. Hodges, 38
Obey, David, 154
Occupy Wall Street movement, 1, 48
offshoring, 5–6, 125–28, 144–48, 166
Okun, Arthur, 9, 32, 63–64
O'Neill, Paul, 116
opportunity, equality of, 39–40
O'Reilly, Bill, 90
Organization of Economic Cooperation and
    Development (OECD), 53, 64, 161,
    179, 181
Organization of Petroleum Exporting
    Countries (OPEC), 160
Osborne, George, 173–74
Owen, Robert, 35
Ozment, Steven, 72

Palestine, 186
panics, 36–37, 97–99
  Panic of 1825, 99
  Panic of 1893, 36, 87
  Panic of 1907, 37
paradox of thrift, 110
Pareto-optimal, 48
Paris Peace Conference (1919), 180
patrimonial capitalism, 48–49
patrimonial class, 52
patriotism, 125–26, 171–73. See also loyalty
Paulson, Henry, 102
Paul VI, Pope, 77

peace, 189
Peace of Westphalia, 138
pension assets, 166–68
perennialists, 132
Perot, H. Ross, 151–52, 167
Perry, Matthew, 25
Piketty, Thomas, 44, 48–56, 64–65, 89–90, 92,
    169
Pinker, Steven, 133
Plato, 20
Pledge of Allegiance (US), 33
Plutarch, 20, 103, 137
Pogge, Thomas, 54, 140–41
political discourse
  liberty in, 38–40
  on loyalty, 126–27
  on moral hazard, 75
  on moral imperatives, 188
  on virtue, 88–91
political freedom. See liberty
politics
  group theory of, 135
  NGO involvement in, 186
Poor Laws (UK), 86–87
Populist movement, 36
Posen, Adam, 62
positive liberty, 39
poverty. See also emerging-market economies
  American values and, 86–93
  deregulation and, 28–31
  globalization and, 58–63, 160
pragmatism, 14–15
primordialists, 132
Prince, Charles, 97
Principles of Responsible Investment (PRI),
    185
prioritarian cosmopolitanism, 138
prisoner's dilemma, 131
privatization, 53
profit shifting, 173–75
Progressive Era, 85
prospect theory, 155
prosperity, inclusive, 2
protectionism, 23–24
Protestant work ethic, 72, 77
protests, antiglobalization, 6, 162
public opinion
  of globalization, 5–6
  of inequality, 6, 44, 55–56
  of trade agreements, 5–6, 150–57
purchasing power parities (PPPs), 56–57, 58f
Putin, Vladimir, 180
Putnam, Robert, 134

Rajan, Raghuram, 63
Rand, Ayn, 27, 91, 133*n*
Rawls, John
    communitarianism and, 135–36
    difference principle, 47, 129–30, 137
    on liberty versus justice, 10, 47–49, 139–41,
      161, 187
    Nozick's critique of, 48–49, 78
Reagan, Ronald, 4, 27, 41, 55, 91–92, 150
reform movements, 83
Reich, Robert, 165, 167
relativism, 130
religious doctrine
    capitalism, 7–8, 76–78
    debt, 72, 103–105
    global financial crisis, 7–8
    justice, 35, 42, 74
    liberty, 20–22
    loyalty, 126
    money making, 5, 52, 76–78
    moral hazard, 100, 103
    social welfare, 28, 86–87, 91
rent seeking, 51–52, 54
Republican Party (US), 84, 101–102
rescues
    moral hazard and, 95–107, 116–17
    virtuous behavior and, 11–12, 74–75
reshoring, 144–46
return on capital, 50–53
r > *g* phenomenon, 50–54, 169
rhetoric of reaction, 90
Ricardo, David, 23, 49, 86–87
Roberts, John, 38
Rockefeller Foundation, 182, 184
Rognlie, Matthew, 51
Romney, Mitt, 11, 43, 81, 88, 127, 163
Roosevelt, Franklin, 11, 38, 72, 87, 101, 109
Roosevelt, Theodore, 36–37, 42, 85
Rothschild, Emma, 24
Rousseau, Jean-Jacques, 33
Rubin, Robert, 29, 31, 95 96, 115 16
Ruggie, John, 185
Russian default (1998), 115
Ryan, Paul, 75, 90–91

Sachs, Jeffrey, 116
Sacks, Lord Jonathan, 21
Saez, Emmanuel, 44
Saint-Simon, Henri de, 35
Salinas de Gortari, Carlos, 151
Samuelson, Paul, 41, 111, 145
Sandel, Michael, 42–43, 79–80, 85, 131, 183
Santelli, Rick, 101–102
Sarkozy, Nicolas, 69, 71, 118

Schäuble, Wolfgang, 72, 173–74
Scheffler, Samuel, 139
Schmidt, Helmut, 73
Schröder, Gerhard, 140
Schuman, Robert, 26, 179
Schumer, Charles, 54
Schumpeter, Joseph, 127
Schwartz, Anna, 99
Scopes, John, 37*n*
Seattle protests (1999), 6, 162
Second Great Depression, 109
self-determination, 134
self-interest, 138
selfish gene, 133
Sen, Amartya, 49
September 11, 2001 attacks, 132, 140, 159
Servan-Schreiber, Jean-Jacques, 168
services sector, 148–49
Shultz, George, 116
Simon, William, 43, 116
Simpson-Bowles commission, 174
Singer, Peter, 140–41, 181–82
slavery, 84
Smith, Adam, 9, 23–24, 74, 84, 98, 141
Smoot-Hawley Tariff (US), 25, 151–52
Social Darwinism, 37, 98, 133
social democracy, 35
social engineering, 135
socialism
    bailouts and, 101–102
    versus capitalism, 26 27
    history of, 35
    poor countries and, 136
    religious doctrine on, 77
social justice, 9–10, 31–32, 135, 187–88. *See
    also* justice
Social Security, 113
society of states, 130
Socrates, 137
Solow, Robert, 50–51
Sorkin, Andrew Ross, 168
South Korea, 114–15
South Sea bubble (1720), 36, 98
sovereign debt restructuring mechanism
    (SDRM), 117
Soviet Union, 26, 61, 134–35, 139, 179
speculative euphoria, 97
Spencer, Herbert, 37, 98
spiteful egalitarianism, 63
stagflation, 27
Stiglitz, Joseph, 29, 31, 44, 63, 115
stock market, 166–68
stock market crash (1929), 98–99
Stolper-Samuelson theory, 145

Suharto, 114–15
Sullivan Principles, 185
Summers, Lawrence
    capital liberalization, 29
    on economic growth, 62
    on financial crises, 32
    on global governance, 183–84
    Mexico debt crisis, 95
    on moral hazard, 119
    on Piketty's theories, 51
    risk management strategy, 115
supply side economics, 52
supranationalism, 180
Supreme Court (US), 37–38
survival of the fittest, 98
sustainable development, 129–30

Talbott, Strobe, 132, 137, 180
taxation
    capital and, 64–65
    corporate tax havens, 173–75
    global system of, 184
    liberty and, 36–37
    supply side economics, 52
    virtue and, 87–88, 91–93
Tea Party (US), 41, 101–102
technology, 144–46
terrorist attacks, 132, 140, 159
Thailand, 114–15
Thaler, Richard, 56
Thatcher, Margaret, 4, 27
Thirty Years' War, 138
Thomas Aquinas, St., 21
Tobin, James, 87
Tocqueville, Alexis de, 34, 39
too big to fail principle, 101–102
trade
    global, 127, 128f
    globalization and, 146–50
    loyalty and, 12
Trade Adjustment Assistance (TAA) program,
        149–50
trade agreements. See also specific agreement
    adverse effects of, 149–50
    employment and, 125–28
    loyalty and, 126, 150–57
    nongovernment organizations in, 183
    poor countries and, 129–30, 159–62
    public opinion of, 5–6, 150–57
trade barriers, arguments against, 20, 23–24,
        162
tradeoffs
    overview, 3, 8–13, 187–91
    liberty versus justice, 10–11 (See also justice;
        liberty)

    loyalty, 12–13 (See also loyalty)
    sustainable development, 129–30
    virtue, 11–12 (See also virtue)
tragedy of the commons, 133
Transatlantic Trade and Investment
        Partnership (TTIP), 154–55
Transcendental movement, 83
transnationalism, 180
Trans-Pacific Partnership (TPP), 5–6, 126,
        149–50, 155
Treaty of Rome, 26, 179
Trilling, Lionel, 130
Troubled Asset Relief Program (TARP), 102
Truman. Harry, 179
Trumka, Richard, 166
Trump, Donald, 163
trust, 74
Tsipras, Alexis, 70–72, 119

ultimatum game, 55–56
unemployment, 96, 97f, 125, 144–50
United Kingdom
    Corn Laws, 24, 146, 152
    debtors' prisons, 105
    Poor Laws, 86–87
United Nations
    development assistance, 59, 161
    Economic and Social Security Council, 184
    role of, 139–41, 180–81
    Sullivan Principles, 185
    Universal Declaration of Human Rights,
        185
United States
    attitude toward globalization in, 5–6, 181
    bankruptcy law, 106–107
    debtors' prisons, 106
    debt relief programs, 107, 114–16
    effects of globalization in, 61
    federal debt, 112–13
    foreign aid, 161–62
    foreign policy, 138–39, 179
    immigration to, 59, 84, 140, 162–64
    inequality in, 44, 63, 143–44
    justice in, 35–42
    liberty in, 24–28, 38–42
    role of government in (See government role)
    trade policies, 149–50
    trade statistics, 127, 128f
    values in, 34, 40, 75, 78–79, 81
United States Conference of Catholic Bishops,
        42, 91
universal economy, doctrine of, 21
universal laws, 19–20
Uruguay Round, 171
utilitarianism, 14, 74, 103

van Heemskerck, Jacob, 19
veil of ignorance, 48
Vernon, Raymond, 169
virtue. *See also* moral hazard
    overview, 11–12, 187–91
    in American society, 81–93
    definitions of, 82–83
    financial crises and, 95–107, 114–19
    role in capitalism, 73–80, 120–21
    role in economic sphere, 75–80
virtue ethics, 74

wages
    immigration and, 163
    minimum, 54–55
    offshoring and, 145, 147–48
Wal-Mart, 171
Walzer, Michael, 134
Warren, Earl, 38
Warren, Elizabeth, 102
Washington Consensus, 28–29
wealth
    philosophy of, 21–22
    public opinion of, 6
    religious doctrine on, 5, 52, 76–78
    sources of, 48–52
wealth redistribution
    economic theory on, 9–10, 32
    government programs for, 51, 54–55,
        63–65, 75, 87–90
Weber, Max, 72, 76–78
Webster, Noah, 33

Welch, Finis, 43
Whig Party (US), 84
White, Harry Dexter, 177–78
Whitman, Walt, 83
Will, George, 80
Williams, Rowan, 8
Wilson, Edward, 133
Wilson, Woodrow, 37, 134
Wolf, Martin, 30, 64, 76, 129, 166
Wolfensohn, James, 161–62
worker displacement, 148
Worker Rights Consortium, 172
working class, 60–61, 144–50
World Bank
    on agricultural subsidies, 162
    creation of, 25, 178
    criticism of, 7
    debt restructuring programs, 28
    poverty statistics, 58–60, 62
    role of, 139–41, 178–82, 189
World Economic Forum (Davos), 182, 184
World Trade Organization (WTO)
    creation of, 26, 29, 178
    criticism of, 7
    Doha Round, 159–60
    role of, 139–41, 178–82
    Seattle demonstrations against, 6
World War I, 25, 180
World War II, 25, 72
Wriston, Walter, 116

Zedillo, Ernesto, 162

Other Publications from the Peterson Institute for International Economics

WORKING PAPERS

94-1   **APEC and Regional Trading Arrangements in the Pacific**
Jeffrey A. Frankel with Shang-Jin Wei and Ernesto Stein

94-2   **Towards an Asia Pacific Investment Code**
Edward M. Graham

94-3   **Merchandise Trade in the APEC Region: Is There Scope for Liberalization on an MFN Basis?**   Paul Wonnacott

94-4   **The Automotive Industry in Southeast Asia: Can Protection Be Made Less Costly?**
Paul Wonnacott

94-5   **Implications of Asian Economic Growth**
Marcus Noland

95-1   **APEC: The Bogor Declaration and the Path Ahead**   C. Fred Bergsten

95-2   **From Bogor to Miami...and Beyond: Regionalism in the Asia Pacific and the Western Hemisphere**   Jeffrey J. Schott

95-3   **Has Asian Export Performance Been Unique?**   Marcus Noland

95-4   **Association of Southeast Asian Nations and ASEAN Free Trade Area: Chronology and Statistics**   Gautam Jaggi

95-5   **The North Korean Economy**
Marcus Noland

95-6   **China and the International Economic System**   Marcus Noland

96-1   **APEC after Osaka: Toward Free Trade by 2010/2020**   C. Fred Bergsten

96-2   **Public Policy, Private Preferences, and the Japanese Trade Pattern**   Marcus Noland

96-3   **German Lessons for Korea: The Economics of Unification**   Marcus Noland

96-4   **Research and Development Activities and Trade Specialization in Japan**
Marcus Noland

96-5   **China's Economic Reforms: Chronology and Statistics**   Gautam Jaggi, Mary Rundle, Daniel H. Rosen, and Yuichi Takahashi

96-6   **US-China Economic Relations**
Marcus Noland

96-7   **The Market Structure Benefits of Trade and Investment Liberalization**
Raymond Atje and Gary Clyde Hufbauer

96-8   **The Future of US-Korea Economic Relations**   Marcus Noland

96-9   **Competition Policies in the Dynamic Industrializing Economies: The Case of China, Korea, and Chinese Taipei**
Edward M. Graham

96-10   **Modeling Economic Reform in North Korea**   Marcus Noland, Sherman Robinson, and Monica Scatasta

96-11   **Trade, Investment, and Economic Conflict Between the United States and Asia**
Marcus Noland

96-12   **APEC in 1996 and Beyond: The Subic Summit**   C. Fred Bergsten

96-13   **Some Unpleasant Arithmetic Concerning Unification**   Marcus Noland

96-14   **Restructuring Korea's Financial Sector for Greater Competitiveness**   Marcus Noland

96-15   **Competitive Liberalization and Global Free Trade: A Vision for the 21st Century**   C. Fred Bergsten

97-1   **Chasing Phantoms: The Political Economy of USTR**   Marcus Noland

97-2   **US-Japan Civil Aviation: Prospects for Progress**   Jacqueline McFadyen

97-3   **Open Regionalism**   C. Fred Bergsten

97-4   **Lessons from the Bundesbank on the Occasion of Its 40th (and Second to Last?) Birthday**   Adam S. Posen

97-5   **The Economics of Korean Unification**
Marcus Noland, Sherman Robinson, and Li-Gang Liu

98-1   **The Costs and Benefits of Korean Unification**   Marcus Noland, Sherman Robinson, and Li-Gang Liu

98-2   **Asian Competitive Devaluations**
Li-Gang Liu, Marcus Noland, Sherman Robinson, and Zhi Wang

98-3   **Fifty Years of the GATT/WTO: Lessons from the Past for Strategies or the Future**
C. Fred Bergsten

98-4   **NAFTA Supplemental Agreements: Four Year Review**   Jacqueline McFadyen

98-5   **Local Government Spending: Solving the Mystery of Japanese Fiscal Packages**
Hiroko Ishii and Erika Wada

98-6   **The Global Economic Effects of the Japanese Crisis**   Marcus Noland, Sherman Robinson, and Zhi Wang

98-7   **The Relationship Between Trade and Foreign Investment: Empirical Results for Taiwan and South Korea**   Li-Gang Liu, The World Bank, and Edward M. Graham

99-1   **Rigorous Speculation: The Collapse and Revival of the North Korean Economy**
Marcus Noland, Sherman Robinson, and Tao Wang

99-2   **Famine in North Korea: Causes and Cures**   Marcus Noland, Sherman Robinson, and Tao Wang

99-3   **Competition Policy and FDI: A Solution in Search of a Problem?**   Marcus Noland

99-4   **The Continuing Asian Financial Crisis: Global Adjustment and Trade**
Marcus Noland, Sherman Robinson, and Zhi Wang

99-5   **Why EMU Is Irrelevant for the German Economy**   Adam S. Posen

99-6   **The Global Trading System and the Developing Countries in 2000**
C. Fred Bergsten

99-7   **Modeling Korean Unification**
Marcus Noland, Sherman Robinson, and Tao Wang

99-8   **Sovereign Liquidity Crisis: The Strategic Case for a Payments Standstill**
Marcus Miller and Lei Zhang

99-9 **The Case for Joint Management of Exchange Rate Flexibility** C. Fred Bergsten, Olivier Davanne, and Pierre Jacquet

99-10 **Does Talk Matter After All? Inflation Targeting and Central Bank Behavior** Kenneth N. Kuttner and Adam S. Posen

99-11 **Hazards and Precautions: Tales of International Finance** Gary Clyde Hufbauer and Erika Wada

99-12 **The Globalization of Services: What Has Happened? What Are the Implications?** Gary Clyde Hufbauer and Tony Warren

00-1 **Regulatory Standards in the WTO** Keith Maskus

00-2 **International Economic Agreements and the Constitution** Richard M. Goodman and John M. Frost

00-3 **Electronic Commerce in Developing Countries** Catherine L. Mann

00-4 **The New Asian Challenge** C. Fred Bergsten

00-5 **How the Sick Man Avoided Pneumonia: The Philippines in the Asian Financial Crisis** Marcus Noland

00-6 **Inflation, Monetary Transparency, and G-3 Exchange Rate Volatility** Kenneth N. Kuttner and Adam S. Posen

00-7 **Transatlantic Issues in Electronic Commerce** Catherine L. Mann

00-8 **Strengthening the International Financial Architecture: Where Do We Stand?** Morris Goldstein

00-9 **On Currency Crises and Contagion** Marcel Fratzscher

01-1 **Price Level Convergence and Inflation in Europe** John H. Rogers, Gary Clyde Hufbauer, and Erika Wada

01-2 **Subsidies, Market Closure, Cross-Border Investment, and Effects on Competition: The Case of FDI on the Telecommunications Sector** Edward M. Graham

01-3 **Foreign Direct Investment in China: Effects on Growth and Economic Performance** Edward M. Graham and Erika Wada

01-4 **IMF Structural Conditionality: How Much Is Too Much?** Morris Goldstein

01-5 **Unchanging Innovation and Changing Economic Performance in Japan** Adam S. Posen

01-6 **Rating Banks in Emerging Markets** Liliana Rojas-Suarez

01-7 **Beyond Bipolar: A Three-Dimensional Assessment of Monetary Frameworks** Kenneth N. Kuttner and Adam S. Posen

01-8 **Finance and Changing US-Japan Relations: Convergence Without Leverage—Until Now** Adam S. Posen

01-9 **Macroeconomic Implications of the New Economy** Martin Neil Baily

01-10 **Can International Capital Standards Strengthen Banks in Emerging Markets?** Liliana Rojas-Suarez

02-1 **Moral Hazard and the US Stock Market: Analyzing the "Greenspan Put"?** Marcus Miller, Paul Weller, and Lei Zhang

02-2 **Passive Savers and Fiscal Policy Effectiveness in Japan** Kenneth N. Kuttner and Adam S. Posen

02-3 **Home Bias, Transaction Costs, and Prospects for the Euro: A More Detailed Analysis** Catherine L. Mann and Ellen E. Meade

02-4 **Toward a Sustainable FTAA: Does Latin America Meet the Necessary Financial Preconditions?** Liliana Rojas-Suarez

02-5 **Assessing Globalization's Critics: "Talkers Are No Good Doers???"** Kimberly Ann Elliott, Debayani Kar, and J. David Richardson

02-6 **Economic Issues Raised by Treatment of Takings under NAFTA Chapter 11** Edward M. Graham

03-1 **Debt Sustainability, Brazil, and the IMF** Morris Goldstein

03-2 **Is Germany Turning Japanese?** Adam S. Posen

03-3 **Survival of the Best Fit: Exposure to Low-Wage Countries and the (Uneven) Growth of US Manufacturing Plants** Andrew B. Bernard, J. Bradford Jensen, and Peter K. Schott

03-4 **Falling Trade Costs, Heterogeneous Firms, and Industry Dynamics** Andrew B. Bernard, J. Bradford Jensen, and Peter K. Schott

03-5 **Famine and Reform in North Korea** Marcus Noland

03-6 **Empirical Investigations in Inflation Targeting** Yifan Hu

03-7 **Labor Standards and the Free Trade Area of the Americas** Kimberly Ann Elliott

03-8 **Religion, Culture, and Economic Performance** Marcus Noland

03-9 **It Takes More than a Bubble to Become Japan** Adam S. Posen

03-10 **The Difficulty of Discerning What's Too Tight: Taylor Rules and Japanese Monetary Policy** Adam S. Posen and Kenneth N. Kuttner

04-1 **Adjusting China's Exchange Rate Policies** Morris Goldstein

04-2 **Popular Attitudes, Globalization, and Risk** Marcus Noland

04-3 **Selective Intervention and Growth: The Case of Korea** Marcus Noland

05-1 **Outsourcing and Offshoring: Pushing the European Model Over the Hill, Rather Than Off the Cliff!** Jacob Funk Kirkegaard

05-2 **China's Role in the Revived Bretton Woods System: A Case of Mistaken Identity** Morris Goldstein and Nicholas R. Lardy

05-3 **Affinity and International Trade** Marcus Noland

05-4 **South Korea's Experience with International Capital Flows** Marcus Noland

05-5 Explaining Middle Eastern
Authoritarianism   Marcus Noland

05-6 Postponing Global Adjustment: An
Analysis of the Pending Adjustment of
Global Imbalances   Edwin M. Truman

05-7 What Might the Next Emerging Market
Financial Crisis Look Like?
Morris Goldstein, assisted by Anna Wong

05-8 Egypt after the Multi-Fiber Arrangement:
Global Approval and Textile Supply
Chains as a Route for Industrial
Upgrading   Dan Magder

05-9 Tradable Services: Understanding the
Scope and Impact of Services Offshoring
J. Bradford Jensen and Lori G. Kletzer

05-10 Importers, Exporters, and Multinationals:
A Portrait of Firms in the US that Trade
Goods   Andrew B. Bernard,
J. Bradford Jensen, and Peter K. Schott

05-11 The US Trade Deficit: A Disaggregated
Perspective   Catherine L. Mann and
Katharina Plück

05-12 Prospects for Regional Free Trade in Asia
Gary Clyde Hufbauer and Yee Wong

05-13 Predicting Trade Expansion under FTAs
and Multilateral Agreements
Dean A. DeRosa and John P. Gilbert

05-14 The East Asian Industrial Policy
Experience: Implications for the Middle
East   Marcus Noland and Howard Pack

05-15 Outsourcing and Skill Imports: Foreign
High-Skilled Workers on H-1B and L-1
Visas in the United States
Jacob Funk Kirkegaard

06-1 Why Central Banks Should Not Burst
Bubbles   Adam S. Posen

06-2 The Case for an International Reserve
Diversification Standard
Edwin M. Truman and Anna Wong

06-3 Offshoring in Europe—Evidence of a Two-
Way Street from Denmark
Peter Ørberg Jensen, Jacob Funk Kirkegaard,
and Nicolai Søndergaard Laugesen

06-4 The External Policy of the Euro Area:
Organizing for Foreign Exchange
Intervention   C. Randall Henning

06-5 The Eurasian Growth Paradox
Anders Åslund and Nazgul Jenish

06-6 Has EMU Had Any Impact on the Degree
of Wage Restraint?   Adam S. Posen and
Daniel Popov Gould

06-7 Firm Structure, Multinationals, and
Manufacturing Plant Deaths
Andrew B. Bernard and J. Bradford Jensen

07-1 The Trade Effects of Preferential
Arrangements: New Evidence from the
Australia Productivity Commission
Dean A. DeRosa

07-2 Offshoring, Outsourcing, and Production
Relocation Labor-Market Effects in the
OECD Countries and Developing Asia
Jacob Funk Kirkegaard

07-3 Do Markets Care Who Chairs the Central
Bank?   Kenneth N. Kuttner and
Adam S. Posen

07-4 Industrial Policy, Innovative Policy, and
Japanese Competitiveness: Japan's Pursuit
of Competitive Advantage   Marcus Noland

07-5 A (Lack of) Progress Report on China's
Exchange Rate Policies   Morris Goldstein

07-6 Measurement and Inference in
International Reserve Diversification
Anna Wong

07-7 North Korea's External Economic
Relations   Stephan Haggard and
Marcus Noland

07-8 Congress, Treasury, and the
Accountability of Exchange Rate Policy:
How the 1988 Trade Act Should Be
Reformed   C. Randall Henning

07-9 Merry Sisterhood or Guarded
Watchfulness? Cooperation Between the
International Monetary Fund and the
World Bank   Michael Fabricius

08-1 Exit Polls: Refugee Assessments of North
Korea's Transitions   Yoonok Chang,
Stephan Haggard, and Marcus Noland

08-2 Currency Undervaluation and Sovereign
Wealth Funds: A New Role for the WTO
Aaditya Mattoo and Arvind Subramanian

08-3 Exchange Rate Economics
John Williamson

08-4 Migration Experiences of North Korean
Refugees: Survey Evidence from China
Yoonok Chang, Stephan Haggard, and
Marcus Noland

08-5 Korean Institutional Reform in
Comparative Perspective   Marcus Noland
and Erik Weeks

08-6 Estimating Consistent Fundamental
Equilibrium Exchange Rates
William R. Cline

08-7 Policy Liberalization and FDI Growth,
1982 to 2006   Matthew Adler and
Gary Clyde Hufbauer

08-8 Multilateralism Beyond Doha
Aaditya Mattoo and Arvind Subramanian

08-9 Famine in North Korea Redux?
Stephan Haggard and Marcus Noland

08-10 Recent Trade Patterns and Modes of
Supply in Computer and Information
Services in the United States and NAFTA
Partners   Jacob Funk Kirkegaard

08-11 On What Terms Is the IMF Worth
Funding?   Edwin M. Truman

08-12 The (Non) Impact of UN Sanctions on
North Korea   Marcus Noland

09-1 The GCC Monetary Union: Choice of
Exchange Rate Regime   Mohsin S. Khan

09-2 Policy Liberalization and US Merchandise
Trade Growth, 1980–2006
Gary Clyde Hufbauer and Matthew Adler

09-3 American Multinationals and American
Economic Interests: New Dimensions to
an Old Debate   Theodore H. Moran

09-4 Sanctioning North Korea: The Political
Economy of Denuclearization and
Proliferation   Stephan Haggard and
Marcus Noland

09-5 Structural and Cyclical Trends in Net Employment over US Business Cycles, 1949–2009: Implications for the Next Recovery and Beyond Jacob Funk Kirkegaard

09-6 What's on the Table? The Doha Round as of August 2009 Matthew Adler, Claire Brunel, Gary Clyde Hufbauer, and Jeffrey J. Schott

09-7 Criss-Crossing Globalization: Uphill Flows of Skill-Intensive Goods and Foreign Direct Investment Aaditya Mattoo and Arvind Subramanian

09-8 Reform from Below: Behavioral and Institutional Change in North Korea Stephan Haggard and Marcus Noland

09-9 The World Trade Organization and Climate Change: Challenges and Options Gary Clyde Hufbauer and Jisun Kim

09-10 A Tractable Model of Precautionary Reserves, Net Foreign Assets, or Sovereign Wealth Funds Christopher D. Carroll and Olivier Jeanne

09-11 The Impact of the Financial Crisis on Emerging Asia Morris Goldstein and Daniel Xie

09-12 Capital Flows to Developing Countries: The Allocation Puzzle Pierre-Olivier Gourinchas and Olivier Jeanne

09-13 Mortgage Loan Modifications: Program Incentives and Restructuring Design Dan Magder

09-14 It Should Be a Breeze: Harnessing the Potential of Open Trade and Investment Flows in the Wind Energy Industry Jacob Funk Kirkegaard, Thilo Hanemann, and Lutz Weischer

09-15 Reconciling Climate Change and Trade Policy Aaditya Mattoo, Arvind Subramanian, Dominique van der Mensbrugghe, and Jianwu He

09-16 The International Monetary Fund and Regulatory Challenges Edwin M. Truman

10-1 Estimation of De Facto Flexibility Parameter and Basket Weights in Evolving Exchange Rate Regimes Jeffrey Frankel and Daniel Xie

10-2 Economic Crime and Punishment in North Korea Stephan Haggard and Marcus Noland

10-3 Intra-Firm Trade and Product Contractibility Andrew B. Bernard, J. Bradford Jensen, Stephen J. Redding, and Peter K. Schott

10-4 The Margins of US Trade Andrew B. Bernard, J. Bradford Jensen, Stephen J. Redding, and Peter K. Schott

10-5 Excessive Volatility in Capital Flows: A Pigouvian Taxation Approach Olivier Jeanne and Anton Korinek

10-6 Toward a Sunny Future? Global Integration in the Solar PV Industry Jacob Funk Kirkegaard, Thilo Hanemann, Lutz Weischer, Matt Miller

10-7 The Realities and Relevance of Japan's Great Recession: Neither Ran nor Rashomon Adam S. Posen

10-8 Do Developed and Developing Countries Compete Head to Head in High Tech? Lawrence Edwards and Robert Z. Lawrence

10-9 US Trade and Wages: The Misleading Implications of Conventional Trade Theory Lawrence Edwards and Robert Z. Lawrence

10-10 Wholesalers and Retailers in US Trade Andrew B. Bernard, J. Bradford Jensen, Stephen J. Redding, and Peter K. Schott

10-11 The Design and Effects of Monetary Policy in Sub-Saharan African Countries Mohsin S. Khan

10-12 Managing Credit Booms and Busts: A Pigouvian Taxation Approach Olivier Jeanne and Anton Korinek

10-13 The G-20 and International Financial Institution Governance Edwin M. Truman

10-14 Reform of the Global Financial Architecture Garry J. Schinasi and Edwin M. Truman

10-15 A Role for the G-20 in Addressing Climate Change? Trevor Houser

10-16 Exchange Rate Policy in Brazil John Williamson

10-17 Trade Disputes Between China and the United States: Growing Pains so Far, Worse Ahead? Gary Clyde Hufbauer and Jared C. Woollacott

10-18 Sovereign Bankruptcy in the European Union in the Comparative Perspective Leszek Balcerowicz

11-1 Current Account Imbalances Coming Back Joseph E. Gagnon

11-2 Too Big to Fail: The Transatlantic Debate Morris Goldstein and Nicolas Véron

11-3 Foreign Direct Investment in Times of Crisis Lauge Skovgaard Poulsen and Gary Clyde Hufbauer

11-4 A Generalized Fact and Model of Long-Run Economic Growth: Kaldor Fact as a Special Case Daniel Danxia Xie

11-5 Integrating Reform of Financial Regulation with Reform of the International Monetary System Morris Goldstein

11-6 Capital Account Liberalization and the Role of the RMB Nicholas R. Lardy and Patrick Douglass

11-7 Capital Controls: Myth and Reality—A Portfolio Balance Approach Nicolas E. Magud, Carmen M. Reinhart, and Kenneth S. Rogoff

11-8 Resource Management and Transition in Central Asia, Azerbaijan, and Mongolia Richard Pomfret

11-9 Coordinating Regional and Multilateral Financial Institutions C. Randall Henning

11-10 The Liquidation of Government Debt Carmen M. Reinhart and M. Belen Sbrancia

11-11 Foreign Manufacturing Multinationals and the Transformation of the Chinese Economy: New Measurements, New Perspectives   Theodore H. Moran

11-12 Sovereign Wealth Funds: Is Asia Different?   Edwin M. Truman

11-13 Integration in the Absence of Institutions: China-North Korea Cross-Border Exchange   Stephan Haggard, Jennifer Lee, and Marcus Noland

11-14 Renminbi Rules: The Conditional Imminence of the Reserve Currency Transition   Arvind Subramanian

11-15 How Flexible Can Inflation Targeting Be and Still Work?   Kenneth N. Kuttner and Adam S. Posen

11-16 Asia and Global Financial Governance   C. Randall Henning and Mohsin S. Khan

11-17 India's Growth in the 2000s: Four Facts   Utsav Kumar and Arvind Subramanian

11-18 Applying Hubbert Curves and Linearization to Rock Phosphate   Cullen S. Hendrix

11-19 Delivering on US Climate Finance Commitments   Trevor Houser and Jason Selfe

11-20 Rent(s) Asunder: Sectoral Rent Extraction Possibilities and Bribery by Multinational Corporations   Edmund Malesky, Nathan Jensen, and Dimitar Gueorguiev

11-21 Asian Regional Policy Coordination   Edwin M. Truman

11-22 China and the World Trading System   Aaditya Mattoo and Arvind Subramanian

12-1 Fiscal Federalism: US History for Architects of Europe's Fiscal Union   C. Randall Henning and Martin Kessler

12-2 Financial Reform after the Crisis: An Early Assessment   Nicolas Véron

12-3 Chinese Investment in Latin American Resources: The Good, the Bad, and the Ugly   Barbara Kotschwar, Theodore H. Moran, and Julia Muir

12-4 Spillover Effects of Exchange Rates: A Study of the Renminbi   Aaditya Mattoo, Prachi Mishra, and Arvind Subramanian

12-5 Global Imbalances and Foreign Asset Expansion by Developing-Economy Central Banks   Joseph E. Gagnon

12-6 Transportation and Communication Infrastructure in Latin America: Lessons from Asia   Barbara Kotschwar

12-7 Lessons from Reforms in Central and Eastern Europe in the Wake of the Global Financial Crisis   Anders Åslund

12-8 Networks, Trust, and Trade: The Microeconomics of China-North Korea Integration   Stephan Haggard and Marcus Noland

12-9 The Microeconomics of North-South Korean Cross-Border Integration   Stephan Haggard and Marcus Noland

12-10 The Dollar and Its Discontents   Olivier Jeanne

12-11 Gender in Transition: The Case of North Korea   Stephan Haggard and Marcus Noland

12-12 Sovereign Debt Sustainability in Italy and Spain: A Probabilistic Approach   William R. Cline

12-13 John Williamson and the Evolution of the International Monetary System   Edwin M. Truman

12-14 Capital Account Policies and the Real Exchange Rate   Olivier Jeanne

12-15 Choice and Coercion in East Asian Exchange Rate Regimes   C. Randall Henning

12-16 Transactions: A New Look at Services Sector Foreign Direct Investment in Asia   Jacob Funk Kirkegaard

12-17 Prospects for Services Trade Negotiations   Jeffrey J. Schott, Minsoo Lee, and Julia Muir

12-18 Developing the Services Sector as Engine of Growth for Asia: An Overview   Marcus Noland, Donghyun Park, and Gemma B. Estrada

12-19 The Renminbi Bloc Is Here: Asia Down, Rest of the World to Go? *Revised Aug. 2013*   Arvind Subramanian and Martin Kessler

12-20 Performance of the Services Sector in Korea: An Empirical Investigation   Donghyun Park and Kwanho Shin

12-21 The Services Sector in Asia: Is It an Engine of Growth?   Donghyun Park and Kwanho Shin

12-22 Assessing Potential Inflation Consequences of QE after Financial Crises   Samuel Reynard

12-23 Overlooked Opportunity: Tradable Business Services, Developing Asia, and Growth   J. Bradford Jensen

13-1 The Importance of Trade and Capital Imbalances in the European Debt Crisis   Andrew Hughes Hallett and Juan Carlos Martinez Oliva

13-2 The Elephant Hiding in the Room: Currency Intervention and Trade Imbalances   Joseph E. Gagnon

13-3 Does High Home-Ownership Impair the Labor Market?   David G. Blanchflower and Andrew J. Oswald

13-4 The Rise of Emerging Asia: Regional Peace and Global Security   Miles Kahler

13-5 Peers and Tiers and US High-Tech Export Controls: A New Approach to Estimating Export Shortfalls   Asha Sundaram and J. David Richardson

13-6 The Hyperglobalization of Trade and Its Future   Arvind Subramanian and Martin Kessler

13-7 How to Measure Underemployment?   David N. F. Bell and David G. Blanchflower

13-8 The Greek Debt Restructuring: An Autopsy   Jeromin Zettelmeyer, Christoph Trebesch, and Mitu Gulati

13-9 Asian and European Financial Crises Compared   Edwin M. Truman

13-10 Why Growth in Emerging Economies Is Likely to Fall   Anders Åslund

13-11 AGOA Rules: The Intended and Unintended Consequences of Special Fabric Provisions   Lawrence Edwards and Robert Z. Lawrence

14-1 Regime Change, Democracy, and Growth   Caroline Freund and Mélise Jaud

14-2 Labor Market Slack in the United Kingdom   David N. F. Bell and David G. Blanchflower

14-3 Oil Prices and Interstate Conflict Behavior   Cullen S. Hendrix

14-4 Demographic versus Cyclical Influences on US Labor Force Participation   William R. Cline with Jared Nolan

14-5 The Federal Reserve Engages the World (1970–2000): An Insider's Narrative of the Transition to Managed Floating and Financial Turbulence   Edwin M. Truman

14-6 Wages and Labor Market Slack: Making the Dual Mandate Operational   David G. Blanchflower and Adam S. Posen

14-7 What Goes into a Medal: Women's Inclusion and Success at the Olympic Games   Marcus Noland and Kevin Stahler

14-8 Official Financial Flows, Capital Mobility, and Global Imbalances   Tamim Bayoumi, Joseph Gagnon, and Christian Saborowski

14-9 Sustainability of Public Debt in the United States and Japan   William R. Cline

14-10 Versailles Redux? Eurozone Competitiveness in a Dynamic Balassa-Samuelson-Penn Framework   Kevin Stahler and Arvind Subramanian

14-11 Understanding Differences in Growth Performance in Latin America and Developing Countries between the Asian and Global Financial Crises   Roberto Alvarez and José De Gregorio

14-12 Foreign Investment and Supply Chains in Emerging Markets: Recurring Problems and Demonstrated Solutions   Theodore H. Moran

15-1 The Economic Scope and Future of US-India Labor Migration Issues   Jacob Funk Kirkegaard

15-2 Myanmar: Cross-Cutting Governance Challenges   Cullen S. Hendrix and Marcus Noland

15-3 Financing Asia's Growth   Gemma B. Estrada, Marcus Noland, Donghyun Park, and Arief Ramayandi

15-4 Maintaining Financial Stability in the People's Republic of China during Financial Liberalization   Nicholas Borst and Nicholas Lardy

15-5 The Financial Sector and Growth in Emerging Asian Economies   William R. Cline

15-6 Financing Productivity- and Innovation-Led Growth in Developing Asia: International Lessons and Policy Issues   Ajai Chopra

15-7 The Future of Worldwide Income Distribution   Tomáš Hellebrandt and Paolo Mauro

15-8 Testing the Modigliani-Miller Theorem of Capital Structure Irrelevance for Banks   William R. Cline

15-9 An Old Boys' Club No More: Pluralism in Participation and Performance at the Olympic Games   Marcus Noland and Kevin Stahler

15-10 Recent Declines in Labor's Share in US Income: A Preliminary Neoclassical Account   Robert Z. Lawrence

15-11 The Resilient Trade Surplus, the Pharmaceutical Sector, and Exchange Rate Assessments in Switzerland   Philip Sauré

15-12 The Tradability of Services: Geographic Concentration and Trade Costs   Antoine Gervais and J. Bradford Jensen

15-13 Enhancing Financial Stability in Developing Asia   Adam S. Posen and Nicolas Véron

15-14 The OECD's "Action Plan" to Raise Taxes on Multinational Corporations   Gary Hufbauer, Euijin Jung, Tyler Moran, and Martin Vieiro

15-15 The Influence of Foreign Direct Investment, Intrafirm Trading, and Currency Undervaluation on US Firm Trade Disputes   J. Bradford Jensen, Dennis P. Quinn, and Stephen Weymouth

15-16 Further Statistical Debate on "Too Much Finance"   William R. Cline

POLICY BRIEFS

98-1 The Asian Financial Crisis   Morris Goldstein

98-2 The New Agenda with China   C. Fred Bergsten

98-3 Exchange Rates for the Dollar, Yen, and Euro   Simon Wren-Lewis

98-4 Sanctions-Happy USA   Gary Clyde Hufbauer

98-5 The Depressing News from Asia   Marcus Noland, Sherman Robinson, and Zhi Wang

98-6 The Transatlantic Economic Partnership   Ellen L. Frost

98-7 A New Strategy for the Global Crisis   C. Fred Bergsten

98-8 Reviving the "Asian Monetary Fund"   C. Fred Bergsten

99-1 Implementing Japanese Recovery   Adam S. Posen

99-2 A Radical but Workable Restructuring Plan for South Korea   Edward M. Graham

99-3 Crawling Bands or Monitoring Bands: How to Manage Exchange Rates in a World of Capital Mobility   John Williamson

99-4 Market Mechanisms to Reduce the Need for IMF Bailouts   Catherine L. Mann

99-5 Steel Quotas: A Rigged Lottery   Gary Clyde Hufbauer and Erika Wada

99-6 China and the World Trade Organization: An Economic Balance Sheet   Daniel H. Rosen

99-7 Trade and Income Distribution: The Debate and New Evidence William R. Cline

99-8 Preserve the Exchange Stabilization Fund C. Randall Henning

99-9 Nothing to Fear but Fear (of Inflation) Itself Adam S. Posen

99-10 World Trade after Seattle: Implications for the United States Gary Clyde Hufbauer

00-1 The Next Trade Policy Battle C. Fred Bergsten

00-2 Decision-Making in the WTO Jeffrey J. Schott and Jayashree Watal

00-3 American Access to China's Market: The Congressional Vote on PNTR Gary Clyde Hufbauer and Daniel H. Rosen

00-4 Third Oil Shock: Real or Imaginary? Consequences and Policy Alternatives Philip K. Verleger, Jr.

00-5 The Role of the IMF: A Guide to the Reports John Williamson

00-6 The ILO and Enforcement of Core Labor Standards Kimberly Ann Elliott

00-7 "No" to Foreign Telecoms Equals "No" to the New Economy! Gary Clyde Hufbauer and Edward M. Graham

01-1 Brunei: A Turning Point for APEC? C. Fred Bergsten

01-2 A Prescription to Relieve Worker Anxiety Lori G. Kletzer and Robert E. Litan

01-3 The US Export-Import Bank: Time for an Overhaul Gary Clyde Hufbauer

01-4 Japan 2001—Decisive Action or Financial Panic Adam S. Posen

01-5 Fin(d)ing Our Way on Trade and Labor Standards? Kimberly Ann Elliott

01-6 Prospects for Transatlantic Competition Policy Mario Monti

01-7 The International Implications of Paying Down the Debt Edwin M. Truman

01-8 Dealing with Labor and Environment Issues in Trade Promotion Legislation Kimberly Ann Elliott

01-9 Steel: Big Problems, Better Solutions Gary Clyde Hufbauer and Ben Goodrich

01-10 Economic Policy Following the Terrorist Attacks Martin Neil Baily

01-11 Using Sanctions to Fight Terrorism Gary Clyde Hufbauer, Jeffrey J. Schott, and Barbara Oegg

02-1 Time for a Grand Bargain in Steel? Gary Clyde Hufbauer and Ben Goodrich

02-2 Prospects for the World Economy: From Global Recession to Global Recovery Michael Mussa

02-3 Sovereign Debt Restructuring: New Articles, New Contracts—or No Change? Marcus Miller

02-4 Support the Ex-Im Bank: It Has Work to Do! Gary Clyde Hufbauer and Ben Goodrich

02-5 The Looming Japanese Crisis Adam S. Posen

02-6 Capital-Market Access: New Frontier in the Sanctions Debate Gary Clyde Hufbauer and Barbara Oegg

02-7 Is Brazil Next? John Williamson

02-8 Further Financial Services Liberalization in the Doha Round? Wendy Dobson

02-9 Global Economic Prospects Michael Mussa

02-10 The Foreign Sales Corporation: Reaching the Last Act? Gary Clyde Hufbauer

03-1 Steel Policy: The Good, the Bad, and the Ugly Gary Clyde Hufbauer and Ben Goodrich

03-2 Global Economic Prospects: Through the Fog of Uncertainty Michael Mussa

03-3 Economic Leverage and the North Korean Nuclear Crisis Kimberly Ann Elliott

03-4 The Impact of Economic Sanctions on US Trade: Andrew Rose's Gravity Model Gary Clyde Hufbauer and Barbara Oegg

03-5 Reforming OPIC for the 21st Century Theodore H. Moran and C. Fred Bergsten

03-6 The Strategic Importance of US-Korea Economic Relations Marcus Noland

03-7 Rules Against Earnings Stripping: Wrong Answer to Corporate Inversions Gary Clyde Hufbauer and Ariel Assa

03-8 More Pain, More Gain: Politics and Economics of Eliminating Tariffs Gary Clyde Hufbauer and Ben Goodrich

03-9 EU Accession and the Euro: Close Together or Far Apart? Peter B. Kenen and Ellen E. Meade

03-10 Next Move in Steel: Revocation or Retaliation? Gary Clyde Hufbauer and Ben Goodrich

03-11 Globalization of IT Services and White Collar Jobs: The Next Wave of Productivity Growth Catherine L. Mann

04-1 This Far and No Farther? Nudging Agricultural Reform Forward Tim Josling and Dale Hathaway

04-2 Labor Standards, Development, and CAFTA Kimberly Ann Elliott

04-3 Senator Kerry on Corporate Tax Reform: Right Diagnosis, Wrong Prescription Gary Clyde Hufbauer and Paul Grieco

04-4 Islam, Globalization, and Economic Performance in the Middle East Marcus Noland and Howard Pack

04-5 China Bashing 2004 Gary Clyde Hufbauer and Yee Wong

04-6 What Went Right in Japan Adam S. Posen

04-7 What Kind of Landing for the Chinese Economy? Morris Goldstein and Nicholas R. Lardy

05-1 A Currency Basket for East Asia, Not Just China John Williamson

05-2 After Argentina Anna Gelpern

05-3 Living with Global Imbalances: A Contrarian View Richard N. Cooper

05-4 The Case for a New Plaza Agreement William R. Cline

06-1 The United States Needs German Economic Leadership Adam S. Posen

06-2 The Doha Round after Hong Kong Gary Clyde Hufbauer and Jeffrey J. Schott

06-3 Russia's Challenges as Chair of the G-8 Anders Åslund

06-4 Negotiating the Korea–United States Free Trade Agreemen Jeffrey J. Schott, Scott C. Bradford, and Thomas Moll

06-5 Can Doha Still Deliver on the Development Agenda? Kimberly Ann Elliott

06-6 China: Toward a Consumption Driven Growth Path Nicholas R. Lardy

06-7 Completing the Doha Round Jeffrey J. Schott

06-8 Choosing Monetary Arrangements for the 21st Century: Problems of a Small Economy John Williamson

06-9 Can America Still Compete or Does It Need a New Trade Paradigm? Martin Neil Baily and Robert Z. Lawrence

07-1 The IMF Quota Formula: Linchpin of Fund Reform Richard N. Cooper and Edwin M. Truman

07-2 Toward a Free Trade Area of the Asia Pacific C. Fred Bergsten

07-3 China and Economic Integration in East Asia: Implications for the United States C. Fred Bergsten

07-4 Global Imbalances: Time for Action Alan Ahearne, William R. Cline, Kyung Tae Lee, Yung Chul Park, Jean Pisani-Ferry, and John Williamson

07-5 American Trade Politics in 2007: Building Bipartisan Compromise I. M. Destler

07-6 Sovereign Wealth Funds: The Need for Greater Transparency and Accountability Edwin M. Truman

07-7 The Korea-US Free Trade Agreement: A Summary Assessment Jeffrey J. Schott

07-8 The Case for Exchange Rate Flexibility in Oil-Exporting Economies Brad Setser

08-1 "Fear" and Offshoring: The Scope and Potential Impact of Imports and Exports of Services J. Bradford Jensen and Lori G. Kletzer

08-2 Strengthening Trade Adjustment Assistance Howard F. Rosen

08-3 A Blueprint for Sovereign Wealth Fund Best Practices Edwin M. Truman

08-4 A Security and Peace Mechanism for Northeast Asia: The Economic Dimension Stephan Haggard and Marcus Noland

08-5 World Trade at Risk C. Fred Bergsten

08-6 North Korea on the Precipice of Famine Stephan Haggard, Marcus Noland, and Erik Weeks

08-7 New Estimates of Fundamental Equilibrium Exchange Rates William R. Cline and John Williamson

08-8 Financial Repression in China Nicholas R. Lardy

09-1 Did Reagan Rule In Vain? A Closer Look at True Expenditure Levels in the United States and Europe Jacob Funk Kirkegaard

09-2 Buy American: Bad for Jobs, Worse for Reputation Gary Clyde Hufbauer and Jeffrey J. Schott

09-3 A Green Global Recovery? Assessing US Economic Stimulus and the Prospects for International Coordination Trevor Houser, Shashank Mohan, and Robert Heilmayr

09-4 Money for the Auto Industry: Consistent with WTO Rules? Claire Brunel and Gary Clyde Hufbauer

09-5 The Future of the Chiang Mai Initiative: An Asian Monetary Fund? C. Randall Henning

09-6 Pressing the "Reset Button" on US-Russia Relations Anders Åslund and Andrew Kuchins

09-7 US Taxation of Multinational Corporations: What Makes Sense, What Doesn't Gary Clyde Hufbauer and Jisun Kim

09-8 Energy Efficiency in Buildings: A Global Economic Perspective Trevor Houser

09-9 The Alien Tort Statute of 1789: Time for a Fresh Look Gary Clyde Hufbauer

09-10 2009 Estimates of Fundamental Equilibrium Exchange Rates William R. Cline and John Williamson

09-11 Understanding Special Drawing Rights (SDRs) John Williamson

09-12 US Interests and the International Monetary Fund C. Randall Henning

09-13 A Solution for Europe's Banking Problem Adam S. Posen and Nicolas Véron

09-14 China's Changing Outbound Foreign Direct Investment Profile: Drivers and Policy Implication Daniel H. Rosen and Thilo Hanemann

09-15 India-Pakistan Trade: A Roadmap for Enhancing Economic Relations Mohsin S. Khan

09-16 Pacific Asia and the Asia Pacific: The Choices for APEC C. Fred Bergsten

09-17 The Economics of Energy Efficiency in Buildings Trevor Houser

09-18 Setting the NAFTA Agenda on Climate Change Jeffrey J. Schott and Meera Fickling

09-19 The 2008 Oil Price "Bubble" Mohsin S. Khan

09-20 Why SDRs Could Rival the Dollar John Williamson

09-21 The Future of the Dollar Richard N. Cooper

09-22 The World Needs Further Monetary Ease, Not an Early Exit Joseph E. Gagnon

10-1 The Winter of Their Discontent: Pyongyang Attacks the Market Stephan Haggard and Marcus Noland

10-2 Notes on Equilibrium Exchange Rates: William R. Cline and John Williamson

10-3 Confronting Asset Bubbles, Too Big to Fail, and Beggar-thy-Neighbor Exchange Rate Policies Morris Goldstein

10-4 After the Flop in Copenhagen Gary Clyde Hufbauer and Jisun Kim

10-5 Copenhagen, the Accord, and the Way Forward Trevor Houser

10-6 The Substitution Account as a First Step Toward Reform of the International Monetary System Peter B. Kenen

10-7   The Sustainability of China's Recovery from the Global Recession
        Nicholas R. Lardy

10-8   New PPP-Based Estimates of Renminbi Undervaluation and Policy Implications
        Arvind Subramanian

10-9   Protection by Stealth: Using the Tax Law to Discriminate against Foreign Insurance Companies   Gary Clyde Hufbauer

10-10   Higher Taxes on US-Based Multinationals Would Hurt US Workers and Exports
        Gary Clyde Hufbauer and Theodore H. Moran

10-11   A Trade Agenda for the G-20
        Jeffrey J. Schott

10-12   Assessing the American Power Act: The Economic, Employment, Energy Security and Environmental Impact of Senator Kerry and Senator Lieberman's Discussion Draft   Trevor Houser, Shashank Mohan, and Ian Hoffman

10-13   Hobbling Exports and Destroying Jobs
        Gary Clyde Hufbauer and Theodore H. Moran

10-14   In Defense of Europe's Grand Bargain
        Jacob Funk Kirkegaard

10-15   Estimates of Fundamental Equilibrium Exchange Rates, May 2010
        William R. Cline and John Williamson

10-16   Deepening China-Taiwan Relations through the Economic Cooperation Framework Agreement   Daniel H. Rosen and Zhi Wang

10-17   Turning Back the Clock: Japan's Misguided Postal Law is Back on the Table   Gary Clyde Hufbauer and Julia Muir

10-18   Dealing with Volatile Capital Flows
        Olivier Jeanne

10-19   Revisiting the NAFTA Agenda on Climate Change   Jeffrey J. Schott and Meera Fickling

10-20   Renminbi Undervaluation, China's Surplus, and the US Trade Deficit
        William R. Cline

10-21   The Road to a Climate Change Agreement Runs Through Montreal   Richard J. Smith

10-22   Not All Financial Regulation Is Global
        Stéphane Rottier and Nicolas Véron

10-23   Prospects for Implementing the Korea US Free Trade Agreement   Jeffrey J. Schott

10-24   The Central Banker's Case for Doing More   Adam S. Posen

10-25   Will It Be Brussels, Berlin, or Financial Markets that Check Moral Hazard in Europe's Bailout Union? Most Likely the Latter!   Jacob Funk Kirkegaard

10-26   Currency Wars?   William R. Cline and John Williamson

10-27   How Europe Can Muddle Through Its Crisis   Jacob Funk Kirkegaard

10-28   KORUS FTA 2.0: Assessing the Changes
        Jeffrey J. Schott

10-29   Strengthening IMF Surveillance: A Comprehensive Proposal
        Edwin M. Truman

10-30   An Update on EU Financial Reforms
        Nicolas Véron

11-1   Getting Surplus Countries to Adjust
        John Williamson

11-2   Corporate Tax Reform for a New Century
        Gary Clyde Hufbauer and Woan Foong Wong

11-3   The Elephant in the "Green Room": China and the Doha Round   Aaditya Mattoo, Francis Ng, and Arvind Subramanian

11-4   The Outlook for International Monetary System Reform in 2011: A Preliminary Report Card   Edwin M. Truman

11-5   Estimates of Fundamental Equilibrium Exchange Rates, May 2011
        William R. Cline and John Williamson

11-6   Revitalizing the Export-Import Bank
        Gary Clyde Hufbauer, Meera Fickling, and Woan Foong Wong

11-7   Logistics Reform for Low-Value Shipments   Gary Clyde Hufbauer and Yee Wong

11-8   What Should the United States Do about Doha?   Jeffrey J. Schott

11-9   Lessons from the East European Financial Crisis, 2008–10   Anders Åslund

11-10   America's Energy Security Options
        Trevor Houser and Shashank Mohan

11-11   Keeping the Promise of Global Accounting Standards   Nicolas Véron

11-12   Markets vs. Malthus: Food Security and the Global Economy   Cullen S. Hendrix

11-13   Europe on the Brink   Peter Boone and Simon Johnson

11-14   IFSWF Report on Compliance with the Santiago Principles: Admirable but Flawed Transparency   Sarah Bagnall and Edwin M. Truman

11-15   Sustainability of Greek Public Debt
        William R. Cline

11-16   US Tax Discrimination Against Large Corporations Should Be Discarded
        Gary Clyde Hufbauer and Martin Vieiro

11-17   Debt Relief for Egypt?   John Williamson and Mohsin Khan

11-18   The Current Currency Situation
        William R. Cline and John Williamson

11-19   G-20 Reforms of the International Monetary System: An Evaluation
        Edwin M. Truman

11-20   The United States Should Establish Normal Trade Relations with Russia
        Anders Åslund and Gary Clyde Hufbauer

11-21   What Can and Cannot Be Done about Rating Agencies   Nicolas Véron

11-22   Oil Exporters to the Euro's Rescue?
        Philip K. Verleger

12-1   The Coming Resolution of the European Crisis   C. Fred Bergsten and Jacob Funk Kirkegaard

12-2   Japan Post: Retreat or Advance?
        Gary Clyde Hufbauer and Julia Muir

12-3   Another Shot at Protection by Stealth: Using the Tax Law to Penalize Foreign Insurance Companies   Gary Clyde Hufbauer

12-4 The European Crisis Deepens Peter Boone and Simon Johnson

12-5 Interest Rate Shock and Sustainability of Italy's Sovereign Debt William R. Cline

12-6 Using US Strategic Reserves to Moderate Potential Oil Price Increases from Sanctions on Iran Philip K. Verleger, Jr.

12-7 Projecting China's Current Account Surplus William R. Cline

12-8 Does Monetary Cooperation or Confrontation Lead to Successful Fiscal Consolidation? Tomas Hellebrandt, Adam S. Posen, and Marilyne Tolle

12-9 US Tire Tariffs: Saving Few Jobs at High Cost Gary Clyde Hufbauer and Sean Lowry

12-10 Framework for the International Services Agreement Gary Clyde Hufbauer, J. Bradford Jensen, and Sherry Stephenson. Assisted by Julia Muir and Martin Vieiro

12-11 Will the World Trade Organization Enjoy a Bright Future? Gary Clyde Hufbauer and Jeffrey J. Schott

12-12 Japan Post: Anti-Reform Law Clouds Japan's Entry to the Trans-Pacific Partnership Gary Clyde Hufbauer and Julia Muir

12-13 Right Idea, Wrong Direction: Obama's Corporate Tax Reform Proposals Gary Clyde Hufbauer and Martin Vieiro

12-14 Estimates of Fundamental Equilibrium Exchange Rates, May 2012 William R. Cline and John Williamson

12-15 Restoring Fiscal Equilibrium in the United States William R. Cline

12-16 The Trans-Pacific Partnership and Asia-Pacific Integration: Policy Implications Peter A. Petri and Michael G. Plummer

12-17 Southern Europe Ignores Lessons from Latvia at Its Peril Anders Åslund

12-18 The Coming Resolution of the European Crisis: An Update C. Fred Bergsten and Jacob Funk Kirkegaard

12-19 Combating Widespread Currency Manipulation Joseph E. Gagnon

12-20 Why a Breakup of the Euro Area Must Be Avoided: Lessons from Previous Breakups Anders Åslund

12-21 How Can Trade Policy Help America Compete? Robert Z. Lawrence

12-22 Hyperinflations Are Rare, but a Breakup of the Euro Area Could Prompt One Anders Åslund

12-23 Updated Estimates of Fundamental Equilibrium Exchange Rates William R. Cline and John Williamson

12-24 Europe's Single Supervisory Mechanism and the Long Journey Towards Banking Union Nicolas Véron

12-25 Currency Manipulation, the US Economy, and the Global Economic Order C. Fred Bergsten and Joseph E. Gagnon

13-1 The World Needs a Multilateral Investment Agreement Anders Åslund

13-2 A Blueprint for Rebalancing the Chinese Economy Nicholas R. Lardy and Nicholas Borst

13-3 Debt Restructuring and Economic Prospects in Greece William R. Cline

13-4 Reengineering EMU for an Uncertain World Ángel Ubide

13-5 From Supervision to Resolution: Next Steps on the Road to European Banking Union Nicolas Véron and Guntram B. Wolff

13-6 Liquefied Natural Gas Exports: An Opportunity for America Gary Clyde Hufbauer, Allie E. Bagnall, and Julia Muir

13-7 The Congress Should Support IMF Governance Reform to Help Stabilize the World Economy Edwin M. Truman

13-8 Crafting a Transatlantic Trade and Investment Partnership: What Can Be Done Jeffrey J. Schott and Cathleen Cimino

13-9 Corporate Taxation and US MNCs: Ensuring a Competitive Economy Gary Clyde Hufbauer and Martin Vieiro

13-10 Four Changes to Trade Rules to Facilitate Climate Change Action Aaditya Mattoo and Arvind Subramanian

13-11 Dealing with Cybersecurity Threats Posed by Globalized Information Technology Suppliers Theodore H. Moran

13-12 Sovereign Damage Control Anna Gelpern

13-13 Sizing Up US Export Disincentives for a New Generation of National-Security Export Controls J. David Richardson and Asha Sundaram

13-14 Shadow Deposits as a Source of Financial Instability: Lessons from the American Experience for China Nicholas Borst

13-15 Estimates of Fundamental Equilibrium Exchange Rates, May 2013 William R. Cline

13-16 Preserving the Open Global Economic System: A Strategic Blueprint for China and the United States Arvind Subramanian

13-17 A Realistic Bridge Towards European Banking Union Nicolas Véron

13-18 Avoiding the "Resource Curse" in Mongolia Theodore H. Moran

13-19 Progress on Sovereign Wealth Fund Transparency and Accountability: An Updated SWF Scoreboard Allie E. Bagnall and Edwin M. Truman

13-20 Role of Apprenticeships in Combating Youth Unemployment in Europe and the United States Natalia Aivazova

13-21 Lehman Died, Bagehot Lives: Why Did the Fed and Treasury Let a Major Wall Street Bank Fail? William R. Cline and Joseph E. Gagnon

13-22 Ukraine's Choice: European Association Agreement or Eurasian Union? Anders Åslund

13-23 How to Form a More Perfect European Banking Union Ángel Ubide

13-24 China's Credit Boom: New Risks Require New Reforms Nicholas Borst

13-25 Governing the Federal Reserve System after the Dodd-Frank Act
Peter Conti-Brown and Simon Johnson

13-26 Financial Services in the Transatlantic Trade and Investment Partnership
Simon Johnson and Jeffrey J. Schott

13-27 US Employment Deindustrialization: Insights from History and the International Experience
Robert Z. Lawrence and Lawrence Edwards

13-28 Stabilizing Properties of Flexible Exchange Rates: Evidence from the Global Financial Crisis   Joseph E. Gagnon

13-29 Estimates of Fundamental Equilibrium Exchange Rates, November 2013
William R. Cline

13-30 Five Challenges for Janet Yellen at the Federal Reserve   David J. Stockton

14-1 Making Labor Market Reforms Work for Everyone: Lessons from Germany
Jacob Funk Kirkegaard

14-2 Addressing Currency Manipulation Through Trade Agreements
C. Fred Bergsten

14-3 Income Inequality Developments in the Great Recession   Tomas Hellebrandt

14-4 Monetary Policy with Abundant Liquidity: A New Operating Framework for the Federal Reserve   Joseph E. Gagnon and Brian Sack

14-5 Is the European Central Bank Failing Its Price Stability Mandate?   Ángel Ubide

14-6 A Proposed Code to Discipline Local Content Requirements   Cathleen Cimino, Gary Clyde Hufbauer, and Jeffrey J. Schott

14-7 Rethinking the National Export Initiative
Caroline Freund

14-8 Women, Sports, and Development: Does It Pay to Let Girls Play?   Barbara Kotschwar

14-9 IMF Reform Is Waiting on the United States   Edwin M. Truman

14-10 Wages and Labor Market Slack: Making the Dual Mandate Operational
David G. Blanchflower and Adam S. Posen

14-11 Managing Myanmar's Resource Boom to Lock in Reforms   Cullen S. Hendrix and Marcus Noland

14-12 Going Beyond Economic Engagement: Why South Korea Should Press the North on Labor Standards and Practices
Marcus Noland

14-13 NAFTA at 20: Misleading Charges and Positive Achievements
Gary Clyde Hufbauer, Cathleen Cimino, and Tyler Moran

14-14 What Should Surplus Germany Do?
Jacob Funk Kirkegaard

14-15 Internationalization of the Renminbi: The Role of Trade Settlement
Joseph E. Gagnon and Kent Troutman

14-16 Estimates of Fundamental Equilibrium Exchange Rates, May 2014
William R. Cline

14-17 Alternatives to Currency Manipulation: What Switzerland, Singapore, and Hong Kong Can Do   Joseph E. Gagnon

14-18 The US Manufacturing Base: Four Signs of Strength   Theodore H. Moran and Lindsay Oldenski

14-19 US Policies toward Liquefied Natural Gas and Oil Exports: An Update
Cathleen Cimino and Gary Clyde Hufbauer

14-20 Debt Sanctions Can Help Ukraine and Fill a Gap in the International Financial System   Anna Gelpern

14-21 Is China's Property Market Heading toward Collapse?   Li-Gang Liu

14-22 Should Korea Join the Trans-Pacific Partnership?   Jeffrey J. Schott and Cathleen Cimino

14-23 Why Bail-In Securities Are Fool's Gold
Avinash D. Persaud

14-24 An Economic Strategy to Save Ukraine
Anders Åslund

14-25 Estimates of Fundamental Equilibrium Exchange Rates, November 2014
William R. Cline

14-26 Rapid Growth in Emerging Markets and Developing Economies: Now and Forever?   Giang Ho and Paolo Mauro

15-1 What Next for the IMF? Edwin M. Truman

15-2 Service Sector Reform in China
Ryan Rutkowski

15-3 Japanese Investment in the United States: Superior Performance, Increasing Integration   Theodore H. Moran and Lindsay Oldenski

15-4 The True Levels of Government and Social Expenditures in Advanced Economies   Jacob Funk Kirkegaard

15-5 How Not to Regulate Insurance Markets: The Risks and Dangers of Solvency II
Avinash Persaud

15-6 From Rapid Recovery to Slowdown: Why Recent Economic Growth in Latin America Has Been Slow   José De Gregorio

15-7 Quantity Theory of Money Redux? Will Inflation Be the Legacy of Quantitative Easing?   William R. Cline

15-8 Estimates of Fundamental Equilibrium Exchange Rates, May 2015 William R. Cline

15-9 Too Much Finance, or Statistical Illusion?   William R. Cline

15-10 Gains from Harmonizing US and EU Auto Regulations under the Transatlantic Trade and Investment Partnership
Caroline Freund and Sarah Oliver

15-11 Hungary under Orbán: Can Central Planning Revive Its Economy?
Simeon Djankov

15-12 From Populist Destabilization to Reform and Possible Debt Relief in Greece
William R. Cline

15-13 Korea and the TPP: The Inevitable Partnership   Jeffrey J. Schott

15-14 Reshoring by US Firms: What Do the Data Say?   Lindsay Oldenski

15-15 Fiscal Tightening and Economic Growth: Exploring Cross-Country Correlations
Paolo Mauro and Jan Zilinsky
15-16 Do Public Development Banks Hurt Growth? Evidence from Brazil
Monica de Bolle
15-17 Chinese Investment and CFIUS: Time for an Updated (and Revised) Perspective
Theodore H. Moran
15-18 Russia's Economy under Putin: From Crony Capitalism to State Capitalism
Simeon Djankov
15-19 Stability Bonds for the Euro Area
Ángel Ubide

* = out of print

POLICY ANALYSES IN INTERNATIONAL ECONOMICS Series

1 The Lending Policies of the International Monetary Fund*   John Williamson
August 1982   ISBN 0-88132-000-5
2 "Reciprocity": A New Approach to World Trade Policy?*   William R. Cline
September 1982   ISBN 0-88132-001-3
3 Trade Policy in the 1980s*   C. Fred Bergsten and William R. Cline
November 1982   ISBN 0-88132-002-1
4 International Debt and the Stability of the World Economy*   William R. Cline
September 1983   ISBN 0-88132-010-2
5 The Exchange Rate System,* 2d ed.
John Williamson
Sept. 1983, rev. June 1985   ISBN 0-88132-034-X
6 Economic Sanctions in Support of Foreign Policy Goals*   Gary Clyde Hufbauer and Jeffrey J. Schott
October 1983   ISBN 0-88132-014-5
7 A New SDR Allocation?*   John Williamson
March 1984   ISBN 0-88132-028-5
8 An International Standard for Monetary Stabilization*   Ronald L. McKinnon
March 1984   ISBN 0-88132-018-8
9 The Yen/Dollar Agreement: Liberalizing Japanese Capital Markets*   Jeffrey Frankel
December 1984   ISBN 0-88132-035-8
10 Bank Lending to Developing Countries: The Policy Alternatives*   C. Fred Bergsten, William R. Cline, and John Williamson
April 1985   ISBN 0-88132-032-3
11 Trading for Growth: The Next Round of Trade Negotiations*   Gary Clyde Hufbauer and Jeffrey J. Schott
September 1985   ISBN 0-88132-033-1
12 Financial Intermediation Beyond the Debt Crisis*   Donald R. Lessard and John Williamson
September 1985   ISBN 0-88132-021-8
13 The United States-Japan Economic Problem*   C. Fred Bergsten and William R. Cline   *Oct. 1985, 2d ed. January 1987*   ISBN 0-88132-060-9

14 Deficits and the Dollar: The World Economy at Risk*   Stephen Marris
Dec. 1985, 2d ed. November 1987   ISBN 0-88132-067-6
15 Trade Policy for Troubled Industries*
Gary Clyde Hufbauer and Howard F. Rosen
March 1986   ISBN 0-88132-020-X
16 The United States and Canada: The Quest for Free Trade*   Paul Wonnacott, with an appendix by John Williamson
March 1987   ISBN 0-88132-056-0
17 Adjusting to Success: Balance of Payments Policy in the East Asian NICs*   Bela Balassa and John Williamson
June 1987, rev. April 1990   ISBN 0-88132-101-X
18 Mobilizing Bank Lending to Debtor Countries*   William R. Cline
June 1987   ISBN 0-88132-062-5
19 Auction Quotas and United States Trade Policy*   C. Fred Bergsten, Kimberly Ann Elliott, Jeffrey J. Schott, and Wendy E. Takacs
September 1987   ISBN 0-88132-050-1
20 Agriculture and the GATT: Rewriting the Rules*   Dale E. Hathaway
September 1987   ISBN 0-88132-052-8
21 Anti-Protection: Changing Forces in United States Trade Politics*   I. M. Destler and John S. Odell
September 1987   ISBN 0-88132-043-9
22 Targets and Indicators: A Blueprint for the International Coordination of Economic Policy   John Williamson and Marcus Miller
September 1987   ISBN 0-88132-051-X
23 Capital Flight: The Problem and Policy Responses*   Donald R. Lessard and John Williamson
December 1987   ISBN 0-88132-059-5
24 United States-Canada Free Trade: An Evaluation of the Agreement*
Jeffrey J. Schott
April 1988   ISBN 0-88132-072-2
25 Voluntary Approaches to Debt Relief*
John Williamson
Sept. 1988, rev. May 1989   ISBN 0-88132-098-6
26 American Trade Adjustment: The Global Impact*   William R. Cline
March 1989   ISBN 0-88132-095-1
27 More Free Trade Areas?* Jeffrey J. Schott
May 1989   ISBN 0-88132-085-4
28 The Progress of Policy Reform in Latin America*   John Williamson
January 1990   ISBN 0-88132-100-1
29 The Global Trade Negotiations: What Can Be Achieved?*   Jeffrey J. Schott
September 1990   ISBN 0-88132-137-0
30 Economic Policy Coordination: Requiem for Prologue?*   Wendy Dobson
April 1991   ISBN 0-88132-102-8
31 The Economic Opening of Eastern Europe*
John Williamson
May 1991   ISBN 0-88132-186-9

32 Eastern Europe and the Soviet Union in the World Economy* Susan Collins and Dani Rodrik
May 1991 ISBN 0-88132-157-5

33 African Economic Reform: The External Dimension* Carol Lancaster
June 1991 ISBN 0-88132-096-X

34 Has the Adjustment Process Worked?* Paul R. Krugman
October 1991 ISBN 0-88132-116-8

35 From Soviet DisUnion to Eastern Economic Community?* Oleh Havrylyshyn and John Williamson
October 1991 ISBN 0-88132-192-3

36 Global Warming: The Economic Stakes* William R. Cline
May 1992 ISBN 0-88132-172-9

37 Trade and Payments after Soviet Disintegration* John Williamson
June 1992 ISBN 0-88132-173-7

38 Trade and Migration: NAFTA and Agriculture* Philip L. Martin
October 1993 ISBN 0-88132-201-6

39 The Exchange Rate System and the IMF: A Modest Agenda Morris Goldstein
June 1995 ISBN 0-88132-219-9

40 What Role for Currency Boards? John Williamson
September 1995 ISBN 0-88132-222-9

41 Predicting External Imbalances for the United States and Japan* William R. Cline
September 1995 ISBN 0-88132-220-2

42 Standards and APEC: An Action Agenda* John S. Wilson
October 1995 ISBN 0-88132-223-7

43 Fundamental Tax Reform and Border Tax Adjustments* Gary Clyde Hufbauer
January 1996 ISBN 0-88132-225-3

44 Global Telecom Talks: A Trillion Dollar Deal* Ben A. Petrazzini
June 1996 ISBN 0-88132-230-X

45 WTO 2000: Setting the Course for World Trade Jeffrey J. Schott
September 1996 ISBN 0-88132-234-2

46 The National Economic Council: A Work in Progress* I. M. Destler
November 1996 ISBN 0-88132-239-3

47 The Case for an International Banking Standard Morris Goldstein
April 1997 ISBN 0-88132-244-X

48 Transatlantic Trade: A Strategic Agenda* Ellen L. Frost
May 1997 ISBN 0-88132-228-8

49 Cooperating with Europe's Monetary Union C. Randall Henning
May 1997 ISBN 0-88132-245-8

50 Renewing Fast Track Legislation* I. M. Destler
September 1997 ISBN 0-88132-252-0

51 Competition Policies for the Global Economy Edward M. Graham and J. David Richardson
November 1997 ISBN 0-88132-249-0

52 Improving Trade Policy Reviews in the World Trade Organization Donald Keesing
April 1998 ISBN 0-88132-251-2

53 Agricultural Trade Policy: Completing the Reform Timothy Josling
April 1998 ISBN 0-88132-256-3

54 Real Exchange Rates for the Year 2000 Simon Wren Lewis and Rebecca Driver
April 1998 ISBN 0-88132-253-9

55 The Asian Financial Crisis: Causes, Cures, and Systemic Implications Morris Goldstein
June 1998 ISBN 0-88132-261-X

56 Global Economic Effects of the Asian Currency Devaluations Marcus Noland, LiGang Liu, Sherman Robinson, and Zhi Wang
July 1998 ISBN 0-88132-260-1

57 The Exchange Stabilization Fund: Slush Money or War Chest? C. Randall Henning
May 1999 ISBN 0-88132-271-7

58 The New Politics of American Trade: Trade, Labor, and the Environment I. M. Destler and Peter J. Balint
October 1999 ISBN 0-88132-269-5

59 Congressional Trade Votes: From NAFTA Approval to Fast Track Defeat Robert E. Baldwin and Christopher S. Magee
February 2000 ISBN 0-88132-267-9

60 Exchange Rate Regimes for Emerging Markets: Reviving the Intermediate Option John Williamson
September 2000 ISBN 0-88132-293-8

61 NAFTA and the Environment: Seven Years Later Gary Clyde Hufbauer, Daniel Esty, Diana Orejas, Luis Rubio, and Jeffrey J. Schott
October 2000 ISBN 0-88132-299-7

62 Free Trade between Korea and the United States? Inbom Choi and Jeffrey J. Schott
April 2001 ISBN 0-88132-311-X

63 New Regional Trading Arrangements in the Asia Pacific? Robert Scollay and John P. Gilbert
May 2001 ISBN 0-88132-302-0

64 Parental Supervision: The New Paradigm for Foreign Direct Investment and Development Theodore H. Moran
August 2001 ISBN 0-88132-313-6

65 The Benefits of Price Convergence: Speculative Calculations Gary Clyde Hufbauer, Erika Wada, and Tony Warren
December 2001 ISBN 0-88132-333-0

66 Managed Floating Plus Morris Goldstein
March 2002 ISBN 0-88132-336-5

67 Argentina and the Fund: From Triumph to Tragedy Michael Mussa
July 2002 ISBN 0-88132-339-X

68 East Asian Financial Cooperation C. Randall Henning
September 2002 ISBN 0-88132-338-1

69 Reforming OPIC for the 21st Century Theodore H. Moran
May 2003 ISBN 0-88132-342-X

70 Awakening Monster: The Alien Tort Statute of 1789 Gary Clyde Hufbauer and Nicholas Mitrokostas
July 2003 ISBN 0-88132-366-7

71 Korea after Kim Jong-il Marcus Noland
January 2004 ISBN 0-88132-373-X

72 Roots of Competitiveness: China's Evolving
Agriculture Interests   Daniel H. Rosen,
Scott Rozelle, and Jikun Huang
July 2004   ISBN 0-88132-376-4

73 Prospects for a US-Taiwan FTA
Nicholas R. Lardy and Daniel H. Rosen
December 2004   ISBN 0-88132-367-5

74 Anchoring Reform with a US-Egypt Free
Trade Agreement   Ahmed Galal and
Robert Z. Lawrence
April 2005   ISBN 0-88132-368-3

75 Curbing the Boom-Bust Cycle: Stabilizing
Capital Flows to Emerging Markets
John Williamson
July 2005   ISBN 0-88132-330-6

76 The Shape of a Swiss-US Free Trade
Agreement   Gary Clyde Hufbauer and
Richard E. Baldwin
February 2006   ISBN 978-0-88132-385-6

77 A Strategy for IMF Reform
Edwin M. Truman
February 2006   ISBN 978-0-88132-398-6

78 US-China Trade Disputes: Rising Tide,
Rising Stakes   Gary Clyde Hufbauer,
Yee Wong, and Ketki Sheth
August 2006   ISBN 978-0-88132-394-8

79 Trade Relations Between Colombia and the
United States   Jeffrey J. Schott, *ed.*
August 2006   ISBN 978-0-88132-389-4

80 Sustaining Reform with a US-Pakistan Free
Trade Agreement   Gary Clyde Hufbauer and
Shahid Javed Burki
November 2006   ISBN 978-0-88132-395-5

81 A US–Middle East Trade Agreement: A
Circle of Opportunity?   Robert Z. Lawrence
November 2006   ISBN 978-0-88132-396-2

82 Reference Rates and the International
Monetary System   John Williamson
January 2007   ISBN 978-0-88132-401-3

83 Toward a US-Indonesia Free Trade
Agreement   Gary Clyde Hufbauer and
Sjamsu Rahardja
June 2007   ISBN 978-0-88132-402-0

84 The Accelerating Decline in America's
High-Skilled Workforce   Jacob F. Kirkegaard
December 2007   ISBN 978-0-88132-413-6

85 Blue-Collar Blues: Is Trade to Blame for
Rising US Income Inequality?
Robert Z. Lawrence
January 2008   ISBN 978-0-88132-414-3

86 Maghreb Regional and Global Integration:
A Dream to Be Fulfilled Gary Clyde Hufbauer
and Claire Brunel, *eds.*
October 2008 ISBN 978-0-88132-426-6

87 The Future of China's Exchange Rate Policy
Morris Goldstein and Nicholas R. Lardy
July 2009   ISBN 978-0-88132-416-7

88 Capitalizing on the Morocco-US Free Trade
Agreement: A Road Map for Success
Gary Clyde Hufbauer and Claire Brunel, eds
September 2009   ISBN 978-0-88132-433-4

89 Three Threats: An Analytical Framework
for the CFIUS Process   Theodore H. Moran
August 2009   ISBN 978-0-88132-429-7

90 Reengaging Egypt: Options for US-Egypt
Economic Relations   Barbara Kotschwar and
Jeffrey J. Schott
January 2010   ISBN 978-088132-439-6

91 Figuring Out the Doha Round
Gary Clyde Hufbauer, Jeffrey J. Schott, and
Woan Foong Wong
June 2010   ISBN 978-088132-503-4

92 China's Strategy to Secure Natural
Resources: Risks, Dangers, and
Opportunities   Theodore H. Moran
June 2010   ISBN 978-088132-512-6

93 The Implications of China-Taiwan
Economic Liberalization   Daniel H. Rosen
and Zhi Wang
January 2011   ISBN 978-0-88132-501-0

94 The Global Outlook for Government Debt
over the Next 25 Years: Implications for the
Economy and Public Policy
Joseph E. Gagnon with Marc Hinterschweiger
June 2011   ISBN 978-0-88132-621-5

95 A Decade of Debt   Carmen M. Reinhart and
Kenneth S. Rogoff
September 2011   ISBN 978-0-88132-622-2

96 Carbon Abatement Costs and Climate
Change Finance   William R. Cline
July 2011   ISBN 978-0-88132-607-9

97 The United States Should Establish
Permanent Normal Trade Relations with
Russia   Anders Åslund and
Gary Clyde Hufbauer
April 2012   ISBN 978-0-88132-620-8

98 The Trans-Pacific Partnership and Asia-
Pacific Integration: A Quantitative
Assessment   Peter A. Petri,
Michael G. Plummer, and Fan Zhai
November 2012   ISBN 978-0-88132-664-2

99 Understanding the Trans-Pacific
Partnership   Jeffrey J. Schott,
Barbara Kotschwar, and Julia Muir
January 2013   ISBN 978-0-88132-672-7

100 Foreign Direct Investment in the United
States: Benefits, Suspicions, and Risks with
Special Attention to FDI from China
Theodore H. Moran and Lindsay Oldenski
August 2013   ISBN 978-0-88132-660-4

101 Outward Foreign Direct Investment and US
Exports, Jobs, and R&D: Implications for
US Policy   Gary Clyde Hufbauer,
Theodore H. Moran, and Lindsay Oldenski,
Assisted by Martin Vieiro
August 2013   ISBN 978-0-88132-668-0

102 Local Content Requirements: A Global
Problem   Gary Clyde Hufbauer,
Jeffrey J. Schott, Cathleen Cimino, Martin
Vieiro, and Erika Wada
September 2013   ISBN 978-0-88132-680-2

103 Economic Normalization with Cuba: A
Roadmap for US Policymakers
Gary Clyde Hufbauer, Barbara Kotschwar,
assisted by Cathleen Cimino and Julia Muir
April 2014   ISBN 978-0-88132-682-6

BOOKS

IMF Conditionality*   John Williamson, ed.
1983   ISBN 0-88132-006-4
Trade Policy in the 1980s*   William R. Cline, ed.
1983   ISBN 0-88132-031-5
Subsidies in International Trade*
Gary Clyde Hufbauer and Joanna Shelton Erb
1984   ISBN 0-88132-004-8
International Debt: Systemic Risk and Policy
Response*   William R. Cline
1984   ISBN 0-88132-015-3
Trade Protection in the United States: 31 Case
Studies*   Gary Clyde Hufbauer, Diane E. Berliner,
and Kimberly Ann Elliott
1986   ISBN 0-88132-040-4
Toward Renewed Economic Growth in Latin
America*   Bela Balassa, Gerardo M. Bueno,
Pedro Pablo Kuczynski, and Mario Henrique
Simonsen
1986   ISBN 0-88132-045-5
Capital Flight and Third World Debt*
Donald R. Lessard and John Williamson, eds.
1987   ISBN 0-88132-053-6
The Canada-United States Free Trade
Agreement: The Global Impact*   Jeffrey J. Schott
and Murray G. Smith, eds.
1988   ISBN 0-88132-073-0
World Agricultural Trade: Building a
Consensus*   William M. Miner and
Dale E. Hathaway, eds.
1988   ISBN 0-88132-071-3
Japan in the World Economy*   Bela Balassa and
Marcus Noland
1988   ISBN 0-88132-041-2
America in the World Economy: A Strategy
for the 1990s*   C. Fred Bergsten
1988   ISBN 0-88132-089-7
Managing the Dollar: From the Plaza to the
Louvre*   Yoichi Funabashi
1988, 2d ed. 1989   ISBN 0-88132-097-8
United States External Adjustment and the
World Economy*   William R. Cline
May 1989   ISBN 0-88132-048-X
Free Trade Areas and U.S. Trade Policy*
Jeffrey J. Schott, ed.
May 1989   ISBN 0-88132-094-3
Dollar Politics: Exchange Rate Policymaking
in the United States*   I. M. Destler and
C. Randall Henning
September 1989   ISBN 0-88132-079-X
Latin American Adjustment: How Much Has
Happened?*   John Williamson, ed.
April 1990   ISBN 0-88132-125-7
The Future of World Trade in Textiles and
Apparel*   William R. Cline
1987, 2d ed. June 1999   ISBN 0-88132-110-9
Completing the Uruguay Round: A Results-
Oriented Approach to the GATT Trade
Negotiations*   Jeffrey J. Schott, ed.
September 1990   ISBN 0-88132-130-3

Economic Sanctions Reconsidered (2 volumes)
Economic Sanctions Reconsidered: Supple-
mental Case Histories   Gary Clyde Hufbauer,
Jeffrey J. Schott, and Kimberly Ann Elliott
1985, 2d ed. Dec. 1990   ISBN cloth 0-88132-115-X/
paper 0-88132-105-2
Economic Sanctions Reconsidered: History
and Current Policy   Gary Clyde Hufbauer,
Jeffrey J. Schott, and Kimberly Ann Elliott
December 1990   ISBN cloth 0-88132-140-0
    ISBN paper 0-88132-136-2
Pacific Basin Developing Countries: Prospects
for the Future*   Marcus Noland
January 1991   ISBN cloth 0-88132-141-9
    ISBN paper 0-88132-081-1
Currency Convertibility in Eastern Europe*
John Williamson, ed.
October 1991   ISBN 0-88132-128-1
International Adjustment and Financing: The
Lessons of 1985-1991*   C. Fred Bergsten, ed.
January 1992   ISBN 0-88132-112-5
North American Free Trade: Issues and
Recommendations*   Gary Clyde Hufbauer and
Jeffrey J. Schott
April 1992   ISBN 0-88132-120-6
Narrowing the U.S. Current Account Deficit*
Alan J. Lenz
June 1992   ISBN 0-88132-103-6
The Economics of Global Warming
William R. Cline
June 1992   ISBN 0-88132-132-X
US Taxation of International Income:
Blueprint for Reform   Gary Clyde Hufbauer,
assisted by Joanna M. van Rooij
October 1992   ISBN 0-88132-134-6
Who's Bashing Whom? Trade Conflict in High-
Technology Industries   Laura D'Andrea Tyson
November 1992 ISBN 0-88132-106-0
Korea in the World Economy*   Il SaKong
January 1993   ISBN 0-88132-183-4
Pacific Dynamism and the International
Economic System*   C. Fred Bergsten and
Marcus Noland, eds.
May 1993   ISBN 0-88132-196-6
Economic Consequences of Soviet
Disintegration*   John Williamson, ed.
May 1993   ISBN 0-88132-190-7
Reconcilable Differences? United States-Japan
Economic Conflict*   C. Fred Bergsten and
Marcus Noland
June 1993   ISBN 0-88132-129-X
Does Foreign Exchange Intervention Work?
Kathryn M. Dominguez and Jeffrey A. Frankel
September 1993   ISBN 0-88132-104-4
Sizing Up U.S. Export Disincentives*
J. David Richardson
September 1993   ISBN 0-88132-107-9
NAFTA: An Assessment   Gary Clyde Hufbauer and
Jeffrey J. Schott, rev. ed.
October 1993   ISBN 0-88132-199-0
Adjusting to Volatile Energy Prices
Philip K. Verleger, Jr.
November 1993   ISBN 0-88132-069-2

The Political Economy of Policy Reform
John Williamson, ed.
January 1994 ISBN 0-88132-195-8

Measuring the Costs of Protection in the United
States Gary Clyde Hufbauer and
Kimberly Ann Elliott
January 1994 ISBN 0-88132-108-7

The Dynamics of Korean Economic
Development* Cho Soon
March 1994 ISBN 0-88132-162-1

Reviving the European Union*
C. Randall Henning, Eduard Hochreiter, and Gary
Clyde Hufbauer, eds.
April 1994 ISBN 0-88132-208-3

China in the World Economy Nicholas R. Lardy
April 1994 ISBN 0-88132-200-8

Greening the GATT: Trade, Environment,
and the Future Daniel C. Esty
July 1994 ISBN 0-88132-205-9

Western Hemisphere Economic Integration*
Gary Clyde Hufbauer and Jeffrey J. Schott
July 1994 ISBN 0-88132-159-1

Currencies and Politics in the United States,
Germany, and Japan C. Randall Henning
September 1994 ISBN 0-88132-127-3

Estimating Equilibrium Exchange Rates
John Williamson, ed.
September 1994 ISBN 0-88132-076-5

Managing the World Economy: Fifty Years
after Bretton Woods Peter B. Kenen, ed.
September 1994 ISBN 0-88132-212-1

Reciprocity and Retaliation in U.S. Trade Policy
Thomas O. Bayard and Kimberly Ann Elliott
September 1994 ISBN 0-88132-084-6

The Uruguay Round: An Assessment*
Jeffrey J. Schott, assisted by Johanna Buurman
November 1994 ISBN 0-88132-206-7

Measuring the Costs of Protection in Japan*
Yoko Sazanami, Shujiro Urata, and Hiroki Kawai
January 1995 ISBN 0-88132-211-3

Foreign Direct Investment in the United States,
3d ed. Edward M. Graham and Paul R. Krugman
January 1995 ISBN 0-88132-204-0

The Political Economy of Korea-United States
Cooperation* C. Fred Bergsten and Il SaKong, *eds.*
February 1995 ISBN 0-88132-213-X

International Debt Reexamined* William R. Cline
February 1995 ISBN 0-88132-083-8

American Trade Politics, 3d ed. I. M. Destler
April 1995 ISBN 0-88132-215-6

Managing Official Export Credits: The Quest for
a Global Regime* John E. Ray
July 1995 ISBN 0-88132-207-5

Asia Pacific Fusion: Japan's Role in APEC*
Yoichi Funabashi
October 1995 ISBN 0-88132-224-5

Korea-United States Cooperation in the New
World Order* C. Fred Bergsten and Il SaKong, *eds.*
February 1996 ISBN 0-88132-226-1

Why Exports Really Matter!* ISBN 0-88132-221-0
Why Exports Matter More!* ISBN 0-88132-229-6
J. David Richardson and Karin Rindal
July 1995; February 1996

Global Corporations and National Governments
Edward M. Graham
May 1996 ISBN 0-88132-111-7

Global Economic Leadership and the Group of
Seven C. Fred Bergsten and C. Randall Henning
May 1996 ISBN 0-88132-218-0

The Trading System after the Uruguay Round*
John Whalley and Colleen Hamilton
July 1996 ISBN 0-88132-131-1

Private Capital Flows to Emerging Markets after
the Mexican Crisis* Guillermo A. Calvo,
Morris Goldstein, and Eduard Hochreiter
September 1996 ISBN 0-88132-232-6

The Crawling Band as an Exchange Rate Regime:
Lessons from Chile, Colombia, and Israel
John Williamson
September 1996 ISBN 0-88132-231-8

Flying High: Liberalizing Civil Aviation in the
Asia Pacific* Gary Clyde Hufbauer and
Christopher Findlay
November 1996 ISBN 0-88132-227-X

Measuring the Costs of Visible Protection
in Korea* Namdoo Kim
November 1996 ISBN 0-88132-236-9

The World Trading System: Challenges Ahead
Jeffrey J. Schott
December 1996 ISBN 0-88132-235-0

Has Globalization Gone Too Far? Dani Rodrik
March 1997 ISBN paper 0-88132-241-5

Korea-United States Economic Relationship*
C. Fred Bergsten and Il SaKong, eds.
March 1997 ISBN 0-88132-240-7

Summitry in the Americas: A Progress Report
Richard E. Feinberg
April 1997 ISBN 0-88132-242-3

Corruption and the Global Economy
Kimberly Ann Elliott
June 1997 ISBN 0-88132-233-4

Regional Trading Blocs in the World Economic
System Jeffrey A. Frankel
October 1997 ISBN 0-88132-202-4

Sustaining the Asia Pacific Miracle:
Environmental Protection and Economic
Integration Andre Dua and Daniel C. Esty
October 1997 ISBN 0-88132-250-4

Trade and Income Distribution
William R. Cline
November 1997 ISBN 0-88132-216-4

Global Competition Policy Edward M. Graham
and J. David Richardson
December 1997 ISBN 0-88132-166-4

Unfinished Business: Telecommunications after
the Uruguay Round Gary Clyde Hufbauer and
Erika Wada
December 1997 ISBN 0-88132-257-1

Financial Services Liberalization in the WTO
Wendy Dobson and Pierre Jacquet
June 1998 ISBN 0-88132-254-7

Restoring Japan's Economic Growth
Adam S. Posen
September 1998 ISBN 0-88132-262-8

Measuring the Costs of Protection in China
Zhang Shuguang, Zhang Yansheng, and Wan
Zhongxin
November 1998 ISBN 0-88132-247-4

Foreign Direct Investment and Development: The New Policy Agenda for Developing Countries and Economies in Transition
Theodore H. Moran
December 1998   ISBN 0-88132-258-X

Behind the Open Door: Foreign Enterprises in the Chinese Marketplace   Daniel H. Rosen
January 1999   ISBN 0-88132-263-6

Toward A New International Financial Architecture: A Practical Post-Asia Agenda
Barry Eichengreen
February 1999   ISBN 0-88132-270-9

Is the U.S. Trade Deficit Sustainable?
Catherine L. Mann
September 1999   ISBN 0-88132-265-2

Safeguarding Prosperity in a Global Financial System: The Future International Financial Architecture, Independent Task Force Report Sponsored by the Council on Foreign Relations
Morris Goldstein, Project Director
October 1999   ISBN 0-88132-287-3

Avoiding the Apocalypse: The Future of the Two Koreas   Marcus Noland
June 2000   ISBN 0-88132-278-4

Assessing Financial Vulnerability: An Early Warning System for Emerging Markets
Morris Goldstein, Graciela Kaminsky, and Carmen Reinhart
June 2000   ISBN 0-88132-237-7

Global Electronic Commerce: A Policy Primer
Catherine L. Mann, Sue E. Eckert, and Sarah Cleeland Knight
July 2000   ISBN 0-88132-274-1

The WTO after Seattle Jeffrey J. Schott, ed.
July 2000   ISBN 0-88132-290-3

Intellectual Property Rights in the Global Economy   Keith E. Maskus
August 2000   ISBN 0-88132-282-2

The Political Economy of the Asian Financial Crisis   Stephan Haggard
August 2000   ISBN 0-88132-283-0

Transforming Foreign Aid: United States Assistance in the 21st Century   Carol Lancaster
August 2000   ISBN 0-88132-291-1

Fighting the Wrong Enemy: Antiglobal Activists and Multinational Enterprises
Edward M. Graham
September 2000   ISBN 0-88132-272-5

Globalization and the Perceptions of American Workers Kenneth Scheve and Matthew J. Slaughter
March 2001   ISBN 0-88132-295-4

World Capital Markets: Challenge to the G-10
Wendy Dobson and Gary Clyde Hufbauer, assisted by Hyun Koo Cho
May 2001   ISBN 0-88132-301-2

Prospects for Free Trade in the Americas
Jeffrey J. Schott
August 2001   ISBN 0-88132-275-X

Toward a North American Community: Lessons from the Old World for the New Robert A. Pastor
August 2001   ISBN 0-88132-328-4

Measuring the Costs of Protection in Europe: European Commercial Policy in the 2000s
Patrick A. Messerlin
September 2001   ISBN 0-88132-273-3

Job Loss from Imports: Measuring the Costs
Lori G. Kletzer
September 2001   ISBN 0-88132-296-2

No More Bashing: Building a New Japan–United States Economic Relationship   C. Fred Bergsten, Takatoshi Ito, and Marcus Noland
October 2001   ISBN 0-88132-286-5

Why Global Commitment Really Matters!
Howard Lewis III and J. David Richardson
October 2001   ISBN 0-88132-298-9

Leadership Selection in the Major Multilaterals
Miles Kahler
November 2001   ISBN 0-88132-335-7

The International Financial Architecture: What's New? What's Missing?   Peter B. Kenen
November 2001   ISBN 0-88132-297-0

Delivering on Debt Relief: From IMF Gold to a New Aid Architecture   John Williamson and Nancy Birdsall, with Brian Deese
April 2002   ISBN 0-88132-331-4

Imagine There's No Country: Poverty, Inequality, and Growth in the Era of Globalization   Surjit S. Bhalla
September 2002   ISBN 0-88132-348-9

Reforming Korea's Industrial Conglomerates
Edward M. Graham
January 2003   ISBN 0-88132-337-3

Industrial Policy in an Era of Globalization: Lessons from Asia   Marcus Noland and Howard Pack
March 2003   ISBN 0-88132-350-0

Reintegrating India with the World Economy
T. N. Srinivasan and Suresh D. Tendulkar
March 2003   ISBN 0-88132-280-6

After the Washington Consensus: Restarting Growth and Reform in Latin America
Pedro-Pablo Kuczynski and John Williamson, eds.
March 2003   ISBN 0-88132-347-0

The Decline of US Labor Unions and the Role of Trade   Robert E. Baldwin
June 2003   ISBN 0-88132-341-1

Can Labor Standards Improve under Globalization?   Kimberly Ann Elliott and Richard B. Freeman
June 2003   ISBN 0-88132-332-2

Crimes and Punishments? Retaliation under the WTO   Robert Z. Lawrence
October 2003   ISBN 0-88132-359-4

Inflation Targeting in the World Economy
Edwin M. Truman
October 2003   ISBN 0-88132-345-4

Foreign Direct Investment and Tax Competition
John H. Mutti
November 2003   ISBN 0-88132-352-7

Has Globalization Gone Far Enough? The Costs of Fragmented Markets   Scott C. Bradford and Robert Z. Lawrence
February 2004   ISBN 0-88132-349-7

Food Regulation and Trade: Toward a Safe and Open Global System Tim Josling, Donna Roberts, and David Orden
March 2004   ISBN 0-88132-346-2

Controlling Currency Mismatches in Emerging Markets   Morris Goldstein and Philip Turner
April 2004   ISBN 0-88132-360-8

Free Trade Agreements: US Strategies and
Priorities   Jeffrey J. Schott, ed.
April 2004   ISBN 0-88132-361-6
Trade Policy and Global Poverty
William R. Cline
June 2004   ISBN 0-88132-365-9
Bailouts or Bail-ins? Responding to Financial
Crises in Emerging Economies   Nouriel Roubini
and Brad Setser
August 2004   ISBN 0-88132-371-3
Transforming the European Economy
Martin Neil Baily and Jacob Funk Kirkegaard
September 2004   ISBN 0-88132-343-8
Chasing Dirty Money: The Fight Against Money
Laundering   Peter Reuter and Edwin M. Truman
November 2004   ISBN 0-88132-370-5
The United States and the World Economy:
Foreign Economic Policy for the Next Decade
C. Fred Bergsten
January 2005   ISBN 0-88132-380-2
Does Foreign Direct Investment Promote
Development?   Theodore H. Moran,
Edward M. Graham, and Magnus Blomström, eds.
April 2005   ISBN 0-88132-381-0
American Trade Politics, 4th ed.   I. M. Destler
June 2005   ISBN 0-88132-382-9
Why Does Immigration Divide America? Public
Finance and Political Opposition to Open
Borders   Gordon H. Hanson
August 2005   ISBN 0-88132-400-0
Reforming the US Corporate Tax
Gary Clyde Hufbauer and Paul L. E. Grieco
September 2005   ISBN 0-88132-384-5
The United States as a Debtor Nation
William R. Cline
September 2005   ISBN 0-88132-399-3
NAFTA Revisited: Achievements and Challenges
Gary Clyde Hufbauer and Jeffrey J. Schott, assisted
by Paul L. E. Grieco and Yee Wong
October 2005   ISBN 0-88132-334-9
US National Security and Foreign Direct
Investment   Edward M. Graham and
David M. Marchick
May 2006   ISBN 978-0-88132-391-7
Accelerating the Globalization of America: The
Role for Information Technology
Catherine L. Mann, assisted by Jacob Funk
Kirkegaard
June 2006   ISBN 978-0-88132-390-0
Delivering on Doha: Farm Trade and the Poor
Kimberly Ann Elliott
July 2006   ISBN 978-0-88132-392-4
Case Studies in US Trade Negotiation, Vol. 1:
Making the Rules   Charan Devereaux,
Robert Z. Lawrence, and Michael Watkins
September 2006   ISBN 978-0-88132-362-7
Case Studies in US Trade Negotiation, Vol. 2:
Resolving Disputes   Charan Devereaux,
Robert Z. Lawrence, and Michael Watkins
September 2006   ISBN 978-0-88132-363-2
C. Fred Bergsten and the World Economy
Michael Mussa, ed.
December 2006   ISBN 978-0-88132-397-9

Working Papers, Volume I   Peterson Institute
December 2006   ISBN 978-0-88132-388-7
The Arab Economies in a Changing World
Marcus Noland and Howard Pack
April 2007   ISBN 978-0-88132-393-1
Working Papers, Volume II Peterson Institute
April 2007   ISBN 978-0-88132-404-4
Global Warming and Agriculture: Impact
Estimates by Country   William R. Cline
July 2007   ISBN 978-0-88132-403-7
US Taxation of Foreign Income
Gary Clyde Hufbauer and Ariel Assa
October 2007   ISBN 978-0-88132-405-1
Russia's Capitalist Revolution: Why Market
Reform Succeeded and Democracy Failed
Anders Åslund
October 2007   ISBN 978-0-88132-409-9
Economic Sanctions Reconsidered, 3d ed.
Gary Clyde Hufbauer, Jeffrey J. Schott, Kimberly
Ann Elliott, and Barbara Oegg
November 2007
ISBN hardcover 978-0-88132-407-5
ISBN hardcover/CD-ROM 978-0-88132-408-2
Debating China's Exchange Rate Policy
Morris Goldstein and Nicholas R. Lardy, eds.
April 2008   ISBN 978-0-88132-415-0
Leveling the Carbon Playing Field: International
Competition and US Climate Policy Design
Trevor Houser, Rob Bradley, Britt Childs, Jacob
Werksman, and Robert Heilmayr
May 2008   ISBN 978-0-88132-420-4
Accountability and Oversight of US Exchange
Rate Policy   C. Randall Henning
June 2008   ISBN 978-0-88132-419-8
Challenges of Globalization: Imbalances and
Growth   Anders Åslund and Marek Dabrowski, eds.
July 2008   ISBN 978-0-88132-418-1
China's Rise: Challenges and Opportunities
C. Fred Bergsten, Charles Freeman, Nicholas R.
Lardy, and Derek J. Mitchell
September 2008   ISBN 978-0-88132-417-4
Banking on Basel: The Future of International
Financial Regulation   Daniel K. Tarullo
September 2008   ISBN 978-0-88132-423-5
US Pension Reform: Lessons from Other
Countries   Martin Neil Baily and
Jacob Funk Kirkegaard
February 2009   ISBN 978-0-88132-425-9
How Ukraine Became a Market Economy and
Democracy   Anders Åslund
March 2009   ISBN 978-0-88132-427-3
Global Warming and the World Trading System
Gary Clyde Hufbauer, Steve Charnovitz, and Jisun
Kim
March 2009   ISBN 978-0-88132-428-0
The Russia Balance Sheet   Anders Åslund and
Andrew Kuchins
March 2009   ISBN 978-0-88132-424-2
The Euro at Ten: The Next Global Currency?
Jean Pisani-Ferry and Adam S. Posen, eds.
July 2009   ISBN 978-0-88132-430-3
Financial Globalization, Economic Growth, and
the Crisis of 2007–09   William R. Cline
May 2010   ISBN 978-0-88132-4990-0

Russia after the Global Economic Crisis
Anders Åslund, Sergei Guriev, and Andrew Kuchins, eds.
June 2010 ISBN 978-0-88132-497-6

Sovereign Wealth Funds: Threat or Salvation?
Edwin M. Truman
September 2010 ISBN 978-0-88132-498-3

The Last Shall Be the First: The East European Financial Crisis, 2008–10 Anders Åslund
October 2010 ISBN 978-0-88132-521-8

Witness to Transformation: Refugee Insights into North Korea Stephan Haggard and Marcus Noland
January 2011 ISBN 978-0-88132-438-9

Foreign Direct Investment and Development: Launching a Second Generation of Policy Research, Avoiding the Mistakes of the First, Reevaluating Policies for Developed and Developing Countries Theodore H. Moran
April 2011 ISBN 978-0-88132-600-0

How Latvia Came through the Financial Crisis
Anders Åslund and Valdis Dombrovskis
May 2011 ISBN 978-0-88132-602-4

Global Trade in Services: Fear, Facts, and Offshoring J. Bradford Jensen
August 2011 ISBN 978-0-88132-601-7

NAFTA and Climate Change Meera Fickling and Jeffrey J. Schott
September 2011 ISBN 978-0-88132-436-5

Eclipse: Living in the Shadow of China's Economic Dominance Arvind Subramanian
September 2011 ISBN 978-0-88132-606-2

Flexible Exchange Rates for a Stable World Economy Joseph E. Gagnon with Marc Hinterschweiger
September 2011 ISBN 978-0-88132-627-7

The Arab Economies in a Changing World, 2d ed. Marcus Noland and Howard Pack
November 2011 ISBN 978-0-88132-628-4

Sustaining China's Economic Growth After the Global Financial Crisis Nicholas R. Lardy
January 2012 ISBN 978-0-88132-626-0

Who Needs to Open the Capital Account?
Olivier Jeanne, Arvind Subramanian, and John Williamson
April 2012 ISBN 978-0-88132-511-9

Devaluing to Prosperity: Misaligned Currencies and Their Growth Consequences Surjit S. Bhalla
August 2012 ISBN 978-0-88132-623-9

Private Rights and Public Problems: The Global Economics of Intellectual Property in the 21st Century Keith E. Maskus
September 2012 ISBN 978-0-88132-507-2

Global Economics in Extraordinary Times: Essays in Honor of John Williamson
C. Fred Bergsten and C. Randall Henning, eds.
November 2012 ISBN 978-0-88132-662-8

Rising Tide: Is Growth in Emerging Economies Good for the United States? Lawrence Edwards and Robert Z. Lawrence
February 2013 ISBN 978-0-88132-500-3

Responding to Financial Crisis: Lessons from Asia Then, the United States and Europe Now
Changyong Rhee and Adam S. Posen, eds
October 2013 ISBN 978-0-88132-674-1

Fueling Up: The Economic Implications of America's Oil and Gas Boom Trevor Houser and Shashank Mohan
January 2014 ISBN 978-0-88132-656-7

How Latin America Weathered the Global Financial Crisis José De Gregorio
January 2014 ISBN 978-0-88132-678-9

Confronting the Curse: The Economics and Geopolitics of Natural Resource Governance
Cullen S. Hendrix and Marcus Noland
May 2014 ISBN 978-0-88132-676-5

Inside the Euro Crisis: An Eyewitness Account
Simeon Djankov
June 2014 ISBN 978-0-88132-685-7

Managing the Euro Area Debt Crisis
William R. Cline
June 2014 ISBN 978-0-88132-678-1

Markets over Mao: The Rise of Private Business in China Nicholas R. Lardy
September 2014 ISBN 978-0-88132-693-2

Bridging the Pacific: Toward Free Trade and Investment between China and the United States
C. Fred Bergsten, Gary Clyde Hufbauer, and Sean Miner. Assisted by Tyler Moran
October 2014 ISBN 978-0-88132-691-8

The Great Rebirth: Lessons from the Victory of Capitalism over Communism
Anders Åslund and Simeon Djankov, eds.
November 2014 ISBN 978-0-88132-697-0

Ukraine: What Went Wrong and How to Fix It
Anders Åslund
April 2015 ISBN 978-0-88132-701-4

From Stress to Growth: Strengthening Asia's Financial Systems in a Post-Crisis World
Marcus Noland; Donghyun Park, eds.
October 2015 ISBN 978-0-88132-699-4

The Great Tradeoff: Confronting Moral Conflicts in the Era of Globalization
Steven R. Weisman
January 2016 ISBN 978-0-88132-695-6

SPECIAL REPORTS

1 Promoting World Recovery: A Statement on Global Economic Strategy* by Twenty-six Economists from Fourteen Countries
December 1982 ISBN 0 88132 013 7

2 Prospects for Adjustment in Argentina, Brazil, and Mexico: Responding to the Debt Crisis* John Williamson, ed.
June 1983 ISBN 0-88132-016-1

3 Inflation and Indexation: Argentina, Brazil, and Israel* John Williamson, ed.
March 1985 ISBN 0-88132-037-4

4 Global Economic Imb alances*
C. Fred Bergsten, ed.
March 1986 ISBN 0-88132-042-0

5 African Debt and Financing* Carol Lancaster and John Williamson, eds.
May 1986 ISBN 0-88132-044-7

6 Resolving the Global Economic Crisis: After Wall Street* by Thirty-three Economists from Thirteen Countries
December 1987 ISBN 0-88132-070-6

7   **World Economic Problems***
Kimberly Ann Elliott and John Williamson, *eds.*
April 1988   ISBN 0-88132-055-2
    Reforming World Agricultural Trade*
by Twenty-nine Professionals from Seventeen
Countries
1988   ISBN 0-88132-088-9
8   **Economic Relations Between the United
States and Korea: Conflict or Cooperation?***
Thomas O. Bayard and Soogil Young, eds.
January 1989   ISBN 0-88132-068-4
9   **Whither APEC? The Progress to Date and
Agenda for the Future***   C. Fred Bergsten, ed.
October 1997   ISBN 0-88132-248-2
10 **Economic Integration of the Korean
Peninsula**   Marcus Noland, ed.
January 1998   ISBN 0-88132-255-5
11 **Restarting Fast Track***   Jeffrey J. Schott, ed.
April 1998   ISBN 0-88132-259-8
12 **Launching New Global Trade Talks: An
Action Agenda**   Jeffrey J. Schott, ed.
September 1998   ISBN 0-88132-266-0
13 **Japan's Financial Crisis and Its Parallels to
US Experience**   Ryoichi Mikitani and
Adam S. Posen, eds.
September 2000   ISBN 0-88132-289-X
14 **The Ex-Im Bank in the 21st Century: A New
Approach**   Gary Clyde Hufbauer and Rita M.
Rodriguez, eds.
January 2001   ISBN 0-88132-300-4
15 **The Korean Diaspora in the World
Economy**   C. Fred Bergsten and
Inbom Choi, eds.
January 2003   ISBN 0-88132-358-6
16 **Dollar Overvaluation and the World
Economy**   C. Fred Bergsten and
John Williamson, eds.
February 2003   ISBN 0-88132-351-9
17 **Dollar Adjustment: How Far? Against
What?** C. Fred Bergsten and John Williamson,
eds.
November 2004   ISBN 0-88132-378-0
18 **The Euro at Five: Ready for a Global Role?**
Adam S. Posen, ed.
April 2005   ISBN 0-88132-380-2
19 **Reforming the IMF for the 21st Century**
Edwin M. Truman, ed.
April 2006   ISBN 978-0-88132-387-0
20 **The Long-Term International Economic
Position of the United States**
C. Fred Bergsten, ed.
May 2009   ISBN 978-0-88132-432-7

21 **Resolving the European Debt Crisis**
William R. Cline and Guntram B. Wolff, eds.
February 2012   ISBN 978-0-88132-642-0
22 **Transatlantic Economic Challenges in an
Era of Growing Multipolarity**
Jacob Funk Kirkegaard, Nicolas Véron, and
Guntram B. Wolff, eds.
June 2012   ISBN 978-0-88132-645-1

PIIE Briefings

14-1   **Flirting With Default: Issues Raised by
Debt Confrontations in the United States**
February 2014
14-2   **The US-China-Europe Economic
Reform Agenda. Papers presented at a
Symposium in Beijing**   *May 2014*
14-3   **NAFTA: 20 Years Later**   *November 2014*
14-4   **Lessons from Decades Lost: Economic
Challenges and Opportunities Facing
Japan and the United States** (with
Sasakawa Peace Foundation USA)
December 2014
14-5   **Rebuilding Europe's Common Future:
Combining Growth and Reform in the
Euro Area**   *December 2014*
15-1   **Toward a US-China Investment Treaty**
February 2015   ISBN 978-0-88132-707-6
15-2   **Raising Lower-Level Wages: When and
Why It Makes Economic Sense**
April 2015   ISBN 978-0-88132-709-3
15-3   **China's EconomicTransformation:
Lessons, Impact, and the Path Forward**
September 2015   ISBN 978-0-88132-709-0
15-4   **India's Rise: A Strategy for Trade-Led
Growth**   C. Fred Bergsten
September 2015   ISBN 978-0-88132-710-6

WORKS IN PROGRESS

**Rich People, Poor Countries: The Rise of
Emerging-Market Tycoons and their Mega
Firms**   Caroline Freund, assisted by Sarah Oliver
**International Monetary Cooperation: Lessons
from the Plaza Accord After Thirty Years**
Russell A. Green and C. Fred Bergsten, editors

Visit our website at: www.piie.com
E-mail orders to: petersonmail@presswarehouse.com